Realism, Naturalism, and Symbolism

Modes of Thought and Expression
in Europe, 1848–1914

DOCUMENTARY HISTORY OF WESTERN CIVILIZATION
Edited by Eugene C. Black and Leonard W. Levy

A volume
in
DOCUMENTARY HISTORY
of
WESTERN CIVILIZATION

Realism, Naturalism, and Symbolism

Modes of Thought and Expression
in Europe, 1848–1914

edited by

ROLAND N. STROMBERG

Harper & Row, Publishers: New York, Evanston, and London

Contents

꧁꧂꧁꧂꧁꧂꧁꧂꧁꧂꧁꧂꧁꧂꧁꧂꧁꧂

II. NATURALISM

III. SYMBOLISM

Chronology

1848   Revolutions in France, Germany, Austria, Italy.
       German national constitutional assembly at Frankfurt
       Karl Marx and Friedrich Engels, *Communist Manifesto*
1849   Alexander Herzen, *From the Other Shore*
       John Ruskin, *Seven Lamps of Architecture*
       Richard Wagner, *Art and Revolution*
       Ernest Renan, *L'Avenir de la science*
1851   Crystal Palace Exhibition in London: age of industrialism
           and bourgeois rule.
       Schopenhauer's Essays
       Napoleon III's coup d'état in France
1852   Charles Dickens, *Bleak House*
       Leo Tolstoy, *The Cossacks*
1857   Charles Baudelaire, *Les fleurs du mal*
       Gustave Flaubert, *Madame Bovary*
       Herzen begins publication of *The Bell*
1859   Charles Darwin, *On the Origin of Species by Means of
           Natural Selection*
       George Eliot, *Adam Bede*
1861   Wagner's opera "Tannhaüser" performed in Paris
1862   Herbert Spencer, *Synthetic Philosophy*
1863   Renan, *Vie de Jésus*
       "Salon des refusés" of painters in Paris
1864   Edmond and Jules Goncourt, *Germinie Lacerteux*
1865   Paul Verlaine, *Poèmes saturniens*
       Matthew Arnold, *Essays in Criticism*
1867   Fyodor Dostoyevsky, *Crime and Punishment*
       Marx, *Capital*
       Henrik Ibsen, *Peer Gynt*
       Walter Bagehot, *The English Constitution*
1868   Robert Browning, *The Ring and the Book*

1894   *Yellow Book* (published 1894–1897)
      George Moore, *Esther Waters*

1895   Theodor Fontane, *Effie Briest*
      Sigmund Freud, *Studies on Hysteria*
      Max Nordau, *Degeneration*
      Hardy, *Jude the Obscure*
      Trial and imprisonment of Oscar Wilde

1896   Henri Bergson, *Matter and Memory*
      A. E. Housman, *A Shropshire Lad*
      Gabriele d'Annunzio, *The Triumph of Death*

1897   Mallarmé, *Divagations*
      Maurice Barrès, *The Uprooted*
      Tolstoy, *What Is Art?*

1898   Zola, *J'Accuse;* Dreyfus case at peak
      Shaw, *Caesar and Cleopatra; The Perfect Wagnerite*

1900   Freud, *Interpretation of Dreams*
      Cahiers de la quinzaine begins.

1901   Death of Queen Victoria

1902   Maxim Gorki, *The Lower Depths*

1903   Thomas Mann, *Tonio Kröger*
      Anton Chekhov, *The Cherry Orchard*

1905   Einstein's first theory of relativity

1908   Graham Wallas, *Human Nature in Politics*

1910   Charles Péguy, *Notre jeunesse; Clio*
      Georgian poets

1911   Exhibition of post-impressionist paintings

1913–1914   First novels of Marcel Proust, D. H. Lawrence, James
      Joyce Imagism

Introduction

I

REALISM, naturalism, and symbolism, three styles or moods in the arts and literature, coincide roughly with three generations of European history from 1848 to 1914. Realism can be said to have lasted from 1848 to 1871, naturalism from 1871 to 1890, symbolism from 1890 to 1914. The dates are approximations, as is always the case in establishing historical periods; there is some overlap and there are many exceptions. But they are adequate generalizations.

These three literary movements may be said to have reflected changing taste, in accordance with the proposition that each generation feels a need to express itself in a new way. The nineteenth century was dynamic and turbulent. During its first few decades, romanticism had overturned the traditional restraints and rules of classicism, introducing a need for constant change and ever-growing subjectivity which some keen observers predicted could only end in anarchy. It is possible to read modern Western history as a record of the breakdown of order leading toward disintegration. Whether or not that is true, nineteenth century writers certainly found repose in no single style, but had to experiment constantly. If it is true that each generation is impelled to assert its individuality, and each individual his uniqueness, it was above all true in the restless century that followed the French Revolution and the romantic revolution.

Literary-artistic schools interacted with political, social, economic, and intellectual developments in this vigorous era. The revolutions of 1848 are a turning point; after them nothing could be the same. In a paroxysm of "social romanticism," writers and intellectuals had thrown themselves into politics and actually led the revolutions which swept Europe from Paris to Rome, Vienna, and Berlin: famous examples include socialist-journalist Louis Blanc and the poet -revolutionary Alphonse Lamartine in France, the eloquent Italian crusader Giuseppe Mazzini, and the professors who gathered at Frankfurt to write the German constitution. The results of such idealistic efforts were so disillusioning that a generation of poets withdrew from the political realm. Art became an asylum, a retreat from an alien society dominated by crass men and crass motives; or, as some put it, by the "vulgar mob."

After Napoleon III's overthrow of the republic, December 2, 1851, politics was not even a permissible path in France unless one wanted to be a revolutionary, and the situation was the same in most other parts of Europe as reaction followed revolution. Writers threw themselves into literary and artistic movements with the passion formerly reserved for political and social causes. Jules Goncourt, though no lover of democracy and socialism, wrote of Napoleon's regime that "it is decadence in its vilest form. . . . a new invasion of the barbarians." The Crystal Palace exhibition of 1851 in London symbolized the complacency of bourgeois "progress" and the advance of mechanized industry. Artists on the whole felt that both of these debased man and destroyed beauty.

The ambiguity of this situation should be noted: the 1850's and 1860's actually were a prosperous and in many ways a progressive period. In these years Europe found its greatest economic stability of the century. The Bonapartist Empire, despised by aesthetes, built broad boulevards, and laid water pipes and sewers. The unification of Italy and Germany, bungled by the idealistic revolutionaries of '48, progressed under the realistic statecraft of Cavour and Bismarck. Science began its triumphal march of discovery. In many ways there was real improvement; so much so that the average man grew to believe uncritically in constant and inevitable progress. And yet artists and writers felt estranged from this "crass," "bourgeois" civilization, and began the chorus of denunciation of what one poet called "this stupid nineteenth century."

"Realism," as a keynote of the 1848–1871 period, sometimes suggests the *Realpolitik* of the German statesman Bismarck, or the brutal creed of businessmen and economists in this heyday of laissez-faire capitalism. It may also mean the shift toward science, or rather "scientism"—the view that scientific knowledge is the only valid kind, and can solve all human problems. Some date this turn toward science at around 1845; certainly almost everyone became aware of it in the heat of the Darwinian controversy after the publication of *The Origin of Species* in 1859. (The debate about evolution had been going on for some years before the Cambridge scientist produced his decisive summation.) At any rate, the change was a sharp one, noticeable all over the Western world as a shift in the primary interests of educated people. Traditional education dominated by the study of the classics came under sharp attack as reactionary and stupid.

The Second Empire in France under Napoleon III was dominated by Positivism. The philosophy that originated with August Comte between 1830 and 1842 was now adopted by distinguished scholars, scientists, and historians, and even by literary figures.[1] Positivists believed in observable facts and in tentative generalizations formed from these observations. They proclaimed the obsolescence of metaphysics and theology. John Stuart Mill in England, and the neo-Kantians or the materialistic disciples of Hegel in Germany such as Ludwig Feuerbach and Karl Marx, offered something similar to their countrymen. There were other schools than Marx's of allegedly scientific history; for example, that of the Englishman Henry Buckle. Other fields besides history had to be "scientific." Even some novelists were influenced by the scientific mystique and held that truths should be observable, experimentally verifiable, clear, exact, and, in addition, show what was really a matter of faith—the unalterable law governing the universe.

So far as the writers are concerned, this mood conveniently interacted with their rejection of romanticism, which had dominated the Western world for roughly the first half of the century. Discontent with certain aspects of romanticism was manifest as early as the 1830's, and by the 1840's the romantics clearly had declined in importance. It is certainly true, as critics have noted, that "romanticism" contained elements of "realism," and continued in various ways to fertilize the work of later writers who covertly kept some of its features while apparently rejecting it—an old story in the

---

[1] D. G. Charlton in his scholarly and perceptive *Positivist Thought in France 1852–1870* (Oxford. Clarendon Press, 1959), finds exceptions to this familiar generalization, but documents the pervasive influence of various modes of Positivism, scientism, and phenomenalism.

history of thought and style. But clearly a reaction had set in; the tide of taste had turned again, youth was in its habitual rebellion against the rebellion of its fathers. "The romantic movement in France was virtually over by the middle of the eighteen-forties," Enid Starkie writes.[2] For such high priests of later romanticism as Sue, Lamartine, and Vigny, the younger generation of writers had little but contempt. The extent of the revulsion may be suggested by Baudelaire's private remarks on George Sand: "I cannot think of this stupid creature without a shudder of horror."[3] The story was much the same in Germany, despite the stronger hold of romanticism there. In England, the Pre-Raphaelites detached themselves from the main body of Victorian literature for similar motives, if with somewhat different devices; while the Eminent Victorians too looked upon the moral irregularities of Shelley's circle with some distaste. (There was less revolution and more evolution in English literature, just as in English politics.)

The reaction against romanticism often went under the name of realism, for the "realists" put aside a variety of "unrealities" such as cloak-and-sword romances, the cult of the exotic (medieval, oriental, the remote and the fairylandish), or seemingly impossible political ideals, or idealism in philosophy. The realists, it is true, turned for their subjects to real people and contemporary social themes, but they also coined a slogan that echoed down the century and may be regarded as an aesthetic retreat from reality: *Art pour l'art*. Art for art's sake was a reply to the didacticism of the romantics. Such artists might become, as did Stendahl, detached, disabused, sceptical, and rather dry. Let the artist ply his craft for its own sake, for the sake of the creation of a work of art, not for some ulterior motive. Let him create a perfect thing, capable of standing by itself, with the professional skill of a craftsman. The artist's subjective state was regarded as an irrelevance.

The artist drew apart from society, for which he felt the greatest contempt. These writers of the 1830's and 1840's, a somewhat disreputable breed led by Théophile Gautier, marked the route that led to Bohemia. They were the forerunners of the giants of the fifties, Baudelaire and Flaubert, who were as alienated as they were

---

[2] Enid Starkie, *From Gautier to Eliot* (London: Hutchinson, 1960), p. 26.
[3] *The Intimate Journals of Charles Baudelaire*, trans. Christopher Isherwood (Boston: Beacon Press, 1957), pp. 33–35.

aloof, and dedicated themselves to the religion of art, in revulsion at the rule of the bourgeoisie. The scandal of the century was now apparent: the greatest writers were the leading enemies of society. "It will no longer be a despot that oppresses the individual, but the masses," said Flaubert. "I shall return to the Bedouins who are free." He did not literally do that, but a young poet named Arthur Rimbaud soon did. Baudelaire, who spoke of a "thickness of vulgarity" that stifled all sensitive men, shared with Flaubert and Rimbaud a défiance of respectable society, and substituted the cult of the Beautiful, the Work of Art, for religion.

This aesthetic withdrawal from society may seem to contradict the cult of "realism;" but there was a psychological kinship and it is exemplified in the leaders of the French literary world, the Goncourt brothers. They were the most fastidious of artists, yet they almost invented the novel of the "lower depths." It is obvious that one could shock the bourgeoisie by this sort of bluntness, and also embarrass them by pointing at the dreadful ugliness and social evil in their civilization. The Goncourts confessed also that the lower depths had an exotic appeal. Sophisticated minds that had exhausted all other subjects found novelty in the wretchedness around the corner.

> It is in the lowest depths [wrote Edmond Goncourt in 1871] during eclipse of a civilization, that the character of things, of persons, of language, of everything is preserved . . . A painter has a thousand times better chance of making a work that has style out of a mud-bespattered streetwalker in the Rue Saint-Honoré than out of a courtesan of the Rue Breda . . . . The riff-raff have for me the particular attraction of races unknown and undiscovered, something of that exotic quality which travellers seek in far-off lands at the cost of many hardships.

How they wrote! The Goncourt brothers, those indefatigable chroniclers to whom we owe so much knowledge about nineteenth century literati, provide an excellent example of those who lived by writing. They worked at it incessantly all their lives, and when they died left their money for a literary prize, the famous Prix Goncourt. Writing every day for a literary newspaper and every week for a literary journal, they produced a score of plays and novels, a social history of the revolution, volumes on eighteenth century biography and art, painting, Japanese art, and a hundred other works as well as their famous Journal. They wrote to shock and annoy the bourgeois public yet were crushed at their failures, outraged at their prosecutions, and indignant with their critics. Their sometime friend and disciple, Émile Zola, soon launched upon a massive twenty-volume novel, the portrait of an age. Paris swarmed with hundreds of scribblers and daubers, creating, intriguing, quarreling, and stealing each other's ideas and mistresses with an intensity which the bourgeoisie reserved for business. The idea of Bohemia was born, the community of those who stood apart from the world of respectability and paid their tribute to the goddess of art.

"The nineteenth century," writes André Billy, "the century of Châteaubriand, Flaubert, Théophile Gautier and the Goncourts, was the century of outstanding excellence in the field of literature. Viewed both as an art and an independent profession, literature then had a prestige and inspired a devotion of which no other period affords a similar example."[4] Some would dispute the claim to priority in quality, preferring perhaps the seventeenth century. But as a social phenomenon, the attitude of the men of letters would seem to be unique: they were, and felt themselves to be, members of an "independent profession" and the focus of a separate culture. "Bohemia," "art pour l'art," and the "alienated" writer are influential aspects of the civilization of modern Europe.

Nietzsche held that the best literature is that of decadent times. Europe after 1848 in some ways seemed far from decadent. It produced wealth as never before. It perfected the largest unit of political association and power yet known, the nation-state. But it also produced class conflict and a dismal ugliness against which the greater writers and artists revolted and protested; likewise its materialism and absence of spiritual culture shocked sensitive souls. The older aristocracy was dead or dying; a crass and cultureless bourgeoisie replaced it. So, too, the old religious faith seemed to be disappearing: "to give oneself the trouble of denying God is the sole disgrace in such matters," Baudelaire remarked. In *Hard Times*, published in 1854, Charles Dickens struck at the bleakness of life

---

[4] *André Billy, The Goncourt Brothers*, trans. Margaret Shaw (New York: Horizon Press, 1960), p. 335.

in cities where uprooted men faced loss of identity as well as squalor and alienation from their labor. Dickens' striking change of mood, from the optimism of his earlier books, to the somber mood of the 1850's expressed in such novels as *Bleak House* and *Hard Times*, can partly be explained by his personal problems and his increasing age. Yet it also certainly reflects the changing times. The great novelist felt a growing sense of dissatisfaction verging on despair as the joyous hopes—the Great Expectations—of his "romantic" youth faded into the sordid realities of a bourgeois industrial-scientific world.

Innumerable writers expressed dissatisfaction and despair similar to Dickens'. Realism and subsequently naturalism in literature aimed at describing unflinchingly the horrors of modern civilization as seen in the lives of the poor wretches who labored in mines or factories, of prostitutes, degenerates, and criminals. "We go into the street, the living swarming street, into empty lots as well as proud forests" (Huysmans).

The realist movement was not only reacting against the romanticism of the previous era, but also the philosophical idealism of the German school, in particular of Hegel. The eloquent hero of Turgenev's early novel *Rudin*, published in 1856, deals confidently in abstractions such as Humanity, Freedom, Duty, but can do nothing when confronted with real situations. Søren Kierkegaard's similar indictment of Hegel's system as a monstrosity of abstractness unsuited for real life is today quite well known. Idealist philosophy like romanticism was rejected by these men of the 1850's because its abstract concepts seemed arid and irrelevant to real life. They thirsted for something more concrete and human, something nearer the lives of actual men and women in actual situations. They would gladly trade all Hegel's World Spirit for a few cases of direct involvement.

II

Some comment on the meaning of literary "realism" and "naturalism" is in order. These terms are quite difficult to define; they appear vague, contradictory, and inconsistent if one thinks of an abstract definition. "Realism has existed as long as literature has existed," one of the French enthusiasts for *réalisme* declared in the 1850's, and proceeded to claim for his school practically every important writer of modern times. All writers describe something that is "real," for even dreams and mystic experiences are in some senses real; and one who abjured material, physical reality might be in tune with psychological reality. Though realism is often said to be the opposite of romanticism, some have spoken of a "romantic realism" (Dickens, Balzac, Stendhal, Dosteyevsky); perhaps the greatest writers are always both.

Realism and naturalism were often defined by their subject matter: the choice of plain people over richer and more "interesting" ones, sordid subjects rather than pleasant ones, tragic tales instead of stories with conventionally happy endings. During the somewhat confused debate about realism, the foes of the school that called itself realist often declared that reality is spiritual as well as material, and that therefore a writer or painter who leaves out the soul is guilty of falsifying reality; and a novelist who depicts only sordid and debased people is untrue to nature, because there are many good people in the world. The realist could and did argue that there are more poor, unhappy, and degraded people than rich, happy, and elevated ones. Still, if this is the criterion one wonders why a better, more precise word than realism was not chosen, for the latter group while admittedly less numerous is not non-existent, and the former group while perhaps neglected is not alone "real" or "natural." One should perhaps have spoken of a proletarian school, or a tragic school, or (as a later American group of painters were indeed dubbed) an ash can school.

There were, in fact, all sorts of realists, ofen at odds with each other. The English novelist George Eliot was a great realist, but the followers of Zola made fun of her moralism and what they considered her bourgeois fixations. She liked to describe the average, rural, middle-class household, delighted in Dutch genre paintings, cultivated the commonplace. She omitted crude sexual passions, violence, class war, and all manner of subjects which were the hallmark of another sort of realism. In claiming that most people "are neither great heroes or great villains, millionaires or ne-er-do-wells," but something unexcitingly in between, she was probably right. By George Eliot's standards, then, Zola could be convicted of offending against reality as much as those who wrote only about the rich and handsome.

At the end of Zola's era, writers like Marcel Proust and Virginia

Woolf accused the so-called realists and naturalists of ignoring true reality, that of the interior mind. They said the naturalists only described externals. Proust, Woolf and other psychological realists turned for their subject matter to the subtle dissection of mental states, and wrote in an entirely different way from their predecessors. Proust wrote about an aristocratic, highly restricted, and artificial social milieu, presumably because psychological nuances are more easily studied in such circles. Here again the term realism hardly defines the difference between the social or externalistic novel and the psychological or interior one, because both concern different manifestations of that protean universal, "reality."

Realism and naturalism were often defined by their methods. Hippolyte Taine and Zola, much impressed by the achievements of science in their age of scientific progress, proclaimed that literature had to become as scientific as medicine: we observe, we experiment, we frame hypotheses and test them, and thus arrive at truth. And indeed, one could agree that both a chemist and a novelist are "investigators" of knowledge. Zola and the Goncourt brothers assiduously collected material by carefully observing people and noting the information accurately and methodically. They should, one supposes, have been historians: the Goncourts indeed thought that social history and the novel were much the same thing. But even the historian soon realizes that history cannot be a "science" in the same sense as the physical sciences. Zola's novels are held together by a vision that has nothing to do with science. This has become a classic comment on his "naturalism." He could approximate the scientific method in collection of "facts"; he could remain morally neutral toward his facts by overtly neither praising nor blaming. But his treatment of his material was another matter. Here, no doubt unconsciously, he used many criteria of selection not drawn from his facts. Underneath the trappings of scientific objectivity, Zola structured his tales much as novelists always have done, using myths, archetypes, value judgments. He faced and made moral choices which no amount of fact could resolve for him. And indeed he had been demonstrably influenced by many others than the scientists. He had acquired socialist values from Fourier, literary skills from Baudelaire. Zola was the heir of centuries and his works reflected this heritage. His books, far from being the clinical observations of a technician, were the creation of a complex mind and imagination.

The objective of realism was sometimes stated to be the immediate, direct and unalloyed representation of people's speech. Some recent writers have used tape recorders in their research; but even they have obviously had to select from their material and hence structure it. The combination of motion pictures and sound recording to reproduce the exact reaction of people unaware that they are being observed, as in a "Candid Camera" show, can give one realism or naturalism. But the presentation of such material without editing and selection would be either meaningless or interminable. Try to write anything, whether a novel or history, and you soon discover that unless you are to put everything in indiscriminately, and thus write an endless and formless tract, you must bring to your task a principle of selection.[5] Realistic observation can provide the materials for art, but it cannot be that art itself. Because the artist must structure his material, and thus impose himself on it, he cannot achieve complete objectivity. Involved in the processes of sorting, sifting, and organizing are the mind of the artist, his purposes and intentions, his ideologies and psychic peculiarities. Any notion he might have of "letting the facts speak for themselves" must vanish. Each artist must decide for himself how he will present the facts that he has deemed important. Flaubert and Turgenev, Zola and Hardy, Proust and Woolf, different artists have made radically different uses of observed phenomena.[6]

Naturalism and realism, especially the former, may be said to reflect a collapse of the traditional value-structure of Western Civilization. This is a familiar modern theme. The writer or artist turns to "nature" when he lacks a principle of selection in his inherited or received values. Zola's huge project, which aimed at overwhelming the mind by its sheer magnitude, was naturalism's classic creation. The art of leaving out, of selecting certain materials

[5] The American naturalistic novelist, Theodore Dreiser, was almost unable to structure the huge chunks of material that flowed from his pen, and the task of editing it for publication had to be performed by a friend.

[6] In a comment on the realists, Nietzsche once made the point that "the smallest fragment in the world is infinite. What does one see, and paint, or write? In the last analysis, what one *wishes* to see, and what one *can* see."

and ignoring the rest, must be based upon a clear understanding of what is and what is not important which in turn we get from an accepted value system. Lacking such a framework of values, or unable to discover one, one may resort to a vivid impressionism that presents random samples of material, seeking to convey these "slices of life" with a feeling for "realism." Earlier novelists, for example Jane Austen, or even George Eliot, formed their stories around a stable society where many values were taken for granted: Christianity, a social heirarchy, and other aspects of an old and firmly knit society. When this framework dissolved, novelists were forced back, as it were, on the expedient of naturalism, reflecting a world without values, possessing "reality" and nothing more. But of course, as we have noted, they could not in fact eliminate all values from their work; they smuggled in a variegated and confused structure of thought even as they proclaimed that they were presenting "nothing but" the facts.

In brief, from a strictly logical point of view, these literary schools are singularly confused. The realists were not defined by their "realism" in any meaningful sense. They were perhaps not realists at all, nor did they form any consistent school. Realism and naturalism must be defined by their historical content. These terms were a shorthand for certain cultural phenomena of the times, and can be grasped only through a study of these phenomena. To repeat, the political reaction from 1848, the rise of an industrial-bourgeois civilization, the trend away from romanticism and the natural revolt of one generation against its fathers, the prestige of scientific Positivism, the collapse of traditional values, the alienation of the artist from society; these are the most important of the cultural phenomena that entered into the literary movements of the period after 1848.

III

"Naturalism" was often regarded as a subdivision or offshoot of realism, sometimes as a separate and rather different school. Naturalism tended to become important at a somewhat later date than realism: beginning in the 1860's, it dominated the 1870's, but in the 1880's confronted a sharp challenge from the symbolists. Impressionism in painting is a parallel phenomenon, and the closeness of the two movements is underlined by the friendship of Émile Zola, the founder and leader of naturalism, with the impressionist painter Paul Cézanne, and by Zola's keen interest in painting.

The 1870's were a harsher decade than the 1860's. France was shattered by defeat at the hands of Prussia in 1870–1871 and the grim civil war that followed (see pp. 000). Prosperity gave way to economic crisis. The Second Empire fell confusedly to the Third Republic, as democracy advanced all over Europe. Socialism, too, arose again. Times were less stable and more violent. Bourgeois industrialism was even more dominant. Reflecting this social milieu, Zola's brand of realism was cruder, both in style and in subject matter, than the work of earlier writers. The Goncourts had been among the first to treat low life in their novels, but Zola greatly enlarged upon them. The more fastidious "realist" Flaubert did not like Zola's "materialism" at all. Zola's critics constantly accused him of wallowing in dirt. His style was humorless and often graceless, but powerful when he dealt with men swept by destiny into tragedy and violence.

The materialism or naturalism of Zola's school was its philosophical belief that man is a creature determined by physical laws and is subject to scientific investigation exactly as material objects and animals are. Writing somewhat later of the American novelist Theodore Dreiser, the critic Stuart Sherman declared the difference between realism and naturalism to be that the former is based upon a theory of human conduct and the latter upon a theory of animal behavior. The shadow of Darwin had intervened between the 1850's and the 1870's.[7] Many people now felt that men were the creatures of instinct, nature an amoral struggle for power. Zola was more directly influenced by the French medical scientist Claude Bernard than by Darwin, yet his works help prove that a spirit of aggressive "scientism" was in the air claiming for the methods of physical science an application to human beings.

Naturalism also carried insinuations of a godless universe. To be "naturalistic" meant, in one important sense, to explain all things without recourse to supernatural power. Traditional religion came under attack not only from Darwinism but from other directions,

---

[7] On this large topic, which is not directly handled in this volume but which profoundly influenced literature as well as everything else, see Gertrude Himmelfarb, *Darwin and the Darwinian Revolution* (London: Chatto & Windus, 1959).

most notably the so-called "higher criticism" which used modern methods of scholarship to study the Bible. Dutch and German scholars led the way in this formidable assault on the underpinnings of faith. Naive acceptance of the Judaic and Christian holy writings as unique, infallible, and divinely inspired was no longer possible for educated men after about 1875. French Positivists such as Ernest Renan, and German Hegelians or post-Hegelians such as David Strauss and Ludwig Feuerbach, assisted this development. The Victorian crisis of faith, the scandal of God's death announced by Nietzsche, the often anguished search for a viable substitute for religion—something that would retain purpose, plan and hope in the universe while sloughing off the discredited fables—are familiar features of the later nineteenth century intellectual landscape.

The position of the writers was often ambivalent. They might take a positive delight in accepting the hard facts of a world where chance, accident, pointless evil prevailed; an amoral universe where good is not rewarded and evil punished, where indeed good and evil have no meaning. As Lucretius had learned long ago, one can find a certain psychological consolation, feel a certain exhilarating liberation, in discarding belief in God and Providence for an atheistic naturalism. And it was a very good way to shock the pious, respectable burgher who still went to church after he had counted his money, and who hoped that God was in his heaven. More often, though, writers substituted the god of scientific naturalism for the Judaeo-Christian God. At the same time as they spoke scornfully of bygone superstitions they wrote in terms of ecstatic admiration for "the army of unalterable law" revealed in scientific findings about nature. Enjoying the discomfiture of the old orthodoxy, they put in its place a new religion of science which smuggled in God without using that name.

On the other hand writers might feel a genuine distress and be aware of the contradictions involved in a shallow scientific optimism *cum* atheism. They might search endlessley and rather despairingly, as did Renan and Samuel Butler, for some God that modern man could believe in, for some scheme of values derived from the scientific method alone.

The variations in this theme were almost endless. From Feuerbach to Butler, from about 1835 to 1885, the awareness grew that man creates his own gods: "An honest God's the noblest work of man!"

Karl Marx scored a direct hit, however crude his weapon, when he declared that religions are but socially expedient ideologies. And in one of the great stories of his later years, "A Simple Heart," Flaubert told of a simple servant woman who came to believe that her stuffed parrot was the Holy Ghost: a fable for the times. Man makes his own myths.

Compared to the realism of the preceding generation, Naturalism was bolder and franker in its treatment of sex and other delicate matters. The original realists had practiced a certain reticence which the naturalists abandoned, though not so boldly as the more recent and frankly pornographic school. In Tolstoy's *Anna Karenina* the seduction scene is discreetly omitted, as it is in the Italian classic by Manzoni, *I Promessi Sposi (The Betrothed)*. One might compare the description of female physique in, say, Tolstoy's *The Cossacks*, with the work of some recent writers. The beauty of the Cossack girl Marianka is central to the story, but all that Tolstoy tells us is that she was tall and had "firm, female curves." As is well known, any secondary trollop in a novel today is likely to receive the detailed anatomical attentions of the author. In this respect Zola's *Nana* almost broke fresh ground, at least in the respectable literary world.

On the whole the naturalists' final position was pessimistic. In the 1890's, with Thomas Hardy, Joseph Conrad, and such profoundly important non-literary figures as Sigmund Freud, we are presented with a bleak universe, deterministic but ruled by blind or evil forces, godless, full of pain and tragedy, where man is helplessly trapped. Perhaps this mood only reflected the condition of civilization, which was becoming increasingly mechanized and dehumanized. At all events, it provoked a revolt against naturalism's hopeless creed. Optimists, if rather terrible ones, arose to affirm the "life force" and *amor fati*, and to proclaim rebellion against determinism and pessimism.

IV

The turn away from naturalism in the 1880's and 1890's reflected dissatisfaction with its results. Some writers, including those who had belonged to the naturalist group, came to believe that it was a dead end. J. K. Huysmans is a good example. Huysmans had once been a follower of Zola and had written naturalist works, but now saw the limitations of naturalism: it offered no criticism of modern life because it offered no ideals. Zola, doubtless, had been a critic, but in defiance of his intellectual system, which declared that the novelist only describes, he does not judge; the novelist does not even regard man as having any will, because man is the mechanical product of heredity and environment. Such a creed was as obnoxious as the brutes it chronicled. It could only further debase man, who was already sinking into the swamps of bourgeois materialism.

So in the 1880's another literary and intellectual revolution occurred, this time against that of a generation before. The symbolists and decadents who lead the literary revolution in the 1880's and 1890's were similar to their predecessors, the naturalists, in that they were equally radical, equally at war with their society (sometimes even more so), equally shocking to the respectable and conventional, if in slightly different ways. If Zola shocked by the coarseness and candor of his revelations of life in the raw in the lower depths, Huysmans and his followers scandalized readers by their more delicate but equally lascivious intimations of far more sophisticated sins. Stylistically and philosophically symbolism and naturalism were at opposite poles. Reverting to romanticism in this respect, symbolists searched out extremely exotic subjects; they dealt with extremely exotic people. In their works there are Oriental goddesses; mysterious hermits, aristocratic misanthropes; above all there are super-refined, tortuously sensitive individuals, lonely and aloof.

"Decadence," the term so often applied to the *fin de siècle* writers, meant the highly refined style of an overripe civilization. That the civilization was old and ultra-sophisticated did not mean that the style was bad. In his essay on Baudelaire Gautier had predicted and defined the phenomenon of decadence as

> art arrived at that point of extreme maturity yielded by the slanting suns of aged civilizations; an ingenious complicated style, full of shades and allusions, constantly pushing back the boundaries of speech . . . struggling to convey the subtleties of neurosis, the dying confessions of passion grown depraved . . . the ultimate utterance of the Word, summoned to final expression and driven to its last hiding-place.

Gautier's words suggest the various manifestations of decadence, so closely related to symbolism: linguistic sophistication, a complex cultural inheritance, the exploration of subtle psychological realms, and a taste for perversities. Such art was delicious, but it could not be shared with the masses; it demanded the attentions of the few really civilized men who were in addition highly skilled literary craftsmen. It had appeared in the twilight periods of Greece and Rome and again among the humanists of the Italian Renaissance, or so it was thought—hence the popularity of Walter Pater's and Jacob Burckhardt's historical studies in Renaissance civilization. If often romantic in his subject matter, the symbolist-decadent was stylistically addicted to the last refinement of classicism, an exquisitely chiseled way of writing that lacked Homeric simplicity but was far from the formless agglomerations of material typical of various forms of naturalism.

Rather than being a cult of the natural, symbolism was a cult of the artificial. "The first duty of life is to be as artificial as possible," Oscar Wilde announced, borrowing this notion from the acknowledged Bible of decadence, Huysmans' *À Rebours (Against the Grain)*. The symbolist-decadent style was as far removed as possible from the huge canvases of Zola, crudely splashed with a broad brush; it preferred exquisite miniatures. Symbolists suggested rather than stated; indeed symbolist works often create a blurred, shadowy effect. They strove to fuse all the senses, to mingle colors, scents, music in a single intangible, bewitching effect. They were purposely ambivalent or suggestive of more than one level of meaning, like a postimpressionist painting. Such delicacy and subtlety were somewhat akin to the styles of Gautier and Baudelaire, the predecessors of symbolism. The realism of Flaubert and of the Parnassian school had also been more stylized and intimate than the realism of Zola. So, in the 1880's and 1890's the symbolist poets, among whom Mallarmé was the foremost, experimented boldly and extensively in the new style; they were speedily imitated by many artists in all lands.

Philosophically, symbolism was vaguely idealist. Mysterious occult forces, sinister but suggestive of a higher realm, haunt the symbolist poem and drama. The symbolists had more extreme ideas of evil than the naturalists: they saw evil within the human soul, even within God. The symbolists and decadents were also more "alienated." They no longer participated in society; they had ceased to think it reformable. The artist withdrew to cultivate his own exquisite feelings, which he felt were the last refuge from and the sole consolation of a dying civilization. He felt absolutely no responsibility to "a hideous society," but even contemplated renouncing all its moral rules. In England the decadent magazine *The Yellow Book*, published in the singular decade of the 'nineties, combined naughtiness with aestheticism, a mood epitomized by Oscar Wilde. On the Continent, where the piercing insights of Nietzsche were beginning to take effect, the mood was more somber. But even in England there was a strain of melancholy, and in some cases an upsurge of religious fervor; many young poets were converted to Catholicism, and some, like John Davidson, committed suicide. They wooed the Absolute in sin and poetry.

In 1837 the German philosopher Friedrich Schlegel suggested that "positive philosophy" is poetry, that the artist alone directly expresses reality. The strange genius Arthur Rimbaud was among the first to attempt to apply this idea to his poetry. His works bypass conceptual thought; in, them the immediate symbols of the imagination reflect a deeper reality—see for example his *Illuminations*, published in 1871. The belief that there is some path to Reality or Being through mystical, intuitive, unconscious or spontaneous apprehension, which escapes the deformations and emasculations of conceptual "rational" thought, has been persistent in the modern world. One finds it in the existentialists as well as the surrealists. It is surely an illusion. We cannot wriggle out of our subjectivity or involvement in the world in this way. Logic may distort reality, but poetry does so equally. Neither through logic nor poetry can man attain the goal of full knowledge of ultimates and essences; such an attainment is impossible for man since he is a part of what he wishes to understand. F. H. Heinemann remarks that for man to understand fully would be like trying to jump over one's own shadow. If the "cold" logic of "abstract" concepts fails to give us reality as it is, the warmth of poetry and concrete imagery must also fail; we have merely shifted from one kind of shadow to another. It is not possible to overcome scepticism by resolving to be irrational. Both realism and idealism alike affirm a conceptual position based on the knowability of the universe, but this is sheer speculation. In retreat from such a position, some recent philosophers have gone "back to immediate experience, or consciousness, back to pure description of the mental world." But such experience must itself somehow be rendered, unless we are to relapse into silence (as did the German philosopher Heidegger). The veil is always there, that veil which Schopenhauer, borrowing from the Hindu, called the Veil of Maya.

The effort to penetrate the veil fascinated the symbolist poets, who in doing so could indulge in an exercise the more piquant because it scorned and ignored the detested multitude. The symbolists were almost deliberately inscrutable, mystical, and obscure. In a society which, as they alleged, now lacked all stability and coherence, they could fall back on the "culte de Moi" (Maurice Barrès' phrase for pure subjectivism). They were, or said they were, altogether cut off from society. They could be as esoteric as they liked, the more so the better, since it infuriated the crowd. "Épater la bourgeoisie"—to bait the vulgar multitude—was the goal of almost all the post-1848 writers, and by the 1880's the best method of doing so had been found. One had to be as *precieux*, as incomprehensible, as subtle as possible.

However, the bourgeois could and did fight back; part of the story of nineteenth century literature and art concerns the efforts of the bourgeoisie to denounce and suppress the symbolist movement. Flaubert and Baudelaire, Ibsen and Zola, Huysmans and Wilde, the respectable howled at them all. Oscar Wilde, symbol of decadence in England, was imprisoned for homosexuality; in prison he was harshly treated and allowed to contract a fatal illness.[8] No wonder "The symbolists hated the public as much as Flaubert hated it," Maurice Bowra remarks.[9]

Symbolists and related *fin de siècle* figures certainly differed from Parnassians and naturalists in being less rational than they. The realist Flaubert had admired the English positivist Herbert Spencer; as we know, Zola fancied that he was making literature into a science; these men were atheists and Positivists. This frame of mind did not cease to exist among men of letters, and H. G. Wells is a good example of a major figure of the 1900's who believed with a

---

[8] See H. Montgomery Hyde, *Oscar Wilde: The Aftermath* (London: Methuen & Co. 1963).

[9] C.M. Bowra, *The Heritage of Symbolism* (New York: Schocken Books, 1961), p. 12.

sort of mystical fanaticism in the value of science as a cure for all the evils of the world. But we do not today see Wells as a truly great writer. Irrationalism and mysticism were in the air. Paradoxically, science and reason themselves often led to a sort of higher irrationalism.

The mordant insights of Nietzsche, preceding slightly those of Sigmund Freud, made it impossible ever again to believe completely in old-fashioned rationalism. Darwin's works had led to a kind of naturalism that saw mind itself as simply a tool of evolutionary survival. Then after Darwin came the discovery of the unconscious, the greatest discovery of the later part of the century.[10] "I am, therefore I think" was the new gospel, reversing Descartes' rationalist formula. Consciousness is an unanalyzable and protean nothingness of which rational thought is only one of the modes.

Science itself deserted the older rationalism in the time of Max Planck and Albert Einstein. These scientists found that Newton had been wrong: time and space do not exist; the universe is not a machine subject to unalterable laws; the ultimate secrets can probably never be wrung from nature by man because he is a part of what he proposes to understand. From 1885 to 1914 was an "age of unreason" whose high priests were not only the half-mad Nietzsche and the still largely unknown Freud, but the respectable and widely influential French philosopher Henri Bergson. Bergson lectured brilliantly at the Sorbonne on the life force that flows through everything, that cannot be grasped by mere conceptual thought but only in the spontaneity of religious or aesthetic experience.

The explosion of 1914 might be related to the intellectual chaos (a "crisis of culture") of the years just preceding it, to the schism in the soul of a civilization that had lost its religion, was hated by its intellectuals, and had evidently declared war on its artists. The amazing technological, scientific, and economic "progress" that took place between 1849 and 1914 covered Europe with railways and steel mills, manufactured new products, linked the entire world in trade, conquered many diseases, increased population and life expectancy, gained fortunes for some and improved even the work-

---

[10] In *The Unconscious before Freud* (London: Tavistock, 1963), Lancelot L. Whyte makes it clear that the unconscious was not strictly a new concept; but it had occupied a most obscure part of the history of thought prior to the age of Nietzsche, Freud, and Jung.

ingman's average standard of life. The writers, artists and intellectuals of Europe remained skeptical, denying the progress and pre-
dicting early doom for a materialistic, valueless civilization. They
rather welcomed the Great War because it offered the chance to
sacrifice for an ideal, and confronted a hateful culture with its Last
Judgment. The malaise of Europe's keepers of the traditional
culture increased in the decade before 1914. The smell of death,
mingled with cruelty and sadism, is present in the ultra-decadents
such as Gabriele d'Annunzio and Octave Mirbeau. The Georgian
poets in Britain fled an abhorrent public reality to seek desperate
solace in the homeliest of quiet country truths, while in Paris the
bohemian life of the cubist artists took a different road to the same
destination—total rejection of the common, public life of a society
grown unendurable to a cultured man.

The German expressionists, convinced that artistic expression is
the only value in a meaningless, irrational universe, were equally
convinced that the artist must express with complete integrity what
his instincts move him to express. He need pay no attention to the
audience. As Nietzsche had said, what has that to do with the
matter? "Our thoughts, our values, our ifs and buts, our yeas and
nays, grow out of us with the same necessity with which a tree
bears its fruit. . . . Suppose they do not please *you*, these fruits of
ours? What concern is that of the trees—or of us philosophers?"
This complete subjectivism was always an ingredient in symbolism,
and it grew stronger, later to lead into phenomena of the 1920's
such as Dadaism and surrealism. It implied a scorn for the public,
for the mass, for all manner of orthodoxy, conformity, institutional-
ized literature and learning. The conversion of the dandy into the
hippy was only a matter of time.

V

These literary movements were European phenomena, crossing
and transcending national boundaries. They took on local coloration, no doubt, but by and large the literati of Europe formed an
international brotherhood. Nietzsche influenced and was influenced
by the French; the French were stimulated by the English and
vice versa; Russia borrowed heavily from the West but repaid
abundantly—the catalogue of influences is endless. Realism, first of
all, appeared in all countries, sometimes in surprisingly similar

forms. Tolstoy's *Anna Karenina* has often been compared to Flaubert's *Madame Bovary*, and both have been compared to the German novelist Theodor Fontane's *Lost Forever (Unwiederbringlich)*, which is also a consummately told story of unhappy marriage and adultery. The Russian novelist Turgenev frequented the society of Flaubert, Daudet, and other Frenchmen, and was also a friend of the English novelist George Eliot. One thinks of the realist and naturalist novel as predominantly French because of France's usual leadership not so much in literature as in ideas, and its flair for formulating movements and schools and for dramatizing them as important, colorful and meaningful. But Flaubert and Zola have their counterparts in every country. In Britain there were George Eliot, George Meredith, Thomas Hardy, George Moore, and Joseph Conrad (by birth a Pole); in Germany Fontane, Theodor Raabe, and Gerhart Hauptmann; in Scandinavia Ibsen and Strindberg. In Russia, of course, we are in the presence of some of the greatest writers of all, such as Turgenev, Dostoyevsky, Tolstoy, Chekhov, and Gorki.[11] These were all men with a European reputation, and sometimes, in accordance with the text about prophets, they received more honor abroad than at home. (Thus, according to Enid Starkie, Richard Wagner's music was prized more by the French than by the Germans, while the Germans adopted Berlioz.) Henrik Ibsen, the Norwegian dramatist, carried Europe by storm in the naturalist epoch of the 1870's and 1880's though his small country did not ordinarily attract much attention in the world of literature and ideas. Leo Tolstoy was probably the most prophetic and charismatic figure in the world in his time. The Irish national literary revival gained fame all over Europe. From Coole Park (the home of Lady Gregory, William Butler Yeats' patroness) to Yasnaya Polyana, Tolstoy's estate, stretched a single kingdom of the mind. Nor should we forget the European influence on American literature; nor for that matter, the influences exerted by American writers, for example that of Edgar Allen Poe on such writers as Baudelaire. Likewise Japan's remarkable Westernization

---

[11] Milada Součkova, in a recent book, *The Parnassian Jaroslav Vrchlický* (The Hague: Mouton, 1965), calls attention to a well-known Czech writer, Positivist, and Parnassian, who admired Gautier (but also Hugo); he was later attacked by the new men of the 1890's who had been strongly influenced by symbolism.

at this time included a considerable absorption of European modes, and some of this influence was reciprocated.

Symbolism also was international. If it originated, again, in France, it quickly gained disciples everywhere. The Belgians, Maurice Maeterlinck and Emile Verhaeren, worshipped at the shrine of Stéphane Mallarmé. The British aesthetes of the 1890's continued the Francophilism of earlier rebels against Victorianism, notably the poet Algernon Charles Swinburne, one of the leading anti-Victorians of the 1860's and 1870's. In Russia Andreyev argued with Gorki in behalf of symbolism, though Tolstoy denounced it. Among the greatest of all symbolist poets was the German, Stefan George; he was joined a little later by Rainer Maria Rilke. The French novelist, Marcel Proust, whose first volume in the series *Remembrance of Things Past* appeared in 1913, found youthful liberation through reading the English Victorian apostle of beauty and hater of industrial society, John Ruskin. In the years just before 1914, the French philosopher Bergson had a strong influence on British writers, especially on the imagist poets. To this list of international exchanges, which could be extended almost indefinitely, one might add as a significant footnote the fact that the young Serbs who plotted the assassination of the Austrian archduke on June 28, 1914, and thus touched the match to the fuse of world war, had been intoxicated by a mixture of European and American literature including Gorki, Andreyev, Walt Whitman, Oscar Wilde, and Ibsen.[12]

The above paragraphs are by way of underscoring a point that should not be forgotten: the essential internationalism of the nineteenth-century European mind. Paradoxically, nationalism was reaching a peak of strength in exactly these years. Nationalism was largely a popular movement. Many writers and intellectuals scorned it as being vulgar, but sometimes even they succumbed and talked about the uniqueness or even the superiority of their national culture: consider for example the French novelist and essayist Maurice Barrès; or Dostoyevsky's cultural Slavophilism, according to which the Russian soul must redeem a corrupt western Europe; or almost any British Victorian in the heyday of Anglo-Saxon smugness.

---

[12] See the interesting article by Vladimir Dedijer, "Sarajevo Fifty Years After," *Foreign Affairs* (July, 1964) (now incorporated in his book, *The Road to Sarajevo*).

However, the point is that the world of ideas and letters was an international and cosmopolitan one in which there were similar trends in every European country, and constant exchanges and cross-influences. Intellectual history, and social, cultural, literary, and artistic history are too often studied in nationalistic isolation, owing to the custom of writing history and literary criticism in terms of national units. Except perhaps for constitutional and the narrower sort of political history, the proper unit of study is not the individual nation but Western civilization as a whole. One can legitimately note local variations, but only after assimilating the general features.

So far we have chiefly discussed literature, but the other arts followed, or tended to follow, a similar pattern. Just as there was a school of painters, among them Turner and Delacroix, who called themselves romantics, so there were those who turned to realism. John Constable, the painter of the Suffolk countryside, was an early rebel against romanticism: he said, "There is still room for a natural painter," and he practiced what he preached. A little later, Victorian England watched in some amazement the emergence of the self-styled Pre-Raphaelite Brotherhood, who somewhat confusedly sought in painting a fresher vision of things-as-they-are; see, for example, the work of John Everett Millais.

In France, it was Gustave Courbet who first announced himself a "realist" and caused a stir in the world of Paris art in the 1850's. Some viewers thought that Courbet had succeeded all too well in painting the commonplace. "Paint only what you can see, not what you can imagine," was his slogan; and it could be a formula for dullness when Courbet saw only funerals and himself in his studio. The Goncourts as well as Baudelaire despised Courbet for his vulgarity; but he became famous and his disciples carried painting on toward the much more successful school of impressionism. He had opened the doorway to the natural world. Though they had to fight a battle against misunderstanding and entrenched custom, impressionists, who shared many qualities with the literary naturalists, made painting more exciting than it had been for two centuries.

Expressionists and other varieties of postimpressionists, including the pioneers of abstract art, corresponded roughly to the symbolist school of poetry. Like the symbolists they were hooted at by an outraged public, and their exhibitions stirred violent controversy on the eve of 1914 from Moscow to Chicago. Their work, like the symbolists' writing, represented a rebellion against naturalism; it abounded in symbols, showed the influence of the new irrationalism, and had a more defiantly anti-social note.

Music, too, was a part of the pattern of aesthetic revolt. The name of Richard Wagner, who deeply influenced almost all the symbolist poets, was a veritable battle cry from 1860 on. Claude Debussy, a tormented genius, set the work of the symbolist poet Mallarmé to music and was close to symbolist circles. In 1913 the performance of Igor Stravinsky's *The Rite of Spring* set off a battle royal in Paris, as Wagner's *Tannhäuser* had done half a century before. Though it must receive here less discussion than it merits, music played a vigorous part in the years between 1848 and 1914, a period which produced many of the great composers most frequently played since then, such as Brahms, Berlioz, Schumann, Liszt, Wagner, Debussy, and Ravel.

The architecture of this same period provoked the savage comment from John Ruskin that in the cities of the nineteenth century, dedicated solely to commerce and choked with "human dust," "no architecture is possible—nay, no desire of it is possible to their inhabitants." To the author of *The Nature of Gothic* and *The Stones of Venice*, as to many other nineteenth century critics, the supreme indictment of bourgeois civilization was that it built only factories and had no style of its own. One of Ruskin's readers was Frank Lloyd Wright: by the end of the century, men were arising who would bravely try to create a modern style in architecture. The moneyed classes in the heyday of industrialism satisfied their deplorable taste with imitations of past styles and with sham-Gothic restorations. This did not change much before 1914, though Wright, Le Corbusier, and Gropius were beginning their brilliant careers in the 1900's. Perhaps one of the reasons why John Ruskin went mad was that so little was done to improve the ugliness surrounding him: although William Morris, a disciple of Ruskin's and a member of the Pre-Raphaelite Brotherhood, tried to stimulate a cult for beauty and craftsmanship by making beautiful furnishings, books, and other objects, in one of the most extraordinary one-man performances of the century.

VI

This estrangement between art and society continues to be a disturbing feature of our age. In his inquiry into the barriers between scientist and humanist, *The Two Cultures*, published in 1959, C. P. Snow noted the scientists' belief that novelists and poets are mad, anti-social, and incomprehensible. This reaction remains typical of "right-thinking," "normal" people, or those engaged in the thoroughly "rational" pursuits of business, administration, science, and technology. Most of these people believe, certainly to their loss and perhaps to the impairment of their personalities, that the realm of serious literature and art is occupied by queer, even crazy people who are often only just distinguishable from the criminally insane. These "right-thinking" people content themselves with paperback sex and violence, with "pop" art, if any, and no contemporary music at all unless they can tolerate their offspring's primitive variety. They laugh at "modern art," and simply are not aware of what goes on in contemporary poetry and music. They may be slightly aware of certain avant gard novels and plays: there may be a rare occasion when some piece of literature manages precariously to bridge the chasm between art and the public. But one could not question the tininess of the group in the United States today that tries to maintain a knowledge and sympathetic awareness of the contemporary arts. Hardly one in a hundred Americans would even recognize the names of outstanding American poets of this generation (the reader might try himself on Louis Simpson, Sylvia Plath, John Berryman).

It must be admitted that many modern poets, novelists, and dramatists arc, by conventional standards, strange people who do unacceptable things; some of them (like some of the 'right-thinking' people, of course) go mad and even commit suicide. What many of them write is grotesque in style and degenerate in content. Some of them hate and reject society so strongly that they make their lives, as well as their art, one continuous exercise in nose-thumbing at everything conventional. Their loss is that they refuse to make any rational effort to understand and participate in society; this distorts their art and renders it sterile. If the author of a recent perceptive study of the American novel can entitle his book *After Alienation*,[13] detecting a trend back toward reconciliation between writer and society, this trend is as yet surely only a cloud no bigger than a man's hand in the sky of alienation. "Beats," dope addicts, pornographers and violent cynics abound in the arts. Nevertheless their commitment to art is sincere, and they are trying to write or paint seriously. They are carrying on the tradition of Baudelaire, Rimbaud (whom some of them worship as a god,[14]) Guillaume Apollinaire the French surrealist poet, and all the others who set up the religion of art as a counterblast to the rule of the "bourgeoisie."

This "schism in the soul" of modern Western civilization may be contrasted to great epochs in the past. From Periclean Greece to the eighteenth century, art was naturally social, and the artist was an esteemed member of the community. One must add that the community of those who truly appreciated beauty and the best of the arts was quite small: it consisted of the leisured and upper classes. However, in earlier nineteenth-century England the artist was not as estranged from his society as he is now, nor was the Victorian poet without honor; consider Tennyson, Browning, Emerson, and Longfellow. Walter Allen, in his history of the English novel, dates the alienation of the artist in England from the time of Thomas Hardy. At that time we enter a different moral universe—bitter, tragic, pessimistic, contemptuous of the shams of respectability. Such alienation had come earlier in France, in the time of Baudelaire, Flaubert and Rimbaud in the 1860's.

Today in the United States, the arts scarcely count, judging by the amount of public money spent subsidizing them, as opposed to the sums ladled out for all kinds of science, even for political theory. Is this alienation the fault of the writers and artists or the fault of society? Objectively we may agree with the social theorists who from Hegel and Comte to Max Weber have pointed out that modern society is "rationalized," the modern mind "positivistic" to a degree that drives art into the margin of society along with religion and other non-rationalistic modes.[15] It is one of the great themes,

[13] Marcus Klein (New York, 1965).

[14] Cf. Henry Miller, *Time of the Assassins: A Study of Rimbaud* (New York, 1956), and René Etiemble, *Le Mythe de Rimbaud* (Paris, 1953).

[15] For a recent commentary see the brilliant lectures by Edgar Wind, *Art and Anarchy* (London: Faber & Faber, 1963).

and surely one of the great tragedies of modern times. Perhaps it may be most hopefully seen as a temporary crisis caused by the democratization of modern society. Sophisticated European intellectuals faced what often seemed to them a "revolt of the masses" against civilization, but which may be the slow progress of those masses from abject degradation to a share in the common culture. The writers showed little understanding of this process. It must be conceded that the situation was one to try their patience.

Julian Benda, a determined foe of "literary Byzantinism" and the artists' withdrawal from society, has remarked that "this *noli me tangere* attitude slapped in the face of common humanity by modern literature seems to have been known neither by Sophocles, nor by Vergil, nor Dante, nor Racine, nor Goethe, nor Hugo, who gave their masterpieces as the sun gives its light, without worrying about who received it. . ."[16] We may wonder whether the masses of peasants and serfs had any knowledge of Vergil, Dante, or Racine—indeed, we know they did not. The eighteenth-century appeal to the common judgment of all men was really based on a consensus among the aristocracy. Even the more popular romantics scarcely reached beyond a middle-class audience. If the Victorian writers were not alienated until the 1890's, it was in part because of Victorian class stratification, which produced a sharply divided world in which the lower classes lived in another moral and intellectual universe than the upper classes. With the emergence of the former into cultural life, the sensitive and the educated would for the time being be driven into isolation. It was perhaps too much to expect that they would be content to hibernate with their Vergil and Racine in an age seething with excitement and change. For they too were a part of that "generous confusion" (as Graham Hough has called the nineteenth century), in the shadow of which we still live.

The readings that follow attempt to illustrate some of the themes discussed above. It is impossible to illustrate them all by adequate selections from all the important writers: such an anthology would run to dozens of volumes. For this was above all a prolific century, teeming with literature, some of it great, most of it interesting. The

[16] Julien Benda, *La France Byzantine, ou le triomphe de la littérature pure* (Paris: Gallimard, 1945), p. 112.

British Victorians in this powerful era are somewhat underrepresented; they will be treated more fully in another volume in this series devoted to the Victorian age. For French literature it is an equally grand era, for Russia it is *the* era, since nothing like the works of Pushkin, Gogol, Herzen, Dostoyevsky, Tolstoy, Chekhov, Turgenev, Gorki and Andreyev had ever appeared in earlier Russian history. Wagner, Nietzsche, Schopenhauer, Marx, Kierkegaard, Freud, and Ibsen, along with others, came explosively out of the Germanic world. For all Europe it was an age of ideas and ideologies, a time of acute spiritual tensions; the most decisive and critical century for modern man. In this book I can display no more than a tiny portion of this; hopefully it will stimulate students to continue the quest.

I. *Realism*

1. The disenchantment of 1848

"No living man can remain the same after such a blow."
Alexander Herzen, "After the Storm," *From the Other Shore*
(1849)[1]

A voluntary exile from his native Russia, Alexander Herzen arrived in Paris as an ardent young liberal tinged with romantic enthusiasms, just in time to witness the European revolutions of 1848. He was a man of great literary talent and one of the leading intellectuals of his day. Later, between 1857 and 1865, his magazine *The Bell* was smuggled into Russia where it had enormous influence; Herzen was the idol of this generation of Russian reformers. The failure of the 1848 revolutions did not crush his revolutionary spirit, but it sobered him considerably, and thereafter he was always suspicious of large abstractions and intellectual systems—a revolutionary without fanaticism, as Isaiah Berlin calls him. "Do not search for any solutions in this book," he wrote to his son concerning *From the Other Shore*. "Only in the distant future will we be able to perceive the good society. For the time being we can only fight against the specific falsehoods that we encounter." The following selection includes the words wrung from him in the bitter hour of defeat when so many of his generous illusions came crashing down. Countless others felt something similar.

In the "June days" to which Herzen refers, the socialist-led Parisian working class, at odds with the bourgeois-dominated national legislature to which the revolution of February had led, rose up in an insurrection which Alexis de Tocqueville, who witnessed it, called "the greatest and most singular which ever there was in our history and perhaps in any other." It was brutally repressed by the republic's military force. The revolution and the republic were destroyed by this civil war within the ranks of the "people," for the slaughter disillusioned the left-

[1] This translation is by L. Navrozov.

wing as much as the insurrection frightened the conservatives. It was a
pattern repeated elsewhere in Europe during the fateful year of 1848.

Women cry to ease their hearts; that consolation is denied us.
For me writing must take the place of tears. I am writing not to
describe or to explain the bloody events, but simply to speak of
them, to give vent to words, thoughts—to my bitterness. What
place is here for description, for a collection of facts, for judgment?
I can still hear the sound of gunshots, the thud of cavalry galloping
by, the hollow, dismal sounds of gun-carriages rolling along the
deserted streets. Snatches of scenes flash through my mind: a
wounded man on a stretcher presses a hand to his side, the blood
trickling down it; omnibuses in the Place de la Bastille; the encamp-
ments at Porte St. Denis, on the Champs-Elysées, and the mournful
call of the night, "Sentinelle, prenez garde à vous. . ." What talk
can there be of description! The brain is too heated, the blood too
bitter.

It is enough to kill you or drive you mad to have to sit in a room
with arms folded, without being able to go outside, and yet to hear
everywhere, near and far, gunshots, cannonades, cries, the roll of
drums, and to know that somewhere nearby blood is being shed,
the people are being knifed, bayoneted—dying. I did not die, but
I have aged. I am recovering from those June days as if after a grave
illness.

And how solemnly they began! On the twenty-third, about four
o'clock, I was taking a walk before dinner-time, along the banks
of the Seine, bound for the Hotel de Ville. The shops were being
shut up. Sinister-looking National Guards were walking in various
directions. The sky was overcast and it was drizzling. . . . I stopped
at Pont-Neuf. A flash of lightning burst out of the cloud; one peal
of thunder followed another, and above them could be heard the
regular, prolonged tolling of the bell of Saint-Sulpice—the proletariat, again betrayed, was calling its brothers to arms. The cathedral and all the buildings along the embankment were strangely lit
up by several rays of the sun which had pierced the clouds. The
drumbeats rolled in from all sides; the artillery was moving from
the Place du Carrousel.

I listened to the thunder and the tocsin and could not tear my
eyes away from the panorama of Paris—I seemed to be taking leave

of it. I passionately loved Paris at that moment; that was my last tribute to the great city; after the June days it became repugnant to me.

Barricades were being built in all the lanes and streets on the opposite bank of the river. Even now I can see the somber faces of those who were carrying stones, children and women helping them. A young engineering student mounted one of the barricades, evidently completed, planted the banner on it, and began to sing the "Marseillaise" softly in a voice full of sad solemnity. Everybody working there joined in, and this magnificent song, resounding from behind the barricade, wrung the heart. . . . The bell continued to toll. In the meantime the artillery rolled on to the bridge and General Bedeau swept his field glasses over the *enemy* position.

There was still time then to prevent what followed; it was still possible to save the republic and the freedom of all Europe. It was still possible to make peace. The imbecile and blundering government was incapable of this; the Assembly did not desire it; the reactionaries called for revenge, for blood, for atonement for February 24, and the strongboxes of the *National* furnished them with the agents to do the work.

Now, what do you say, my dear Prince Radetzky and you, Your Excellency, Count Paskevich-Erivansky? You are unfit to serve under Cavaignac. Metternich and all the members of the Third Department in his chancellery are *bons enfants* compared to the assembly of enraged shopkeepers.[2]

On the evening of June 26, after the victory of the *National* over Paris, we heard salvos with brief, regular intervals between them. . . . We glanced at each other; everybody was green in the face. "These are executions," we said in unison and looked away. I pressed my forehead to the windowpane. Such moments kindle hatred for a dozen of years, call for lifelong vengeance. *Woe betide those who forgive such moments!*

After the slaughter which lasted four days, quiet was restored. It was a truce during a stage of siege. The streets were still cordoned off and only very occasionally could you meet a carriage. Arrogant

---

[2] Herzen refers to Austrian reactionaries, notorious in Europe for their repression of all liberal causes, and suggests in bitter irony that they could not hold a candle to the bourgeoisie of the French Republic. Cavaignac was the general who led the military force against the workers (Ed.).

National Guards, with ferocious, bestial faces, guarded the shops, brandishing bayonets and rifle butts. Hilarious crowds of drunken militia marched up and down the boulevards, singing "Mourir pour la patrie," boys of sixteen and seventeen bragged of their brothers' blood, caked dry on their hands; middle-class tradeswomen, running out of their shops to hail the conquerors, pelted them with flowers. Cavaignac displayed in his carriage some scoundrel who had killed dozens of Frenchmen. The bourgeoisie were triumphant. And in the meantime the houses in the suburbs of Saint-Antoine were still burning. The shelled walls collapsed, and the exposed interior revealed stone wounds, broken furniture smoldering, glittering pieces of shattered mirrors. . . . But where were the owners, the tenants? No one gave them a thought. Sand had been sprinkled here and there, but the blood showed through all the same. The Pantheon, damaged by shells, was closed to the public. Tents had been pitched along the boulevards; horses nibbled the carefully tended trees of the Champs-Élysées; the Place de la Concorde was littered with hay, the cuirasses of the cavalry and saddles were lying about. Soldiers cooked soup near the railing of the Jardin des Tuileries. Paris saw nothing like it even in 1814.

A few more days passed and Paris began to assume its usual aspect: crowds of idlers again made their appearance on the boulevards; fashionably dressed women in carriages and cabriolets came *to have a look at* the scene of ruins and the signs of desperate battle. The frequent patrols and columns of prisoners alone called to mind those terrible days. Only then did the situation begin to clear up. You will find in Byron a description of a battle waged at night. Its details are veiled by the darkness. At dawn, long after the battle has ended, you can see what had been left behind: a sword here, a blood-soaked rag there. This was the dawn that invaded the soul; it threw light on the frightful havoc. Half of our hopes, half of our faith were done to death; ideas of renunciation, of despair passed through the mind and took root. Who could have thought that our soul, which had been so sorely tried by existing scepticism, still contained so much that was destructible?

No living man can remain the same after such a blow. He either turns more religious, clinging desperately to his creed and finding a kind of consolation in despair, and, struck by the thunderbolt, his heart yet again sends forth new shoots. Or else, manfully, though reluctantly, he parts with his last illusions, taking an even more sober view and loosening his grip on the last withered leaves being whirled away by the biting autumnal wind.

Which is preferable? It is hard to say.

One leads to the bliss of folly, the other to the misery of knowledge.

Make your own choice. One is extremely substantial because it leaves you nothing; the other guarantees nothing, but gives much. I prefer to know even if it deprives me of the last consolation. I shall make my way, a spiritual beggar, through the world, my childish hopes and adolescent aspirations uprooted. Let them all appear before the court of incorruptible reason.

Man houses a permanent, revolutionary tribunal within himself, an implacable Fouquier-Tinville, and even a guillotine. Sometimes judges fall asleep, the guillotine rusts, the false notions, outdated, romantic and feeble, come to life and make themselves at home when all of a sudden some terrific blow rouses the heedless judge and the dozing executioner, and then comes the savage retribution, for the slightest concession, the slightest mercy or pity shown leads back to the past and leaves the chains intact. There is no choice: either execute and go forward, or grant a reprieve and stop midway.

Who doesn't remember his own logical romance, who doesn't remember how the first seeds of doubt, of audacious investigation, entered his heart, and how there they grew riotously until they reached its innermost recesses? That is precisely what it means to stand before the terrible court of the mind. It is not as easy as it seems to execute one's convictions: it is hard to part company with thoughts which grew up with us, and became part of us, which cherished and consoled us; how ungrateful it would be to give them up! Yes, but there is no gratitude at that tribunal; nothing is held sacred, and if the revolution, like Saturn, devours its own children, then negation, like Nero, assassinates its own mother to disembarrass itself of the past. People are afraid of their logic and, having rashly summoned to court the church, the state, the family and morality, good and evil, they endeavor to save some scraps, fragments of the old. While rejecting Christianity, they retain immortality of the soul, idealism, providence. And so people who have marched together, here part ways: some go to the right, others to the left. And still others come to a standstill; like mile posts, they show how much

ground has been covered. But there are those who discard the last
ballast of the past and march boldly forward. In passing from the
old world to the new, one can take nothing along.

Reason, like the Convention, is inexorable and impartial. It recoils
at nothing, and demands that the most supreme being should be
placed on the prisoner's bench—the good king of theology is to
have his January 21. This trial is like the one over Louis XVI, the
touchstone for Girondins. All that is weak and incomplete either
flees or lies; either does not vote at all or else votes without conviction. Meanwhile those who pronounced the sentence believe that
with the execution of the king there is nothing more to condemn;
that from January 22 onwards they shall have a republic, all ready
and perfect. As if atheism was enough in itself to do away with
religion; as if the execution of Louis XVI was enough to do away
with monarchy. There is an astounding similarity between the
phenomenology of terror and logic. Terror began right after
the execution of the king; following him on to the scaffold came the
noble sons of the revolution: brilliant, eloquent, feeble. We pity
them but there was no saving them, and their heads fell; after them
rolled the leonine head of Danton and that of Camille Desmoulins,
the pet of the revolution. Now, at long last, is it all over? No, now
it is the turn of the incorruptible executioners; they will be executed
because they believed in the possibility of democracy being established in France, because they put men to death in the name of
equality; yes, they were executed like Anacharsis Cloots who
dreamed of the fraternity of peoples a few days before the Napole-
onic epoch, and a few years before the Vienna Congress.

There will be no liberty in the world until everything religious
and political is transformed into something human, simple, subject
to criticism and negation. Logic which had reached maturity finds
canonized doctrines detestable; it unfrocks these saints and makes
them human; it transforms sacred mysteries into plain truths; it
holds nothing sacred and if the republic claims those rights that
were held by the monarchy, it despises the republic as it did the
monarchy. Nay, infinitely more! There is no sense in monarchy—
it maintains itself by violence; while the very name "republic"
makes the heart beat faster. Monarchy is in itself a religion, while
the republic has no mystic apologies, no divine rights, it is on our

own level. It is not enough to hate the crown; one must equally lose one's veneration for the Phrygian cap; it is not enough to hold that lèse-majesté is a crime. It is time that man brought to the bar of justice the republic, legislation, representation, all concepts of the citizen and his relation to others and to the state. There will be many executions; one must be ready to sacrifice what is near and dear. It doesn't require very much to sacrifice what we detest! What is hard is to sacrifice what we love once we are convinced that it is not the truth. Therein lies the real task. We are to be executioners of the past. It is not for us to gather the fruit! To us is left the task of persecuting and identifying the past no matter what disguise it assumes and of executing it and laying it on the altar of the future. It triumphs in fact—let us, in the name of human thought, kill it in idea, in conviction. No concessions to anyone! The tricolor of concessions is no good, for it will take a long time before the blood of the June days comes off. And whom, indeed, shall we spare? All the elements of the crumbling world appear in all their wretched absurdity and repulsive folly. What is it you respect? Surely not a government of the *people?* Whom is it you pity? Surely not Paris?

For three whole months the representatives of the people, elected by universal suffrage, elected by all of France, did absolutely nothing and then suddenly rose to their feet in order to show the world an amazing spectacle—eight hundred men acting as one huge monster. Blood flowed like water but not a word did they find of love or conciliation; everything human and generous was overshadowed by the clamor for revenge and fury. The voice of the dying Affre[3] could not move this many-tongued Caligula, this Bourbon changed into copper coins. They pressed to their heart the National Guards who shot down the unarmed. Senard blessed Cavaignac, and Cavaignac was moved to tears as he carried out all the crimes indicated by the judicial finger of the representatives. In the meantime the formidable minority went into hiding. The mountain hid behind the clouds, content that it had not been executed or sent to rot in the dungeons. It silently suffered citizens to be disarmed and decrees

---

[3] Archbishop Affre was shot at the barricade near the Place de la Bastille while trying to make peace (Ed.).

on deportation to be passed; people to be imprisoned for anything in the world, and especially for refusing to shoot their own brothers.

Murder became, in these fearful days, a duty; he who did not stain his hands with the blood of the proletariat became suspect to the middle class. The majority had the courage of their crimes. And those wretched friends of the people, those rhetoricians, those blank hearts? There was one courageous outcry, one great outburst of indignation, and that was uttered outside the Assembly Chamber. The terrible curse of old Lamennais[4] fell on the head of the heartless cannibals and showed up all the more plainly on the brow of the cowards who, in uttering the word "republic," were terrified by its meaning.

Paris! How long has this name been a lodestar to people! Who did not love and worship it? But its time has passed. Let it leave the stage. In the June days it engaged in a bitter contest which it cannot consummate. Paris has aged and its youthful dreams no longer become it. Rejuvenation calls for great shocks: massacres of Saint Bartholomew, the days of September. However, the horrors of June did not bring about recovery. Where will this decrepit vampire obtain more blood of the just, that blood which, on June 27, reflected the fire of the lampions lit by the exultant middle class? Paris adores playing soldiers. It made an emperor of a lucky soldier; it applauded a monstrosity named victory; it erected statues. After fifteen years it again placed the bourgeois figure of the little corporal on a pedestal; it reverentially brought back the ashes of the founder of slavery. Now, too, it hoped to find in soldiers the anchor of salvation against freedom and equality; it summoned the savage hordes of Africans to fight its brothers so as not to share the spoils with them, and cut and stabbed with the steady hand of the assassin. Let it, then, pay for its deeds and its errors.

Paris shot people without trial. . . . What will be the outcome of this bloodshed?—who knows? But whatever it is, it is enough that in this fury of madness, of revenge, of conflict and retribution, the world which stands in the way of the new man, preventing him

[4] Famous proponent of democratic and social Catholicism, a Breton priest whose *Words of a Believer* was one of the most widely read tracts of the 1830's (Ed.).

from living and establishing the future, will fall. And this is splendid! So, long live chaos and destruction!

Vive la mort!

And let the future come!

Paris, July 27, 1848

2. The pessimistic view

"It is physical power alone which has any effect on men. . . ."
Schopenhauer, "Government," *Parerga and Paralipomena*, (1851)[1]

As a brash young man, Arthur Schopenhauer came to Berlin in 1820 and announced that he was going to lecture at the same hour as the great Hegel. Unhappily very few listeners came, and the first edition of his book *The World as Will and Idea* attracted little notice. Already eccentric, Schopenhauer became increasingly misanthropic and lived a very irregular life. However, he continued to write essays and to augment his book in further editions. He treated all the German idealist philosophers with disdain, save Kant whom he respected. Schopenhauer began to collect a following after 1848, when the hour was ripe for his pessimistic outlook, and by the time of his death in 1860 he had grown famous. That he was a gifted writer and an extremely interesting philosopher is not questioned today.

His philosophy was distinctive in its stress on irrational will as the foundation of the cosmos. He agreed with idealism in that he saw basic reality as a non-material unity. But unlike the idealists he did not view this absolute as reason, but rather as a blind, striving force which he called will. There is no logic or sense in the universe, just an endless wanting, a driving energy like man's own restless appetites. Nietzsche would name this force the will to power; Bergson called it the life force; Freud defined it as Eros or the libido: they all could trace their basic conception back to Schopenhauer, and indeed this view of the universe also bears some resemblance to Darwin's vision of struggle and chance. Unlike these thinkers, however, Schopenhauer drew from this idea wholly pessimistic conclusions. He saw no escape from a cruel, meaningless world except in aesthetic contemplation, or in the extinction of the will. Schopenhauer had early fallen under the influence of the recently translated Hindu philosophic-religious classics and appar-

---

[1] Schopenhauer's essay is available in paperback, in a reprint of the old, very good translation by T. Bailey Saunders, used here: *The Essential Schopenhauer* (New York: Barnes and Noble, 1951).

ently adopted their goal of Nirvana, the state of blissful nothingness in which the self is blended into the all.

Schopenhauer was a cultivated man, he wrote with wit and verve and is most readable and widely read. The following essay, published in 1851 in his collection of essays *Parerga and Paralipomena*, on the subject of government, reveals something of the mood of disenchanted realism that made Schopenhauer popular with the post-1848 generation.

I T IS a characteristic failing of the Germans to look in the clouds for what lies at their feet. An excellent example of this is furnished by the treatment which the idea of *natural right* has received at the hands of professors of philosophy. When they are called upon to explain those simple relations of human life which make up the substance of this right, such as right and wrong, property, state, punishment and so on, they have recourse to the most extravagant, abstract, remote and meaningless conceptions, and out of them build a Tower of Babel reaching to the clouds, and taking this or that form according to the special whim of the professor for the time being. The clearest and simplest relations of life, such as effect us directly, are thus made quite unintelligible, to the great detriment of the young people who are educated in such a school. These relations themselves are perfectly simple and easily understood—as the reader may convince himself if he will turn to the account which I have given of them in the *Foundation of Morality*, § 17, and in my chief work, bk. i., § 62 [*The World as Will and Idea*.] But at the sound of certain words, like right, freedom, the good, being—this nugatory infinitive of the cupola—and many others of the same sort, the German's head begins to swim, and falling straightway into a kind of delirium he launches forth into high-flown phrases which have no meaning whatever. He takes the most remote and empty conceptions, and strings them together artificially, instead of fixing his eyes on the facts, and looking at things and relations as they really are. It is these things and relations which supply the ideas of right and freedom, and give them the only true meaning that they possess.

The man who starts from the preconceived opinion that the conception of right must be a positive one, and then attempts to define it, will fail; for he is trying to grasp a shadow, to pursue a specter, to search for what does not exist. The conception of right is a negative one, like the conception of freedom; its content is mere negation. It is the conception of wrong which is positive; wrong has the same significance as *injury—laesio—*in the widest sense of the term. An injury may be done either to a man's person or to his property or to his honor; and accordingly a man's rights are easy to define: everyone has a right to do anything that injures no one else.

To have a right to do or claim a thing means nothing more than to be able to do or take or use it without thereby injuring anyone else. *Simplex sigillum veri.* This definition shows how senseless many questions are; for instance, the question whether we have the right to take our own life. As far as concerns the personal claims which others may possibly have upon us, they are subject to the condition that we are alive, and fall to the ground when we die. To demand of a man, who does not care to live any longer for himself, that he should live on as a mere machine for the advantage of other is an extravagant pretension.

Although men's powers differ, their rights are alike. Their rights do not rest upon their powers, because right is of a moral complexion; they rest on the fact that the same will to live shows itself in every man at the same stage of its manifestation. This, however, only applies to that original and abstract right, which a man possesses as a man. The property, and also the honor, which a man acquires for himself by the exercise of the powers, depend on the measure and kind of power which he possesses, and so len'd his right a wider sphere of application. Here, then, equality comes to an end. The man who is better equipped, or more active, increases by adding to his gains, not his Right, but the number of the things to which it extends.

In my chief work[2] I have proved that the state in its essence is merely an institution existing for the purpose of protecting its members against outward attack or inward dissension. It follows from this that the ultimate ground on which the state is necessary is the acknowledged lack of right in the human race. If right were there, no one would think of a state; for no one would have any fear that his rights would be impaired; and a mere union against the attacks of wild beasts or the elements would have very little analogy with what we mean by a state. From this point of view it

[2] Bk. ii., ch. xlii.

is easy to see how dull and stupid are the philosophasters who in pompous phrases represent that the state is the supreme end and flower of human existence. Such a view is the apotheosis of philistinism.

If it were right that ruled in the world, a man would have done enough in building his house, and would need no other protection than the right of possessing it, which would be obvious. But since wrong is the order of the day, it is requisite that the man who has built his house should also be able to protect it. Otherwise his right is *de facto* incomplete; the aggressor, that is to say, has the right of might—*Faustrecht;* and this is just the conception of right which Spinoza entertains. He recognizes no other. His words are: *unusquisque tantum juris habet quantum potentia valet;* each man has as much right as he has power. And again *uniuscuisque jus potentia eius definitur;* each man's right is determined by his power. Hobbes seems to have started this conception of right, and he adds the strange comment that the right of the good Lord to all things rests on nothing but His omnipotence.

Now this is a conception of right which, both in theory and in practice, no longer prevails in the civic world; but in the world in general, though abolished in theory, it continues to apply in practice. The consequences of neglecting it may be seen in the case of China. Threatened by rebellion within and foes without, this great empire is in a defenseless state, and has to pay the penalty of having cultivated only the arts of peace and ignored the arts of war.

There is a certain analogy between the operations of nature and those of man which is a peculiar but not fortuitous character, and is based on the identity of the will in both. When the herbivorous animals had taken their place in the organic world, beasts of prey made their appearance—necessarily a late appearance—in each species, and proceeded to live upon them. Just in the same way, as soon as by honest toil and in the sweat of their faces men have won from the ground what is needed for the support of their societies, a number of individuals are sure to arise in some of these societies, who, instead of cultivating the earth and living on its produce, prefer to take their lives in their hands and risk health and freedom by falling upon those who are in possession of what they have honestly earned, and by appropriating the fruits of their labor. These are the beasts of prey in the human race; they are the conquering peoples whom we find everywhere in history, from the most ancient to the most recent times. Their varying fortunes, as at one moment they succeed and at another fail, make up the general elements of the history of the world. Hence Voltaire was perfectly right when he said that the aim of all war is robbery. That those who engage in it are ashamed of their doings is clear by the fact that governments loudly protest their reluctance to appeal to arms except for purposes of self-defense. Instead of trying to excuse themselves by telling public and official lies, which are almost more revolting than war itself, they should take their stand, as bold as brass, on Macchiavelli's doctrine. The gist of it may be stated to be this: that whereas between one individual and another, and so far as concerns the law and morality of their relations, the principle, *Don't do to others what you wouldn't like done to yourself,* certainly applies, it is the converse of this principle which is appropriate in the case of nations and in politics: *What you wouldn't like done to yourself do to others.* If you do not want to be put under a foreign yoke, take time by the forelock, and put your neighbor under it himself; whenever, that is to say, his weakness offers you the opportunity. For if you let the opportunity pass, it will desert one day to the enemy's camp and offer itself there. Then your enemy will put you under his yoke; and your failure to grasp the opportunity may be paid for, not by the generation which was guilty of it, but by the next. This Macchiavellian principle is always a much more decent cloak for the lust of robbery than the rags of very obvious lies in a speech from the head of the state; lies, too, of a description which recalls the well-known story of the rabbit attacking the dog. Every state looks upon its neighbors as at bottom a horde of robbers, who will fall upon it as soon as they have the opportunity. . . .

The great mass of mankind, always and everywhere, cannot do without leaders, guides and counselors, in one shape or another, according to the matter in question; judges, governors, generals, officials, priests, doctors, men of learning, philosophers, and so on, are all a necessity. Their common task is to lead the race, for the greater part so incapable and perverse, through the labyrinth of life, of which each of them according to his position and capacity has obtained a general view, be his range wide or narrow. That these guides of the race should be permanently relieved of all bodily labor as well as all discomfort; nay, that in proportion to their much greater achievements they should necessarily own and enjoy more than the common man, is natural and reasonable. Great merchants should also be included in the same privileged class, whenever they make farsighted preparations for national needs.

The question of the sovereignty of the people is at bottom the same as the question whether any man can have an original right to rule a people against its will. How that proposition can be reasonably maintained I do not see. The people, it must be admitted, is sovereign; but it is a sovereign who is always a minor. It must have permanent guardians, and it can never exercise its rights itself, without creating dangers of which no one can foresee the end; especially as like all minors, it is very apt to become the sport of designing sharpers, in the shape of what are called demagogues.

Voltaire remarks that the first man to become a king was a successful soldier. It is certainly the case that all princes were originally victorious leaders of armies, and for a long time it was as such that they bore sway. On the rise of standing armies princes began to regard their people as a means of sustaining themselves and their soldiers, and treated them, accordingly, as though they were a herd of cattle, which had to be tended in order that it might provide wool, milk, and meat. The why and wherefore of all this, as I shall presently show in detail, is the fact that originally it was not right, but might, that ruled in the world. Might has the advantage of having been the first in the field. That is why it is impossible to do away with it and abolish it altogether; it must always have its place; and all that a man can wish or ask is that it should be found on the side of right and associated with it. Accordingly says the prince to his subjects: "I rule you in virtue of the power which I possess. But, on the other hand, it excludes that of anyone else, and I shall suffer none but my own, whether it comes from without, or arises within by one of you trying to oppress another. In this way, then, you are protected." The arrangement was carried out; and just because it was carried out the old idea of kingship developed with time and progress into quite a different idea, and put the other one in the background, where it may still be seen, now and then, flitting about like a specter. Its place has been taken by the idea of the king as father of his people, as the firm and unshakable pillar which alone supports and maintains the whole organization of law and order, and consequently the rights of every man.[3] But a king can accomplish this only by inborn prerogative which reserves authority to him and to him alone—an authority which is supreme, indubitable, and beyond all attack, nay, to which everyone renders instinctive obedience. Hence the king is rightly said to rule "by the grace of God." He is always the most useful person in the state, and his services are never too dearly repaid by any Civil List, however heavy. . . .

Right in itself is powerless; in nature it is might that rules. To enlist might on the side of right, so that by means of it right may rule, is the problem of statesmanship. And it is indeed a hard problem, as will be obvious if we remember that almost every human breast is the seat of an egoism which has no limits, and is usually associated with an accumulated store of hatred and malice; so that at the very start feelings of enmity largely prevail over those of friendship. We have also to bear in mind that it is many millions of individuals so constituted who have to be kept in the bonds of law and order, peace and tranquillity; whereas originally everyone had a right to say to everyone else: *I am just as good as you are!* A consideration of all this must fill us with surprise that on the whole the world pursues its way to peacefully and quietly, and with so much law and order as we see to exist. It is the machinery of state which alone accomplishes it. For it is physical power alone which has any direct action on men; constituted as they generally are, it is for physical power alone that they have any feeling or respect.

If a man would convince himself by experience that this is the case, he need do nothing but remove all compulsion from his fellows, and try to govern them by clearly and forcibly representing to them what is reasonable, right, and fair, though at the same time it may be contrary to their interests. He would be laughed to scorn; and as things go that is the only answer he would get. It would soon be obvious to him that moral force alone is powerless. It is, then, physical force alone which is capable of securing respect.

[3] We read in Stobaeus, *Florileguim*, ch. xliv., 41, of a Persian custom, by which, whenever a king died, there was a five days' anarchy, in order that people might perceive the advantage of having kings and laws.

Now this force ultimately resides in the masses, where it is associated with ignorance, stupidity and injustice. Accordingly the main aim of statesmanship in these difficult circumstances is to put physical force in subjection to mental force—to intellectual superiority, and thus to make it serviceable. But if this aim is not itself accompanied by justice and good intentions, the result of the business, if it succeeds, is that the state so erected consists of knaves and fools, the deceivers and the deceived. That this is the case is made gradually evident by the progress of intelligence among the masses, however much it may be repressed; and it leads to revolution. But if, contrarily, intelligence is accompanied by justice and good intentions, there arises a state as perfect as the character of human affairs will allow. It is very much to the purpose if justice and good intentions not only exist, but are also demonstrable and openly exhibited, and can be called to account publicly, and be subject to control. Care must be taken, however, lest the resulting participation of many persons in the work of government should affect the unity of the state, and inflict a loss of strength and concentration on the power by which its home and foreign affairs have to be administered. This is what almost always happens in republics. To produce a constitution which should satisfy all these demands would accordingly be the highest aim of statesmanship. But, as a matter of fact, statesmanship has to consider other things as well. It has to reckon with the people as they exist, and their national peculiarities. This is the raw material on which it has to work, and the ingredients of that material will always exercise a great effect on the completed scheme.

Statesmanship will have achieved a good deal if it so far attains its object as to reduce wrong and injustice in the community to a minimum. To banish them altogether, and to leave no trace of them, is merely the ideal to be aimed at; and it is only approximately that it can be reached. If they disappear in one direction, they creep in again in another; for wrong and injustice lie deeply rooted in human nature. Attempts have been made to attain the desired aim by artificial constitutions and systematic codes of law; but they are not in complete touch with the facts—they remain an asymptote, for the simple reason that hard and fast conceptions never embrace all possible cases, and cannot be made to meet individaul instances. Such conceptions resemble the stones of a mosaic rather than the delicate shading in a picture. Nay, more: all experiments in this matter are attended with danger; because the material in question, namely, the human race, is the most difficult of all material to handle. It is almost as dangerous as an explosive.

No doubt it is true that in the machinery of the state the freedom of the press performs the same function as a safety valve in other machinery; for it enables all discontent to find a voice; nay, in doing so, the discontent exhausts itself if it has not much substance; and if it has, there is an advantage in recognizing it betimes and applying the remedy. This is much better than to repress the discontent, and let it simmer and ferment, and go on increasing until it ends in an explosion. On the other hand, the freedom of the press may be regarded as a permission to sell poison—poison for the heart and the mind. There is no idea so foolish but that it cannot be put into the heads of the ignorant and incapable multitude, especially if the idea holds out some prospect of any gain or advantage. And when a man has got hold of any such idea what is there that he will not do? I am, therefore, very much afraid that the danger of a free press outweighs its utility, particularly where the law offers a way of redressing wrongs. In any case, however, the freedom of the press should be governed by a very strict prohibition of all and every anonymity.

Generally, indeed, it may be maintained that right is of a nature analogous to that of certain chemical substances, which cannot be exhibited in a pure and isolated condition, but at the most only with a small admixture of some other substances, which serves as a vehicle for them, or gives them the necessary consistency; such as fluorine, or even alcohol, or prussic acid. Pursuing the analogy we may say that right, if it is to gain a footing in world and really prevail, must of necessity be supplemented by a small amount of arbitrary force, in order that, notwithstanding its merely ideal and therefore ethereal nature, it may be able to work and subsist in the real and material world, and not evaporate and vanish into the clouds, as it does in Hesiod. Birthright of every description, all heritable privileges, every form of national religion, and so on, may be regarded as the necessary chemical base or alloy; inasmuch as it is only when right has some such firm and actual foundation that it can be enforced and consistently vindicated. They form for right a sort of ὅς μοι ποῦ στῶ—a fulcrum for supporting its lever.

Linnaeus adopted a vegetable system of an artificial and arbitrary character. It cannot be replaced by a natural one, no matter how reasonable the change might be, or how often it has been attempted to make it, because no other system could ever yield the same certainty and stability of definition. Just in the same way the artificial and arbitrary basis on which, as has been shown, the constitution of a state rests, can never be replaced by a purely natural basis. A natural basis would aim at doing away with the conditions that have been mentioned: in the place of the privileges of birth it would put those of personal merit; in the place of the national religion, the results of rationalistic inquiry, and so on. However agreeable to reason this might all prove, the change could not be made; because a natural basis would lack that certainty and fixity of definition which alone secures the stability of the commonwealth. A constitution which embodied abstract right alone would be an excellent thing for natures other than human, but since the great majority of men are extremely egoistic, unjust, inconsiderate, deceitful, and sometimes even malicious; since in addition they are endowed with very scanty intelligence, there arises the necessity for a power that shall be concentrated in one man, a power that shall be above all law and right, and be completely irresponsible, nay, to which everything shall yield as to something that is regarded as a creature of a higher kind, a ruler by the grace of God. It is only thus that men can be permanently held in check and governed.

The United States of North America exhibit the attempt to proceed without any such arbitrary basis; that is to say, to allow abstract right to prevail pure and unalloyed. But the result is not attractive. For with all the material prosperity of the country what do we find? The prevailing sentiment is a base utilitarianism with its inevitable companion, ignorance; and it is this that has paved the way for a union of stupid Anglican bigotry, foolish prejudice, coarse brutality, and a childish veneration of women. Even worse things are the order of the day: most iniquitous oppression of the black freemen, lynch law, frequent assassination often committed with entire impunity, duels of a savagery elsewhere unknown, now and then open scorn of all law and justice, repudiation of public debts, abominable political rascality towards a neighboring state, followed by a mercenary raid on its rich territory—afterwards sought to be excused, on the part of the chief authority of the state, by lies which every one in the country knew to be such and laughed at—an ever-increasing ochlocracy, and finally all the disastrous influence which this abnegation of justice in high quarters must have exercised on private morals. This specimen of a pure constitution on the obverse side of the planet says very little for republics in general, but still less for the imitations of it in Mexico, Guatemala, Colombia and Peru.

A peculiar disadvantage attaching to republics—and one that might not be looked for—is that in this form of government it must be more difficult for men of ability to attain high position and exercise direct political influence than in the case of monarchies. For always and everywhere and under all circumstances there is a conspiracy, or instinctive alliance, against such men on the part of all the stupid, the weak, and the commonplace; they look upon such men as their natural enemies, and they are firmly held together by a common fear of them. There is always a numerous host of the stupid and the weak, and in a republican constitution it is easy for them to suppress and exclude the men of ability, so that they may not be outflanked by them. They are fifty to one; and here all have equal rights at the start.

In a monarchy, on the other hand, this natural and universal league of the stupid against those who are possessed of intellectual advantages is a one-sided affair; it exists only from below, for in a monarchy talent and intelligence receive a natural advocacy and support from above. In the first place, the position of the monarch himself is much too high and too firm for him to stand in fear of any sort of competition. In the next place, he serves the state more by his will than by his intelligence; for no intelligence could ever be equal to all the demands that would in his case be made upon it. He is therefore compelled to be always availing himself of other men's intelligence. Seeing that his own interests are securely bound up with those of his country; that they are inseparable from them and one with them, he will naturally give the preference to the best men, because they are his most serviceable instruments, and he will bestow his favor upon them—as soon, that is, as he can find them; which is not so difficult, if only an honest search be made. Just in the same way even ministers of state have too much advantage over rising politicians to need to regard them with jealousy; and accordingly for analogous reasons they are glad to single out distinguished men and set them to work, in order to make use of their powers for themselves. It is in this way that intelligence has always under a monarchical government a much better chance against its irreconcilable and ever-present foe, stupidity; and the advantage which it gains is very great.

In general, the monarchical form of government is that which is natural to man; just as it is natural to bees and ants, to a flight of cranes, a herd of wandering elephants, a pack of wolves seeking prey in common, and many other animals, all of which place one of their number at the head of the business in hand. Every business in which men engage, if it is attended with danger—every campaign, every ship at sea—must also be subject to the authority of one commander; everywhere it is one will that must lead. Even the animal organism is constructed on a monarchical principle: it is the brain alone which guides and governs, and exercises the hegemony. Although heart, lungs, and stomach contribute much more to the continued existence of the whole body, these Philistines cannot on that account be allowed to guide and lead. That is a business which belongs solely to the brain; government must proceed from one central point. Even the solar system is monarchical. On the other hand, a republic is as unnatural as it is unfavorable to the higher intellectual life and the arts and sciences. Accordingly we find that everywhere in the world, and at all times, nations, whether civilized or savage, or occupying a position between the two, are always under monarchical government. The rule of many, as Homer said, is not a good thing: let there be one ruler, one king:

Οὐκ ἀγαθὸν πολυκοιρανίη· εἷς κοίρανος ἔστω
Εἷς βασιλεύς.[4]

How would it be possible that, everywhere and at all times, we should see many millions of people nay, even hundreds of millions, become the willing and obedient subjects of one man, sometimes even one woman, and provisionally, even, of a child, unless there were a monarchical instinct in men which drove them to it as the form of government best suited to them? This arrangement is not the product of reflection. Everywhere one man is king, and for the most part his dignity is hereditary. He is, as it were, the person-

[4] *Iliad*, ii., 204.

ification, the monogram, of the whole people, which attains an individuality in him. In this sense he can rightly say: *l'état c'est moi*. It is precisely for this reason that in Shakespeare's historical plays the kings of England and France mutually address each other as *France* and *England*, and the Duke of Austria goes by the name of his country. It is as though the kings regarded themselves as the incarnation of their nationalities. It is all in accordance with human nature; and for this very reason the hereditary monarch cannot separate his own welfare and that of his family from the welfare of his country; as, on the other hand, mostly happens when the monarch is elected, as, for instance, in the states of the church.[5] The Chinese can conceive of a monarchical government only; what a republic is they utterly fail to understand. When a Dutch legation was in China in the year 1658, it was obliged to represent that the Prince of Orange was their king, as otherwise the Chinese would have been inclined to take Holland for a nest of pirates living without any lord or master. Stobaeus, in a chapter in his *Florilegium*, at the head of which he wrote *That monarchy is best*, collected the best of the passages in which the ancients explained the advantages of that form of government. In a word, republics are unnatural and artificial; they are the product of reflection. Hence it is that they occur only as rare exceptions in the whole history of the world. There were the small Greek republics, the Roman and the Carthaginian; but they were all rendered possible by the fact that five-sixths, perhaps even seven-eighths, of the population consisted of slaves. In the year 1840, even in the United States, there were three million slaves to a population of sixteen millions. Then, again, the duration of the republics of antiquity, compared with that of monarchies, was very short. Republics are very easy to found, and very difficult to maintain, while with monarchies it is exactly the reverse. If it is Utopian schemes that are wanted, I say this: the only solution of the problem would be a despotism of the wise and the noble, of the true aristocracy and the genuine nobility, brought about by the method of generation—that is, by the marriage of the noblest men with the cleverest and most intellectual women. This is my Utopia, my Republic of Plato.

[5] The Papal states in Italy, later (1860–1870) absorbed into a united Italy (Ed.).

Constitutional kings are undoubtedly in much the same position as the gods of Epicurus, who sit upon high in undisturbed bliss and tranquillity, and do not meddle with human affairs. Just now they are the fashion. In every German duodecimo-principality a parody of the English constitution is set up, quite complete, from Upper and Lower Houses down to the Habeas Corpus Act and trial by jury. These institutions, which proceed from English character and English circumstances, and presuppose both, are natural and suitable to the English people. It is just as natural to the German people to be split up into a number of different stocks, under a similar number of ruling princes, with an emperor over them all, who maintains peace at home, and represents the unity of the state board. It is an arrangement which has proceeded from German character and German circumstances. I am of opinion that if Germany is not to meet with the same fate as Italy, it must restore the imperial crown, which was done away with by its archenemy, the first Napoleon; and it must restore it as effectively as possible.[6] For German unity depends on it, and without the imperial crown it will always be merely nominal, or precarious. But as we no longer live in the days of Günther of Schwarzburg, when the choice of emperor was a serious business, the imperial crown ought to go alternately to Prussia and to Austria, for the life of the wearer. In any case, the absolute sovereignty of the small states is illusory. Napoleon I did for Germany what Otto the Great did for Italy: he divided it into small, independent states, on the principle, *divide et impera.*

The English show their great intelligence, among other ways, by clinging to their ancient institutions, cutoms and usages, and by holding them sacred, even at the risk of carrying this tenacity too far, and making it ridiculous. They hold them sacred for the simple reason that those institutions and customs are not the invention of an idle head, but have grown up gradually by the force of circumstance and the wisdom of life itself, and are therefore suited to them as a nation. On the other hand, the German allows himself to be persuaded by his schoolmaster that he must go about in an English dresscoat, and that nothing else will do. Accordingly he

[6] Written in the 1850's, before the German unification movement, directed by Bismarck, had begun its drive toward the Second Reich of 1871 (Ed.).

has bullied his father into giving it to him; and with his awkward manners this ungainly creature presents in it a sufficiently ridiculous figure. But the dress coat will some day be too tight for him and incommode him. It will not be very long before he feels it in trial by jury. This institution arose in the most barbarous period of the Middle Ages—the times of Alfred the Great, when the ability to read and write exempted a man from the penalty of death. It is the worst of all criminal procedures. Instead of judges, well versed in law and of great experience, who have grown gray in daily un-raveling the tricks and wiles of thieves, murderers and rascals of all sorts, and so are well able to get at the bottom of things, it is gossip-ing tailors and tanners who sit in judgment; it is their coarse, crude, unpracticed, and awkward intelligence, incapable of any sustained attention, that is called upon to find out the truth from a tissue of lies and deceit. All the time, moreover, they are thinking of their cloth and their leather, and longing to be at home; and they have absolutely no clear notion at all of the distinction between probabil-ity and certainty. It is with this sort of a calculus of probabilities in their stupid heads that they confidently undertake to seal a man's doom.

The same remark is applicable to them which Dr. Johnson made of a court-martial in which he had little confidence, summoned to decide a very important case. He said that perhaps there was not a member of it who, in the whole course of his life, had ever spent an hour by himself in balancing probabilities. Can any one imagine that the tailor and the tanner would be impartial judges? What! the vicious multitude impartial! as if partiality were not ten times more to be feared from men of the same class as the accused than from judges who knew nothing of him personally, lived in another sphere altogether, were irremovable, and conscious of the dignity of their office. But to let a jury decide on crimes against the state and its head, or on misdemeanors of the press, is in a very real sense to set the fox to keep the geese.

Everywhere and at all times there has been much discontent with governments, laws and public regulations; for the most part, how-ever, because men are always ready to make institutions responsible for the misery inseparable from human existence itself; which is, to speak mythically, the curse that was laid on Adam, and through him on the whole race. But never has that delusion been proclaimed

in a more mendacious and impudent manner than by the demagogues of the *Jetztzeit*—of the day we live in. As enemies of Christianity, they are of course, optimists: to them the world is its own end
and object, and accordingly in itself, that is to say, in its own
natural constitution, it is arranged on the most excellent principles,
and forms a regular habitation of bliss. The enormous and glaring
evils of the world they attribute wholly to governments: if governments, they think, were to do their duty, there would be a
heaven upon earth; in other words, all men could eat, drink, propa-
gate and die, free from trouble and want. This is what they mean
when they talk of the world being "its own end and object"; this
is the goal of that "perpetual progress of the human race," and the
other fine things which they are never tired of proclaiming.

Formerly it was *faith* which was the chief support of the throne;
nowadays it is *credit*. The pope himself is scarcely more concerned
to retain the confidence of the faithful than to make his creditors
believe in his own good faith. If in times past it was the guilty debt
of the world which was lamented, now it is the financial debts of
the world which arouse dismay. Formerly it was the Last Day
which was prophesied; now it is the σεισάχθεια, the great repudiation, the universal bankruptcy of the nations, which will one day
happen; although the prophet, in this as in the other case, entertains
a firm hope that he will not live to see it himself.

From an ethical and a rational point of view, the *right of possession* rests upon an incomparably better foundation than the *right
of birth;* nevertheless, the right of possession is allied with the right
of birth and has come to be part and parcel of it, so that it would
hardly be possible to abolish the right of birth without endangering
the right of possession. The reason of this is that most of what a man
possesses he inherited, and therefore holds by a kind of right of
birth; just as the old nobility bear the names only of their hereditary
estates, and by the use of those names do no more than give expression to the fact that they own the estates. Accordingly all
owners of property, if instead of being envious they were wise,
ought also to support the maintenance of the rights of birth.

The existence of a nobility has, then, a double advantage: it helps
to maintain on the one hand the rights of possession, and on the
other the right of birth belonging to the king. For the king is the

first nobleman in the country, and, as a general rule, he treats the nobility as his humble relations, and regards them quite otherwise than the commoners, however trusty and well beloved. It is quite natural, too, that he should have more confidence in those whose ancestors were mostly the first ministers, and always the immediate associates, of his own. A nobleman, therefore, appeals with reason to the name he bears, when on the occurrence of anything to rouse distrust he repeats his assurance of fidelity and service to the king. A man's character, as my readers are aware, assuredly comes to him from his father. It is a narrow-minded and ridiculous thing not to consider whose son a man is.

3. Science, the new god

(a) "The true world which science reveals to us is much superior
to the fantastic world created by the imagination."
Ernest Renan, *The Future of Science* (1848-1849)*

The Future of Science (*L'Avenir de la Science*), written in 1848–1849, was a youthful declaration of faith in science by Ernest Renan (1823–1892), French philologist, historian, essayist, and all-round man of letters in the best tradition of the nineteenth century. Perhaps Renan's most successful book was his *Life of Jesus*, which passed through innumerable editions in the later nineteenth century. He also wrote other works of "higher criticism," taking a critical approach to religious and biblical history. Like so many other Victorians, Renan was a religious seeker, troubled by his inability to believe in the old faith and earnestly trying to find a new one which might be less ill-adjusted to reason. When he wrote the following selection, Renan believed that science could be the new religion or metaphysics, providing moral values as well as certain foundations in the physical realm. The student should take into account the various meanings of the word "science" in this exposition.

W ITHOUT doubt, the patient investigations of the observer, the calculations accumulated by astronomy, the long enumerations of the naturalist, seem hardly able to awaken the sentiment of the beautiful. The beautiful is not in analysis; but the real beauty, which is not based on human fictions and fantasies, is hidden in the results of analysis. To dissect the human body is to destroy

* The translation which follows is by Jane Lilienfeld.

its beauty; and yet, by this dissection science arrives at knowledge of a superior order, knowledge which may not have appeared to a more superficial view. Doubtless this enchanted world where humanity lived before arriving at the life of contemplation, this world which men conceived as moral, passionate, full of life and sentiment, had an inexpressible charm, and it is possible that faced by the severe and inflexible nature which rationalism has created for us, some have begun to long for the miraculous and to reproach experience for having banished it from the universe. This attitude can only result from an incomplete view of the results of science. Because the true world which science reveals to us is much superior to the fantastic world created by the imagination. Had one dared the human spirit to conceive of more astonishing marvels, had one freed it from the limitations which fulfillment of them always imposes on our ideals, the human spirit would not have dared conceive the thousandth fraction of the splendors which observation has revealed. In vain we have inflated our conceptions, we have only fathered fragments at the enormous price of the reality of things. Is it not a strange fact that all the ideas by which primitive science explained the world appear to us narrow, paltry, ridiculous next to those which are true? The earth was similar to a disc, to a column, to a cone, the sun was as big as Peloponnesus, or seen as a simple continuously burning meteor, the stars in concentric spheres pursued their courses in a solid vault, *a closed universe*, suffocating, walled, a narrow curvature against which the instinct of the infinite was bruised; such are the most brilliant hypotheses arrived at by the human spirit. Beyond, it is true, lay the world of angels with its eternal splendors, but even there what narrow limits, what finite conceptions! The temple of our God, has it not been enlarged since our science has discovered the infinity of worlds? And even though one was free to create marvels, one worked in such plain material if I may so; observation did not hinder fantasy, but it was the scientific method (which some are pleased to represent as narrow and without ideals) which revealed to us not that metaphysical infinity the idea of which is the basis of human reason, but the real infinity which was never even glimpsed in the hardiest excursions of fantasy. Therefore let us say without fear that if fiction's marvels seemed up to now necessary for poetry, nature's marvels when laid bare in all their splendor will constitute a poetry a thousand times more sublime, a poetry which will be reality itself, which will be science and philosophy simultaneously.

    (b) "Scarcely anything . . . remains a mystery." Emil du Bois-Reymond, *Natural Science and the History of Culture* (1878)[1]

Emil du Bois-Reymond, despite the French origin of his name,[2] was a German scientist, a professor at the University of Berlin who attained considerable renown as a popularizer of the scientific outlook, sharing that honor with such pundits of the day as Thomas Huxley and Ernest Haeckel. The following short selection, from his *Kulturgeschichte und Naturwissenschaft* (*Natural Science and the History of Culture*), 1878, reveals some of the rather elephantine eloquence this theme inspired in him. Its exultant clichés and arrogant claims were typical of the age and would have secured the unquestioning assent of most people. They must have caused the artistic minority to grind its teeth. Yet such "scientism" affected even the novelists between 1850 and 1890.

It would be a difficult task to describe the revolution which natural science has peacefully wrought in the condition of mankind during the last century. As it lifted from our heads the oppressive lid of a physical firmament, so also did it free us spiritually. For everyone who hearkened to its teachings, the dream of the poet came true—the great disciple of Epicurus [Vergil] who, amid the splendor of the Roman world empire in the time of Octavius, reflected:

    Happy is he who is permitted to understand the grounds of things,
    He conquers fear, inexorable fate, even greedy Death's mad fury.

In place of miracle, science puts law. Ghosts and phantoms pale before it as before the dawning day. It broke the tyranny of the old holy lies. It extinguished the funeral piles of witches and heretics. Historical criticism armed it. But it shied away from excesses of speculation. It revealed the limits of knowledge and its disciples learned to look down without giddiness from the lofty peaks of sovereign scepticism. How light and free one breathes up there!

---

[1] The following translation is by the editor.

[2] French names in Prussia normally denote descent from the Huguenot refugees who were persecuted in France in the later seventeenth century and found asylum in Protestant Prussia.

How scarcely audible to an intellectual ear are the buzzings of the vulgar tumult in the hot lowlands below, the sound of diseased ambitions, the battle cries of the common herd! Along with the anthropocentric perspective, science has left behind the Europe-centered. As it opened the ghetto, the fetters of black men burst also. How differently it conquered the world than did Alexander and the Romans in an earlier time! If literature is the true bond within nations, science is the great *international* bond. Voltaire could find Shakespeare detestable, but bowed before Newton. The triumph of scientific methods will appear to posterity as just such a landmark in the development of humanity as the triumph of mono-theism 1800 years earlier. It does not matter that the people were not ripe for this form of religion; have they ever realized the ideal of Christianity?

If one considers where one first stumbles upon this new mode of thought in literature, the answer is clear: with Voltaire. The intel-lectual trait peculiar to Voltaire (not sufficiently stressed by David F. Strauss), his scientific outlook, which he brought from England and developed at Cirey, enabled him to perceive vividly the distinc-tion between political history, heretofore the only kind, and cul-tural history; and within the latter it was the scientific element that with his usual boldness and clarity he threw into relief. In a hun-dred essays, letters, philosophical novels, this basic idea springs to life; but by virtue of the astonishing suppleness of his mind he at times, as in the *History of Charles XII*, considers things from a human perspective, while at others, as in *Micromegas*, from an Archimedean one.

In conjunction with Voltaire the encyclopedists developed this mode of thought. Even more decidely than he, they pointed the way to methodical procedures which in their orderly operation open the door to power over nature. Thence came that technical interest found in Dìderot, as also in his kindred spirit, the father of utilitarianism on the other side of the Atlantic, Benjamin Franklin.

What they dreamed has come to pass. Man has developed from a tool-making animal, which he was in the very beginning, to a rational animal, who travels by steam, writes with the lightning, paints with the sun's rays. The conversion of sunlight, stored up in coal, into energy, increases his strength a millionfold. The seven wonders of the ancient world, the works of the Romans, vanish beside the daily achievement of modern man. The circumference of the planets becomes too narrow for him. Scarcely anything in the heights or the depths remains a mystery to him. Wherever something to be physically achieved remains withheld from man, there the calculus of his spirit presses forward with its magic key. In the blackest night, in the wildest ocean, his ship steers the shortest route, cleverly escaping the destructive whirlwinds of the typhoon. What the wishing wand did by magic, geology performs: freely it brings forth water, salt, coal, petroleum. The number of metals continues to increase, and though as yet chemistry has not found the philosopher's stone, tomorrow perhaps it will. For the present it vies with organic nature in the production of the useful and pleasing. From the black stinking heaps of refuse, which turn every city into a Baku, it borrows the colors by comparison with which the magnificence of tropical feathers turns pale. It prepares perfumes without sun or flowers. Has it not even solved Simson's riddle, how to make sweet things out of loathsome material?

Gay-Lussac's[3] preserving art has not merely wiped out the difference between the seasons on rich men's tables. The poison-monger sees with angry despair his tricks unmasked. The scourges of smallpox, plague, scurvy are under control. Lister's bandage protects the wounds of soldiers from the entrance of deadly germs. Chloral spreads the wings of God's sleep over the soul in pain, indeed chloroform laughs, if we wish, at the biblical curse of womanhood.

So were Bacon's prophetic words fulfilled: knowledge is power. All the peoples of Europe, of the Old and the New Worlds, travel along this road. A noted art critic recently advanced the opinion that the measure of the peak attained by mankind up to the present time is the development of the plastic arts. In this respect the periods from Phidias to Lysippus [ancient Greece] and the Cinquecento [Italian Renaissance] witnessed the highest level attained by mankind, hardly to recur; at best, a mere flare-up of culture would be possible to our era through the drawings of Cornelius![4]

---

[3] Joseph L. Gay-Lussac, versatile French scientist (1778–1850); the reference here is to his contributions to food preservative chemistry (Ed.).

[4] Peter Joseph Cornelius (1783–1867), German artist, illustrator of Goethe's *Faust* and painter of churches (Ed.).

Thus to take a single side of human activity as characteristic, and to measure the heights of human development by it, is false in itself, and moreover other judgments are equally justified, for example the one-sided ethical view of man on the part of the Jews. But if there is one criterion which for us indicates the progress of humanity, it is much more the level attained of power over nature. Accidental circumstances may influence the progress of art at any time, e.g., talent, taste, wealth, patronage. Only in scientific research and power over nature is there no stagnation; knowledge grows steadily, the shaping strength develops unceasingly. Here alone each new generation stands on the preceding one's shoulders. Here alone no *ne plus ultra* of the Schools intervenes, no dictum of authority oppresses, while even mediocrity finds an honorable place, if it only seek the truth diligently and sincerely. Finally it is not art that defends civilization from recurrent breakdowns. Art with all its splendor would today, under similar circumstances, as so often earlier, yield helplessly to the barbarians, if science did not endow us with a security, the causes of which we hardly any longer think about: so accustomed are we to regard it as the natural condition of the life of the modern civilized community.

4. The bourgeois world

(a) "What grows upon the world is a certain matter-of-factness."
Walter Bagehot, *The English Constitution* (1867)[1]

One of the best snapshot descriptions of the bourgeois world was written by the erudite economist, banker, literary critic, and student of politics, Walter Bagehot. Bagehot was truly an Eminent Victorian, as remarkable for his versatility as for his polished style and penetrating judgments, and *The English Constitution*, from which this extract is taken, is an enduring classic. His social commentary on Victorian society is invariably shrewd.

[1] Walter Bagehot's *The English Constitution* (first edition, 1867; second edition, with additional chapter, 1872) has seldom been out of print. It is available in paperback from Oxford University Press, Cornell University Press, and Doubleday Anchor. Norman St. John Stevas has recently edited Bagehot's *Collected Works* (2 vols., Cambridge: Harvard University Press, 1965).

W HAT grows upon the world is a certain matter-of-factness. The test of each century, more than of the century before, is the test of results. New countries are arising all over the world where there are no fixed sources of reverence; which have to make them; which have to create institutions which must generate loyalty by conspicuous utility. This matter-of-factness is the growth even in Europe of the two greatest and newest intellectual agencies of our time. One of these is business. We see so much of the material fruits of commerce, that we forget its mental fruits. It begets a mind desirous of things, careless of ideas, not acquainted with the niceties of words. In all labor there should be profit, is its motto. It is not only true that we have "left swords for ledgers," but war itself is made as much by the ledger as by the sword. The soldier—that is, the great soldier—of today is not a romantic animal, dashing at forlorn hopes, animated by frantic sentiment, full of fancies as to a lady-love or a sovereign; but a quiet, grave man, busied in charts, exact in sums, master of the art of tactics, occupied in trivial detail; thinking, as the Duke of Wellington was said to do, *most* of the shoes of his soldiers, despising all manner of éclat and eloquence; perhaps, like Count Moltke, "silent in seven languages." We have reached a "climate" of opinion where figures rule, where our very supporter of divine right, as we deemed him, our Count Bismarck, amputates kings right and left, applies the test of results to each, and lets none live who are not to do something. There has in truth been a great change during the last five hundred years in the predominant occupations of the ruling part of mankind; formerly they passed their time either in exciting action or inanimate repose. A feudal baron had nothing between war and the chase—keenly animating things both—and what was called "inglorious ease." Modern life is scanty in excitements, but incessant in quiet action. Its perpetual commerce is creating a "stock-taking" habit—the habit of asking each man, thing, and institution, "Well, what have you done since I saw you last?"

Our physical science, which is becoming the dominant culture of thousands, and which is beginning to permeate our common literature to an extent which few watch enough, quite tends the same way. The two peculiarities are its homeliness and its inquisitiveness: its value for the most "stupid" facts, as one used to call them, and its incessant wish for verification—to be sure, by tiresome seeing and hearing, that they are facts. The old excitement of thought has half died out, or rather it is diffused in quiet pleasure over a life, instead of being concentrated in intense and eager spasms. An old philosopher—a Descartes, suppose—fancied that out of primitive truths, which he could by ardent excogitation know, he might by pure deduction evolve the entire universe. Intense self-examination, and intense reason would, he thought, make out everything. The soul, "itself by itself," could tell all it wanted if it would be true to its sublimer isolation. The greatest enjoyment possible to man was that which this philosophy promises its votaries—the pleasure of being always right, and always reasoning—without ever being bound to look at anything. But our most ambitious schemes of philosophy now start quite differently. Mr. Darwin begins:

> When on board H.M.S. *Beagle,* as naturalist, I was much struck with certain facts in the distribution of the organic beings inhabiting South America, and in the geological relations of the present to the past inhabitants of that continent. These facts, as will be seen in the latter chapters of this volume, seemed to throw some light on the origin of species—that mystery of mysteries, as it has been called by one of our greatest philosophers. On my return home, it occurred to me, in 1837, that something might perhaps be made out on this question by patiently accumulating and reflecting on all sorts of facts which could possibly have any bearing on it. After five years' work I allowed myself to speculate on the subject, and drew up some short notes; these I enlarged in 1844 into a sketch of the conclusions which then seemed to me probable: from that period to the present day I have steadily pursued the same object. I hope that I may be excused for entering on these personal details, as I give them to show that I have not been hasty in coming to a decision.

If he hopes finally to solve his great problem, it is by careful experiments in pigeon fancying, and other sorts of artificial variety making. His hero is not a self-enclosed, excited philosopher, but "that most skillful breeder, Sir John Sebright, who used to say, with respect to pigeons, that he would produce any given feathers in three years, but it would take him six years to obtain a head and a beak." I am not saying that the new thought is better than the old; it is no business of mine to say anything about that; I only wish to bring home to the mind, as nothing but instances can bring it home, how matter-of-fact, how petty, as it would at first sight look, even our most ambitious science has become.

In the new communities which our emigrating habit now constantly creates, this prosaic turn of mind is intensified. In the American mind and in the colonial mind there is, as contrasted with the old English mind, a *literalness*, a tendency to say, "The facts are so-and-so,whatever may be thought or fancied about them." We used before the civil war to say that the Americans worshipped the almighty dollar; we now know that they can scatter money almost recklessly when they will. But what we meant was half right—they worship visible value; obvious, undeniable, intrusive result. And in Australia and New Zealand the same turn comes uppermost. It grows from the struggle with the wilderness. Physical difficulty is the enemy of early communities, and an incessant conflict with it for generations leaves a mark of reality on the mind—a painful mark almost to us, used to impalpable fears and the half-fanciful dangers of an old and complicated society. The "new Englands" of all latitudes are bare-minded (if I may so say) as compared with the "old."

When, therefore, the new communities of the colonized world have to choose a government, they must choose one in which *all* the institutions are of an obvious evident utility. We catch the Americans smiling at our queen with her secret mystery, and our Prince of Wales with his happy inaction. It is impossible, in fact, to convince their prosaic minds that constitutional royalty is a rational government, that it is suited to a new age and an unbroken country, that those who start afresh can start with it. The princelings who run about the world with excellent intentions, but an entire ignorance of business, are to them a locomotive advertisement that this sort of government is European in its limitations and medieval in its origin; that though it has yet a great part to play in the old states, it has no place or part in new states. The *réalisme impitoyable* which good critics find in a most characteristic part of the literature of the nineteenth century, is to be found also in its politics. An ostentatious utility must characterize its creations.

(b) "The degradation of the heart. . . ."
Charles Baudelaire, *Intimate Journal* (1851)[1]

Incensed by a society he despised, which did not accord him adequate recognition, Charles Baudelaire pictured the poet in the modern world as an albatross—a bird dazzling in the air but helpless and awkward on land. The poet is equally at a loss in bourgeois society. He must exile himself to the heights to live freely. Alienated, anti-social, introverted, Baudelaire was the first of the nineteenth and twentieth-century *poètes maudits*. This moody genius died in 1867 at the age of forty-six. In the following passage from his papers Baudelaire gives vent to all his hatred for society as it existed in the mid-nineteenth century—and today?

T HE world is about to end. The only reason that it goes on is that it exists. How feeble is this reason, compared to all those that announce the opposite, particularly this: what under the sun is there to do hereafter? Supposing that the world continues to exist materially, would this be an existence worthy of the name and of history? I do not say that the world will be reduced to the expedients and to the clownish disorder of South American republics, or even that perhaps we shall return to the state of savagery, and wander across the grassy ruins of our civilization, gun in hand, in search of food. No, because this fate and these adventures would still presuppose a certain vital energy, echo of the first ages. New examples and new victims of the inexorable moral laws, we shall perish by that which we believed was what we lived by. Machinery will so far have Americanized us, progress will have so thoroughly atrophied in us the spiritual element, that not even the bloody reveries and unnatural sacrileges of the utopians will be comparable to the results. I ask any thinking man to show me what there is left of life. It is useless to speak of religion, or to search for its relics, since to give oneself the trouble of denying God is the sole disgrace in these matters. Property virtually vanished with the elimination of the rights of the eldest son; but the time will come when human-

---

[1] Baudelaire's *Intimate Journals (Journaux Intimes)* was unpublished in his lifetime, and in fact was published in France only in 1920. It was translated into English by Christopher Isherwood and published by the Blackamore Press, London, in 1930; reprinted in 1957, it is now available in a Beacon Press paperback. The translation which follows here was made by the editor.

ity, like an avenging ogre, will strip the last shred from those who believe themselves to be the legitimate heirs of the revolution. And even that will not be the end.

Human imagination can without difficulty conceive of republics or other communitarian states able to attain a certain glory, if they are led by aristocrats and holy men. It is not in political institutions primarily that the universal ruin, or the universal progress—the name matters little—will appear. It will appear in the degradation of the heart. Need I describe how the last vestiges of statesmanship will struggle painfully in the grasp of universal bestiality, how rulers will be forced, in order to maintain themselves and create a semblance of order, to resort to measures which would make our men of today, hardened as they are, shudder? Then, the son will flee the family not at eighteen but at twelve, emancipated by his precocious gluttony; he will flee it not to seek heroic adventures, not to free a beautiful prisoner from a tower, not to immortalize an attic with sublime thoughts, but to found a business, to enrich himself and to compete with his infamous father, and perhaps to establish and own a journal which will spread "enlightenment," compared to which the *Le Siècle* of that time will be considered an agent of superstition. Then the sinners, the outcasts, women who have had many lovers . . . these women will embody a pitiless wisdom, a wisdom which condemns everything except money, everything, even the crimes of the senses. Then any remnant of virtue, anything which is not worship of Pluto, will be an object of utter ridicule. Justice, if at that fortunate epoch justice can still exist, will be forbidden to those citizens who do not know how to make a fortune. Your wife, O bourgeois—your chaste better half, whose legitimacy seems poetic to you . . . vigilant and loving guardian of your strongbox, will be no more than the absolute type of the kept woman. Your daughter, with an infantile nubility, will dream in her cradle that she sells herself for a million—and you yourself, O bourgeois, even less of a poet than you are today, you will find no fault in that, you will regret nothing. For there are some qualities in a man that grow strong and prosper in proportion as others diminish and grow less; thanks to future progress, nothing will remain of the bowels of compassion but the guts! That time is perhaps very near; who knows if it has not already come and if the crudeness of our perceptions is not the sole obstacle which keeps us from appreciating the kind of air we breathe?

As for myself, who sometimes feel within me the absurdity of a prophet, I know that I shall never achieve the charity of a physician. Lost in this vile world, jostled aside by the crowd, I am like a man worn out, who sees in the years behind him only disappointment and bitterness, and ahead of him only a confusion in which there is nothing new either of enlightenment or suffering. In the evening when such a man has stolen from his fate a few hours of pleasure, when, lulled by the process of digestion, he forgets as far as possible the past and resigns himself to the future; then, exhilarated by his own nonchalance and dandyism, proud that he is less degenerate than the passers-by, he says to himself, as he contemplates the smoke of his cigar, What does it matter to me what becomes of these perceptions?

I believe I have wandered into what those of the trade call a digression. Nevertheless, I will let these pages stand, since I wish to record my days of anger.

(c) "The object of men is not life, but labor."
John Ruskin, "The Study of Architecture in Our Schools" (1865)[1]

John Ruskin, most famous for his art history and criticism, was at his best in passages of eloquent rage at the ugliness of modern civilization. Such ugliness Ruskin always related to society's loss of a religious, i.e. poetic, attitude toward life. While modern industry mechanized men's bodies, modern science mechanized their souls; together industry and science worked to destroy beauty in nature and life. A magnificent prophet who thundered jeremiads at Victorian England, Ruskin's fulminations often contained keen insights. He was like Nietzsche in this respect, and also in that he was a liberating force on dozens of important writers, artists and thinkers: Tolstoy, William Morris, George Bernard Shaw, Marcel Proust, the British Labour party, Gandhi, and Frank Lloyd Wright were all influenced by Ruskin.

It should be added that Ruskin was a foe of literary realism as he

[1] John Ruskin's "The Study of Architecture in Our Schools," an address delivered in 1865, may be found on p. 138 of John D. Rosenberg (ed.), *The Genius of John Ruskin* (New York: Brazilier, 1963). It resembles similar Ruskin statements in *The Seven Lamps of Architecture* and *The Crown of Wild Olive*. In addition to Rosenberg's excellent Ruskin anthology, see Robert L. Herbert (ed.), *Art Criticism of Ruskin* (New York: Doubleday, Anchor paperback, 1964).

understood it. He deplored the writers who descended to the gutter for their material (among whom he included even George Eliot), and contrasted this "foul" fiction with the "fair" fiction of writers who held aloft high ideals. Ruskin was a belated romantic or an early symbolist. Yet he lived long enough to participate in a famous controversy with James McNeill Whistler, whom he accused in 1878 of "flinging a pot of paint in the public's face" because Whistler departed too far from strict realism. Ruskin fully shared in the abhorrence of bourgeois society that writers of all sorts felt after 1848.

All lovely architecture was designed for cities in cloudless air; for cities in which piazzas and gardens opened in bright populousness and peace, cities built that men might live happily in them, and take daily delight in each other's presence and powers. But our cities, built in black air which, by its accumulated foulness, first renders all ornament invisible in distance, and then chokes its interstices with soot; cities which are mere crowded masses of store, and warehouse, and counter, and are therefore to the rest of the world what the larder and cellar are to a private house; cities in which the object of men is not life, but labor; and in which all chief magnitude of edifice is to enclose machinery; cities in which the streets are not the avenues for the passing and procession of a happy people, but the drains for the discharge of a tormented mob, in which the only object in reaching any spot is to be transferred to another; in which existence becomes mere transition, and every creature is only one atom in a drift of human dust, and current of interchanging particles, circulating here by tunnels underground, and there by tubes in the air; for a city, or cities, such as this no architecture is possible—nay, no desire of it is possible to their inhabitants.

5. The realism of Flaubert

"A true work of art has no need of summing up."
Charles Baudelaire, essay on *Madame Bovary* (1857)[1]

In France, what was called realism in the arts emerged in the 1840's, associated with the names of Champfleury and Courbet. Neither Baudelaire, the author of the following essay, nor Flaubert, the subject of that essay, were ever "realists" in the narrower sense. Charles Baudelaire sympathized with realism at first, but came to reject it as too pedestrian and trivial. He found it "rustic, coarse, dishonest, boorish"; the sort of realism that seeks only to depict the world as it is does not rise to the true function of poetry and art. Poe taught Baudelaire to disdain utilitarianism in literature; and Baudelaire came to believe in a poetry of "correspondences." His idea that "This world is a dictionary of hieroglyphics" made Baudelaire the father of the symbolists.

Baudelaire here discusses Gustave Flaubert's novel *Madame Bovary*, published in 1857. Flaubert once declared "I hate what is conventionally called realism, though people regard me as one of its high priests." He was closer in spirit to the school labeled "Parnassian," whose hallmark was a neoclassical concern for stylistic clarity along with a desire to break away from the subjectivity and emotional wallowings of romanticism. Flaubert was a master of understatement, of the ironic, detached, and oblique. He kept his distance from the commonplace with an aristocratic fastidiousness. He hated smut. Indeed, Flaubert hated mankind itself, or the great majority of it. He spoke of returning to the Bedouins (see p. xiii) in his dislike of mid-nineteenth-century Europe. Intensely idealistic, like so many nineteenth-century figures he sought some religious faith to replace a Christianity he could no longer accept.

As Baudelaire suggests in the following essay, *Madame Bovary* burst upon the artistically somnolent 1850's like a bomb. Conservatives felt that its flawless structure and style concealed a message of sheer anarchy. The real secret was that *Madame Bovary* inspired no hope, contained no moral.

---

[1] Baudelaire wrote this some months after *Madame Bovary* first appeared in 1857. This essay, and his essay on Wagner (see p. 245), were first printed in book form in the collection of his criticism, *L'Art romantique*, published in 1869 after his death. The most useful edition of Baudelaire's works in French is the one-volume *Oeuvres complètes*, published by Gallimard in the *Bibliothèque de la Pléiade*. Some of Baudelaire's essays have been translated by Lois B. Hyslop and Francis E. Hyslop, unfortunately not very well, in *Baudelaire as a Literary Critic* (Pennsylvania State University Press, 1964). The translation which follows here is by the editor.

In the matter of criticism, the situation of the writer who follows everybody else, the belated critic, carries advantages which the one who announces success, the prophet-critic, does not have. . . . M. Gustave Flaubert no longer needs championing, if indeed he ever needed it. Numerous artists, among them the finest and most respected, have honored and garlanded his excellent book. It only remains then for criticism to indicate some overlooked points of view, and to insist a little more strongly upon some traits and highlights which I believe have not been sufficiently praised and explained. This position of the critic who comes late, outdistanced by opinion, has, as I was trying to suggest, a paradoxical charm. Freer, because he trails the field all by himself, has the air of one who sums up the debate and who, constrained to avoid the passions of the prosecution and the defense, has a mandate to open a new way, without any other instigation than the love of beauty and justice.

Since I have pronounced that splendid and terrible word, justice, may I be permitted—as I am also most happy—to thank the French court for the shining example of impartiality and good taste which it has provided in this case. Moved by a blind and too vehement zeal for morality, by a spirit that took the wrong ground—faced with a novel, the work of a writer previously unknown—a novel, and what a novel! completely honest and impartial—a subject, banal like all subjects, lashed, soaked, like nature itself, by all the winds and all the storms—the court, I repeat, showed itself as honest and impartial as the book which was placed before it as a sacrifice. And still better: one supposes, if it is permitted to conjecture on the basis of the opinions which accompanied the court's ruling, that if the judges had discovered anything really reprehensible in the book, they would have forgiven it in gratitude for and recognition of the beauty with which it is adorned. This remarkable concern for beauty on the part of men whose faculties are summoned forth only for the just and the true is a very touching symptom, compared with the ardent covetousness of this society which has completely abjured all spiritual love and which, neglecting its heart of former times, is concerned only with its stomach. In sum, it may be said that this decision, through its strong poetic inclination, was definitive; that the Muse has been vindicated, and that all writers, all those worthy of the name at least, have been acquitted in the person of M. Gustave Flaubert.[2]

Let us not say, then, as so many affirm with a thoughtless and unconscious ill temper, that the book owes its great popularity to the trial and the acquittal. Had the book not been persecuted it would have aroused the same curiosity, it would have created the same astonishment, the same stir. Moreover it had already for a long time been receiving the acclaim of the literary world. It had already excited keen interest when it appeared in its first version in the *Revue de Paris,* where unwise deletions destroyed its harmony. Flaubert's position, as one so suddenly become famous, was at the same time excellent and bad; and for this equivocal position, over which his faithful and marvelous talent has been able to triumph, I am going to give the various reasons as best I can.

Excellent: for since the departure of Balzac, that prodigious meteor who will cover our country with a cloud of glory, like a strange and unusual sunrise, like a polar dawn spreading its fairy lights over the icy wastes—all interest in the novel had abated and was sleeping. Striking experiments had been made, one must admit. [Baudelaire refers to works by the Marquis de Custine, author of *Aloys, Ethel,* and *The World as It Is;* to works by Barbey D'Aurevilly, *An Old Mistress, The Bewitched,* and *Les Diaboliques;* and to the writings of Champfleury, Charles Barbara, and Paul Féval.] But the rich gifts of the author of *Mysteries of London* and *Bossu* [Féval] could not accomplish, any more than those of so many other first-rate minds, the deft and sudden miracle of this poor little provincial adulteress, whose story, without complexity, is composed of sorrows, disgusts, sighs and some feverish fits snatched from a life cut short by suicide.

I shall not make a crime of the fact that these writers, some turned toward Dickens, others modeled after Byron or Bulwer [Lytton], too gifted perhaps, too haughty, have not been able, like a simple Paul de Koch, to storm the shaky threshold of Popularity, the only hussy that asks to be violated—nor shall I give them a eulogy; at the same time I do not resent it that M. Gustave Flaubert

[2] Flaubert and Baudelaire both faced criminal prosecution in 1857, the latter for his *Flowers of Evil* of which six poems were judged obscene. So Baudelaire's ironic comments on Flaubert's trial have a special edge (Ed.).

has obtained at the first try that which others search for all their lives. At most I see here a sign of his superior power, and I shall attempt to define the reasons which have made this author's mind move in one way rather than another.

But I also said that the situation of a newcomer was bad; alas, for a lugubriously simple reason. For several years the public's interest in intellectual matters has been singularly diminishing; its budget of enthusiasm has been steadily dwindling. The last years of Louis Philippe's reign saw the last explosions of a spirit still capable of being stimulated by the games of the imagination; but the new novelist found himself faced with a completely jaded society—worse than jaded, it was brutalized and gluttonous ,abhorring fiction and in love only with material possessions.

Under such conditions a well nurtured mind, a lover of the beautiful, but accustomed to vigorous fencing, weighing the good and the bad sides of the case, must have said: "What is the surest way of stirring up these dry old souls? They don't really know what they like; they have a positive distaste only for the great; simple and ardent passion, poetic abandon, embarrasses and offends them. Let us then choose a vulgar subject, since too lofty a one is considered an impertinence by the nineteenth century reader. And also let us take care not to give ourselves away or to speak with our own voice. We will be ice cold in describing the passions and adventures which most people treat with warmth; we will be, as the school[3] says, objective and impersonal.

"Likewise, since our ears have been harassed in recent times with the childish babbling of a school, since we have heard of a certain literary method called *realism*—a disgusting insult thrown in the face of every rational person, a vague and elastic word which signifies for the vulgar not a new method of creation but a minute description of trivialities—we will profit from the confusion of mind and the universal ignorance. We will spread a nervous, picturesque, subtle, exact style upon a banal canvas. We will enclose the warmest, the most boiling emotions in the most trivial episode.

[3] The reference is to the Art for Art's Sake school, whose chief leader was Théophile Gautier, and from which both Flaubert and Baudelaire learned much. In opposition to Romantic sloppiness and subjectivity it demanded craftsmanship, precision, objectivity. It grew into the Parnassian school of the 1860's (Ed.).

The most solemn, the most decisive words will issue from the most stupid mouths.

"Where is the home of foolishness, the most stupid milieu, the place most productive of absurdities, the most abundant in intolerant imbeciles?"

"The provinces."

"Who are the most insufferable people there?"

"The petty souls who flutter about performing petty functions which warp their minds."

"What theme is the most hackneyed, the most prostituted, the stalest old tune?"

"Adultery."

"I have no need to make my heroine a heroine," the poet continues to himself. "If she is sufficiently pretty, has energy, ambition, and a fierce desire to rise in the world, she will be interesting. The *tour de force*, besides, will be all the better, and our little sinner will have at least this merit, comparatively quite rare, of being different from the pompous praters of the epoch preceding ours.

"I have no need to be preoccupied with style, picturesque settings, or description of places; I possess all these qualities in superabundant power; I will proceed supported upon analysis and logic, and I will thus show that all subjects are indifferently good or bad, depending on the manner in which they are handled, and that the most commonplace ones can become the best."

And so *Madame Bovary*—a wager, a real wager, a bet, like every work of art—was created.

To accomplish this *tour de force* in its entirety it only remained for the author to divest himself (as far as possible) of his sex and make himself a woman. The result is a marvel; it is apparent that for all his zeal as an actor the author has not been able to avoid infusing a virile blood into the veins of his creature, so that Madame Bovary, in what is most forceful and ambitious in her, and also the most contemplative, has remained a man. Like Pallas Athena armed, issued from the head of Zeus, this bizarre androgyne has preserved all the attractions of a man-like soul in the charming body of a woman.

Several critics have said that this work, truly fine in the detail and vivacity of its descriptions, does not contain a single person who represents morality, who bespeaks the conscience of the author. Where is the proverbial and legendary character charged with explaining the moral and directing the intelligence of the reader? In other words, where is the summing up?

Nonsense! Eternal and incorrigible confusion of functions and categories! A true work of art has no need of a summing up. The logic of the work is enough for all the claims of morality, and it is for the reader to draw his own conclusions from it.

As for the character in the story who is intimate and profound, that is unquestionably the adulteress; she alone, the dishonored victim, possesses all the qualities of a hero. A moment ago I said that she was almost male, and that the author had endowed her (perhaps unconsciously) with all the virile qualities.

Let us examine attentively:

1. The imagination, supreme and tyrannical faculty, substituted for the heart, or what one calls the heart, from which reasoning is ordinarily excluded, and which usually rules in the woman as in the animal;

2. Sudden energy of action, rapidity of decision, mystic fusion of reason and passion, which characterize men created for action;

3. Immoderate taste for seduction, for domination and even for all the crudest means of seduction, extending as far as charlatanism of costume, perfumes, cosmetics—all of which can be summed up in two words: dandyism,[4] exclusive love of domination.

And nevertheless Madame Bovary gives herself; carried away by the vagaries of her imagination, she gives herself magnificently, generously, in a manner quite masculine, to clowns who are not her equals, exactly as poets deliver themselves to jades.

A fresh proof of the fully masculine blood which flows in her veins is that this unfortunate woman cares less about the visible external defects of her husband, and his distracting provincialisms, than about his total absence of genius, his mental inferiority so well revealed in the stupid operation on the club foot.

And on this subject, re-read the pages which contain this episode, so unjustly branded as irrelevant, whereas in fact it serves to cast in

[4] For Baudelaire's conception of the dandy, see Ellen Moers, *The Dandy: Brummell to Beerbohm* (New York, 1960), Chapter XII. The term meant to Baudelaire something very desirable: sensibility, refinement, disdain for vulgarity and mediocrity, hatred of the bourgeoisie, etc. (Ed.)

a vivid light the whole character of the person. A black anger, long suppressed, breaks out in Madame Bovary; doors slam; the amazed husband, who has not known how to give any spiritual joy to his romantic wife, is banished to his room; he is being punished, the ignorant culprit! and Madame Bovary, despairing, cries out like a lesser Lady Macbeth mated with an inadequate master: "Ah! why am I not at least the wife of one of those old scholars, bald and stooped, whose eyes shielded by green eyeshades are always glued on some scientific document! I could lean on his arm proudly; I would at least be in the company of an intellectual giant; but to be the bond companion of this imbecile who cannot even straighten the foot of a cripple! oh!"

Truly this woman is very sublime in her way, in her small circle bounded by petty horizons.

4. Even in her convent education I find proof of the equivocal temperament of Madame Bovary.

The good sisters noticed in this girl an astonishing aptitude for life, for exploiting life, guessing its pleasures—there you see the man of action!

The girl was intoxicated by the color of the stained glass, by the oriental hues that the long windows threw on her school prayer-book; she gorged herself on the solemn vesper music, and, by a paradox the source of which was entirely nerves, she substituted in her soul for the true God a God of her imagination, the God of the future and of chance, a vignette God with spurs and a mustache. Behold the hysterical poet!

Hysteria! Why not make this physiological mystery the basis of a literary work, this mystery which the Academy of Medicine has not yet solved and which, manifesting itself in women by the sensation of an ascending and suffocating lump in the throat (I speak only of the chief symptom), expresses itself in nervous men by impotence and also by an inclination to every sort of excess?

In sum, this woman is truly great, she is above all pitiable, and despite the systematic hardness of the author, who has made every effort to keep outside his work and play the part of a puppet-master, all women of intellect will be grateful to him for having elevated the female to so high a level, so far from the pure animal and so near to the ideal man, as well as for having caused her to participate in that double character of calculation and dream which constitutes the perfect being.

It is said that Madame Bovary is ridiculous. Indeed, look at her, now taking for a hero out of Walter Scott a certain fellow—shall I say even a country gentleman?—who wears hunting jackets and mismatched clothes! and again, see her lovesick over a little law clerk (who does not even know how to commit a dangerous action for his mistress), and finally the poor creature, this bizarre Pasiphæ, restricted to the narrow confines of a village, pursues her ideal in the dance-halls and taverns of the prefecture. What does it matter? Let us say it, avow it, she is a Caesar at Carpentras; she pursues the ideal!

I shall certainly not say, like the werewolf of insurrectional memory, that rebel who abdicated: "With all the platitudes and all the insanities of the present day, do we not still have cigarette paper and adultery?"[5] But I shall affirm that after all, everything considered, even with the most precise scales, our world is pretty harsh for one engendered by Christ; that it is hardly entitled to cast stones at adultery, and that a few Minotaurized persons more or less will not speed up the rotation of the spheres nor advance by one second the final destruction of the universe. It is time to put an end to an increasingly contagious hypocrisy, and to consider it absurd for men and women, corrupted to the point of triviality, to cry "Shame!" upon an unfortunate author who has dared in chaste language to cast a golden glow over the adventures of the boudoir, always repugnant and grotesque when poetry does not caress them with the splendour of its opal light.

If I allowed myself to go on in this analytical vein, I would never finish with Madame Bovary; this book, essentially suggestive, could inspire a volume of observations. I will limit myself, for the time being, to the remark that several of the most important episodes have been either neglected or condemned by the early critics. For example: the episode of the botched operation on the club foot, and

---

[5] A reference to Pétrus Borel, "Champavert the Lycanthrope," a morose and misanthropic late Romantic—a kind of mid-nineteenth century Beatnik—about whom Baudelaire wrote a short article, and who perhaps influenced him. See Enid Starkie, Pétrus Borel. (London, 1954). (Ed.).

the one, so remarkable, so full of sadness, so truly *modern*, where the future adulteress—still only at the beginning of her fall, the unhappy woman—goes to ask help from the church, from the divine Mother, from that one which has no excuses for not being always ready, from that pharmacy where no one has the right to sleep! The good priest Bournisien, preoccupied solely with his rascals of the catechism class who are doing gymnastics all over the stalls and chairs of the church, replies with frankness: "Since you are sick, madame, and since M. Bovary is a doctor, *why don't you go and find your husband?*"

What woman confronted by such priestly inadequacy would not go, an amnestied maniac, to plunge her head under the turbulent waters of adultery—and which one among us, in a more innocent age and in troubled circumstances, has not inevitably come to know the incompetent priest?

6. Optimistic realism

"Count it a crime to let a truth slip."
Robert Browning, "Fra Lippo Lippi" (1855)

Realism could mean various things. Critics alleged that some "realists" used the term as an excuse for muckraking. To others, like Flaubert, realism meant more nearly the amoral attitude, showing life-as-it-often-is with clinical detachment. Other realists, such as the English poet Robert Browning, gloried in "God's plenty," and delighted in catching as exactly as possible the true shape and hue of everything. In a land afflicted with fewer apparent political and social tensions than France, Robert Browning felt less alienated from society than did Baudelaire and Flaubert. Nevertheless, Browning rarely confronted directly the ills of the nineteenth-century society. It is significant that most of his greatest poems take place in the Italian Renaissance, whereas Baudelaire and Flaubert usually write of contemporary France. Browning may not have Flaubert's clinical detachment, but neither of them makes overt moral judgments on his characters.

In the following passage from "Fra Lippo Lippi," Browning puts into the Renaissance painter's mouth the creed of the realist or naturalist. Though a monk, "poor brother Lippo" is a sensualist; indeed, at the beginning of the poem he is caught emerging from a whorehouse. "The world means intensely, and it means good," according to this more optimistic kind of realism.

You understand me: I'm a beast I know.
But see, now—why, I see as certainly
As that the morning-star's about to shine,
What will hap some day. We've a youngster here
Comes to our convent, studies what I do,
Slouches and stares and lets no atom drop:
His name is Guidi—he'll not mind the monks—
They call him Hulking Tom, he lets them talk—
He picks my practice up—he'll paint apace,
I hope so—though I never live so long,
I know what's sure to follow. You be judge!
You speak no Latin more than I, belike;
However, you're my man, you've seen the world
—The beauty and the wonder and the power,
The shapes of things, their colors, lights, and shades,
Changes, surprises,—and God made it all!
—For what? Do you feel thankful, ay or no,
For this fair town's face, yonder river's line,
The mountain round it and the sky above,
Much more the figures of man, woman, child,
These are the frame to? What's it all about?
To be passed over, despised? or dwelt upon,
Wondered at? oh, this last of course!—you say.
But why not do as well as say,—paint these
Just as they are, careless what comes of it?
God's works—paint any one, and count it crime
To let a truth slip. Don't object, "His works
Are here already; nature is complete:
Suppose you reproduce her—(which you can't)
There's no advantage! you must beat her, then."
For, don't you mark? We're made so that we love
First when we see them painted, things we have passed
Perhaps a hundred times nor cared to see;
And so they are better, painted—better to us,
Which is the same thing. Art was given for that;
God uses us to help each other so,
Leading our minds out. Have you noticed, now
Your cullion's changing face? A bit of chalk,
And trust me but you should, though! How much more

If I drew higher things with the same truth!
That were to take the Prior's pulpit-place,
Interpret God to all of you! Oh, oh
It makes me mad to see what men shall do
And we in our graves! This world's no blot for us
Nor blank; it means intensely, and means good:
To find its meaning is my meat and drink.

7. Russian realism

Fyodor Dostoyevsky, *The Devils* (1871)[1]

Erich Auerbach remarks of the Russian realistic novel that it displayed a "passionate intensity of experience" beyond that of western Europe, as if emotions in this huge land were as outsize as Russian geography. Auerbach's remark leads one to think above all of Fyodor Dostoyevsky, who was artist, psychologist, metaphysician, even prophet, as well as novelist. Dostoyevsky's combination of acute perception of physical and psychological detail with great depth of thought makes him perhaps the greatest of all nineteenth century novelists. His ability to lead us straight into a scene and inside a character, a truly Dickensian talent, is supplemented by a serious interest in a wide range of ideas. Dostoyevsky's world, with its intense, brooding characters, may seem strange at first, but few readers can fail to be fascinated by it.

Dostoyevsky wrote *The Devils* (or *The Possessed*, as it is often translated) between 1869 and 1871 against a background of political ferment in Russia. Revolutionary terrorist movements were springing up, organized by liberals disillusioned with the tsar's reform program that had begun bravely with the freeing of the serfs in 1861 but had then faltered. Though contemptuous of the Russian aristocracy, Dostoyevsky was hostile to this revolutionary spirit. He put his faith in the tsardom and became a Slavophile and anti-westerner, rejecting imitation of Europe as the correct path for Russia and urging her to develop her own unique national soul and mission. "Let the nihilists and the Westerners scream that I am a reactionary!" he wrote privately at the time. "To hell with them. I shall say everything to the last word."

The Devils was based on a real incident, the arrest and trial of a

---

[1] *The Devils*, first published in 1871, has been translated into many languages. This translation is by David Magarshack (Harmondsworth: Penguin Books, 1953).

revolutionary anarchist named Nechayev who, together with four others, had murdered a member of their group for allegedly betraying them. Nechayev becomes Peter Verkhovensky in the novel, and Shatov the victim. Chief among the other characters is Nicholas Stavrogin, through whom Dostoyevsky critically views the aristocracy. In part, however, Stavrogin is a metaphysically troubled character, in much the same way as are the leading characters in another great novel by Dostoyevsky, *The Brothers Karamazov*. Another compelling character is Kirilov, a man of deep integrity who eventually commits suicide as a consequence of his atheism. Many of the other characters in the Russian village where the action takes place are evidently under the spell of the unscrupulous but able revolutionary, Verkhovensky. Virginsky, Liputin, and Lyamshin took part in the subsequent murder plot, while Stavrogin and Shigalyov backed out. The scene described below is at Virginsky's house, where a number of "liberal" people have gathered. Mrs. Virginsky, a midwife by profession, is the village atheist. Her husband's sister is a brash young lady down from the university with the latest nihilist ideas.

VERKHOVENSKY sprawled with amazing unconcern in the chair at the head of the table almost without greeting anyone politely, but in spite of the fact that everybody was waiting for them, they all, as though by a word of command, pretended that they had scarcely noticed them. Mrs. Virginsky turned severely to Stavrogin as soon as he took his seat.

"Stavrogin, do you want tea?"

"Yes, thank you," he replied.

"Tea for Stavrogin," she ordered her sister. "And," she turned to Verkhovensky, "what about you?"

"Thanks, I'll have some tea, of course. What a question to ask your visitors! And let me have some cream too, please. You always give one such horrible stuff instead of tea, and at a name-day party, too."

"Why, do you recognize name-days?" the girl student laughed suddenly. "We were just discussing it."

"Old stuff," the schoolboy muttered from the other end of the table.

"What is old stuff? To get rid of prejudices, even the most innocent, isn't old-fashioned. On the contrary, it's still quite a new thing, to everyone's disgrace," the girl student declared promptly darting forward in her chair. "Besides, there are no innocent prejudices," she added fiercely.

"I merely wanted to say," cried the schoolboy, getting terribly excited, "that prejudices, of course, are old-fashioned and ought to be extirpated, but that so far as name-days are concerned everybody knows already that they are stupid and very old-fashioned, indeed, a sheer waste of time, which is being wasted as it is, so that you could have employed your wits on a more useful subject."

"You go on and on, but one can't understand a word you are saying," the girl student cried.

"It seems to me that everyone has the same right to express an opinion as everyone else, and if I wish to express my opinion like anyone else, then—"

"No one deprives you of your right to express an opinion," Mrs. Virginsky herself interrupted sharply. "You were only asked not to mumble because no one can understand you."

"I must say you don't seem to treat me with any respect. If I could not finish what I had to say, it is not because I had nothing to say, but because I had too much to say," the schoolboy muttered almost in despair, becoming completely muddled.

"If you don't know how to talk, you'd better shut up," the girl student snapped.

The schoolboy jumped up from his chair.

"All I wanted to say," he cried, his cheeks burning with shame and afraid to look around, "is that you merely wanted to show how clever you are because Mr. Stavrogin has just come in—that's it!"

"That's a filthy and immoral thing to say, and merely shows that you're suffering from arrested mental development. I'll thank you not to address yourself to me again," the girl student rattled on.

"Stavrogin," Mrs. Virginsky began, "before you came they'd been having a furious discussion about the rights of the family. This army officer here," she nodded towards her relation the major, "and of course I shouldn't dream of bothering you with such old-fashioned rubbish which has long been disposed of. But how could the conception of the rights and duties of the family have arisen in the form of the superstitious nonsense in which they appear to us now? That is the question. What's your opinion?"

"What do you mean by how they could have arisen?"

"What she means is that, for instance, we know that the superstition about God arose from thunder and lightning," said the girl student, throwing herself again into the fray and staring at Stavrogin with her eyes almost popping out of her head. "It's a well-known fact that primitive man, terrified by thunder and lightning, deified the invisible enemy, being aware of his own weakness before it. But how did the superstition about the family arise? How did the family itself arise?"

"That's not at all what I meant—" Mrs. Virginsky made an attempt to stop her.

"I suppose the answer to such a question would be rather indiscreet," replied Stavrogin.

"What do you mean," the girl student asked, darting forward.

But a tittering was heard in the group of the teachers, which was at once echoed by Lyamshin and the schoolboy at the other end of the table, followed by a hoarse chuckle from the Major.

"You should be writing vaudevilles," Mrs. Virginsky observed to Stavrogin.

"A remark like that hardly does you credit, sir—I don't know what your name is," the girl student rapped out with positive indignation.

"Don't you be too cheeky, madam," the Major blurted out. "You're a young lady, and you ought to behave modestly, but you seem to be sitting on needles."

"Hold your tongue, please, and don't you dare to speak to me in so familiar a tone, sir, with your disgusting comparisons. I've never seen you before, and I don't care whether you're a relative of mine or not."

"But I'm your uncle. I used to carry you about in my arms when you were a baby."

"What do I care what you used to carry about? I didn't ask you to carry me about, did I? Which means that you liked carrying me about as a baby. And let me add that I strongly object to your familiar tone unless it's as a fellow citizen. Otherwise I forbid you to talk to me like that once and for all."

"They're all like that now!" the Major addressed Stavrogin, who was sitting opposite, banging the table with his fist. "And let me tell you, sir, that I am fond of liberalism and modern ideas and I'm fond of listening to intelligent conversation, but, mind you, only to men's. As for listening to women, sir, to these modern forward minxes—no sir, I just can't put up with 'em. They're a pain in the neck, that's what they are, sir. Don't fidget, madam!" he shouted at the girl student, who was fidgeting on her chair. "No, sir, I, too, demand to be heard. I've been insulted, sir!"

"You're only interfering with the others," Mrs. Virginsky muttered indignantly. "You can't say anything yourself."

"Oh, no, sir, I shall most certainly say what's in my mind," the Major cried agitatedly, addressing Stavrogin. "I'm counting on you, Mr. Stavrogin, because you have only just come in, though I haven't the honor of knowing you. Without men they'll perish like flies, sir; that's what I think. All their woman question is just lack of originality. I assure you, sir, that all this woman question has been invented for them by men, out of sheer stupidity, as if they hadn't enough trouble in the world. Thank God, I'm not married! No sense of discrimination, sir, none whatever. Can't invent a dress pattern of their own. Even that men invent for them! Take her, sir; take that girl. I used to carry her about in my arms, used to dance the mazurka with her when she was ten years old, and when she arrived today I naturally rushed to embrace her, but all she had to say to me—and before I had time to speak a word, mind you—was that there was no God. If she had just waited a little, and not got it out as soon as she opened her mouth! But, you see, she was in such a devil of a hurry! Well, I suppose intelligent people don't believe; but if they don't, it's because they're brainy chaps. But you, I said to her, you dumpling, what do you know about God? Why, I said to her, I'm damned if it wasn't some student who taught you all this, and if he had taught you to light the lamp before an icon, you'd jolly well have lighted it."

"You're always telling stories," the girl student retorted disdainfully and as though she were ashamed to waste too many words on a man like him. "You're a very spiteful person, and only a few moments ago I proved to you conclusively that you're quite incapable of conducting a rational argument. In fact, I told you just now that we have all been taught in the catechism that if you honor your father and your mother, you will live long and be given riches. That's in the ten commandments. If God found it necessary to offer rewards for love, then your God must be immoral. That's how I proved it to you, and not at all the moment I opened my mouth. I did it because you asserted your rights. It's not my fault if you're stupid and haven't grasped it yet. You feel hurt and you're angry—that's what's really the matter with your generation."

"You're a silly goose!" said the Major.

"And you're a silly fool!"

"Call me names!"

"But, look here, sir," Liputin squeaked from the end of the table, "didn't you tell me yourself that you don't believe in God?"

"Well, what if I did? I'm quite a different matter! Perhaps I do believe, but not altogether. And though I do not entirely believe, it would never occur to me to say that God ought to be shot. I thought about God while I served in the Hussar regiment. It is the accepted thing in poetry to pretend that hussars only drink and make merry. Well, sir, I might have been drinking; but, believe me, sir, I used to jump out of bed at night in my socks and start crossing myself before the icon so that God should give me faith, because even then I was worried by the question whether there was a God or not. I had a bad time of it, I can tell you! In the morning, of course, you'd amuse yourself and your faith would apparently be gone again. I've noticed that, as a rule, your faith tends to evaporate a little in the mornings."

"Haven't you any cards?" Verkhovensky asked their hostess, yawning heartily.

"I'm entirely, entirely in sympathy with your question," the girl student put in quickly, blushing with indignation at the Major's words.

"We're wasting precious time listening to stupid talk," Mrs. Virginsky rapped out with a severe look at her husband.

The girl student pulled herself up.

"I should like to tell the meeting about the sufferings and the protest of the students, but as our time is being wasted in immoral conversations—"

"There's no such thing as moral or immoral," the schoolboy declared, unable to restrain himself, as soon as the girl student began.

"I knew that long before they taught it to you, Mr. Schoolboy," said the girl student.

"And what I say is," the schoolboy rasped out in a fury, "that you are a child who has just arrived from Petersburg to enlighten us all, while we know it all ourselves. As for the commandment 'Honor thy father and thy mother,' which you misquoted, everyone in Russia knows that it is immoral since Belinsky's days."

"Will this never end?" Mrs. Virginsky addressed her husband in a firm tone of voice.

As the hostess she blushed at the triviality of the conversation, especially as she had noticed that some of the newly invited guests smiled, and even looked bewildered.

"Ladies and gentlemen," Virginsky suddenly raised his voice, "if anyone would like to say anything more pertinent to our business, or if anyone has any statement to make, I propose that he does so without wasting more time."

"I should like, if I may, to ask one question," the lame teacher who had been sitting very decorously till then, without uttering a word, said quietly. "I should like to know whether we constitute a meeting here now, or whether we are just a collection of ordinary mortals who have come to a party? I'm asking it just as a matter of form, and because I don't want to remain in ignorance."

The "crafty" question created an impression; they all exchanged glances, as though everyone were expecting an answer from everyone else, and suddenly, as though at a word of command, they all turned round to Verkhovensky and Stavrogin.

"I simply propose that we should take a vote on the question whether we are a meeting or not," Mrs. Virginsky said.

"I second it," Liputin concurred, "though the proposal is a little vague."

"I second it, too, and I," they cried.

"I, too, think that it will be more in order," Virginsky confirmed.

"Let's take a vote, then," Mrs. Virginsky declared. "Lyamshin, will you please sit down at the piano? you can vote from there."

"Not again?" Lyamshin cried. "Haven't I been thumping it long enough?"

"Go on, please. I beg you to sit down at the piano and play. Don't you want to be useful to the cause?"

"But I assure you, my dear Mrs. Virginsky, that no one is eavesdropping on us. It's just your imagination. Besides, your windows are so high, and who would be able to make anything out even if he did eavesdrop?"

"We can't make anything out ourselves," someone muttered.

"And I'm telling you that precautions are always necessary. I mean, in case there should be spies," she explained, turning to Verkhovensky, "let them hear from the street that we are having a birthday party and music."

"Damnation!" Lyamshin swore, sitting down at the piano and beginning to play a waltz, banging on the keys almost with his fists.

"Those who are in favor of having a meeting, please raise their right hands," Mrs. Virginsky proposed.

Some raised their hands, others did not. Some raised them and put them down, others put them down and raised them again.

"Damn it all, I don't understand a thing," one army officer cried.

"I don't either," another one cried.

"Well, I do," cried a third one. "If it's *yes*, then up with your hand."

"But what does *yes* mean?"

"It means a meeting."

"No, it doesn't mean a meeting."

"I voted for a meeting," the schoolboy cried, turning to Mrs. Virginsky.

"Then why didn't you raise your hand?"

"I was looking at you: you didn't raise yours, so I didn't raise mine."

"How silly! I didn't raise mine because I was the proposer. Ladies and gentlemen, I propose we do it the other way round: those who are in favor of a meeting, sit quietly and don't raise your hands, and those who are not in favor of it, raise your right hands."

"Those not in favor?" the schoolboy repeated the question.

"You're not saying that on purpose, are you?" Mrs. Virginsky cried angrily.

"No, please, who is in favor or who is not in favor, because you have to define it more precisely?" two or three voices cried.

"Those not in favor, *not* in favor."

"Very well, but what have we to do? Must we put up our hands or not if we are *not* in favor?" the officer asked.

"Ah, well," the Major remarked; "it seems we haven't got used to a constitution yet."

"Mr. Lyamshin, would you mind not banging away so much?" the lame teacher observed. "It's impossible to hear anything."

"But, really, Mrs. Virginsky, no one is listening," Lyamshin cried, jumping up. "I haven't the slightest wish to play. I've come here as a guest, and not as a piano thumper."

"Ladies and gentlemen, will you answer verbally—are we or are we not a meeting?" Virginsky proposed.

"We are, we are!"

"Well, if so, there's no need to vote. Are you satisfied, ladies and gentlemen, or do you still wish to vote?"

"No, no! We understand!"

"Is there anyone here who does not want a meeting?"

"No, no, we all want it."

"But what is a meeting?" someone asked; but he received no reply.

"We must elect a chairman," people cried from different parts of the room.

"Our host, of course, our host!"

"Ladies and gentlemen," the elected chairman began, "if so, I should like to move my first proposal: if there's anyone here who'd like to say anything more pertinent to the business in hand, or if there's anyone who'd like to make a statement, let him do so without wasting any more time."

No one spoke. Everyone in the room again turned to Verkhovensky and Stavrogin.

"Verkhovensky, have you no statement to make?" Mrs. Virginsky asked him directly.

"None whatever," he replied, yawning and stretching on his chair. "I'd like a glass of cognac, though."

"Stavrogin, what about you?"

"No, thank you. I don't drink."

"I mean would you like to speak or not? I didn't mean cognac."

"Speak? What about? No, I don't want to."

"They'll bring you your cognac," she said, addressing Verkhovensky.

The girl student got up. She had been jumping up from her chair several times.

"I have come to make a statement about the sufferings of our unfortunate students and the ways of rousing them everywhere to protest. . . ."

But she stopped short; at the other end of the table a rival had appeared, and everbody's eyes turned to him. Long-eared Shigalyov slowly rose from his seat, looking grim and gloomy, and, with a melancholy expression, put down a thick, closely written notebook on the table. He remained standing in silence. Many people looked in bewilderment at his notebook, but Liputin, Virginsky, and the lame teacher seemed to be pleased about something.

"I ask leave to address the meeting," Shigalyov said gloomily but firmly.

"Please," Virginsky gave his permission.

The orator sat down, said nothing for half a minute, then uttered in a solemn voice:

"Ladies and gentlemen!"

"Here's the cognac," Mrs. Virginsky's relation who had been pouring out tea and gone to fetch the brandy snapped distastefully and contemptuously, placing a bottle of brandy and a glass, which she had not put on a tray or a plate, before Verkhovensky.

The interrupted orator waited with a dignified air.

"Never mind, go on, I'm not listening," Verkhovensky cried, pouring himself out a glass.

"Ladies and gentlemen," Shigalyov began again, "in calling for your attention and, as you will see later, in asking for your assistance in a matter of first-class importance, I must first of all say a few words by way of an introduction."

"Mrs. Virginsky, have you any scissors?" Verkhovensky asked suddenly.

"What do you want scissors for?" Mrs. Virginsky glared at him.

"I've forgotten to cut my nails—been meaning to for the last three days," he replied, examining his long and dirty nails imperturbably.

Mrs. Virginsky flushed, but Miss Virginsky seemed pleased at something.

"I believe I saw them on the window sill a short while ago," she said, getting up from the table.

She went up to the window, found the scissors, and brought them back at once. Verkhovensky did not even glance at her. He took the scissors and began busying himself with them. Mrs. Virginsky realized that there was sound method in Verkhovensky's request, and was ashamed of her touchiness. The people exchanged silent glances. The lame teacher was watching Verkhovensky enviously and angrily. Shigalyov went on:

"Having devoted all my energies to the study of the social organization of the society of the future which is to replace our present one, I have come to the conclusion that all the inventors of social systems, from the ancient times to our present year, have been dreamers, storytellers, fools who contradicted themselves and had no idea of natural science or that strange animal called man. Plato, Rousseau, Fourier, aluminum pillars, all that is only good for sparrows, and not for human society. But as the future form of society is of the utmost importance now that we at last are all ready to act, I am submitting to you my own system of the world organization so as to make any further thinking unnecessary. Here it is!" he exclaimed, tapping the notebook. "I intended to explain the contents of my book to this meeting in most abbreviated form possible. I'm afraid, however, that I shall have to add a great many verbal explanations, and that the whole of my exposition will therefore take up at least ten evenings, one evening for each chapter of my book." (There was laughter in the room.) "In addition, I should like to state beforehand that my system is not yet complete." (Again laughter.) "I'm afraid I got rather muddled up in my own data, and my conclusion is in direct contradiction to the original idea with which I start. Starting from unlimited freedom, I arrived at unlimited despotism. I will add, however, that there can be no other solution of the social formula than mine."

The laughter in the room grew louder and louder, but it was mostly the young people who laughed and, as it were, the uninitiated visitors. Mrs. Virginsky, Liputin, and the lame teacher looked annoyed.

"If you couldn't work out your system yourself, and are in despair about it, what do you expect us to do?" an officer observed cautiously.

"You are right, my dear serving officer," Shigalyov said, turning to him sharply, "and most of all because you used the word despair. Yes, I was in despair. Nevertheless, everything I say in my book is irrefutable, and there is no other solution. No one can invent anything else. And that is why I should like, without wasting any time, to invite you, ladies and gentlemen, to express your opinion after you have heard the contents of my book during the next ten evenings. If, however, the members of our society refuse to listen to me, let us part at the very beginning, the gentlemen to carry on with their official duties and the ladies to go back to their kitchens, for if you reject my solution, you will find no other. None whatever! By missing their opportunity, they'll have only themselves to blame, for they are bound to come back to it again sooner or later."

The people began to stir. "What's the matter with him? Is he mad?" voices could be heard asking.

"What it comes to, " Lyamshin concluded, "is Shigalyov's despair, and the important question seems to be: should he or should he not be in despair?"

"The fact that Shigalyov is so near to despair is a personal question," the schoolboy declared.

"I move that a vote should be taken how far Shigalyov's despair affects our common cause and, at the same time, whether it is worth listening to him or not," an officer suggested gaily.

"It's not that at all," the lame teacher at last intervened, speaking, as was his wont, with rather an ironic smile, so that it was difficult to say whether he was serious or joking. "This, ladies and gentlemen, isn't the point at issue at all. Mr. Shigalyov is too much devoted to his task and, besides, he is too modest. I know his book. He proposes as a final solution of the problem to divide humanity into two unequal parts. One-tenth is to be granted absolute freedom and unrestricted powers over the remaining nine-tenths. Those must give up their individuality and be turned into something like a herd, and by their boundless obedience will by a series of regenerations attain a state of primeval innocence, something like the original paradise. They will have to work, however. The measures the author proposes for depriving the nine-tenths of humanity of their true will and their transformation into a herd by means of the re-education of whole generations, are very remarkable. They are based on the facts of nature and very logical. It is possible not to agree with some of his conclusions, but it is impossible to doubt the author's intelligence or knowledge. It is a pity that his stipulation that we should devote ten evenings to his theory is impracticable, or we might hear a great deal that is interesting."

"Are you really serious?" Mrs. Virginsky turned to the lame

teacher in some alarm. "I mean if that man, not knowing what to do with people, turns nine-tenths of them into slaves? I've suspected him for a long time."

"Do you mean your brother?" asked the lame teacher.

"Family relationship? Are you laughing at me?"

"And, besides, to work for the aristocrats and obey them as if they were gods—that's an odious suggestion!" the girl student observed fiercely.

"What I'm offering you is not odious suggestions, but paradise, paradise on earth; for there can be no other one on earth," Shigalyov concluded peremptorily.

"For my part," Lyamshin cried, "instead of putting them into paradise, I'd take these nine-tenths of humanity, if I didn't know what to do with them, and blow them up, leaving only a small number of educated people who'd live happily ever after in accordance with scientific principles."

"Only a clown could talk like that!" the girl student cried, flushing.

"He is a clown, but he's useful," Mrs. Virginsky whispered to her.

"And very likely that is the best solution of the problem," Shigalyov said, addressing Lyamshin heatedly. "I don't expect you even realize what a profound thing you've just said, my dear, merry friend. But as it is practically impossible to carry out your idea, we must, I'm afraid, be content with the earthly paradise, since that's what it has been called."

"What awful rot!" Verkhovensky could not help saying, without raising his eyes, though he went on cutting his nails unconcernedly.

"But why is it rot?" the lame teacher took it up at once, as though he had been expecting him to say something in order to attack him. "Why rot? Mr. Shigalyov is rather a fanatic lover of mankind; but remember that Fourier, Cabet, and particularly Proudhon himself have proposed many more despotic and fantastic solutions of the problem. Mr. Shigalyov's solution is perhaps far more sober. I assure you that, having read his book, it is almost impossible not to agree with certain things in it. He is perhaps much nearer to realism than anyone, and his earthly paradise is almost the real one, the same one, for the loss of which mankind is sighing, if it ever existed."

"Well, I knew I'd get it in the neck," Verkhovensky muttered again.

"Allow me to point out, sir," the lame teacher went on, getting more and more excited, "discussions on the future social organization of mankind are almost an urgent necessity for all modern thinking men. Herzen spent his whole life worrying about it. Belinsky—and I know it for a fact—used to spend whole evenings with his friends debating and solving the smaller, as it were, domestic details of the future social organization of mankind."

"Some even go off their heads," the Major suddenly remarked.

"Anyway, you are more likely to arrive at something by talking than by sitting about without uttering a word as if you were dictators," Liputin hissed, as though at last plucking up courage to start his attack.

"I didn't mean Shigalyov when I said it was rot," Verkhovensky mumbled. "You see, ladies and gentlemen"—he raised his eyes a little —"in my view all these books, Fourier, Cabet, all this talk about the 'right to work,' all this Shigalyov business—all are like novels, of which you can write a hundred thousand. An aesthetic pastime. I realize that in this provincial hole of a town you are bored, and so you rush to pick up any piece of paper that has something written on it."

"If you don't mind my saying so, sir," said the lame teacher, fidgeting on his chair, "we may be provincials, and I daresay that we deserve to be pitied on that account alone, but we do know that so far nothing new has happened in the world to make us shed tears because we've missed it. We are urged, for instance, in the various leaflets of foreign make which are distributed among us, to close our ranks and form groups with the sole purpose of bringing about general destruction on the pretext that however much you tried to cure the world, you would never succeed in curing it, while by adopting the radical measure of chopping off a hundred million heads we should ease our burden and be able to jump over the ditch with much less trouble. It's an excellent idea, but one at any rate which is as incompatible with reality as the Shigalyov 'theory,' which you referred to just now with such contempt."

"I'm afraid I haven't come here to engage in discussions," Verkhovensky let drop a significant hint and, as though completely unaware of the slip he had made, drew the candle nearer to him to see better.

"It is a pity, a great pity, that you haven't come here to engage in discussions, and don't you think it's an even greater pity that you should be preoccupied with your toilet now?"

"What's my toilet got to do with you?"

"It's as difficult to cut off a hundred million heads as it is to change the world by propaganda. Much more difficult, perhaps, especially in Russia," Liputin ventured again.

"It's Russia they pin all their hopes on now," said an army officer.

"Yes, we've heard about that, too," the lame teacher put in. "We know that a mysterious *index* finger is pointing to our fair country as the country most suitable for accomplishing the great task. Except for this: in the event of a gradual solution of the problem by propaganda I, at any rate, might gain something personally. I mean, I might enjoy some pleasant talk at least, and even obtain some reward from the Government for my services to social advancement. But in the event of the second solution by the rapid method of cutting off a hundred million heads, I don't stand to gain anything, do I? If you started propagating that, you might end up by having your tongue cut out."

"Yours certainly would be," said Verkhovensky.

"Ah, so there you are, sir. And since it is quite impossible, even in the most favorable circumstances, to complete such a massacre in less than fifty, or at most thirty years, for they are not sheep and they wouldn't allow themselves to be slaughtered, wouldn't it be be better to collect your pots and pans and emigrate overseas to some Pacific islands and there close your eyes in peace? Believe me" —he tapped his finger significantly on the table—"all you're likely to achieve by such propaganda is mass emigration and nothing more!"

He concluded looking very pleased with himself. He was one of the intellectuals of our province. Liputin was smiling craftily. Virginsky listened a little dejectedly, but all the others followed the discussion with great attention, especially the ladies and the officers. They all realized that the upholders of the hundred million heads theory had been pushed against a wall, and they waited to see what would come of it.

"You certainly put it very well," Verkhovensky mumbled more unconcernedly than ever, looking as though he were bored. "Emigration is a good idea. And yet if, in spite of the obvious disadvantages you foresee, the number of people who are ready to fight for the common cause grows daily, we shall be able to do without you. For what is happening here, my dear sir, is that a new religion is taking the place of the old one, and that is why we are getting so many new fighters and it is such a big thing. You can emigrate! And, you know, I'd advise you to go to Dresden, and not to the Pacifiic islands. For, in the first place, it is a city which has never been visited by any epidemics, and as you're an educated man, you're quite certainly afraid of death; secondly, it is near the Russian border, so that you will be able to receive your income from your beloved country more easily; thirdly, it contains what are known as treasures of art, and you're an aesthetic fellow, a former teacher of literature, I believe; and, finally, it is a sort of miniature Switzerland—and that will provide you with poetic inspiration, for I am sure you write verse. In a word, it's a treasure in a snuffbox."

There was a general stir, especially among the officers. Another second and they would all have begun talking at once. But the lame man rose to the bait irritably.

"No, sir, perhaps I won't run away from the common cause. You must realize, sir, that—"

"Do you really mean that you would agree to join the group of five if I proposed it to you?" Verkhovensky suddenly rapped out, and he put the scissors down on the table.

They all looked startled. The mysterious man had shown his hand too suddenly. He had even spoken openly about "the group of five."

"Everyone feels himself to be an honest man and will not shrink from his responsibility for the common cause," the lame teacher tried to wriggle out of it, "but—"

"No, sir, this isn't any longer a question of *but*," Verkhovensky interrupted him sharply and peremptorily. "Ladies and gentlemen, I demand a straight answer. I realize very well that having come here and having called you together myself, I'm obliged to give you some explanations" (another unexpected disclosure), "but I can't possibly give you any before I find out what your frame of mind is. Disregarding all this talk—for we can't just go on talking for another thirty years as people have done for the last thirty—let me ask you which you prefer: the slow way consisting of the composition of social novels and the dry, unimaginative planning of the destinies of mankind a thousand years hence, while despotism swallows the morsels of roast meat which would fly into your mouths of themselves, but which you fail to catch; or are you in favor of a quick solution, whatever it may be, which will at last untie your hands and which will give humanity ample scope for ordering its own social affairs in a practical way and not on paper? They shout: a hundred million heads; well, that may be only a metaphor, but why be afraid of it if with the slow paper daydreams despotism will in a hundred or so years devour not a hundred but five hundred million heads? And please note that a man suffering from an incurable illness will not be cured, whatever prescriptions are written for him on paper; on the contrary, if there is any delay, he will go on festering so much that he will infect us all and corrupt all the healthy forces on which we can count now, so that in the end we shall all come to grief. I entirely agree that to chatter liberally and eloquently is an exceedingly pleasant pastime, and that to act is a little dangerous. Anyway, I'm afraid I'm not very good at talking. I came here with certain communications, and I should, therefore, like to ask all of you, ladies and gentlemen, not to vote, but to tell me frankly and simply which appeals to you more—a snail's pace in a swamp or full steam ahead across it?"

"I'm all for crossing at full steam!" the schoolboy cried enthusiastically.

"Me, too," said Lyamshin.

"Well, of course," an officer, followed by another and by someone else, muttered, "there can be no doubt as to the choice."

What struck them most was that Verkhovensky had some "communications" to make and that he had promised to speak at once.

"Ladies and gentlemen, I see that almost all of you have decided to act in the spirit of the leaflets," he said, scanning everybody in the room.

"All, all," a majority of voices cried.

"I must confess that I am more in favor of a humane policy," said the Major, "but as all are in favor of yours, I am with the rest too."

"It would seem, therefore, that even you are not against it," Verkhovensky addressed the lame man.

"I'm not really," said the cripple, blushing, "but if I agree with the others now, it's solely because I don't want to upset the—"

"You're all like that! He's ready to argue for six months to show off his liberal eloquence, but he ends up by voting with the rest! Think it over, ladies and gentlemen. Are you really all ready?"

(Ready for what? A vague, but very tempting question.)

"Of course all—" they cried, but not without watching each other.

"But afterwards perhaps you'll be sorry for having agreed so quickly? That's how it almost always happens with you, you know."

They grew excited for different reasons, very excited. The lame teacher flew at Verkhovensky.

"I should like to point out," he said, "that the answer to such questions depend on certain conditions. Even if we have given our decision, the question which was put to us in so strange a fashion, you must realize—"

"In what strange fashion?"

"A fashion such questions are not asked in."

"Tell me how, please. But, you know, I was sure that you'd be the first to take offense."

"You've extracted from us an answer about our readiness for immediate action, but what right had you to do so? What authority had you to ask us such questions?"

"You should have thought of asking that question before! Why did you answer my question? First you agree and then you change your mind."

"If you ask me, I think that the irresponsible frankness of your principal question shows that you've neither the authority nor the right to ask it, but you did so out of personal curiosity."

"What are you driving at?" Verkhovensky cried, as though he were beginning to be greatly disturbed.

"What I am driving at is that new members are, anyway, recruited with the utmost secrecy, and not in the company of twenty people one doesn't know!" the lame teacher blurted out.

He had put all his cards on the table, but then he was in a state of uncontrollable irritation. Verkhovensky turned quickly to the company with a well-simulated expression of alarm.

"Ladies and gentlemen, I deem it my duty to announce to you all that all this is nonsense and that our conversation has gone too far. I have recruited no members so far, and no one has the right to say of me that I am recruiting members. We were simply discussing our opinions. Isn't that so? But be that as it may"—he turned to the lame man,—"you, sir, alarm me greatly. I never thought that such innocent things had to be discussed in secrecy here. Or are you afraid that the police may be informed? Do you really think that there is an informer among us?"

They became terribly excited; everybody was talking.

"Ladies and gentlemen, if that is the case," Verkhovensky went on, "then I have compromised myself more than anybody, and, therefore, I must ask you to answer one question, if you care to, of course. It's entirely up to you."

"What question? What question?" they all began to shout.

"A question that will make it absolutely clear whether we are to remain together or take our hats and go our several ways in silence."

"The question, the question?"

"If any of us knew of the existence of a proposed political murder, would he inform the police about it, in view of all the consequences, or would he stay at home and wait to see what happened? There can be all sorts of opinions about that. The answer to the question will tell us clearly whether we are to separate or whether we are to remain together, and that not for this evening only. May I ask you for your answer first?" He turned to the lame teacher.

"Why me first?"

"Because you started it all. Please don't try to wriggle out of it. Cleverness won't help you. Still, just as you like. It's entirely up to you."

"I'm sorry, but such a question is an insult."

"No, sir, that's not good enough. Please be more explicit."

"I've never been an agent of the secret police," the lame teacher said, wriggling more than ever.

"Please be more explicit, and don't keep us waiting."

The lame man got so angry that he wouldn't even reply. He glared furiously at his tormentor from under his glasses without uttering a word.

"Yes or no? Would you or would you not inform the police?" Verkhovensky cried.

"Of course I would *not*," the lame teacher shouted twice as loudly.

"No one would inform the police! Of course not!" many voices cried.

"May I ask you, Major, whether you would inform the police or not?" Verkhovensky went on. "And, mind, I ask you on purpose."

"No, sir, I would not inform."

"But if you knew that someone wished to rob and murder a man, an ordinary mortal, you would inform the police, wouldn't you?"

"Yes, sir, but that would be merely a case of civil law, while what we are discussing is a political matter. I've never been an agent of the secret police."

"No one here has," voices cried again. "An unnecessary question. Everyone can give only one answer. There are no informers here!"

"What's that gentleman getting up for?" the girl student cried.

"That's Shatov. Why did you get up, Shatov?" Mrs. Virginsky cried.

Shatov had really got up. He held his hat in his hand and was looking at Verkhovensky. It seemed as though he wanted to say something to him, but was hesitating. He looked pale and angry, but he controlled himself and walked to the door without saying a word.

"Shatov, that won't do you any good, you know," Verkhovensky shouted enigmatically after him.

"But it will do you good, you dirty spy and scoundrel," Shatov shouted back at him from the doorway and went out.

More cries and exclamations.

"So that's the test, is it?" a voice cried.

"Came in useful!" cried another.

"I hope it isn't too late," remarked a third.

"Who asked him to come? Who received him? Who is he? Who's Shatov? Will he inform the police or not?"—questions were fired from all over the room.

"If he were an informer, he'd have pretended not to be one, but he had his say and went out," someone observed.

"Stavrogin, too, is getting up," the girl student cried. "Stavrogin hasn't answered the question, either."

Stavrogin actually got up, and after him Kirilov, too, got up at the other end of the table.

"I'm sorry, Mr. Stavrogin," Mrs. Virginsky addressed him sharply, "but we've all answered the question, but you are leaving without a word."

"I see no necessity to answer the question which interests you so much," Stavrogin murmured.

"But we've compromised ourselves and you haven't," a few voices cried.

"What do I care whether you've compromised yourselves or not?" Stavrogin said with a laugh, but his eyes flashed.

"What do you care? What do you care?" several voices exclaimed.

Many people jumped up from their chairs.

"I say, ladies and gentlemen, I say," the lame teacher cried, "Mr. Verkhovensky hasn't answered the question, either; he's merely asked it."

His words produced an extraordinary sensation. They all exchanged glances with one another. Stavrogin laughed aloud in the lame man's face and went out, followed by Kirilov. Verkhovensky rushed out into the hall after them.

"What are you doing to me?" he murmured, seizing Stavrogin's hand and squeezing it with all his might.

Stavrogin pulled his hand away without a word.

"Wait for me at Kirilov's. I'll be there. It's absolutely necessary! Absolutely!"

"There's no need for me to be there!" Stavrogin cut him short.

"Stavrogin will be there," Kirilov observed with an air of finality. "Stavrogin, it is necessary for you to be there. I'll explain it to you there."

They went out.

8. Social realism

"Today when the novel has assumed the methods and the duties of science, it is entitled to claim the liberties and frankness of science."
Edmond and Jules Goncourt, Preface to *Germinie Lacerteux* (1864)[1]

The partnership of the inseparable Edmond and Jules Goncourt ended tragically in 1870 when Jules, the younger brother, died at only forty. Edmond lived to a ripe old age, continuing the diary the two had kept ever since 1851. Completely dedicated to the literary life, the

[1] The translation which follows is by the editor. The Preface can be read in full in the anthology edited by Eugen Weber, *Paths to the Present* (New York: Dodd, Mead & Co., 1960).

brothers Goncourt were part of the Parisian world of writers who sometimes starved in garrets, sometimes soared to wealth and fame, but never dreamed of any other sort of existence.

The Goncourts were extraordinarily versatile. They wrote history, art criticism, plays, and novels and many other kinds of books. For a time they edited a literary newspaper, and they always kept up the famous *Journal* which, when it was published in part in Edmond's lifetime, scandalized Paris by its frankness. But the Goncourts were never a popular success. Some of the acid in the *Journal* is obviously Edmond's jealousy of those who, like his friend and protégé Émile Zola, used the Goncourt method of probing the lower depths to win himself fame and fortune.

The Goncourt *Journal* affords more insight into the nineteenth-century French literati than any other document. The Goncourts' utter dedication to literature lived on in the prize provided for by Edmond's will; and the Prix Goncourt remains one of France's most sought-after literary honors.

Though aspiring to an almost proletarian realism, the Goncourts were fastidious intellectual aristocrats whose style was too aesthetic for the masses. But they could well claim to have inaugurated the truly naturalistic novel with Germinie Lacerteux in 1864. This novel is a candid tale of life in the lower depths.

W‍E MUST ask the public's pardon for offering it this book, and warn it of what will be found inside.

The public likes false novels; this one is true.

It loves stories that pretend to take place in "society"; this one comes from the streets.

It likes smutty little books, the memoirs of prostitutes, boudoir confessions, erotic dirt, scandal hitching up its skirt in bookstore windows; the pages it is about to read are severe and pure. Let it not expect a picture of Pleasure, exposing her breasts; what follows is a clinical study of love.

The public also loves vapid, bland stuff, adventures with a happy ending, fantasies that do not spoil its digestion nor disturb its peace of mind; this book with its tragedy and violence is designed to upset the public's habits and challenge its complacency.

Why then have we written it? Simply to shock the public and offend its taste?

No.

Living in the nineteenth century, in a time of universal suffrage, democracy, liberalism, we asked ourselves whether what are called "the lower classes" do not have a right to the novel; whether these lower depths of society, the "people," must remain under a literary ban, subject to the scorn of writers who heretofore have kept silent about whatever heart and soul the people may have. We asked ourselves whether in this age of equality there should still exist classes too unworthy, miseries too base, dramas too squalid, catastrophes too ignoble to record. We began to wonder whether tragedy, the traditional literary form of an ancient literature and a vanished society, was really dead for all time; whether, in a country without castes and a legal aristocracy, the sufferings of the poor and humble could arouse interest, emotion, and pity to the same degree as the sufferings of the rich and powerful; whether, in a word, the tears shed down below could make us cry as easily as those which are shed on high.

These thoughts encouraged us to produce our unworthy novel *Soeur Philomène* in 1861; today [1864] they lead us to publish *Germinie Lacerteux*.

Now, it matters little to us if this book is slandered. Today when the Novel is expanding and growing, when it is beginning to be the great, serious, impassioned, living form of literary work and social inquiry, when by means of its analytical methods and psychological research it is becoming contemporary Moral History; today when the Novel has assumed the methods and the duties of science, it is entitled to claim the liberties and frankness of science. Let it aim at Art and Truth; let it reveal to the more fortunate Parisians sufferings which they should not be allowed to forget; let it show the fashionable world things that Sisters of Charity do not shrink from, things which the queens of former times allowed their children to see in hospitals and almshouses: human suffering, vibrant and immediate, which teaches charity. Let the novel's religion be that which the last century called by the broad and ample name of *Humanity*. Here is a sufficient cause; here is the novel's law.

9. Social realism and socialist realism

(a) The Paris Commune of 1871: "Government is passing from the hands of the haves to those of have-nots." Edmond Goncourt, *Journal* (1870-1871)[1]

Defeated by the Prussians at the Battle of Sedan in 1870, the French army soon surrendered and an armistice was signed bringing to an end the war which everyone had expected France to win. This was in the fall of 1870. A new National Assembly, elected after the abdication of Emperor Napoleon III to make peace with the victorious Germans, moved the capital from Paris to Versailles and signed a humiliating treaty.

The Parisians, stirred by memories of the revolutions of 1789 and 1848, and furious with the royalist "capitulards" who had taken the capital away from Paris, revolted and set up a revolutionary communal government, determined to carry on the war as well as to enact legislation favoring the workers. It was a gallant but foolhardy attempt. The rest of France soon took its vengeance on the Parisian radicals whom it considered to be perennial destroyers of property and moral order. The "June Days" of 1848 were repeated in the "Bloody Week" of May 21–29, 1871, when the troops of the regular French army under orders from Adolphe Thiers, the new president, besieged and attacked the Parisian Communards, captured Paris street by street, and executed thousands. An estimated twenty thousand persons died either in combat or by execution in Paris, many more than during the 1789 Reign of Terror. The episode shocked Europe, dealt radicalism a deathly blow, and intensified bitter class divisions in France. It may not be too much to say that its effects have hardly yet worn off.

In the midst of war, starvation, and suffering, the artist in Edmond Goncourt was always present, stopping to admire a spectacle. Jean-Paul Sartre has reproached Goncourt for not fighting on the side of the Parisian Communards. It is difficult to imagine the aristocratic Edmond fighting at all, but if he had it would undoubtedly have been on the other side. With the realist's passion for exact observation and precise expression, Goncourt draws living pictures. Sneering at the rabble who run the Commune, he still suffers in watching "the end of the greatness of France." What barbarians these Germans are after all, and what a tragedy for France! But he is happier when he feels the "taste for literature" gradually coming back to him as the crisis draws to an end. Years later, when the *Journal* was published. Renan complained

---

[1] This translation is taken from *The Goncourt Journals*, ed. and trans. Robert Baldick (London: Oxford University Press, 1962).

bitterly, as well he might, that Goncourt had misquoted him about the Germans. But Edmond stoutly insisted on the essential accuracy of his account, which he had written down the next day.

3 September, 1870

WHAT a sight, that of Paris this evening, with the news of Mac-Mahon's defeat and the capture of the Emperor spreading from group to group! Who can describe the consternation written on every face, the sound of aimless steps pacing the streets at random, the anxious conversations of shopkeepers and concierges on their doorsteps, the crowds collecting at street-corners and outside town-halls, the siege of the newspaper kiosks, the triple line of readers gathering around every gas-lamp, and on chairs at the back of shops the dejected figures of women whom one senses to be alone and deprived of their men?

Then there is the menacing roar of the crowd, in which stupe-faction has begun to give place to anger. Next there are great crowds moving along the boulevards, led by flags and shouting: "Down with the Empire! Long live Trochu!" And finally there is the wild, tumultuous spectacle of a nation determined to perish or to save itself by an enormous effort, by one of those impossible feats of revolutionary times.

4 September

This was the scene outside the Chamber about four o'clock to-day. Against its grey façade, from which the sunlight had faded, around its columns and all the way down its steps, there was a crowd, a vast multitude of men, in which smocks formed blue and white patches among the black coats. Many were carrying branches in their hands and had green leaves fastened to their hats. There were a few soldiers with twigs tied to the barrels of their rifles.

A hand rose above the heads of the crowd and chalked the names of the members of the Provisional Government in big red letters on one of the columns. On another column somebody had already written: *The Republic has been proclaimed.* There was shouting and cheering; hats were thrown into the air; people clambered on to the pedestals of the statues, clustering together beneath the figure of Minerva; a man in a smock was calmly smoking his pipe on the knees of Chancellor de L'Hospital; bunches of women were hanging on the railing facing the Pont de la Concorde.

All around one could hear people greeting each other with the excited words: "It's happened!" And right at the top of the façade, a man tore the blue and white stripes from the tricolor, leaving only the red waving in the air. On the terrace overlooking the Quai d'Orsay, infantrymen were stripping the shrubs and handing green branches over the parapet to women fighting to take them.

At the gate of the Tuileries, near the great pool, the gilt "N"'s were hidden beneath old newspapers, and wreaths of immortelles hung in the place of the missing eagles.

Tuesday, 6 September

At the Café Brébant, [Ernest] Renan was sitting all by himself at the big table in the red drawing room, reading a newspaper and making despairing gestures.

Saint-Victor came in, sat down heavily on a chair, and exclaimed: "The Apocalypse! . . . Behold a pale horse, and his name that sat on him was Death. . . ."

Then Charles-Edmond, Du Mesnil, Nefftzer, and Berthelot arrived, and we sat down to dinner to the accompaniment of sad remarks on every side.

We spoke of the great defeat, of the impossibility of putting up an adequate defense, of the incompetence of the eleven men in the Government of National Defense, of the deplorable lack of weight they carry with the diplomatic corps and the neutral governments.

Somebody remarked: "Precision weapons are contrary to the French temperament. Shooting fast and charging with a bayonet, that's what our soldier needs to do. If he can't do that, then he's paralyzed. The mechanization of the individual is not for him. And that is where the Prussian soldier is superior at present."

Renan looked up from his plate.

"In all the subjects I have studied, I have always been struck by the superiority of the German mind and German workmanship. It is not surprising that in the art of war, which is an art after all, inferior but complicated, they should have achieved the superiority which, I repeat, I have observed in all the subjects I have studied and with which I am familiar. . . . Yes, gentlemen, the Germans are a superior race!"

"Oh, come now!" everyone shouted.

"Yes, very superior to us," Renan went on, warming to his theme. "Catholicism cretinizes the individual; the education given by the Jesuits or the brothers of the Christian School arrests and constricts the mental faculties, whereas Protestantism develops them."

Berthelot's soft, sickly voice brought our thoughts down from sophistical speculation to menacing reality.

"You may not be aware, gentlemen," he said, "that we are surrounded by enormous stocks of petroleum which are stored at the gates of Paris, and not allowed in because of the city toll. If the Prussians get hold of this petroleum and empty it into the Seine, they will turn it into a river of fire which will burn both banks. That was how the Greeks set fire to the Arab fleet."

"But why not warn Trochu?"

"Has he got time?"

Berthelot went on: "Unless they blow up the locks along the Marne canal, all the big Prussian siege artillery will come sailing up to the walls of Paris. The locks are mined, I believe, but will they remember to blow them up? . . . I could go on telling you about things like that until the cows come home."

Renan, clinging stubbornly to his thesis of the superiority of the German people, was expounding it to his two neighbors when Du Mesnil interrupted him to say: "As for the independent spirit of your German peasants, all I can say is that when I was shooting in Baden, we used to send them to pick up the game with a kick in the arse!"

"Well," retorted Renan, dropping the main argument of his thesis, "I would rather have peasants you kicked in the arse than peasants like ours, whom universal suffrage has made our masters, peasants—the very dregs of civilization—who were responsible for inflicting that government on us for twenty years!"

Berthelot went on with his dispiriting revelations, at the end of which I exclaimed:

"So it's all over? There's nothing left for us to do but rear a new generation to exact vengeance?"

"No, no," cried Renan, standing up and going red in the face, "no, not vengeance! Let France perish, let the Nation perish: there is a higher ideal of Duty and Reason!"

"No, no," howled the whole company, "there is nothing higher than the Nation!"

"No," shouted Saint-Victor, louder and more angrily than the rest, "let's have no quibbling and aestheticizing. There is nothing higher than the Nation!"

Renan had got up and begun walking round the table rather unsteadily, waving his little arms in the air, quoting Holy Writ, and saying that it was all there. Then he went over to the window, beneath which Paris life was going on in apparent unconcern, and said to me: "That is what will save us: the flabbiness of that people."

And the company broke up, with everyone thinking: "Perhaps, a fortnight from now, it will be the Prussians who will be dining at this table and sitting in our places."

8 September

Empire or Republic, nothing really changes. It is annoying to hear people saying all the time: "It is the Emperor's fault." If our generals have shown themselves to be inefficient, if our officers are ignorant, if our troops have had their moments of cowardice, that is not the Emperor's fault. Moreover, a single man cannot have so great an influence on a nation, and if the French nation had not been disintegrating, the Emperor's extraordinary mediocrity would not have robbed it of victory. Let us not forget that sovereigns always reflect the nation over which they rule, and that they would not remain on their thrones for three days if they were at variance with its soul. . . .

Tuesday, 27 September

A serious expression comes over the faces of the people strolling along the street who go up to the white posters gleaming in the gaslight. I see them read carefully and then walk away slowly, silent and thoughtful. These posters are the statutes of the courts-martial set up at Vincennes and Saint-Denis. One stops short at these words: "Sentence will be executed forthwith by the squad detailed to guard the courtroom." And one realizes with a slight shudder that we are entering the summary, dramatic atmosphere of a siege.

Saturday, 1 October

Horsemeat is sneaking slyly into the diet of the people of Paris. The day before yesterday, Pélagie brought home a piece of fillet which, on account of its suspicious appearance, I did not eat. Today, at Peter's restaurant, I was served some roast beef that was watery, devoid of fat, and streaked with white sinews; and my painter's eye noticed that it was a dark red color very different from the pinky red of beef. The waiter could give me only a feeble assurance that this horse was beef.

Monday, 3 October

Paris has never known an October like this. The clear, starry nights are like nights in the south of France. God loves the Prussians.

Tuesday, 4 October

The bombardment seems imminent. Yesterday somebody came to my house to ask if I had a stock of water on every floor. Today I noticed barrels of water in every alleyway, and in front of the church in the Rue de la Chaussée-d'Antin a huge iron cylinder, mounted on piles, which is apparently a municipal reservoir.

Next to the pavement, standing in the gutter, erect, immobile, seeing nothing, hearing nothing, heedless of the carriages brushing past her, there was an old countrywoman wearing a tile-shaped bonnet and wrapped, in her petrified rigidity, in folds which resembled the ledgerstones at Bruges. She carried within her such stupefied grief that I went up to her and spoke to her. Then this woman, slowly coming to, said to me in a voice like a groan: "I thank you for your kindness. I am not in need. I am simply unhappy."

Monday, 10 October

This morning I went to get a card for my meat ration. It seemed to me that I was looking at one of those queues in the great Revolution which my poor old cousin Cornélie used to describe to me, in that patient line of heterogeneous individuals, of ragged old women, of men in peaked caps, of small shopkeepers, cooped up in those improvised offices, those whitewashed rooms, where you recognized, sitting round a table, omnipotent in their uniforms of officers of the National Guard and supreme dispensers of your food, your far from honest tradesmen.

I came away with a piece of blue paper, a typographical curiosity for future Goncourts and times to come, which entitles me and my

housekeeper to buy every day two rations of raw meat or two portions of food cooked in the municipal canteens. There are coupons
up to 14 November: a good many things may happen between now
and then. . . .

Monday, 31 October

On people's faces and in their attitudes one could read the effect
of the great and terrible things that are in the air. Standing behind a
group of people questioning a National Guard, I heard the words
revolver shots, rifle shots, wounded. Outside the Théâtre-Français,
Lafontaine told me the official news of Bazaine's capitulation.

The Rue de Rivoli was packed with people, and the crowd,
sheltering under umbrellas, grew thicker as one approached the
Hôtel de Ville. There, there was a throng, a multitude, a mêlée of
people of all sorts and conditions, through which National Guards
would force their way now and then, waving their rifles in the air
and shouting: "The Commune for ever!" The building was in darkness, with time moving heedlessly round the illuminated clock-face,
the windows all wide open, and the workmen who had led the
movement of 4 September sitting on the sills with their legs dangling outside. The square was a forest of rifle butts raised in the air,
the metal plates gleaming in the rain.

On every face could be seen distress at Bazaine's capitulation, a
sort of fury over yesterday's reverse at Le Bourget, and at the
same time an angry and rashly heroic determination not to make
peace. Some workmen in bowler hats were writing in pencil, on
greasy pocket-books, a list a gentleman was dictating to them.
Among the names I heard those of Blanqui, Flourens, Ledru-Rollin,
and Mottu. "Things are going to move now!" said one workman, in
the midst of the eloquent silence of my neighbors; and I came
across a group of women already talking fearfully of the division of
property.

It seemed, as I had guessed from the workmen's legs dangling
from the windows of the Hôtel de Ville, that the Government had
been overthrown and the Commune established, and that the list of
the gentleman in the square was due to be confirmed by universal
suffrage within twenty-four hours. It was all over. Today one could
write: *Finis Franciae.* . . .

Shouts of "The Commune for ever!" went up all over the square, and fresh battalions went rushing off down the Rue de Rivoli, followed by a screaming, gesticulating riff-raff. . . . Poor France, to have fallen under the control of those stupid bayonets! Just then an old lady, seeing me buy the evening paper, asked me—oh, the irony of it!—whether the price of Government stock was quoted in my paper.

After dinner, I heard a man in a workman's smock say to the tobacconist whom I had asked for a light: "They can't go on fooling us like that for ever! There'll be a '93 before long, with everybody hanging everybody else!"

The Boulevard was in darkness, the shops were all shut, and there were no passers-by. A few groups of people, each person holding a parcel of food tied with a string cutting into one finger, stood in the gaslight coming from stalls and cafes whose owners kept coming to the door, uncertain as to whether to close or not. The call to arms was sounded. An apoplectic old National Guard went by, cap in hand, shouting: "The scum!" An officer of the National Guard appeared at the door of the Café Riche and called for the men in his battalion. The rumor went round that General Tamisier was a prisoner of the Commune. The call to arms went on sounding insistently. A young National Guard went running along the middle of the Boulevard, shouting at the top of his voice: "To arms, damn you!"

Civil war, with starvation and bombardment, is that what tomorrow holds in store for us?

. . .

Monday, 5 December

Saint-Victor, in his article yesterday, said in a striking fashion that France had to rid herself of the idea which she had entertained until now of Germany, of that country which she had been accustomed to consider, on the strength of its poetry, as the land of innocence and good nature, as the sentimental nest of platonic love. He recalled that the ideal, fictional world of Werther and Charlotte, of Hermann and Dorothea, had produced the toughest of soldiers, the wiliest of diplomats, the craftiest of bankers. He might have added the most mercenary of courtesans. We must be on our guard against that race, which arouses in us the idea of childlike innocence: their fair hair is the equivalent of the hypocrisy and sly determination of the Slav races.

Saturday, 31 December

In the streets of Paris, death passes death, the undertaker's wagon drives past the hearse. Outside the Madeleine today I saw three coffins, each covered with a soldier's greatcoat with a wreath of immortelles on top.

Out of curiosity I went into Roos's, the English butcher's shop on the Boulevard Haussmann, where I saw all sorts of weird remains. On the wall, hung in a place of honor, was the skinned trunk of young Pollux, the elephant at the Zoo; and in the midst of nameless meats and unusual horns, a boy was offering some camel's kidneys for sale.

The master-butcher was perorating to a group of women: "It's forty francs a pound for the fillet and the trunk. . . . Yes, forty francs. . . . You think that's dear? But I assure you I don't know how I'm going to make anything out of it. I was counting on three thousand pounds of meat and he has only yielded two thousand, three hundred. . . . The feet, you want to know the price of the feet? It's twenty francs. . . . For the other pieces, it ranges from eight francs to forty. . . . But let me recommend the black pudding. As you know, the elephant's blood is the richest there is. His heart weighed twenty-five pounds. . . . And there's onion, ladies, in my black pudding."

I fell back on a couple of larks which I carried off for my lunch tomorrow.

Friday, 6 January [*1871*]

The shells have begun falling in the Rue Boileau and the Rue La Fontaine. Tomorrow, no doubt, they will be falling here; and even if they do not kill me, they will destroy everything I still love in life, my house, my knick-knacks, my books.

On every doorstep, women and children stand, half frightened, half inquisitive, watching the medical orderlies going by, dressed in white smocks with red crosses on their arms, and carrying stretchers, mattresses, and pillows.

Saturday, 7 January

The sufferings of Paris during the siege. A joke for two months. In the third month the joke went sour. Now nobody finds it funny any more, and we are moving fast towards starvation or, for the moment at least, towards an epidemic of gastritis. Half a pound of horsemeat, including the bones, which is two people's ration for three days, is lunch for an ordinary appetite. The prices of edible chickens or pies put them out of reach. Failing meat, you cannot fall back on vegetables; a little turnip costs eight sous and you have to pay seven francs for a pound of onions. Nobody talks about butter any more, and every other sort of fat except candle-fat and axle-grease has disappeared too. As for the two staple items of the diet of the poorer classes—potatoes and cheese—cheese is just a memory, and you have to have friends in high places to obtain potatoes at twenty francs a bushel. The greater part of Paris is living on coffee, wine, and bread.

This evening, at the station, when I asked for my ticket to Auteuil, the clerk told me that as from today trains would not run beyond Passy. Auteuil is no longer part of Paris. . . .

Wednesday, 18 January
It is no longer a case of a stray shell now and then as it has been these last few days, but a deluge of cast iron gradually closing in on me and hemming me in. All around me there are explosions fifty yards away, twenty yards away, at the railway station, in the Rue Poussin, where a woman has just had a foot blown off, and next door, where a shell had already fallen the day before yesterday. And while, standing at the window, I try to make out the Meudon batteries with the aid of a telescope, a shell-splinter flies past me and sends mud splashing against my front door.

At three o'clock I was going through the gate at the Étoile when I saw some troops marching past and stopped to look. The monument to our victories, lit by a ray of sunshine, the distant cannonade, the immense march-past, with the bayonets of the troops in the rear flashing beneath the obelisk, all this was something theatrical, lyrical, epic in nature. It was a grandiose, soul-stirring sight, that army marching towards the guns booming in the distance, an army with, in its midst, gray-bearded civilians who were fathers, beardless youngsters who were sons, and in its open ranks women carrying their husband's or their lover's rifle slung across their backs. And it is impossible to convey the picturesque touch brought to the war by this citizen multitude escorted by cabs, unpainted omnibuses, and removal vans converted into army provision wagons.

Thursday, 26 January

The shells are coming closer. New batteries seem to be opening fire. Shells are exploding every few minutes along the railway line, and people cross our boulevard on their hands and feet.

You can see everybody performing the painful mental operation of accustoming the mind to the shameful idea of capitulation. Yet there are some strong-minded men and women who go on resisting. I have been told of some poor women who, even this morning, were shouting in the queues outside the bakers' shops: "Let them cut our ration again! We're ready to suffer anything! But don't let them surrender!"

Monday, 30 January

In a newspaper giving the news of the capitulation, I read the news of King William's enthronement as emperor of Germany at Versailles, in the Hall of Mirrors, under the nose of the stone Louis XIV in the courtyard outside. That really marks the end of the greatness of France. . . .

Sunday, 5 March,

The peace conditions strike me as so oppressive, so crushing, so mortal for France, that I am afraid war may break out again before we are ready to wage it.

Sunday, 19 March

In the train, people around me were saying that the army was retiring towards Versailles and that Paris was in the grip of insurrection.[2]

The embankment and the two big streets leading to the Hôtel de Ville were blocked by barricades, with cordons of National Guards lined up on front. One was overcome with disgust at the sight of their stupid, abject faces, in which triumph and intoxication created a sort of dissolute radiance. Every now and then they could be seen, their caps cocked over one ear, staggering out of the half-open door of some wine shop, the only sort of shop open today. Around these barricades there was a pack of street corner Diogenes and fat

[2] This marked a Government withdrawal which permitted the Commune two months of revolutionary life before it was crushed.

bourgeois of dubious professions, with clay pipes in their mouths and their wives on their arms.

Above the Hôtel de Ville, a red flag was flying; and down below, the square was swarming with an armed mob behind three guns.

On the way home, I read on people's faces dazed indifference, sometimes melancholy irony, most often sheer consternation, with old gentlemen raising their hands in despair and whispering among themselves after looking cautiously all around.

Tuesday, 28 March

The newspapers see nothing in what is going on but a question of decentralization: as if it had anything to do with decentralization! What is happening is nothing less than a conquest of France by the worker and the reduction to slavery under his rule of the noble, the bourgeois, and the peasant. Government is passing from the hands of the have's to those of the have-not's, from those who have a material interest in the preservation of society to those who have no interest whatever in order, stability, or preservation. Perhaps, in the great law of change that governs all earthly things, the workers are for modern society what the Barbarians were for ancient society, the convulsive agents of dissolution and destruction.

Sunday, 2 April

The sound of gunfire, about ten o'clock, in the direction of Courbevoie. Thank God, civil was has broken out! When things have reached this pass, civil war is preferable to hypocritical skull-duggery. The firing dies down. Has Versailles been beaten? Alas, if Versailles suffers the slightest reverse, Versailles is lost! Somebody calls to see me and says that from remarks he has overheard he fears a defeat.

I set out straight away for Paris, studying people's faces, which are a sort of barometer of events in revolutionary times; I see in them a hidden satisfaction, a sly joy. Finally a newspaper tells me that the Belleville troops have been beaten! I am filled with a jubilation which I savor at length. Let tomorrow bring what it will.

Wednesday, 12 April

On awaking this morning, I saw that the fort at Issy, which I thought had been taken, was still flying the red flag. So the Versailles troops have been thrown back again.

Why this stubborn resistance which the Prussians did not encounter? Because the idea of the motherland is dying. Because the formula: "The nations are brothers" has done its work, even in this time of invasion and cruel defeat. Because the International's doctrines of indifference to nationality have penetrated the masses.

Why this stubborn resistance? Because in this war, the common people are waging their own war and are not under the Army's orders. This keeps the men amused and interested, with the result that nothing tires or discourages or dispirits them. One can get anything out of them, even heroism.

Tuesday, 18 April

In the Place Vendôme, the scaffolding has been put up in readiness for the demolition of the Column.[3] The square is the center of a fantastic tumult and a medley of amazing uniforms. There are some extraordinary National Guards to be seen there, including one who looks like a Velasquez dwarf, dressed in a military greatcoat with his twisted feet poking out at the bottom.

From all I hear, the employees of the Louvre are extremely worried. The Venus de Milo is hidden—guess where—at the Prefecture of Police. She is even hidden very deep down, and concealed underneath another hiding-place filled with police dossiers and papers calculated to stop any searchers in their investigations. All the same, it is thought that Courbet is on her track, and the silly employees fear the worst if the fanatical modernist lays his hands on the classical masterpiece.

Wednesday, 19 April

Charles-Edmond told me yesterday that it was estimated that seven hundred thousand people had left Paris since the elections.

All day long, there was a great deal of movement on the part of the National Guards. I saw some battalions coming back wearing bunches of lilac, but looking rather sheepish. On the Quai Voltaire

[3] The Vendôme column, a symbol of Bonapartism, was demolished by the Commune on May 16, 1871.

there was a smell of gunpowder carried up the Seine by the wind. For a long time I stood listening to the gunfire from the end of the waterside terrace, behind the figure of Fame riding side-saddle on her stone horse and standing out all white against a showery, smoky sky with great purple clouds scudding across it.

Sunday, 21 May

I spent the whole of the day dreading a defeat for Versailles, and remembering a remark which Burty had kept repeating: "The Versailles troops have been thrown back seven times."

Sad and worried, I set off this evening for my usual place of observation, the Place de la Concorde. When I got to the square I saw a huge crowd surrounding a cab with an escort of National Guards. "What is it?" I asked. "It's a gentleman they've just arrested," a woman replied. "He was shouting out of the window that that Versailles troops had entered the city." I remembered the little groups of National Guards I had just met in the Rue Saint-Florentin, running along as if in full retreat. But there have been so many mistakes and disappointments that I placed no confidence in the good news, though I was deeply stirred and agitated by that sickly condition which doctors call precordial anxiety.

I wandered around for a long time in search of information. . . . Nothing, nothing at all. The people who were still in the streets were like the people I saw yesterday. They were just as calm, just as dazed. Nobody seemed to have heard about that shout in the Place de la Concorde. Another rumor!

I returned home and went to bed in despair. I could not sleep. Through my hermetically closed curtains I seemed to be able to hear a confused murmur in the distance. I got up and opened the window. In a street some way off there was the usual noise of one company relieving another, as happened every night. I told myself I had been imagining things and went back to bed . . . but this time there was no mistaking the sound of drum and bugle! I rushed back to the window. The call to arms was sounding all over Paris, and soon, drowning the noise of the drums and the bugles and the shouting and the cries of "To Arms!" came the great, tragic, booming notes of the tocsin being rung in all the churches—a sinister sound which filled me with joy and sounded the death-kneel of the odious tyranny oppressing Paris.[4]

Monday, 22 May

I could not stay indoors today, I simply had to see and know.

Coming out, I found everybody standing in the carriage gateways in angry, excited groups hoping for the best and already plucking up the courage to taunt the mounted orderlies.

All of a sudden, a shell exploded on the Madeleine and all the tenants promptly went back indoors. Near the new Opera I saw a National Guard being carried along with his thigh broken. In the square, in a few scattered groups, they were saying that the Versailles troops had reached the Palace of Industry. The National Guards, coming back in small bands, and looking tired and shamefaced, were obviously demoralized and discouraged.

I came to call on Burty and found myself a prisoner in his apartment for I do not know how long. It was not safe to go out, as anybody seen in the streets by the National Guards was promptly enrolled and forced to work on the barricades. Burty started copying out extracts of the *Correspondence found at the Tuileries* while I buried myself in his *Delacroix* to the sound of exploding shells coming gradually nearer.

Soon they were falling very close. The house in the Rue Vivienne on the other side of the street had its porch shattered. Another shell smashed the street-lamp opposite. And a final shell, falling during dinner, exploded right outside and shook us on our chairs.

A bed was made up for me and I threw myself on to it, fully dressed. Under the windows I could hear the noise of drunken National Guards and their hoarse voices challenging every passerby. At daybreak I fell into a sleep haunted by nightmares and explosions.

Tuesday, 23 May

Today the sound of firing came nearer and nearer. We could distinctly hear rifleshots in the Rue Drouot. Suddenly a squad of

---

[4] May 21 marked the entrance of the Versailles Government's troops into Paris and the beginning of the "bloody week" when the Commune was destroyed in brutal fighting.

workers appeared who had been ordered to block the boulevard on a level with the Rue Vivienne and to build a barricade under our windows. Their hearts were not in it. Some of them took up two or three paving-stones from the roadway, and the others, as if for form's sake, gave a few blows with a pickax at the asphalt pavement. But almost immediately bullets started raking the boulevard and passing over their heads, and they downed tools. Burty and I saw them disappear down the Rue Vivienne with a sigh of relief. We were both thinking of the National Guards who would have come into the house to fire from the windows, trampling our collections under their feet.

Then a large band of National Guards appeared with their officers, falling back slowly and in good order. Others followed, marching faster. And finally some more came rushing along in a general stampede, in the midst of which we saw a dead man with his head covered in blood, whom four men were carrying by his arms and legs like a bundle of dirty washing, taking him from door to door without finding a single one open.

On the other side of the boulevard there was a man stretched out on the ground of whom I could see only the soles of his boots, and a bit of gold braid. There were two men standing by the corpse, a National Guard and a lieutenant. The bullets were making the leaves rain down on them from a little tree spreading its branches over their heads. I was forgetting a dramatic detail: behind them, in front of the closed doors of a carriage entrance, a woman was lying flat on the ground, holding a peaked cap on one hand.

At last our boulevard was in the hands of the Versailles troops. We had ventured out on to our balcony to have a look at them when a bullet struck the wall just above us. It was a fool of a tenant who had taken it into his head to light his pipe at his window.

The shells started falling again—this time shells fired by the Federates [i.e. Communards] at the positions captured by the Versailles troops. We camped in the anteroom. Renée's little iron bed was pulled into a safe corner. Madeleine lay down on a sofa near her father, her face lit up by the lamp and silhouetted against the white pillow, her thin little body lost in the folds and shadows of a shawl. Mme Burty sank into an armchair. As for myself, I kept listening to the heartrending cries of a wounded infantryman who had dragged himself up to our door and whom the concierge, out of a cowardly fear of compromising himself, refused to let in.

Now and then I went to the windows overlooking the boulevard, to look out at that black night of Paris, unrelieved by a gleam of gaslight or lamplight, and whose deep, fearful darkness concealed those of the day's dead who had not been collected.

Wednesday, 24 May

When I awoke I looked for the corpse of the National Guard who had been killed yesterday. It had not been removed. It had simply been partly covered with the branches of the tree under which he had been killed.

The fires burning all over Paris were creating a light like the light of an eclipse.

There was a pause in the bombardment. I took advantage of it to leave Burty and go to the Rue de l'Arcade. There I found Pélagie, who had had the courage to cross the whole battlefield yesterday, holding a big bunch of roses from my *Gloire de Dijon* rose-tree, helped and protected by the Versailles officers, who in their admiration for this woman advancing fearlessly through the rifle-fire and grapeshot, had guided her through the breaches opened up by the engineers near the Expiatory Chapel.

We set off for Auteuil, trying to get a glimpse of the Tuileries on the way. A shell which exploded practically at our feet in Place de la Madeleine forced us to fall back along the Faubourg Saint-Honoré, where we were followed by splinters striking the walls above our heads and to the left and right of us.

All evening, through a gap in the trees, I watched the fire of Paris, a fire which, against the night sky, looked like one of those Neapolitan gouaches of an eruption of Vesuvius on a sheet of black paper.

Thursday, 25 May

All day long, the guns and rifles have gone on firing. I spent the day walking round the ruins of Auteuil, where the damage and destruction is such as might have been caused by a whirlwind.

Carriages kept going by along the road from Saint-Denis to Versailles, taking back to Paris people whose stay in the country had made them positively archaic.

Paris is decidedly under a curse! After a drought lasting a whole month, there is now a wind of hurricane force blowing across the burning city.

Friday, 26 May

Today I was walking beside the railway line near Passy station when I saw some men and women surrounded by soldiers. I plunged through a gap in the fence and found myself at the edge of the road on which the prisoners were waiting to be taken to Versailles. There were a great many prisoners there, for I heard an officer say to the colonel, as he handed over a piece of paper: "Four hundred and seven, including sixty-six women."

The men had been split up into lines of seven or eight and tied to each other with string that cut into their wrists. They were just as they had been captured, most of them without hats or caps, and with their hair plastered down on their foreheads and faces by the fine rain that had been falling ever since this morning. There were men of the people there who had made themselves head coverings out of blue check handkerchiefs. Others, drenched to the skin by the rain, were holding thin overcoats tight across their chests, with a bulge where they were carrying a hunk of bread. They came from every class of society: hard-faced workmen, bourgeois in socialist hats, National Guards who had not had time to change out of their uniforms, and a couple of infantrymen with ghostly-white faces— stupid, fierce, indifferent, mute figures.

There was the same variety among the women. There were women wearing kerchiefs next to women in silk gowns. I noticed housewives, working-girls, and prostitutes, one of whom was wearing the uniform of a National Guard. And in the midst of them all there stood out the bestial head of a creature whose face was half-covered with an enormous bruise. Not one of these women showed the apathetic resignation of the men. There was anger and scorn on their faces, and many of them had a gleam of madness in their eyes.

Among these women, there was one who was singularly beautiful, with the implacable beauty of a young Fate. She was a girl with dark, curly hair, steely eyes, and cheekbones red with dried tears. She stood frozen as it were in a defiant posture, hurling insults at officers and men from a throat and lips so contracted by anger that they were unable to form sounds or words. Her mute, twisted mouth masticated abuse without being able to spit it out. "She's just like the girl who stabbed Barbier!" a young officer said to one of his friends.

Everyone was ready to go when pity, which can never entirely abandon man, induced some of the soldiers to hold out their water-bottles to the women, who with graceful movements turned their heads and opened parched mouths to drink, at the same time keeping a wary eye on the scowling face of an old gendarme. The signal for departure was given and the pitiful column moved off on its journey to Versailles under a watery sky.

Sunday, 28 May

Driving along the Champs-Élysées in a cab, I saw, in the distance, legs running in the direction of the great avenue. I leaned out of the window. The whole avenue was filled by a huge crowd between two lines of troopers. I got out and joined the people running to see what it was. It was the prisoners who had just been taken at the Buttes-Chaumont, walking along in fives with a few women in their midst. "There are six thousand of them," a trooper in the escort told me. "Five hundred were shot on the spot." At the head of this haggard multitude a nonagenarian was walking along on trembling legs.

Despite all the horror one felt towards these men, one was saddened by the sight of this dismal procession, in the midst of which one could see some soldiers, army deserters, who had their tunics on inside out, with their grey cloth pockets hanging by their sides, and who seemed to be already half stripped for the firing-squad.

I met Burty in the Place de la Madeleine. We walked along the streets and boulevards, suddenly crowded with people who had emerged from their cellars and hiding-places, thirsting for light and sunshine, and wearing on their faces the joy of liberation. We went to collect Mme Burty, whom we persuaded to come out for a stroll. While Burty, who had suddenly been stopped in the street by Mme Verlaine, was discussing ways and means of concealing her husband, Mme Burty told me a secret which Burty had kept from me. One of his friends on the Public Committee, whose name she did not mention, had told Burty, four or five days ago, that the Government no longer had control over anything and that they were going to enter all the houses in Paris, confiscate the valuables they contained, and shoot all the householders.

I took leave of the Burtys and went to see how much of Paris had been burnt by the Federates. The Palais-Royal has been burnt down, but the pretty façade of the two wings overlooking the square are intact; money will have to be spent on reconstructing the interior. The Tuileries need to be rebuilt along the garden and overlooking the Rue de Rivoli.

There is smoke everywhere, the air smells of burning and varnish, and on all sides one can hear the hissing of hose-pipes. In a good many places there are still horrible traces of the fighting: here a dead horse; there, beside the paving-stones from a half-demolished barricade, a peaked cap swimming in a pool of blood.

The large-scale destruction begins at the Châtelet and carries on from there. Behind the burnt-out theatre, the custumes have been spread out on the ground: carbonized silk in which, here and there, one catches sight of the gleam of golden spangles, the sparkle of silver.

On the other side of the embankment, the Palais de Justice has had the roof of its round tower decapitated. There is nothing left of the new buildings but the iron skeleton of the roof. The Prefecture of Police is a smoldering ruin, in whose bluish smoke the brand-new gold of the Sainte-Chapelle shines brightly.

By way of little paths made through barricades which have not yet been demolished, I eventually reached the Hôtel de Ville.

It is a splendid, a magnificent ruin. All pink and ash-green and the color of white-hot steel, or turned to shining agate where the stonework has been burnt by paraffin, it looks like the ruin of an Italian palace, tinted by the sunshine of several centuries, or better still like the ruin of a magic palace, bathed in the theatrical glow of electric light. With its empty niches, its shattered or truncated statues, its broken clock, its tall window-frames and chimneys still standing in mid-air by some miracle of equilibrium, and its jagged silhouette outlined against the blue sky, it is a picturesque wonder which ought to be preserved if the country were not irrevocably condemned to the restorations of M. Viollet-le-Duc. The irony of chance! In the utter ruin of the whole building there shines, on a marble plaque intact in its new gilt frame, the lying inscription: *Liberty, Equality, Fraternity.*

Monday, 29 May

Posted up on all the walls I see MacMahon's proclamation announcing that it was all over at four o'clock yesterday afternoon.

This evening one can hear the movement of Parisian life starting up again, and its murmur like a distant tide: the hours no longer fall into the silence of the desert.

(b) "The struggle of the producing against the appropriating class."
Karl Marx, "The Historic Significance of the Commune,"
The Civil War in France (1871)[1]

The Commune of 1871 began as a patriotic republican Parisian protest against national humiliation and conservative rule, and ended in a working-class myth. Marx's essay helped create this myth. This angry man of socialism scorned Goncourt's aristocratic detachment; though supposedly a "social scientist," Marx was emotionally committed to the cause of the "proletariat" with a passion rarely matched. And he thought he saw in the short-lived Commune of 1871 the historical debut of the most momentous event in human history: the dictatorship of the proletariat. Although it is dubious history, *The Civil War in France* reveals Marx's wonderful capacity for polemic. One may well compare his sort of "realism" with the other varieties exhibited in this section. This selection is Chapter III of his *The Civil War in France*, written at white heat soon after the event and published under the auspices of the First International Workingmen's Association.

O N THE dawn of the 18th of March, Paris arose to the thunderburst of "Vive la Commune!" What is the Commune, that sphinx so tantalizing to the bourgeois mind?

"The proletarians of Paris," said the Central Committee in its manifesto of the 18th of March, "amidst the failures and treasons of the ruling classes, have understood that the hour has struck for them to save the situation by taking into their own hands the direction of public affairs. . . . They have understood that it is their imperious duty and their absolute right to render themselves masters of their own destinies, by seizing upon the governmental power." *But the working class cannot simply lay hold of the ready-made state machinery, and wield it for its own purposes.*

[1] First published in 1871, Karl Marx's *The Civil War in France* was reprinted by the Communist publishing house, International Publishers, New York, 1933; they still have it in print as a paperback.

The centralized state power, with its ubiquitous organs of standing army, police, bureaucracy, clergy, and judiciary—organs wrought after the plan of a systematic and hierarchic division of labor—originates from the days of absolute monarchy, serving nascent middle-class society as a mighty weapon in its struggles against feudalism. Still, its development remained clogged by all manner of medieval rubbish, seigniorial rights, local privileges, municipal and guild monopolies, and provincial constitutions. The gigantic broom of the French Revolution of the eighteenth century swept away all these relics of bygone times, thus clearing simultaneously the social soil of its last hindrances to the superstructure of the modern state edifice raised under the First Empire, itself the offspring of the coalition wars of old semifeudal Europe against modern France. During the subsequent regimes[2] the government, placed under parliamentary control—that is, under the direct control of the propertied classes—became not only a hotbed of huge national debts and crushing taxes; with its irresistible allurements of place, pelf, and patronage, it became not merely the bone of contention between rival factions and adventurers of the ruling classes; but its political character changed simultaneously with the economic changes of society. At the same pace at which the progress of modern industry developed, widened, intensified the class antagonism between capital and labor, *the state power assumed more and more the character of the national power of capital over labor, of a public force organized for social enslavement, of an engine of class despotism.* After every revolution marking a progressive phase in the class struggle, the purely repressive phase in the state power stands out in bolder and bolder relief. The revolution of 1830, resulting in the transfer of government from the land-

---

[2] Marx gives his own characteristic interpretations of the several French regimes between 1800 and 1871, which were: the First Empire, of Napoleon I, to 1814–1815; restored Bourbon monarchy with extremely limited legislature, 1815–1830; the Orleanist monarchy of King Louis Philippe, brought in by the revolution of 1830 and giving political power to the upper bourgeoisie; the short-lived Second Republic which came to power as a result of the revolution of 1848, giving way in 1851 to the Second Empire of Napoleon III after a coup d'état, on which Marx had also written a burning philippic. Napoleon III abdicated after the disastrous battle of 1870 against the Prussians at Sedan (Ed.).

lords to the capitalists, transferred it from the more remote to the more direct antagonists of the working men. The bourgeois republicans, who, in the name of the revolution of 1848, took the state power, used it for the June massacres, in order to convince the working class that "social" republic meant the republic ensuring their social subjection, and in order to convince the royalist bulk of the bourgeois and landlord class that they might safely leave the cares and emoluments of government to the bourgeois "republicans." However, after their one heroic exploit of June, the bourgeois republicans had, from the front, to fall back to the rear of the "Party of Order"—a combination formed by all the rival fractions and factions of the appropriating class in their now openly declared antagonism to the producing classes. The proper form of their joint stock government was the *Parliamentary Republic*, with Louis Bonaparte for its president. Theirs was a regime of avowed class terrorism and deliberate insult towards the "vile multitude." If the Parliamentary Republic, as M. Thiers said, "divided them [the different fractions of the ruling class] least," it opened an abyss between that class and the whole body of society outside their spare ranks. The restraints by which their own divisions had under former regimes still checked the state power, were removed by their union; and in view of the threatening upheaval of the proletariat, they now used that state power mercilessly and ostentatiously as the *national war engine of capital against labor. In their uninterrupted crusade against the producing masses they were,* however, bound not only to invest the executive with continually increased powers of repression, but at the same time to divest their own parliamentary stronghold—the National Assembly—one by one, of all its own means of defense against the executive. The executive, in the person of Louis Bonaparte, turned them out. The natural offspring of the "Party-of-Order" republic was the Second Empire.

The empire, with the coup d'etat for its certificate of birth, universal suffrage for its sanction, and the sword for its scepter, professed to rest upon the *peasantry, the large mass of producers not directly involved in the struggle of capital and labor.* It professed to save the working class by breaking down parliamentarism, and, with it, the undisguised subserviency of government to the propertied classes. It professed to save the propertied classes by upholding their economic supremacy over the working class; and, finally, it professed to unite all classes by reviving for all the chimera of national glory. In reality, it was the only form of government possible at a time when the bourgeoisie had already lost, and the working class had not yet acquired, the faculty of ruling the nation. It was acclaimed throughout the world as the savior of society. Under its sway, bourgeois society, freed from political cares, attained a development unexpected even by itself. Its industry and commerce expanded to colossal dimensions; financial swindling celebrated cosmopolitan orgies; the misery of the masses was set off by a shameless display of gorgeous, meretricious, and debased luxury. The state power, apparently soaring high above society, was at the same time itself the greatest scandal of that society and the very hotbed of all its corruptions. Its own rottenness, and the rottenness of the society it had saved, were laid bare by the bayonet of Prussia, herself eagerly bent upon transferring the supreme seat of that regime from Paris to Berlin. *Imperialism is, at the same time, the most prostitute and the ultimate form of the state power which nascent middle-class society had commenced to elaborate as a means of its own emancipation from feudalism, and which fullgrown bourgeois society had finally transformed into a means for the enslavement of labor by capital.*

The direct antithesis to the empire was the Commune. The cry of "Social Republic," with which the revolution of February was ushered in by the Paris proletariat, did but express a vague aspiration after a republic that was not only to supersede the monarchical form of class rule, but class rule itself. The Commune was the positive form of that republic.

Paris, the central seat of the old governmental power, and, at the same time, the social stronghold of the French working class, had risen in arms against the attempt of Thiers and the Rurals to restore and perpetuate that old governmental power bequeathed to them by the empire. Paris could resist only because, in consequence of the siege, it had got rid of the army and replaced it by a National Guard, the bulk of which consisted of workingmen. This fact was now to be transformed into an institution. The first decree of the Commune, therefore, was the suppression of the standing army, and the substitution for it of the armed people.

The Commune was formed of the municipal councilors, chosen by universal suffrage in various wards of the town, responsible and revocable at short terms. The majority of its members were naturally workingmen, or acknowledged representatives of the working class. The Commune was to be a working, not a parliamentary, body, executive and legislative at the same time. Instead of continuing to be the agent of the central government, the police was at once stripped of its political attributes and turned into the responsible and at all times revocable agent of the Commune. So were the officials of all other branches of the administration. *From the members of the Commune downward, the public service had to be done at "workmen's wages."* The vested interests and the representation allowances of the high dignitaries of state disappeared along with the high dignitaries themselves. Public functions ceased to be the private property of the tools of the central government. Not only municipal administration, but the whole initiative hitherto exercised by the state was put into the hands of the Commune.

Having once got rid of the standing army and the police, the physical force elements of the old government, the Commune was anxious to break the spiritual force of repression, the "parson power," by the disestablishment and disendowment of all churches as proprietary bodies. The priests were sent back to the recesses of private life, there to feed upon the alms of the faithful in imitation of their predecessors, the apostles. All educational institutions were opened to the people gratuitously, and at the same time cleared of all interference of church and state. Thus, not only was education made accessible to all, but science itself freed from the fetters which class prejudice and governmental force had imposed upon it.

The judicial functionaries were to be divested of that sham independence which had but served to mask their abject subserviency to all succeeding governments to which, in turn, they had taken, and broken, the oaths of allegiance. *Like the rest of public servants, magistrates and judges were to be elective, responsible, and revocable.*

The Paris Commune was, of course, to serve as a model to all the great industrial centers of France. The communal regime once established in Paris and the secondary centers, the old centralized government would in the provinces, too, have to give way to the self-government of the producers. In a rough sketch of national organization which the Commune had no time to develop, it is clearly stated that the commune was to be the political form of even the smallest country hamlet, *and that in the rural districts the standing army was to be replaced by a national militia, with an extremely short term of service.* The rural communes of each district were to administer their common affairs by an assembly of delegates in the central town, and these district assemblies were again to send deputies to the National Delegation in Paris, each delegate to be at any time revocable and bound by the *mandat impératif (formal instructions) of his constituents.* The few but important functions which still would remain for a central government were not to be suppressed, as has been intentionally misstated, but were to be discharged by communal, and therefore strictly responsible, agents. The unity of the nation was not to be broken; but, on the contrary, to the organized by the Communal constitution, and to become a reality by the destruction of the state power which claimed to be the embodiment of that unity independent of, and superior to, the nation itself, from which it was but a parasitic excrescence. *While the merely repressive organs of the old governmental power were to be amputated, its legitimate functions were to be wrested from an authority usurping preeminence over society itself, and restored to the responsible agents of society.* Instead of deciding once in three or six years which member of the ruling class was to represent the people in Parliament, universal suffrage was to serve the people, constituted in Communes, as individual suffrage serves every other employer in the search for the workmen and managers in his business. *And it is wellknown that companies, like individuals, in matters of real business generally know how to put the right man in the right place, and, if they for once make a mistake, to redress it promptly. On the other hand, nothing could be more foreign to the spirit of the Commune than to supersede universal suffrage by hierarchic investiture.*

It is generally the fate of completely new historical creations to be mistaken for the counterpart of older and even defunct forms of social life, to which they may bear a certain likeness. Thus, this new Commune, which breaks the modern state power, has been mistaken for a reproduction of the medieval communes, which first preceded, and afterwards became the substratum of, that very state power. The Communal constitution has been mistaken for an attempt to break up into a federation of small states, as dreamt of by Montesquieu and the Girondins, that unity of great nations which, if originally brought about by political force, has now become a powerful coefficient of social production. The antagonism of the Commune against the state power has been mistaken for an exaggerated form of the ancient struggle against overcentralization. Peculiar historical circumstances may have prevented the classical development, in France, of the bourgeois form of government, and may have allowed, in England, the great central state organs to be supplemented by corrupt vestries, jobbing councilors, and ferocious Poor Law guardians in the towns, and virtually hereditary magistrates in the counties. The Communal constitution would have restored to the social body all the forces hitherto absorbed by the state parasite feeding upon, and clogging the free movement of, society. By this one act it would have initiated the regeneration of France. The provincial French middle class saw in the Commune an attempt to restore the sway their order had held over the country under Louis Philippe, and which, under Louis Napoleon, was supplanted by the pretended rule of the country over the towns. *In reality, the Communal constitution brought the rural producers under the intellectual lead of the central towns of their districts, and there secured to them, in the workingmen, the natural trustees of their interests. The very existence of the Commune involved, as a matter of course, local municipal liberty,* but no longer as a check upon the now superseded state power. It could only enter into the head of a Bismarck—who, when not engaged on his intrigues of blood and iron, always likes to resume his old trade, so befitting his mental caliber, of contributor to *Kladderadatsch* (the Berlin *Punch*) —it could only enter into such a head, to ascribe to the Paris Commune aspirations after the caricature of the old French municipal organization of 1791, the Prussian municipal constitution, which degrades the town governments to mere secondary wheels in the police machinery of the Prussian state. The Commune made that catchword of bourgeois revolutions, cheap government, a reality, by destroying the two greatest sources of expenditure—the standing army and state bureaucratism. Its very existence presupposed the nonexistence of monarchy, which, in Europe at least, is the normal encumbrance and indispensable cloak of class rule. It supplied the republic with the basis of really democratic institutions.

But neither cheap government nor the "true republic" was its ultimate aim; they were its mere concomitants.

The multiplicity of interpretations to which the Commune has been subjected, and the multiplicity of interests which construed it in their favor, show that it was a thoroughly flexible political form, while all previous forms of government had been emphatically repressive. Its true secret was this. *It was essentially a working-class government, the product of the struggle of the producing against the appropriating class, the political form at last discovered under which to work out the economic emancipation of labor.*

Except on this last condition, the Communal constitution would have been an impossibility and a delusion. The political rule of the producer cannot coexist with the perpetuation of his social slavery. The Commune was therefore to serve as a lever for uprooting the economic foundations upon which rests the existence of classes, and therefore of class rule. With labor emancipated, every man becomes a workingman, and productive labor ceases to be a class attribute.

It is a strange fact. In spite of all the tall talk and all the immense literature, for the last sixty years, about emancipation of labor, no sooner do the workingmen anywhere take the subject into their own hands with a will, than up rises at once all the apologetic phraseology of the mouthpieces of present society with its two poles of capital and wage slavery (the landlord now is but the sleeping partner of the capitalist), as if capitalist society was still in its purest state of virgin innocence, with its antagonisms still undeveloped, with its delusions still unexploded, with its prostitute realities not yet laid bare. The Commune, they exclaim, intends to abolish property, *the basis of all civilization!* Yes, gentlemen, the Commune intends to abolish that class property which makes the labor of the many the wealth of the few. It aimed at the expropriation of the expropriators. It wanted to make individual property a truth by transforming the means of production, *land* and *capital*, now chiefly the means of enslaving and exploiting labor, into mere instruments of free and associated labor. But this is Communism, "impossible" Communism! Why, those members of the ruling classes who are intelligent enough to perceive the impossibility of continuing the present system—and they are many—have become the obtrusive and full-mouthed apostles of cooperative production. If cooperative production is not to remain a sham and a snare; if it is to supersede the capitalist system; if united cooperative societies are to regulate national production upon a common plan, thus taking it under their own control, and putting an end to the constant anarchy and periodical convulsions which are the fate of capitalist production—what else, gentlemen, would it be but Communism, "possible" Communism?

The working class did not expect miracles from the Commune. They have no ready-made utopias to introduce *par décret du peuple*. They know that in order to work out their own emancipation, and along with it that higher form to which present society is irresistibly tending, by its own economic agencies, they will have to pass through long struggles, through a series of historic processes, transforming circumstances and men. They have no ideals to realize, but to set free the elements of the new society with which the old collapsing bourgeois society itself is pregnant. In the full consciousness of their historic mission, and with the heroic resolve to act up to it, the working class can afford to smile at the coarse invective of the gentlemen's gentlemen with the pen and inkhorn, and at the didactic patronage of well-wishing bourgeois doctrinaires, pouring forth their ignorant platitudes and sectarian crotchets in the oracular tone of scientific infallibility.

When the Paris Commune took the management of the revolution in its own hands; when plain workingmen for the first time dared to infringe upon the governmental privilege of their "natural superiors," and, under circumstances of unexampled difficulty, performed their work modestly, conscientiously, and efficiently—performed it at salaries the highest of which barely amounted to one-fifth of what, according to high scientific authority, is the minimum required for a secretary to a certain metropolitan school board—the old world writhed in convulsions of rage at the sight of the Red Flag, the symbol of the Republic of Labor, floating over the Hôtel de Ville.

And yet, this was the first revolution in which the working class was openly acknowledged as the only class capable of social initiative, even by the great bulk of the Paris middle class—shopkeepers, tradesmen, merchants—the wealthy capitalist alone excepted. The Commune had saved them by a sagacious settlement of that ever recurring cause of dispute among the middle class themselves—the debtor and creditor accounts. The same portion of the middle class, after they had assisted in putting down the workingmen's insurrection of June, 1848, had been at once unceremoniously sacrificed to their creditors by the then Constituent Assembly. But this was not their only motive for now rallying round the working class. They felt there was but one alternative—the Commune, or the empire, under whatever name it might reappear. The empire had ruined them economically by the havoc it made of public wealth, by the wholesale financial swindling it fostered, by the props it lent to the artificially accelerated centralization of capital, and the concomitant expropriation of their own ranks. It had suppressed them politically, it had shocked them morally by its orgies, it had insulted their Voltairianism by handing over the education of their children to the *Frères Ignorantins*, it had revolted their national feeling as Frenchmen by precipitating them headlong into a war which left only one equivalent for the ruins it made—the disappearance of the empire. In fact, after the exodus from Paris of the high Bonapartist and capitalist *Bohème*, the true middle-class Party of Order came out in the shape of the *Union Républicaine*, enrolling themselves under the colors of the Commune and defending it against the willful misconstruction of Thiers. Whether the gratitude of this great body of the middle class will stand the present severe trial, time must show.

The Commune was perfectly right in telling the peasants that "its victory was their only hope." Of all the lies hatched at Versailles and reechoed by the glorious European penny-a-liner, one of the most tremendous was that the Rurals represented the French peasantry. Think only of the love of the French peasant for the men to whom, after 1815, he had to pay the billion of indemnity.[3] In the eyes of the French peasant, the very existence of a great landed proprietary is in itself an encroachment on his conquests of 1789. The bourgeoisie, in 1848, had burdened his plot of land with the additional tax of forty-five centimes in the franc; but then it

---

[3] After the overthrow of Napoleon and the restoration of the monarchy in 1815 many of those who had emigrated from France during the revolution returned and tried to reclaim property taken from them. They did not usually succeed in regaining their property but were reimbursed to some extent by a controversial act of the legislature.

did so in the name of the revolution; while now it had fomented
a civil war against the revolution, to shift on the peasant's shoulders
the chief load of the five billions of indemnity to be paid to the
Prussian. The Commune, on the other hand, in one of its first proc-
lamations, declared that the true originators of the war would be
made to pay its cost. The Commune would have delivered the
peasant from the blood tax, would have given him a cheap government, transformed his present blood-suckers, the notary, advocate,
executor, and other judicial vampires, into salaried communal
agents, elected by, and responsible to, himself. It would have freed
him of the tyranny of the *garde champêtre*, the gendarme, and the
prefect; would have put enlightenment by the schoolmaster in
the place of stultification by the priest. As the French peasant is,
above all, a man of reckoning, he would find it extremely reasonable
that the pay of the priest, instead of being extorted by the tax-
gatherer, should only depend upon the spontaneous action of the
parishioners' religious instincts. Such were the great immediate
boons which the rule of the Commune, and that rule alone, held
out to the French peasantry. It is, therefore, quite superfluous here
to expatiate upon the more complicated but vital problems which
the Commune alone was able, and at the same time compelled, to
solve in favor of the peasant, viz., the hypothecary debt (mort-
gage), lying like an incubus upon his parcel of soil, the *proletariat
foncier* (land-holding proletariat), daily growing upon the land,
and his expropriation from it enforced, at a more and more rapid
rate, by the very development of modern agriculture and the competition of capitalist farming.

The French peasant had elected Louis Bonaparte president of
the republic; but the Party of Order created the empire. What the
French peasant really wants he commenced to show in 1849 and
1850, by opposing his mayor to the government's prefect, his
schoolmaster to the government's priest, and himself to the government's gendarme. All the laws made by the Party of Order in
January and February, 1850, were avowed measures of repression
against the peasant. The peasant was a Bonapartist, because the
Great Revolution, with all its benefits to him, was, in his eyes,
personified in Napoleon. This delusion, rapidly breaking down
under the Second Empire (and in its very nature hostile to the

Rurals), this prejudice of the past, how could it have withstood the appeal of the Commune to the living interests and urgent wants of the peasantry?

The Rurals—this was, in fact, their chief apprehension—knew that three months' free communication of Communal Paris with the provinces would bring about a general rising of the peasants, and hence their anxiety to establish a police blockade around Paris, so as to stop the spread of the rinderpest.

If the Commune was thus the true representative of all the healthy elements of French society, and therefore the truly national government, it was, at the same time, a workingmen's government; as the bold champion of the emancipation of labor, it was emphatically international. Within sight of the Prussian army that had annexed to Germany two French provinces, the Commune annexed to France the working people all over the world.

The Second Empire had been the jubilee of cosmopolitan blacklegism, the rakes of all countries rushing in at its call for a share in its orgies and in the plunder of the French people. Even at this moment the right hand of Thiers is Ganesco, the foul Wallachian, and his left hand is Markowski, the Russian spy. The Commune admitted all foreigners to the honor of dying for the immortal cause. Between the foreign war lost by their treason, and the civil war fomented by their conspiracy with the foreign invader, the bourgeoisie had found the time to display their patriotism by organizing police hunts upon the Germans in France; the Commune made a *German workingman its Minister of Labor*. Thiers, the bourgeoise, the Second Empire, had all continually deluded Poland by loud professions of sympathy, while in reality betraying her to, and doing the dirty work of, Russia; the Commune honored the heroic sons of Poland by placing them at the head of the defenders of Paris. And, to broadly mark the new era of history it was conscious of initiating, under the eyes of the conquering Prussians on the one side and of the Bonapartist army, led by Bonapartist generals, on the other, the Commune pulled down that colossal symbol of martial glory, the Vendôme column.

The great social measure of the Commune was its own working existence. Its special measures could but betoken the tendency of a government of the people by the people. *Such were the abolition of the nightwork of journeyman bakers;* the prohibition, under penalty, of the employers' practice to reduce wages by levying upon their *workpeople fines under manifold pretexts—a process in which the employer combines in his own person the parts of legislator, judge, and executioner, and filches the money to boot.* Another measure of this class was the surrender, to associations of workmen, under reserve of compensation, of all closed workshops and factories, no matter whether the respective capitalists had absconded or preferred not to work.

The financial measures of the Commune, remarkable for their sagacity and moderation, could only be such as were compatible with the state of a besieged town. Considering the colossal robberies committed upon the city of Paris by the great financial companies and contractors, under the protection of Haussmann, the Commune would have had an incomparably better title to confiscate their property than Louis Napoleon had against the Orleans family. The Hohenzollerns and the English oligarchs, who both have derived a good deal of their estates from church plunder, were, of course, greatly shocked at the Commune clearing but eight thousand francs out of secularization.

While the Versailles government, as soon as it had recovered some spirit and strength, used the most violent means against the Commune; while it put down the free expression of opinion all over France, even to the forbidding of meetings of delegates from the large towns; while it subjected Versailles and the rest of France to an espionage far surpassing that of the Second Empire; while its gendarme inquisitors burned all papers printed at Paris, and sifted all correspondence from and to Paris; while in the National Assembly the most timid attempts to put in a word for Paris were howled down in a manner unknown even to the *Chambre introuvable* of 1816; with the savage warfare of Versailles outside, and its attempts at corruption and conspiracy inside Paris—would the Commune not have shamefully betrayed its trust by affecting to keep up all the decencies and appearances of liberalism as in a time of profound peace? Had the government of the Commune been akin to that of M. Thiers, there would have been no more occasion to suppress Party-of-Order papers at Paris than there was to suppress Communal papers at Versailles.

It was irritating, indeed, to the Rurals that at the very same time they declared the return to the church to be the only means of salvation for France, the infidel Commune unearthed the peculiar mysteries of the Picpus nunnery and of the St. Laurent Church. It was a satire upon M. Thiers that, while he showered grand crosses upon the Bonapartist generals, in acknowledgment of their mastery in losing battles, signing capitulations, and turning cigarettes at Wilhelmshöhe, the Commune dismissed and arrested its generals whenever they were suspected of neglecting their duties. The expulsion from, and arrest by, the Commune of one of its members who had slipped in under a false name, and had undergone at Lyons six days' imprisonment for simple bankruptcy, was it not a deliberate insult hurled at the forger, Jules Favre, then still the Foreign Minister of France, still selling France to Bismarck, and still dictating his orders to that paragon government of Belgium? But, indeed, the Commune did not pretend to infallibility, the invariable attribute of all governments of the old stamp. It published its doings and sayings, it initiated the public into all its shortcomings.

In every revolution there intrude, at the side of its true agents, men of a different stamp; some of them survivors of and devotees to past revolutions, without insight into the present movement, but preserving popular influence by their known honesty and courage, or by the sheer force of tradition; others mere bawlers, who by dint of repeating year after year the same set of stereotyped declamation against the government of the day, have sneaked into the reputation of revolutionists of the first water. After March 18 some such men did also turn up, and in some cases contrived to play preeminent parts. As far as their power went, they hampered the real action of the working class, exactly as men of that sort have hampered the full development of every previous revolution. They are an unavoidable evil; with time they are shaken off; but time was not allowed to the Commune.

Wonderful, indeed, was the change the Commune had wrought in Paris! No longer any trace of the meretricious Paris of the Second Empire. No longer was Paris the rendezvous of British landlords, Irish absentees, American ex-slaveholders and shoddy men, Russian ex-serf owners, and Wallachian boyards. No more corpses at the morgue, no nocturnal burglaries, scarcely any robberies; in fact, for the first time since the days of February, 1848, the streets of Paris were safe, and that without any police of any kind. "We," said a member of the Commune, "hear no longer of assassination, theft, and personal assault; it seems, indeed, as if the police had dragged along with it to Versailles all its conservative friends." The *cocottes* had followed the scent of their protectors—the absconding men of family, religion, and, above all, of property. In their stead, the real women of Paris showed again at the surface— heroic, noble, and devoted, like the women of antiquity. Working, thinking, fighting, bleeding Paris—almost forgetful, in its incubation of a new society, of the cannibals at its gates—radiant in the enthusiasm of its historic initiative!

Opposed to this new world at Paris, behold the old world at Versailles—that assembly of the ghouls of all defunct régimes; Legitimists and Orleanists, eager to feed upon the carcass of the nation—with a tail of antediluvian republicans, sanctioning, by their presence in the Assembly, the slaveholders' rebellion, relying for the maintenance of their parliamentary republic upon the vanity of the senile mountebank at its head, and caricaturing 1789 by holding their ghastly meetings in the *Jeu de Paume*. There it was, this Assembly, the representative of everything dead in Franc, propped up into a semblance of life by nothing but the swords of the generals of Louis Bonaparte. Paris all truth, Versailles all lie; and that lie vented through the mouth of Thiers.

Thiers tells a deputation of the mayors of the Seine-et-Oise— "You may rely upon my word, which I have *never* broken!" He tells the assembly itself that "it was the most freely elected and most liberal assembly France ever possessed"; he tells his motley soldiery that it was "the admiration of the world, and the finest army France ever possessed"; he tells the provinces that the bombardment of Paris by him was a myth: "If some cannonshots have been fired, it is not the deed of the army of Versailles, but of some insurgents trying to make believe that they are fighting, while they dare not show their faces." He again tells the provinces that "the artillery of Versailles does not bombard Paris, but only cannonades it." He tells the archbishop of Paris that the pretended executions and reprisals (!) attributed to the Versailles troops were all moonshine. He tells Paris that he was only anxious "to free it from the hideous tyrants who oppress it," and that, in fact, the Paris of the Commune was "but a handful of criminals."

The Paris of M. Thiers was not the real Paris of the "vile multitude," but a phantom Paris, the Paris of the *francs fileurs*, the Paris of the Boulevards, male and female—the rich, the capitalist, the gilded, the idle Paris, now thronging with its lackeys, its blacklegs, its literary *bohême*, and its *cocottes* at Versailles, Saint-Denis, Rueil, and Saint-Germain; considering the civil war but an agreeable diversion, eyeing the battle going on through telescopes, counting the rounds of cannon, and swearing by their own honor and that of their prostitutes that the performance was far better got up than it used to be at the Porte St. Martin. The men who fell were really dead; the cries of the wounded were cries in good earnest; and, besides, the whole thing was so intensely historical.

This is the Paris of M. Thiers, as the Emigration of Coblenz was the France of M. de Calonne.

II. *Naturalism*

❦❦❦❦❦❦❦❦❦❦❦❦

10. The continuing march of science

"Dykes have been burst; boundaries removed; we hardly know the old landmarks." David Masson, *Recent British Philosophy* (1867)

David Masson (1822–1907) was a Scottish literary historian and biographer, a student of what we would today call the history of ideas, and a writer in whose occasionally slightly purple prose one can easily hear echoes of his great fellow Scot, Thomas Carlyle, whom he greatly admired. His appraisal of trends in British philosophy in 1867 stressed John Stuart Mill and William Hamilton, the leading representatives of British empiricism and German transcendentalism. But he saw that the new scientific discoveries and theories—evolution was the greatest of these, but there was also the discovery of the second law of thermodynamics and other theories about the cosmos—completely changed the terms of discourse and rendered the old systems obsolete. Something of the bewilderment these new perspectives brought to the mid-Victorians may be sensed in the following passage. Naturalism was chiefly influenced by these scientific ideas, revealing man in the dimensions of cosmic determinism, no longer a unique creature possessing an immortal soul and the object of God's special providence. Masson ends with several verses of Alfred Tennyson's poem of anguished Victorian doubt, *In Memoriam*.

In no age so conspicuously as in our own has there been a crowding in of new scientific conceptions of all kinds to exercise a perturbing influence on speculative philosophy. They have come in almost too fast for Philosophy's powers of reception. She has visibly reeled amid their shocks, and has not yet recovered her equilibrium. Within those years alone which we are engaged in surveying there have been developments of native British science, not to speak of influxes of scientific ideals, hints, and probabilities from without, in the midst of which British Philosophy has looked about her scared and bewildered, and has felt that some of her oldest statements about herself, and some of the most important terms in her vocabulary, require re-explication. I think that I can even mark the precise year 1848 as a point whence the appearance of an unusual amount of unsteadying thought may be dated—as if, in that year of simultaneous European irritability, not only were the nations agitated politically, as the newspapers saw, but conceptions of an intellectual kind that had long been forming themselves underneath in the depths were shaken up to the surface in scientific journals and books. There are several vital points on which no one can now think, even were he receiving four thousand a year for doing so, as he might very creditably have thought seventeen years ago. There have been during that period, in consequence of revelations by scientific research in this direction and in that, some most notable enlargements of our views of physical nature and of history —enlargements even to the breaking down of what had formerly been a wall in the minds of most, and the substitution on that side of a sheer vista of open space. . . .

The influx upon philosophy of new and disorganizing scientific conceptions has never been greater than during the seventeen years since 1848. Scientific conceptions unknown to the physiologists of the earlier part of this century, unknown to the phrenologists, and not to be found even in the *Cours de Philosophie Positive* of M. Comte—scientific conceptions, I say, till recently unheard of, or existing only in the form of certain vague drifts and conjectures of the scientific mind—have of late years poured in upon us in full flood. Dykes have been burst; boundaries removed; we hardly know the old landmarks. Now, upon none of our previous modes of thought, whether among philosophers or among people at large, has the aggregate influence of these new conceptions been greater than precisely upon that notion of man or humanity as a whole over which, as we have said, there might have been a general opinion among the bystanders that the battle of empiricism and transcendentalism might at last be fought out. Lo! ere the battle could be begun, the very notion over which it was to be fought is dissolved, agitated out of definite shape, or rolled away, on one side of it, into an edgeless mist! No flagstaff, we are now told, can we plant at any one spot, however far back, in earthly time, and say that at that point humanity is to be considered as beginning—that all before was a world prehuman, but all after is a history with man in it. In the first place, what of all those recent speculations as to the antiquity of the human species? It is not for me here to discuss these speculations, or even to enumerate them in their mutual relations; but to be speaking of recent British Philosophy, and not to recognize the vast question of Science so raised as bearing upon British Philosophy, and as compelling her in some way or other to new explications of herself, would be a piece of hypocritical cowardliness. How our popular system of chronology is faring, or may ultimately fare, at the hands of the new archaeologists, let time (which is the party principally concerned) itself determine. It will fare as truth would have it, and no otherwise. But it is more than the question of human chronology that is now in agitation. Behind that question as to the antiquity of the human species lies the question as to the origin of all species, as to the place and connections of man in the entire scheme of animated nature in our planet. Raised long ago in all varieties of ways by naturalists whose particular theories are exploded, this question has been raised again, and notably among ourselves, in forms that have brought our scientific chiefs into earnest debate, and gathered almost the whole population round them as spectators. The issue here too it is not for me to forecast. But observe how, if the views so recently announced should become general in any modification of them, Condillac's resolution of all human thought, feeling, belief, or faculty, into transformed sensation reappears in the world with its scope enlarged. Humanity itself then shades off by indefinite gradations into preceding forms of life. It is not at any particular point, however far back, assumed as the beginning of human history, that empiricism need then abandon the battle, from the impossibility of accounting empirically for the then incipient organism, however poor and wretched it was. That organism itself, with all its stock of powers, was still, empiricism might say, only transformed or concreted experience. Seas, ages, aeons of experience had preceded it, whose essence was conserved and elaborated in its structure; and specimens of the intermediate organisms through which this one had been reached, and also the wrecks and shapes of myriads of others, lay strewn about, showing the measureless

energy of Nature, and the enormous struggle of sentient inven-
tiveness which she had carried in her bosom, during periods anterior
to the farthest ken of man. And so, on and on, bursting the verte-
brate in the way, bursting type after type, Imagination, growing
dizzier and dizzier in her ascent through an animated vagueness of
she knows not what, pursues and still pursues that ideal of a bypast
eternity, at which Reason, following in her train, can take his
stand and say, "Here we may stop; here experience begins; nothing
here is a priori." Utterly in vain! Whither goes the last fantasy of
Science, still holding by the principle of continuity, transformation
out of prior elements, the resolution of what is into what was?
Whither but beyond conceivable sentiency itself on our earth,
nay beyond aught of a slush of vegetation conceivable as preceding
sentiency, on through theories of a sheerly mineral geology, to
alight at last on the steaming crust of a desolate planet of molten
rotundity, itself the convolved shred of what was once a space-
filling nebula? Here, from sheer fatigue, the imagination does rest
for the present; here, if anywhere, it seems possible to whisper to
oneself a faint persuasion as if one need not think of anything a
priori to such a milk of thinness. Suppose the last word of science
then to be that all that exists is transformed nebula. With a thou-
sandfold more energy . . . may Mr. Mill utter his protest. Is it such
a mighty thing, such a stroke of universal explanation, simply to
gather up the world and all its glories and to *call* them "transformed
nebula?" No; but the particular question is as to the ultimate rest-
ing place of that theory of experience which Mr. Mill himself holds.
If water is oxygen and hydrogen, why should we fear to say so?
We want to trace experience to its fountainhead.

It seems to me, I repeat, that by the recent crowding in of such
new scientific conceptions there has been a disturbance of the
relations of recent British empiricism as represented hitherto in
Mill and recent British transcendentalism as thrown into form by
Hamilton. Neither system seems to present its leading principle
bent as one would like to see it into the curves and junctures of the
most anxious thought of our time. Possibly Mr. Mill's system, from
its comparative abstinence hitherto from the attempt to do so—from
its being so much more the rich forthgoing of a philosophy the
principles of which are avowed than a metaphysical wrestle for
these principles—will have less difficulty in shaping itself to what it

may recognize as the new requirements. It is by *metaphysical deficiency* that it falls short of such a system of more developed empiricism as one can conceive offering itself in the midst of these requirements. On the other hand, from the very elaborateness and exactness of the metaphysical part of Hamilton's philosophy, from its consisting so peculiarly of a system of metaphysics, it is possible that the complaint against it may be that of *positive incompatibility* at many points with present requirements. One can conceive a system of transcendentalism that should be provided with answers to some questions, different from those which sufficed for Hamilton ere yet the questions had taken their present shape. Might not that Kantian scheme of the mind of man, for example, which represents it as a complex organism of so many a priori forms, neither more nor fewer,[1] encounter nowadays a kind of opposition that could not have been ready for it when it was first promulgated? Might not Science, in one of her new moods, object that it isolates man as the last term of a series from all the preceding—nay, that it gives an account of man fixed down, as it were, for inspection and analysis, at one moment (two or three thousand years long perhaps, but still a moment) of his own nominal existence? Is the organism itself stable? May not the very constituting *forms* of human thought have increased themselves, or changed perceptibly by a touch here and there, even within historic time, and may not the best present list that could be given of these forms be inapplicable to man in the future? So I can conceive Science interrogating Transcendentalism, and perhaps explaining her meaning by means of a series of human crania chronologically arranged; and I do not think that such replies as Transcendentalism could give would suggest themselves easily out of Hamilton. . . .

Is it not precisely in the form of an alteration, or of alterations, of the cosmological conceptions that had served for us before, that the recent abundance of new scientific teachings and revelations has most visibly taken effect? What is that battle of faith now going on among us, and painfully exercising so many minds, but a struggle between the expanded sort of cosmological conception

[1] Kant's categories of the understanding, or a priori concepts, with which each human mind is equipped and which enable it to know the objects of knowledge, as listed by him were exactly twelve, three each under the headings of quantity, quality, relation, and modality. (Ed.)

which science has seemed to be making imperative on the imaginations of us all and the little heap of propositions we have heretofore guarded so fondly at the center as the true epitome to the reason of the whole physical vast of things? And what expanded sort of cosmological conception does science seem to have been making imperative? We have just been speaking of it. In running back the difference of the two psychological theories to the extreme point to which science seemed to be driving it up, we ended in a tumult of cosmology. Whither had we run ourselves back? Why—and this only because there seemed a defiance of any conceivable going farther—to a universal nebula! Let rhythm re-suggest what prose is too shame-faced to repeat:

> *Our* hour is now: Erst, space was nebulous;
> It whirled, and in the whirl the luminous milk
> Broke out in rifts and curdled into orbs—
> Whirled and still curdled, till the azure rifts
> Severed and shored vast systems, all of orbs.
> Each orb has had its history. For ours,
> It blazed and steamed, cooled and contracted, till,
> Tired of mere vapouring within the grasp
> Of ruthless condensation, it assumed
> Its present form, proportions, magnitude—
> Our tidy ball, axled eight thousand miles.

And so, on and on, Geology taking up the wondrous tale, and navigating our ball and furbishing it, as she only knows how, through the boundless series of ages of her possession of it, till at length, not so very long ago, History meets her emerging into a glimmering light, and, the ball somehow having bred or been covered with populations of human beings, some of whom had made great advances, and formed civilizations, and taught themselves to read and write and think of high matters, we see at last a Greek Herodotus walking musingly round the margin of the Mediterranean, and collecting those legends of the past and those scraps of information respecting manners, customs, and monuments, for which we bless him and think of him with love! Thenceforward till now the voyage has been in a more familiar sea, and all has been simpler sailing.

Instead of trying, by farther description, and by involving each of the more important recent speculations of science in its proper place and measure, to body forth the cosmological image which is becoming prevalent in educated minds, let me despatch the matter more swiftly by saying that any change or expansion of the cosmological image that has recently taken place seems to be the result of a synthesis of three notions, each having its origin in scientific research:

1. There is the notion of *evolution*, as a fact or law holding universally throughout existence. It is the notion that every existing state has grown entirely out of an immediately preceding state, has been evolved out of that state by using up all its elements or constituents. I need not stay to illustrate the notion. It is now tolerably familiar to most. A crude form of the notion existed long ago, and still figures, with a quantity of haze around it, in the word *progress*. But, though *progress* is a very good word, and may still most usefully be kept in service as expressing that advance from a worse state of things to a better which is the sort of evolution to be preferred and striven for, yet, for the general meaning now in view, *progress*, both from its excess and its deficiency, is not nearly so good a word as its later substitute. *Evolution*, accordingly, has become the common word; it is more and more showing itself in our literature, and carrying the exact notion it expresses along with it. And the result of the diffusion of this notion, and of the exercise of it in the minds that have received it, has been that more men have been accustomed to *think back*, as it were, all the heterogeneous universe which we now behold, including our human society in the heart of it, through its preceding series of states making a complete rendition of all the contents of each state into the body of its predecessor, still in the direction of that simplest and homogeneous unity out of which all may be conceived as evolved. Observe, in this very statement of the notion of evolution, the implied sub-notion that the course or method of evolution is the gradual presentation of what was once simple and homogeneous in states more and more complex and heterogeneous. A name has been given to this sub-notion too. It has been called *differentiation*.

2. There is a notion which has not come into such distinct recognition as to have received a special name, but the existence and working of which in many minds may certainly be detected, and

which is hinted at in many current forms of speculation. I will call it the notion of *interplanetary*, or even *interstellar, reciprocity.* Imperceptibly, by the action of many suggestions from different quarters, men have of late contracted or recovered a habit of interplanetary recollectiveness in their thoughts about things—a habit of consciously extending their regards to the other bodies of our solar system, and even to other sidereal systems, and feeling as if somehow *they* were not to go for nothing in the calculation of our earth's interests and fortunes. Not of course the sort of interplanetary recollectiveness involved in the old dream of astrology, during the prevalence of which dream men did, with an intensity which we seldom realize, though History would be a fool to forget it, bring down the high heavens into their being and carry the very stars as golden bees in their bonnets. It is not that we are becoming Guy Mannerings in ruined towers and again casting horoscopes. Nor is the habit of thought dependent on any continuance or revival of the old controversy as to the plurality of worlds. We are compelled to interplanetary recollectiveness in quite new ways. Seeing how we have conquered our little earth physically, and brought it thoroughly into grasp with telegraphs and railroads, it has even been a whimsy of some minds that we might begin to foresee a time when terrestrial work alone would not suffice for the activity of the developed race of earth's sons, and, in answer to their passionate longings, Nature might be bound to furnish them an outlet of enterprise in interplanetary connections. But, such mere whimsies apart, very stringent teachings of real science are compelling to what may be called an interplanetary habit of consciousness. Those extraordinary recent revelations by spectrum-analysis, as to the constitution of the sun and of other celestial bodies, are they the curiosities merely of chemical speculation? No; the general thought of man drinks them in, and is different, with them, through a thousand correspondences, from what it would have been without them. Or, again, has no action of a vital kind been exerted upon general thought by those marvelous calculations, founded on the doctrine of the correlation of forces, as to probable endurance of that heat of the sun on which science finds that all the movements, all the actions, all the life of our earth and the rest of the solar system depend, and of which it views them as but conversions? I remember, indeed, that, when one of our most distinguished scientific men put forth a popular paper on the age of the sun's heat, stating the probability that in so many hundred millions of years the whole stock of heat would be exhausted, and we or our posterity should have to take the consequences, an English newspaper seriously objected to the publishing of such things, on the ground that, as the catastrophe was so far off, it could concern neither man nor beast to think about it. Here was an instance of a kind of pigheadedness, or indifference to ideas, which possess to a disastrous extent the current literature of Britain, and would move to indignation if it were not so comical. As if any man into whose mind this idea of the exhaustibility of the sun's heat, and consequently of the force energizing our system, had once entered, could ever think a thought about anything whatsoever that should not, in shape and color, be influenced by that idea? In short, just as Science has made general, or is beginning to make general, by her teachings, the notion of the evolution of all the present cosmical variety and complexity of things from some vast indistinct beginning, so, by some of her late teachings, she has been persuading men to embrace in their regards all parts of the present complexity as still vibrating together, and to think of planets and stars and all starry systems, despite their enormous interspaces, as glittering dispersed in one entanglement.

3. Distinct from either the notion of the past evolution of all things physical from some one homogeneous beginning, or from the notion of their present inter-entanglement in all their places throughout the purlieus of immensity, as still holding from that beginning by the threads of its mazy outrush—distinct from both these notions, but completing them and rounding them off towards the future, is the notion of the tendency of all things to *ultimate and universal collapse*. M. Comte, if I remember rightly, has an inkling of this speculation in one of its particular forms. Anticipating for the human race an almost indefinite career of farther development on this earth, thinking humanity yet not near midway of the course of its mighty collective life, he nevertheless considers himself bound to announce it as an inevitable conclusion of strict science, that even this collective life of humanity cannot go on forever—that there must come a period, however far distant, when all the elements of the collective organism of humanity shall have been used up or brought into equilibrium, and when consequently

the organism, like any other, must begin to decay. Some day, unless for a reserve of interferences of which we can foresee nothing, our earth will be carrying not its present freight of nations, with their civilizations, governments, agricultures, literatures, and libraries, but only the unrecognizable wrecks of what had once been such, crawling over its surface, and degenerating, through stages of meaner and meaner vitality, back into shapelessness and extinction. But this prognostication of M. Comte's is as nothing compared with the prognostications to which science has been led by the same principle. One might suppose, in considering M. Comte's antic- ipation, the coming in, ere the period arrived for its fulfillment, of such a reserve of interferences, now unimaginable, as should hand on man and his belongings, together with the tradition of our for- saken planet, into some wider mode of existence. But it is the col- lapse or winding-down of the whole solar system that recent science, conjecturing onwards through time, has been prognosticat- ing as inevitable in the distance. By a process which has been named the equilibration of forces, and which is slowly going on, it seems to be foreseen that a period will come when all the energy locked up in the solar system, and sustaining whatever of motion or life there is in it, will be exhausted, when the vivid play of its actions and interactions shall cease, and all its parts through all their present variousness will be stiffened or resolved, as regards each other, in a defunct and featureless community of rest and death. Nor is this all. Speculation dares to go with her mathematics beyond the bounds of the solar system itself, and, though professing to grope here in a region the possibilities of which transcend her accustomed grasp and make it falter and tremble, yet sees no other end but that all the immeasurable entanglement of all the starry systems shall also run itself together at last in an indistinguishable equilibrium of ruin, as beads or fleeces of oily substance hung in some gauze-work would trickle together in burning tears at the touch of fire, and be consumed in a steam. Thus, to something like that universal nebula out of which all things are fancied as evolved does Science, at her utmost daring, conceive of them as tending to be resolved again. Universal dissolution, universal rest, universal death, is her last dream of the drift of things in the infinite future. Or, if she will not let it be finally a dream of universal death, but will arouse herself even as she dreams, is it not by an act which she confesses to be incompetent to herself as yet—by a kind of convulsive shudder of her being at the touch of a ghostly hand, and an unconscious turning in her sleep? To this, however, there are some who think she ought to consent. Hence, with some, the notion of the tendency of all things back to a universal homogeneousness and collapse is relieved by the farther speculation that, when that state is reached, the process of evolution will somehow begin again. Again the nebula will whirl; again there will be spun forth some wondrous entanglement of starry systems through a blue immensity; again there will be dances of orbs round their central suns; again the orbs will have their strange particular histories; and again, when the maximum of diversity and speciality is reached, there will be a beginning of the revoke of all things into involution and integration again. This is introduced into the cosmological conception, as far as science can carry it or consent that it can be carried, the ultimate notion or imagination of a vast *periodicity*. The universe is a recurring beat or pulsation. It is a rhythm of alternate evolution and involution, expansion and contraction. It is the opening and shutting of a hand. It is a nothing ever manifesting itself as a something, and a something ever returning into a nothing. . . .

To this most excruciating pass, as it must appear to British souls, science at the utmost seems to have conducted metaphysics. How well the Laureate has expressed the real pain of the crisis! Always one of *his* peculiar merits is that he receives and ponders to the utmost the last scientific informations of the time, letting them sway his thoughts and occultly shape even the phrasing of his song; and no reader of the *In Memoriam* but must have noted this noble elegy, and its full philosophical significance:

'So careful of the type?' But no.
From scarpèd cliff and quarried stone
She cries, 'A thousand types are gone:
I care for nothing, all shall go.

'Thou makest thine appeal to me:
I bring to life, I bring to death:
The spirit does but mean the breath:
I know no more.' And he, shall he,

Man, her last work, who seemed so fair,
     Such splendid purpose in his eyes,
     Who rolled the psalm to wintry skies,
Who built him fanes of fruitless prayer,

Who trusted God was love indeed
     And love Creation's final law—
     Though Nature, red in tooth and claw
With ravine, shrieked against his creed—

Who lived, who suffered countless ills,
     Who battled for the True, the Just,
     Be blown about the desert dust,
Or sealed within the iron hills?

No more? A monster then, a dream,
     A discord. Dragons in the prime,
     That tare each other in their slime,
Were mellow music matched with him.

O life as futile, then, as frail!
     O for thy voice to soothe and bless!
     What hope of answer, or redress?
Behind the veil, behind the veil.

11. The book of despair

Winwood Reade, *The Outcasts* (1875)

The sad story of Arthur Elliott's loss of faith, told below, describes an experience shared by many sensitive and thoughtful Victorians. Darwin's theory pointed remorselessly to a cruel and probably godless world, ruled by chance. The realm of scientific naturalism took on a grimmer look after 1859, though men such as Henry Drummond and Josiah Royce came forward with formulae to explain away the darkness. The story of Darwin and his shattering impact on the world, when people saw themselves no longer as creatures endowed with an immortal soul and watched over by a benevolent deity but as one branch of the tailless apes who happened to survive because of certain favorable physical traits, has been told many times. In one important sense, "naturalism" was almost the same thing as applied Darwinism.

Arthur Elliott was the only son of a wealthy landed proprietor, one of my nearest neighbors, and a brother magistrate. Arthur had a most amiable nature, and was tenderly loved, not only by his parents, but by all who knew him intimately. His attainments were remarkable, as I can testify; for we read much together. He was an excellent classical scholar, but his favorite study was that of metaphysics, from which he was led to the study of natural science. But religion was the poetry and passion of his life; and though of a different belief, it afforded me pleasure to hear him discourse on the grandeur and benevolence of God. Sometimes when we were together in a deep green wood on a sultry summer afternoon; or sometimes walking at night beneath the glorious starlit sky; or sometimes, when reading the dialogues of Plato, some divine thought rose from the book like an immortal spirit from the grave, and passed into the soul, then the tears would stream from his eyes, and falling on his knees he would utter praises or prayers in words of surpassing eloquence, and with a voice of the sweetest melody. And often—how well I remember it now—often at such times his gestures grew wild and almost furious, his utterance was choked, and a strange bubbling sound came from his mouth. . . .

One day he came to me in trouble. He had been reading the great work of Malthus—the *Essay on Population*—and said that it made him doubt the goodness of God.[1] I replied with the usual commonplace remarks; he listened to me attentively, then shook his head, and went away. A little while afterwards he read *The Origin of Species*, which had just come out, and which proves that the law of population is the chief agent by which evolution has been produced.[2] From that time he began to show symptoms of insanity—which disease it is thought he inherited from one of his progenitors. He dressed always in black, and said that he was in mourning for mankind. The works of Malthus and Darwin, bound in somber

[1] According to Malthus' essay, population will always increase as wealth increases, so that the bulk of mankind can never improve their condition but will always remain at a bare level of subsistence. Malthus saw a way out if by education and restraint the birth rate could be diminished (Ed.).

[2] I.e., there is always a superabundance of individual organisms in any species and natural selection eliminates some and saves others. Darwin said that he first conceived his theory of evolution via natural selection when reading Malthus (Ed.).

covers, were placed on a table in his room; the first was lettered outside, *The Book of Doubt,* and the second *The Book of Despair.* . . .

In the grey hour of dawn they heard a struggle in the room, and a choked kind of cry, They pushed the door, but it had been secured from within by a small piece of wood wedged in underneath. They forced it open at last, and the body of the unfortunate young man was found hanging from the window bar. Life was extinct.

12. Life in the raw

Émile Zola, *Germinal* (1885)[1]

According to an entry in the Goncourts' *Journal* (1870), Zola remarked that

> After the analysis of the smallest subtleties of feeling, such as Flaubert did in *Madame Bovary,* after the analysis of things artistic, plastic, and neurotic, such as you have done, after these jewelled works, these chiselled volumes, there is no room for the young, nothing for them to do, no characters left for them to conceive and construct. It is only by the bulk of their work, the power of their creation that they can appeal to the public.

Flaubert and Baudelaire, who had wondered what was left for a writer to do after Hugo, had invented a new style; Zola knew that coming after Flaubert he must develop a new way of seeing and presenting life. Zola's temperament suited the new mode of novel writing. His prose was journalistic rather than poetic. He outdid the older writers by sheer bulk, by the grandiosity of his conceptions, and by the brutal frankness of his realism. Flaubert had little taste for this more exuberant brand of realism which came to be known as naturalism, and which was almost a monopoly of the tremendously prolific Zola: "Such materialism infuriates me . . . . after the realists we have the naturalists and the impressionists. What progress!" Zola proclaimed himself the scientist of literature. Using Claude Bernard's ideas for his own purposes, Zola declared that literature can be just as much a science as medicine. The novelist observes life; then he experiments with his characters. He knows that human nature is a calculable product of

[1] Trans. L.W. Tancock (Harmondsworth: Penguin Books, 1954).

heredity and environment. And he is not concerned with morality, but only with truth. This philosophy, which Zola set forth in his tract *Le Roman Experimental*, published in 1880, has struck almost everyone then and since as extremely naive, because Zola's novels are obviously much more than scientific tracts (see the Introduction, p. xvii).

Yet with this creed in mind Zola set out to study the history of an entire family in a huge series of twenty novels called *Les Rougon-Macquart* or *Histoire naturelle et sociale d'une famille sous le Second Empire*. Perhaps Zola was inspired in his attempt by Balzac's great sequence, *La Comedie Humaine*. His was the forerunner of many other mammoth novels (by Proust, Jules Romains, and John Galsworthy, for example). *Germinal*, published in 1885, was the thirteenth of the series. Two strains of blood appear in the family, going back to a single ancestress—an unstable, psychotic woman who had children both by a peasant, Rougon, and by a brutal criminal, Macquart. The latter line is condemned by its sinister blood to produce abnormal types, usually vicious and depraved, but occasionally revealing artistic genius. Among earlier figures in Zola's gallery of degenerates was the grand-daughter of Macquart, Gervaise, of *L'Assommoir* (the gin-mill, or grog-shop), alcoholic mother of numerous illegitimate children who lived and died in squalor and misery. One of her children was the celebrated *Nana*, Parisian prostitute. Étienne Lantier, of *Germinal*, was the son of Gervaise and the half-brother of Nana; one of his two full brothers was a murderous madman and the other was a great artist who finally committed suicide.

In studying Étienne, Zola confronts the social question—the conditions of the working class, in this case the coal miners. Less abnormal than the rest of his ill-starred family, but penniless and friendless, Étienne takes a job in the mines of northern France. The first eleven chapters of *Germinal* cover his first day in Montsou, and carefully describe the people and the surroundings. It is a grim picture of poverty and degradation. But Zola was not naive enough to make it a heroes-and-villains tale in which the virtuous workers are simply robbed by the cruel capitalists. There is vice as well as virtue on both sides, and in fact all are trapped in the same web of circumstances. The tragic climax of *Germinal* is a strike brought on, ironically, by a change designed to make the mines safer. Zola's naturalism is pessimistic; but he sees heroism, courage, and above all an abundance of vitality in his wretched victims of fate. Zola was at his best in scenes of mass action. The following selection comes near the climax of the book.

ALL THE entrances to Le Voreux had been sealed, and the only door left open was guarded by sixty soldiers standing with ordered arms. This was the way into the pit top, by a narrow flight of steps on to which the doors of the locker-room and deputies' room opened. The captain had lined them up two deep against the brick wall so that they could not be attacked from the rear.

At first the band of miners from the village kept its distance. There were not more than thirty-five of them and they were arguing violently among themselves.

Maheude had been the first to arrive, all disheveled, with a kerchief tied hastily round her head and Estelle asleep in her arms. She was furiously repeating:

"Don't let anybody go in or come out! Catch them all inside!"

Maheu was backing his wife up when old Mouque came along from Réquillart. They tried to prevent his going through, but he insisted, saying that his horses went on eating oats just the same and didn't care two hoots about a revolution. Besides, a horse had died, and he had to see about bringing it up. Étienne managed to free the old ponyman, whom the soldiers allowed into the pit. A quarter of an hour later, as the band of strikers was growing larger and more threatening, a wide door opened on the ground floor and some men appeared, hauling out the dead animal, a pitiful carcass still tied up in the rope net, and they left it in the middle of the puddles of melted snow. The sensation was so great that nobody thought of preventing their going in again and barricading the door behind them. For they had all recognized the horse, his head stiff and bent back against his side, and whispers ran round:

"It's Trompette, isn't it? Yes, it's Trompette."

It was. He had never been able to accustom himself to life underground and had remained dismal and unwilling to work, tortured by longing for the daylight he had lost. In vain had Bataille, the father of the pit, given him friendly rubs with his side and nibbled his neck so as to give him a little of his own resignation after ten years underground. Caresses only made him more doleful and his skin quivered when his friend who had grown old in the darkness whispered secrets in his ear. And whenever they met and snorted together they both seemed to be lamenting—the old one because he could not now remember, and the young one because he could not forget. They lived side by side in the stable, lowering their heads into the same manger and blowing into each other's nostrils, comparing their unending dreams of daylight, their visions of green pastures, white roads, and golden sunlight for ever and ever. Then, as Trompette, bathed in sweat, lay dying on his straw, Bataille had begun to sniff at him with heartbroken little sniffs, like sobs. He felt his friend grow cold, the pit was taking his last joy away, this friend who had come from up there, all fresh with lovely smells that brought back his own young days in the open air. And when he saw that the other was lying still he broke his tether, whinneying with fear.

Mouque had been warning the overman for a week. But who bothered about a sick horse at such a time? In any case these gentlemen disliked moving the horses about. But now they had got to make up their minds to move him. The day before Mouque and two men had spent an hour roping Trompette up. Bataille was harnessed to haul him to the shaft. Slowly the old horse dragged his dead friend along through such a narrow gallery that he had to proceed by little jerks, at the risk of grazing the skin of the corpse, and he shook his head in distress as he heard the long brushing sound of this mass of flesh bound for the knacker's yard. When they unharnessed him at pit bottom he watched with melancholy gaze the preparations for the ascent, as the body was pushed on to cross-beams over the sump and the net was tied to the bottom of a cage. Then at last the onsetters rang the meat-call, and he raised his head to see his friend go, gently at first and then with a rush up into darkness—lost for ever up the black hole. There he stood craning his neck, his shaky old memory recalling, maybe, some of the things of the earth. It was all over now, and his friend would never see anything again, and he would be done up himself into a dreadful bundle when the day came for him to go up there. His legs began to shake and the open air from that far country seemed to catch his throat, and he plodded back to the stable unsteadily as though he were drunk.

Up in the yard the miners stood round sadly looking at Trompette's body. One woman said softly:

"At any rate a man only goes down there if he wants to!"

A new crowd was coming down from the village, led by Levaque, followed by his wife and Bouteloup. Levaque was shouting:

"Death to the Belgians! No foreigners here! Down with them!"

They all surged forward, and Étienne had to check them. He went up to the captain, a tall, thin young man not more than twenty-eight, looking desperate but determined, and reasoned with him, trying to win him over, watching the effect of his words. Why risk useless slaughter? Was not justice on the miners' side? They were all brothers, and ought to work together. When Étienne mentioned the word republic the captain made a nervous gesture, but he kept his military stiffness and rapped out:

"Stand back! Don't force me to do my duty!"

Étienne tried three times, but his friends behind him were getting restive. The word ran round that Monsieur Hennebeau was at the pit and somebody suggested letting him down by the neck to see if he would hew his own coal. But the rumor was false; only Négrel and Dansaert were there, and they both appeared for a moment at a window of the pit top, the overman keeping in the background, for he had been very subdued since his adventure with Pierronne. The engineer, however, boldly looked down at the crowd with his sharp little eyes, smiling with the contemptuous mockery with which he regarded all men and all things. But he was booed and they both disappeared. The only face that could now be seen was that of the fair-haired Souvarine. He was on duty, not having left his machine for a single day throughout the strike. But he had become more and more taciturn and absorbed in some fixed idea, which seemed to gleam like steel in his pale eyes.

"Stand back!" shouted the captain again. "No, I can't listen to anything. My orders are to guard this pit and I'm going to guard it. And don't start hustling my men, or I'll find some way of making you get back!"

But in spite of his firm tone he was becoming increasingly uneasy as he saw the ever rising tide of miners. He was due to be relieved at noon, but fearing that he would not be able to hold out until then he had just sent a pit-boy off to Montsou for reinforcements.

He was answered by a storm of yells.

"Down with the foreigners! Death to the Belgians! We want to be masters in our own pit!"

Étienne turned back, sick at heart. So it had come to this, and there was nothing left to do but fight and die. He gave up trying to hold his mates back and the crowd rushed the little detachment of troops. There were nearly four hundred of them now, and more were pouring out of the neighboring villages and running down to swell the numbers. They were all shouting the same war-cry, and Maheu and Levaque were furiously addressing the soldiers:

"Go away! We've no quarrel with with you. Go away!"

"This is nothing to do with you," added Maheude. "You let us mind our own business!"

Behind her la Levaque screamed in her more violent way: "Have we got to kill you so as to get past? Just you bugger off!"

And even the shrill little voice of Lydie could be heard coming from the thickest part of the fray, where she and Bébert had managed to worm themselves:

"Look at those silly old sausages of soldiers!"

Catherine was standing a little in the rear and listening in bewilderment to all this new violence into which ill-luck had thrown her. Hadn't she had enough trouble already? What had she done to be constantly dogged by misfortune? Even up till yesterday she had not really understood what all the anger of the strikers was about, thinking that when you have your own fair share of beatings it is silly to go looking for more. But now her heart was full of hatred, and remembering what Étienne used to say during those evening talks at home she tried to understand what he was now saying to the soldiers. For he was treating them as friends, reminding them that they were men of the people too, and that they should side with the people against the exploiters of the people's sufferings.

Just then the crowd swayed violently and an old woman emerged. It was Ma Brûlé in all her skinny hideousness, neck and arms outstretched and running so fast that wisps of gray hair blew into her eyes.

"By Christ, I'm in this!" she panted. "That rat Pierron tried to keep me locked in the cellar!"

Without more ado she fell upon the soldiers, belching abuse from her black mouth:

"You lot of blackguards! You dirty lot of sods! Look at them! They lick their masters' boots and can only be brave against poor people!"

The others joined in the volleys of insults. A few still shouted: "Up with the soldiers! Throw the officer down the shaft!" But soon the only shout was: "Down with the red trousers!" However, these men who had heard appeals for fraternity and friendly attempts to enlist them on the people's side with still, impressive faces, not batting an eyelid, kept their same passive stiffness under the storm of abuse. Behind them the captain had drawn his sword, and as the crowd closed in more and more, threatening to crush them against the wall, he gave the order to present bayonets. They obeyed, and a double hedge of steel blades pointed at the chests of the strikers.

"The bloody bastards!" screamed Ma Brûlé, but she fell back.

But they all returned to the charge immediately, heedless of death in their frenzy. Women rushed forward, Maheude and la Levaque shouted:

"That's right! Kill us, kill us! We want our rights."

Levaque, at the risk of cutting himself, took three bayonets in his hands and tried to pull them towards him and wrench them off the rifles. In his rage he stood there twisting them with ten times his normal strength, but Bouteloup, regretting having followed his mate, stood quietly on one side, watching.

"Come and have a look at this! Come on, look at this if you are good chaps!" said Maheu.

And he unbuttoned his coat and opened his shirt, displaying his bare chest, hairy and tattooed with coal. In a terrible outburst of insolent bravado he pressed himself against the points of the bayonets and forced the soldiers back. One point pricked him in the nipple and so maddened him that he forced it further in so as to hear his ribs crack.

"Cowards! you daren't do it! There are ten thousand more behind us. Yes, you can kill us, but there'll be ten thousand more to kill as well!"

The soldiers' position was becoming critical, for they had had strict orders not to use their arms except in a desperate emergency. But how could they prevent these madmen from running themselves through? Moreover there was no room left, as they now had their backs to the wall and could not retire any further. The little handful of men held firm against the rising tide of miners, however, coolly carrying out their captain's brief commands. He stood there nervous and tightlipped, with only one fear: that all this abuse would make his men lose their tempers. Already a young sergeant, a lanky fellow whose four hairs of moustache were bristling, was blinking his eyes in an ominous manner, and near him a veteran, tanned in a score of campaigns, had turned pale on seeing his bayonet twisted like a straw. Yet another, probably a recruit, still smelling of the farmyard, flushed crimson every time he was called a shit and a blackguard. But the abuse went on and on, with waving fists and abominable words: shovelfuls of accusations and threats hit them in the face. It needed all the force of their orders to keep them standing there in the lofty, gloomy silence of military discipline.

Just as a collision seemed inevitable, Richomme the deputy could be seen coming out behind the soldiers. His kindly white head was bowed down with emotion. He addressed them in a loud voice.

"Oh, for God's sake! This is getting silly! This damn nonsense can't go on!"

He threw himself between the bayonets and the miners.

"Listen, mates. You know I'm an old workman and that I've always been on your side! Very well, then, I promise you that if they don't deal fair with you I'll tell the bosses some home truths myself. But you're going too far, and it won't do you any good to bawl a lot of filthy words at these good chaps and try to get your own bellies ripped open."

They listened and hesitated. But as ill-luck would have it Négrel's strong profile appeared again just then at an upper window. No doubt he was afraid they would accuse him of having sent out a deputy instead of risking his own skin, and he tried to speak. But his voice was drowned in such a frightful outcry that he could only shrug his shoulders and leave the window again. From then onwards it was useless for Richomme to try to reason with them on his own account and repeat that the matter should be settled between friends; he was suspect and shouted down. But he stuck to his guns and stayed with them.

"What the hell! I don't care if I'm smashed up with you, but so long as you are so stupid I shall stick to you!"

Étienne, whom he had asked to help him make them see reason, made a gesture of impotence. It was too late now; there were more than five hundred of them, and not only the fanatics who had charged down the hill to turn out the Belgians, but onlookers and people who thought the battle was a good lark. Some way back Zacharie and Philomène were standing in the middle of a group watching as if it were a show, and so unconcerned that they had brought the two children, Achille and Désirée. A new wave of strikers arrived from Réquillart, including Mouquet and Mouquette; he at once went and clapped his friend Zacharie's shoulders with a grin, but she was very worked up and ran off to join the front row of the malcontents.

The captain was continually glancing towards the Montsou road. The reinforcements he had requested had not yet come, and his sixty men could not hold out much longer. It occurred to him to stage a demonstration that would strike the imagination of the mob, and he ordered his men to load their rifles in full view. The soldiers obeyed, but it only increased the tension and gave rise to further mockeries and provocations.

"Look, they're off to target practice!" sneered the women, Ma Brûlé, la Levaque and the rest.

Maheude, holding Estelle to her breast (she had woken up and was crying) came so near that the sergeant asked her what she thought she was doing, with a poor little kid and all.

"Mind your own bloody business!" was her answer. "Shoot her if you dare!"

The men shook their heads in scorn. Nobody believed they could be fired at.

"They've only got blank cartridges," said Levaque.

"Do you take us for Cossacks or what?" shouted Maheu. "You don't fire at Frenchmen, dammit!"

Others said that when you had served in the Crimea you weren't afraid of lead, and they all went on throwing themselves at the rifles. If these had gone off at that moment the mob would have been mown down.

Mouquette, now in the front row, was almost speechless with indignation at the idea that soldiers could mean to cut open women's bodies. She had exhausted all her obscene vocabulary on them, and could not think of anything when suddenly she bethought herself of the supreme insult to fire at the troops, and showed them her backside. She lifted her skirts with both hands and displayed her great round buttocks, making them as huge as she could.

"Look, that's for you, and it's too clean by half, you lot of swine!"

She bobbed and somersaulted and turned about so that everybody had a good view, and at each thrust of her bum she repeated:

"That's for the officer! That's for the sergeant! That's for the privates!"

A storm of laughter went up, and Bébert and Lydie were convulsed. Even Étienne, despite his gloomy forebodings, applauded this insulting exhibition. Everybody, scoffers and fanatics alike, now joined in booing the soldiers as though they were splashed all over with excrement, and only Catherine stood apart, on some old timber, saying nothing, but feeling such bitter hatred rising within her that her breast seemed about to burst.

There was a scuffle. The captain had decided to take a few prisoners in order to give his men something to do to relieve their feelings. With one bound Mouquette darted off between some of the men's legs and was gone. Three miners, including Levaque, were seized from the thick of the fray and taken off under guard to the deputies' room. Négrel and Dansaert called from above to the captain to come in and barricade himself with them, but he refused, feeling that these buildings, the doors of which had no locks to them, were bound to be taken by assault and that he would have the humiliation of being disarmed. Already his little company was chafing with impatience, and they could not run away from a rabble in clogs. Once again the sixty were back to the wall and facing the mob with loaded rifles.

At first the strikers were impressed by this display of force and fell back in silence. But then a shout went up demanding the immediate release of the prisoners. Somebody said that they were being killed in there. And at once, without any sort of concerted action, everybody had the same impulse, the same thirst for revenge, and they all made a dash for the stacks of bricks nearby. The marly soil provided the clay, and these bricks were baked on the premises. Children carried them one by one, women filled their skirts with them, and soon everybody had his own ammunition dump at his feet and the stoning began.

Ma Brûlé was the first to join battle. She broke the bricks across her bony knee and hurled the two pieces with her right and left hands together. La Levaque nearly dislocated her shoulders, for being so fat and soft she had to go very near in order to aim straight, heedless of the pleadings of Bouteloup, who tried to pull her back in the hope of taking her home now that her husband was out of the way. The women all warmed up to the job, and Mouquette, finding it annoying to be all bleeding through trying to break bricks over her soft, fat thighs, had given it up and was throwing them whole. Even the children entered the fray, Bébert showing Lydie how to bowl them underarm. The thudding bricks made a noise like gigantic hailstones. Suddenly Catherine appeared in the midst of the furies, waving her arms in the air and hurling her bricks with all the strength of her young arms. Though she could never have explained why, she was bursting with an impulse to slaughter everybody. Wouldn't this accursed life of misery soon be over? She had had enough of it, what with being beaten and cast off by her man, paddling about the muddy roads like a stray cur and not even being able to ask her own father for a bite or a sup because he was starving as well. Things had never taken a turn for the better, but had gone on getting worse ever since she had known anything. So she broke her bricks and flung the pieces anywhere with the one idea of smashing everything up. She saw red and did not care whose jaw she broke.

Étienne, still standing in front of the soldiers, nearly had his head split open. His ear began to swell up, and he turned round and realized with a shock that the brick had come from Catherine's frenzied hands. At the risk of his life he stayed there and watched her. Similarly many others were so enthralled by the battle that they simply stood by with their arms dangling by their sides. Mouquet was adjudicating the throws as though it were a cork-throwing contest: oh, well aimed! or oh, hard luck! He was entering into the fun of the thing, nudging Zacharie, who was having words with Philomène because he had clouted Achille and Désirée and refused to take them up on his shoulders to give them a better view. In the background the road was lined with crowds of onlookers. At the top of the hill, where the village began, old Bonnemort had just come into view, hobbling along on his stick, and his motionless form was now outlined against the rust-colored sky.

As soon as the brick-throwing had begun, Richomme had taken up his stand again between the soldiers and the mob, entreating one side and exhorting the other, heedless of danger and so heartbroken that great tears were running down his cheeks. But the noise drowned his words, and only his big gray mustache could be seen moving up and down.

The hail of bricks became thicker, for the men had now followed the women's example.

At that moment Maheude noticed Maheu standing in the rear, sullen and empty-handed.

"Here, what's up with you?" she shouted. "Are you scared?

Are you going to stand there and let your mates be taken to prison? If I hadn't got the child I'd show you!"

Estelle was clutching her cheek and bawling her head off, preventing her mother from joining Ma Brûlé and the others. And as her husband still did not seem to understand she kicked some bricks towards his legs.

"Are you going to pick them up, for God's sake? Have I got to spit in your face in front of everybody so as to put a bit of pluck into you?"

He went very red and broke some bricks and threw the pieces. She lashed him on with her tongue, dazed him with words, stood behind him howling for death and almost crushed the life out of the child at her breast, until he had moved forward right in front of the rifles.

The little squad was nearly lost to sight under the hail of stones. Fortunately they landed too high and merely pitted the wall above. What was to be done? For a moment the captain considered retreating into the buildings, but the very thought of showing his back to the mob made his pale face flush—and in any case it was no longer practicable for if they made the slightest movement they would be lynched. A brick had just broken the peak of his cap and blood was trickling down his forehead. Several of his men were wounded, and he realized that they were at the end of their tether and had reached the stage of instinctive self-defense when they would no longer obey their superiors. The sergeant had let out an oath when his shoulder had nearly been put out and his skin bruised by a heavy thud that sounded like a dolly banging the washing. The recruit had been grazed in two places, his thumb was smashed and his right knee was smarting: how much longer were they going to put up with this? One brick had bounced up and hit the veteran in the groin, and he had turned green and was raising his rifle with his thin arms. Three times the captain was on the point of ordering them to fire. He was torn with perplexity, and for some seconds an apparently endless struggle within him shook all his ideas, his sense of duty, and his beliefs as a man and a soldier. The bricks rained thicker still, and just as he was opening his mouth to shout "Fire!" the rifles went off of their own accord; first three shots, then five, then the whole volley of a platoon and then, long afterwards, a single shot in the midst of silence.

There was a moment of stupefaction. They had really fired, and the crowd stood motionless, unable to believe it. Then piercing shrieks arose, while the bugle sounded to cease fire. And then a wild panic like the stampede of cattle before machine guns, a frantic rush through the mud.

With the first three shots Bébert and Lydie collapsed on each other, the girl shot in the face and the boy with a hole under the left shoulder. She was killed instantly and lay still. But he went on moving for a while, and in his dying convulsions seized her in his arms as though wanting to take her again as he had taken her in the dark retreat where they had spent their last night on earth. At that moment Jeanlin, still puffy with sleep, came skipping along from Réquillart through the smoke, just in time to see Bébert embrace his little wife and die.

The other five shots which followed had brought down Ma Brûlé and the deputy Richomme. He had been shot in the back while still imploring his mates, and had sunk to his knees. He fell on one side and lay gasping on the ground, with his eyes still full of tears. As for the old woman, her breast had been torn open and she had fallen stiff, crashing like a bundle of dry wood, vomiting a final oath with her life-blood.

Then the volley swept the whole area, mowing down the groups of onlookers as they were enjoying the battle and laughing a hundred paces away. A bullet went into Mouquet's mouth and bowled him over with his face smashed in. He fell at the feet of Zacharie and Philomène, whose children were spattered with red spots. At the same moment Mouquette had two bullets in the stomach. She had seen the soldiers raise their rifles, and, good soul that she was, she had instictively flung herself in front of Catherine, warning her to look out. With a loud scream she fell on her back, knocked clean over by the blow. Étienne rushed up meaning to lift her and carry her away, but she waved him off as though to say she was done for anyway. Then she hiccoughed, still smiling at them both to show she was happy to see them together now that she was going.

All was over, or so it seemed, and the bullets were all spent, some of them as far away as the walls of the village, when the last single shot went off.

It went through Maheu's heart. He spun round and fell with his face in a puddle of black water.

Maheude stooped down, bewildered.

"Here, come on, old chap, get up! It's nothing, is it?"

She was still encumbered with Estelle, and had to tuck her under one arm so as to turn her husband's head.

"Say something, do! Where does it hurt?"

His eyes were staring expressionless and a bloody foam was coming from his mouth. She understood. He was dead. And she sat down in the mud, with her baby still under her arm like a bundle, looking at her old chap, dazed.

The pit had been cleared. The captain had nervously taken off his cap which had been cut by a stone, and then put it on again, but even in the face of the great tragedy of his life he kept his stiff military bearing, while his men silently reloaded their rifles. The horrified faces of Négrel and Dansaert could be seen at the window. Behind them was standing Souvarine, his brow deeply furrowed as though the answer to his terrible problem had etched itself there. On the horizon at the edge of the plateau Bonnemort was still standing, leaning on his stick with one hand and shading his eyes with the other so as to see more clearly the slaughter of his own flesh and blood down below. The wounded were groaning and the dead freezing into twisted postures, muddy with the liquid mire of the thaw and sinking in places into the inky patches of coal now reappearing here and there out of the wastes of dirty snow. In the midst of these human corpses, looking so small and pinched and poor, lay the corpse of Trompette, a huge and pitiful heap of dead flesh.

Étienne had not found death. He was still waiting for it by the side of Catherine who had collapsed with fatigue and grief, when a sonorous voice made him start. It was abbé Ranvier coming back from his Mass. There he stood with arms raised like an inspired prophet of old, calling down the wrath of God upon the murderers, foretelling the age of justice and the coming extermination of the bourgeoisie by fire from heaven, since now it had committed the foulest crime of all and caused the workers and the penniless of this world to be slain.

13. The natural history of morality

"The slave revolt in morals begins with resentment becoming
creative and giving birth to values." Friedrich Nietzsche,
"The Slave Revolt in Morals," *The Genealogy of Morals* (1887)[1]

One important application of Darwinism, and a significant variety of
naturalism, was the exploration of the thesis that all man's ideals, his
religion, and morality, are only products of historical evolution and
are to be viewed not as absolutes but as means of survival. Karl Marx
declared religions to be the tools of the ruling class in their subjection
of the oppressed. Friedrich Nietzsche, as the following extract shows,
held almost the opposite: religion was the revenge of the weak on the
strong. Where Marx and Nietzsche agreed was in seeing religion and
morality as the outgrowth of impulses to domination, urges to power—
as weapons in the human struggle for survival. They were thus given
a naturalistic explanation.

The perverse genius of Freidrich Nietzsche combined naturalism
with a most startling analysis of the sickness of European civilization.
Nietzsche thought that when men were forced to form society, their
instinctive and healthy animality had turned inward. The result was
morality and religion, which Nietzsche explained as the revenge of the
weak on the strong, of herd-spirit on leadership. He found the whole
Judaic-Christian tradition to be scarcely more than a disease, a triumph
of sickness over life. Freud later put in more comprehensible terms
some of Nietzsche's concepts: civilization repressed the animal instincts
of the "Id," and thus brought on neurosis by creating a conflict between natural sexual appetites and socially accepted morality. Nietzsche

---

[1] Horace B. Samuel's translation of *Genealogy of Morals*, included in
The Philosophy of Nietzsche (Modern Library, 1927), and Francis Golf-
fing's translation of the same work, which appears together with *The Birth
of Tragedy* in a Doubleday Anchor edition, are both available today. These,
especially the latter, are not very distinguished translations. Walter Kaufmann (ed.), *The Portable Nietzsche* (New York: Viking, 1954), includes
very little of this work. The most convenient German edition of Nietzsche
is the three-volume *Werke* (Munich: C. Hanser, 1960). *Joyful Wisdom* is
not in the Modern Library edition, and only part of it is the Viking *The
Portable Nietzsche*, but it is available in translation by Thomas Common
(New York: Ungar). The old Oscar Levy translation of the *Complete
Works* has recently been reprinted (18 vols., New York: Russell & Russell,
1964), but this translation, too, leaves something to be desired. The translation which follows is by the editor.

also thought that Judaism, Christianity, and democracy are bad because they glorify the weak and incompetent ("the bungled and botched" of natural selection) and that aristocracy is good because it is creative. Modern European civilization's frightful decadence is the result of too much religion and morality and herd-spirit. The only remedy lies in producing and then giving complete freedom of action to aristocratic blond-beast "supermen" who may re-establish culture on a sound basis by acting "beyond good and evil." To say the least, these ideas were considerably muddled and obscure in Nietzsche's frenetic speculations. Yet the brilliance of his style, and the often piercing insights of his completely original mind, made Nietzsche a leading oracle of the period from about 1880 to 1914.

O NE WILL already have guessed how easily the priestly modes of value diverge from the knightly-aristocratic ones and then evolve into the very opposite. An impulse of this sort especially exists when the priestly caste and the warrior caste strive against each other jealously and fall into disagreements. The aristocratic value-judgments presuppose a strong physique, a blooming, abundant, even overly exuberant health, together with that which its maintenance implies, war, adventure, hunting, games, tournaments, and everything that embraces strong, free, cheerful actions. The priestly value modes have, as we have seen, other presuppositions: a bad thing for them, if it is a question of war! Priests, as is well known, make the most dangerous of enemies—why? Because they are the most impotent. Out of this impotence grows a hate that is monstrous, terrible, profound, and poisonous. All the greatest haters in history have been priests, also the brainest ones: compared with the intelligence of priestly vengeance all other intelligence is as nothing. Human history would be quite a tedious thing without the intelligence which emerges from its impotent ones. Let us take the outstanding example. Everything that has been done on earth against the "superior folk," "the powerful," the lords, the "power structure," is trivial compared to what the *Jews* have done against them; the Jews, that priestly race who were able to gain compensation from their enemies and conquerors at last by a radical reversal of their values, a kind of spiritual revenge. This was uniquely suitable for a priestly people, a people of the most pronounced priestly resentments. It was the Jews who, against the aristocratic equation of values (good-noble-strong-beautiful-happy-favored-of-God), dared with a frightening consistency to reverse this and with the fangs of unfathomable hatred (the hatred of the impotent) to hold fast to the doctrine that "the miserable alone are good; the poor, the powerless, the base alone are good; the suffering, the deprived, the sick, the ugly are the only worthy folk, the only godly ones, for these alone is there holiness—and on the other hand you wellborn and mighty, you are for all eternity the evil ones, the cruel, the greedy, the lustful, the godless, you will forever be unholy, accursed, and damned!" . . . We know who has received the inheritance of this Jewish reversal of values. . . .[2] In connection with this terrible and boundlessly fateful initiative which the Jews launched with this most basic of all declarations of war, I recall the statement I made on another occasion [*Beyond Good and Evil*] that *the slave revolt in morals* began with the Jews: a revolt which has two thousand years of history behind it and which even today is concealed from our eyes, because—it has triumphed so completely. . . .

But you do not understand this? You have no eyes for something that required two millennia to bring it to fruition? This is not strange: all *long* things are hard to see, to see in their entirety. This however is the eventuality: out of the trunk of this tree of Jewish revenge and hatred—the deepest and most sublime, ideal-creating and value-shaping hatred which has ever appeared on earth—grew something just as incomparable, a *new love*, the deepest and most sublime of all kinds of love—and from what other trunk could this have grown? Can one believe that this grew up as the negation of that thirst after vengeance, as the opposite of that Jewish hatred? No, the reverse is true. This love grew out of that hatred as its cröwn, as the triumphant crown spreading in purest light and sunshine, shaped by the same impulse and working toward the same goals, toward victory, booty, seduction, as does that hate whose roots are sunk always more solidly and greedily into all that was deeply evil. This Jesus of Nazareth, as the bodily Gospel of Love,

---

[2] Nietzsche is of course telling his Christian audience that Christianity as the offshoot of Judaism is in exactly the same boat. It should be noted that Nietzsche is not anti-Semitic in the more usual sense of despising the Jews from a Christian or racial viewpoint, but is suggesting that they invented the slave morality which has prevailed over all of Western civilization since ancient times (Ed.).

this "Redeemer" who brought holiness and triumph to the poor, the sick, and the sinners—was he not precisely the seduction in its most sinister and irresistible form, a devious route to those same Jewish values and innovations of ideals? Has not Israel attained the final goal of her sublime vindictiveness exactly by this "Redeemer," her apparent opponent and liquidator? Does it not fit into the secret black art of a truly great politics of vengeance, a farseeing, subterranean, slow-working and foresighted vengeance, that Israel had to deny the true instrument of her vengeance, publicly, as a deadly enemy and nail him to the cross so that the whole world (meaning the enemies of Israel) would unthinkingly swallow this bait? And could anyone by the most refined wit think up a more dangerous trap? Anything that could equal in alluring, intoxicating, stupefying, seductive strength this symbol of "holy cross," this shattering paradox of a "crucified God," this mystery of an unthinkable last extreme cruelty and self-crucifixion of God *for the salvation of mankind?* . . . It is at least certain that *sub hoc signo* Israel with her vengeance and reversal of all previous values triumphed again, triumphed over all other ideals, all *nobler* ideals.

"But what is all this talk about *nobler* ideals? Let us face facts: the people have triumphed—or the "slaves," the "rabble," the "herd," whatever you want to call them—and if this came about by means of the Jews, well then! never did a people have such a world-historical mission. The nobility is done for; the morality of the common man has triumphed. I don't deny that one may construe this triumph as a poisoning of the blood (it has thoroughly mixed the races); but unquestionably this madness has *succeeded.* The "redemption" of mankind (i.e., from the lords) is well on its way; everybody is Judaized or Christianized or rabble-ized (what matters the term?) The progress of this poisoning through the whole body of mankind seems unstoppable; its tempo and pace may even become slower, less apparent, more circumspect from now on—there's all the time in the world. . . . Does the church today still have a *necessary* function in this regard or even a right of existence? Or could it be dispensed with? *Quaeritur.* It appears that it hinders and holds back this progress, instead of hastening it? Even in that could lie its usefulness. . . . Certainly it has gradually become something coarse and crude, repellent to a sharp intellect, a really modern taste. Should it not at least refine itself somewhat? It puts more people off today than it attracts. Which of us would be a freethinker, were it not for the church? The church, not its poison, antagonizes us. Apart from the church we too love the poison. . . ." This was the epilogue of a "freethinker" to my argument, an honest chap, as he has abundantly proved, moreover a democrat; he had been listening to me up until then and could not stand to hear me grow silent. You know I have a great deal to be silent about in this matter.

The slave revolt in morals begins with resentment becoming creative and giving birth to values: the resentment of beings whose proper activity is frustrated and who compensate by an imaginary revenge. While all aristocratic morality stems from a triumphant yea-saying to itself, the slave morality begins by saying No to something outside, to an Other, to a Not-self, and this No is its creative act. This reversal of valuational directions, this *necessary* looking outward instead of into the self, is basic to resentment: the slave morality always needs an opposing outer world in order to begin, it needs an external stimulus, psychologically speaking, in order to act. Its action is in the nature of a reaction. The reverse is true of aristocratic modes of valuation: they act and grow spontaneously, they seek out opposition only in order to affirm themselves the more joyously and thankfully. Their negative idea "base," "common," "wretched," is only a pallid one born later as a contrast to their positive, thoroughly passionate and vital basic idea "We aristocrats, we good, beautiful, happy ones!" If aristocratic values go astray and sin against reality, this happens in spheres with which they are not sufficiently familiar, against knowledge of which they even shield themselves; the mistake occurs in the area they hold in contempt, that of the common man, the lower classes; on the other hand we may consider that in any case the feeling of contempt, of looking down, of superiority, supposing that it does falsify the image of those held in contempt, does so far less than does the vindictiveness of the impotent when it pours its suppressed hatred on its enemies (naturally only in effigy). In fact there is in this contempt too much of nonchalance and casualness, too much disregard and impatience, even too much gaiety, for it to make of its object a complete caricature or object of horror. One cannot

miss the almost benevolent nuances, for example, which the Greek
nobility put into all the words with which it described the lower
classes; how a sort of pity, regard, and indulgence constantly entered and softened the picture until in the end almost all the words
used to describe the common man survive as expressions for "unhappy," "pitiable" . . . . On the other hand "bad," "base," "unhappy," have never ceased to have for the Greek ear similar
connotations, with "unhappy" predominating: this as a heritage
from the old aristocratic valuations, which even the despised accepted. . . . The "wellborn" felt themselves to be the "happy" ones;
they did not have to create their happiness artificially by looking
at their enemies, as resentful people must do; and likewise they
knew, being strong, active people, that happiness is inseparable
from action—activity was a necessary part of happiness for them.
All very much the opposite of "happiness" among the impotent
and oppressed, festering in their poisonous feelings of hostility, to
whom it appears as a narcotic, a drug, peace, calm, the Sabbath,
soul's-ease, stretching out the legs, in brief *passively*. While the
aristocrat lives for himself with confidence and openness . . . the
resentful man is neither sincere nor yet honest and straightforward
with himself. His soul squints; his mind loves hiding places, secret
paths, and back doors; everything hidden impresses him as *his*
world, *his* security, *his* comfort; he knows silences, not-forgetting,
waiting, self-depreciation, self-humiliation. A race of such resentful
men in the end will of necessity be cleverer than any aristocratic
race; they will honor cunning to a much greater degree, as a vital
condition of their survival, whereas to an aristocratic people braini-
ness savors slightly of decadence and over-refinement, and is not
nearly so substantial a quality as the perfect functioning of regula-
tive unconscious instincts, or even a certain thoughtlessness, perhaps
a brave recklessness in the face of danger or the enemy; or that
enthusiastic suddenness of anger, love, awe, gratitude and vengeance for which in all times aristocratic spirits have been noted.
When resentment appears in aristocratic men it fulfills and spends
itself in an immediate reaction, and therefore does not *poison* them;
nor does it appear at all in numerous cases where it would unfailingly
occur among weak and impotent men. Their enemies, their misfor-
tunes, even their misdeeds they cannot long take seriously—this is
the sign of a strong, full nature, in which there is an excess of plas-

tic, molding, healing and forgetting strength. (A good example of this in modern history is Mirabeau, who retained no recollection of insults and mean actions done to him, and who could not forgive simply because he had forgotten.) Such a man simply shakes off vermin with a shrug, which would get under another's skin; here alone it is possible, if it is possible anywhere, to speak of "loving your enemy." How much respect a nobleman has for his foe! And such respect is already a bridge to love. . . . Indeed he needs his enemy, as his mark of distinction, nor could he bear to have any other enemy than one in whom there is nothing to scorn and very much to honor. Against this consider "the enemy" as the resentful man conceives him—here precisely is his creative achievement, in conceiving the "wicked enemy," the "wicked," as a fundamental idea, from which as a copy and counterpart he derives a "good" one —himself!

This is the exact opposite of the aristocrats, who create the idea of "good" spontaneously and then derive from this a conception of the "bad." This aristocratic "bad", and that "wicked" which springs from the cauldron of frustrated hate—how different are these two apparently similar concepts! The idea of "good" is not the same in both cases. We must ask who exactly the wicked are, in the conception of the vindictive morality. The answer is clear: they are the good of the other morality, they are the aristocratic, the strong, the commanding—but colored, reinterpreted, seen in reverse with the poisoned eye of resentment. And here at once we will so far recant as to admit that whoever knew these "good" ones only as foes would find them very evil foes indeed; the same men who among themselves, *inter pares,* are so restricted by ethical custom, honor, obligation, and even more by their jealousy of each other, who in their relationships to one another are so full of respect, self-control, delicacy, loyalty, pride and friendship, are toward others, toward the strangers, not much better than uncaged beasts. There they enjoy freedom from all social compulsions, they compensate for the strain which long enclosure and confinement in the peace of the community has caused, they revert to the amorality of wild animals, becoming rampaging monsters who may return from an orgy of murder, destruction, rape, torture, with elation and serenity of soul, as if they had perpetrated no more than a student prank, convinced that the poets now for a long time to come will have something to sing and boast about. At the bottom of all these noble races is the beast of prey, the "blond beast" lusting after booty and conquest; this basic urge needs an outlet from time to time, the beast must be let out to roam again in the wilderness—whether Roman, Arabian, German, or Japanese nobility, Homeric heroes, Scandinavian Vikings, the need is the same for all. The noble races have left traces of the idea "barbarian" wherever they have been; an awareness of this and even a pride in it betrays itself in their highest culture, as for example when Pericles in that famous funeral oration tells his Athenians that "to every land and sea our boldness has broken a path, erecting imperishable monuments everywhere to itself both good *and evil*." This boldness of noble blood, headstrong, absurd, impulsive, expressing itself unpredictably and even improbably in its enterprises—Pericles commends the Athenians especially for their Pαθυμια—this indifference to and contempt for security, life and limb, comfort, this shocking depth of taste for destruction, cruelty, lust of conquest—all this is contained in the picture of "barbarians" and "wicked enemies," a combination of Goths and Vandals, formed by their victims. That deep, icy mistrust which the German arouses as soon as he attains power, seen again today, is an eternal echo of the inextinguishable horror with which for centuries Europe witnessed the fury of the blond Germanic beast (although between the old Germans and us modern ones hardly any connection in thought or blood remains.) I once called attention to the embarrassment of Hesiod when he tried to formulate the sequence of historical epochs and expressed them as gold, silver, and bronze ages; he was not able to cope with the contradiction which the world of Homer presented to him, splendid yet also so terrible and brutal as it was, except by making one age into two and putting one before the other—first the age of heroes and demigods of Troy and Thebes, as remembered by the noble tribes who traced their ancestry to it, and then the bronze age, the same world as it appeared to the descendants of the downtrodden, despoiled, mistreated, uprooted and enslaved: as an age of bronze, hard, cold, cruel, insecure, bruised and encrusted with blood. If it be true, as is nowadays believed, that the meaning of culture is to make a tame and civilized animal, a domestic animal, out of the human wild beast, then we must consider all these instincts of reaction and resentment, with whose help the noble tribes together with their ideals have finally been overpowered and destroyed, as the true agents of civilization; which would still not be.to say that these agents themselves represent civilization. The opposite is not only much more probable, it is today obvious. These carriers of leveling and revenge-seeking instincts, these descendants of all European and non-European slaves, especially of the pre-Aryan population, represent the *retrogression* of humanity! These "agents of civilization" are a disgrace to the human race and even an argument against civilization. One may well be right to fear the primitive element that lies deep in every aristocratic race, and be on guard against it; but who would not a hundred times rather know fear, if it is accompanied by admiration, than *not* to fear at the cost of being forever condemned to the nauseating sight of mediocrity, pettiness, decadence? And is this not our fate? What causes our disgust at human nature today? (There is no doubt that such disgust does exist.) Not fear of it; rather, that we have nothing more to fear from it; human worms swarm over the earth; the "tame man," the heroless mediocrity, considers himself as the zenith and goal of civilization of history; not without a certain justice, insofar as he feels himself to contrast with the crowd of failures, weaklings, and invalids the odor of whom is beginning to fill Europe, compared to whom he has at least a little vitality. . . .

Here I do not suppress a sigh and a final conviction. Exactly what is it I find really intolerable? What is it I cannot cope with, that stifles me and sickens me? Foul air! The failures around me, the smell of failed souls. . . . Who would not rather endure want, privation, ill-health, toil, loneliness? In the end all the rest can be faced, born as one is to an underground and embattled existence; one always comes again into the light, always experiences his golden hours of triumph—and then one stands there, as one is born, unshakeable, eager, ready to face new, strange, and difficult things, like a bow drawn ever tighter. But from time to time, grant me (if there be, beyond good and evil, any Granters of Favors) a glance, grant me *one* glance only at something perfect, wholly achieved, happy, powerful, triumphant, something still capable of inspiring awe! A man who will justify mankind, a fulfilling and redeeming happy accident of a man, who can restore one's faith in mankind!

... Thus it is: the depreciation and leveling down of European man is our greatest danger, this is the prospect that depresses us. ... Today we see nothing that wants to become greater, we suspect that ALL goes ever downward, downward, becoming thinner, more placid, "smarter," cosier, more ordinary, more indifferent, more Chinese, more Christian—man, there is no doubt, becomes always "better" .... Exactly here lies Europe's crisis: with the fear of man we have lost also the love of man, reverence for him, hope in him, indeed the *will* to him. The human prospect wearies us—what is the current nihilism, if it is not *that?* We are tired of man.

But to resume: the problem of the *other* origin of "good," of Good as the resentful people have conceived it, asks to be completed. That lambs are averse to the great birds of prey is not strange; but that is no ground for persuading the birds of prey that they should not seize little lambs. And if the lambs say to each other, "These birds of prey are wicked; and those who resemble birds of prey as little as possible, indeed are their opposites, namely lambs, aren't they then good?", there is nothing to object to in such an erection of ideals; however, the birds of prey are likely to look scornful at this and say, "*We* are not hostile to these good lambs, we love them very much—nothing so tasty as a tender lamb." To expect of strength that it not express itself as strength, that it not be a vanquishing will, a subjugating will, a thirst for enemies and obstacles and triumphs, is just as foolish as to expect of weakness that it express itself as strength. A quantum of strength is a quantum of drive, will, activity, indeed it is nothing at all other than just so much drive, will, activity, and only the deception of language (and the fallacies of reason embedded in it), which misconstrues all activity as conditioned by an agent or subject, can make it appear otherwise. Just as ordinary people separate the lightning from its light and view the latter as the work of a subject they call the lightning, so folk morality separates the strength from the expression of that strength, as if it were a neutral substratum, at liberty to express or not to express strength. But there is no such substratum; there is no "essence" behind the doing, the acting, the becoming; the "doer" has simply been added to the deed by the imagination—the doing is everything. The average man doubles the act,

when he makes the lightning flash; he states the same event once as
cause and then again as effect. The scientist does no better when he
says "energy moves, energy produces" and the like—all our science
in spite of its coolness and freedom from emotion is still a victim of
the deceptions of language and has never got rid of those ephemeral
things, "subjects." (The *atom* for example is such a will-o-the-wisp,
resembling the Kantian "thing in itself.") What wonder that the
repressed, deeply smoldering emotions of vengeance and hatred
make use of these beliefs and at bottom hold to no belief more
ardently than that it is within the power of the strong to be weak,
the bird of prey to be a lamb—whereby they win for themselves the
right to call the bird of prey to account for being a bird of prey. . . .
When the oppressed and downtrodden, with the vindictive cunning
of the impotent, exhort each other as follows: "Let us be different
from those wicked ones, that is, let us be good! And good is everything that does not oppress, that hurts no one, that does not attack,
does not revenge, leaves vengeance to God, holds itself like us in
obscurity, walks away from wickedness and generally desires little
from life, like us, the patient, the humble, the righteous"—this
means, considered coolly and without prejudice, really nothing
more than this: "We weak ones are in fact weak; it will be well for
us if we do nothing which we are not strong enough to do." But
these evident facts, this intelligence of the lowest rank which even
insects possess (in danger they feign death), thanks to the duplicity
and self-deception of the impotent has clothed itself in the splendor
of resigned, quiet, patient virtue, as though the weakness of the
weak— i.e., their nature, their being, their whole and inevitable and
unchangeable reality— is a free choice, something willed and therefore deserving. This sort of man has the belief in the indifferent
freely willing subject which is necessary to an instinct of self-
preservation, in which every lie takes care to sanctify itself. The
subject, or, as it is popularly called the *soul*, has been until now the
best tenet of belief perhaps because it makes possible for the majority of mortals, the weak and downtrodden of every sort, that sublime self-deception which sees weakness as freedom and anyone's
nature as meritorious service.

Does anyone want to look for a while into that secret place
where they *manufacture ideals* on earth? Who has the courage?

Well then! Here is an opening through which to peer into this dark workshop. Wait a minute, Mr. Inquisitive, your eyes must first get used to the uneven light. So! Ready? Tell me what's going on down there. Tell us what you see, man of dangerous curiosity—I'm listening.

"I don't see anything, but I can hear something. There is a low, spiteful muttering and whispering in every nook and corner. It seems to me that everyone is lying; a cloying softness sticks to every sound. Weakness is being turned into righteousness, no doubt about it—it's just as you said—"

"Go on."

"—and impotence into 'good'; timid baseness into 'humility,' submission before those one hates into 'obedience' (to one who they say commands their submission, they call him God). The passiveness of a weakling, the very cowardice of which he is full, his standing-at-the-door, his inevitable waiting around, is here given a good name; indeed, as "patience," it is elevated to the chief of virtues. Not being able to avenge oneself is called not *wanting* to avenge oneself ,perhaps even forgiveness ('for they know not what they do—only *we* know what they do!'). Also there's talk of 'loving thine enemy'—accompanied by much sweat."

"Go on."

"Undoubtedly they are miserable, all these whisperers and hole-in the-corner counterfeiters, though they huddle together for warmth, yet they tell me this misery is a sign of their being God's chosen ones, one beats the dog he loves best; perhaps this misery is also a schooling, a test, a preparation, perhaps even more, something for which they will be compensated with tremendous interest, not in gold but in happiness. They call this 'salvation.' "

"Go on."

"Now they are giving me to understand that they are not only better than the powerful, the lords of the earth, whose spittle they must lick (*not* from fear, of course, certainly not, but rather because to honor authority is God's command)—not only are they better, but also better *off*, or at least they will be one day. But enough! I can't stand any more. What foul air! This shop where they manufacture ideals seems to me to stink of unmitigated lies."

"No, a moment more, please. You have not told me anything yet about the masterpiece of this black art, which transmits black into

white, milk, and innocence; haven't you noticed their most perfect,
their boldest, finest, cleverest trick? Watch! These vermin, full
of hatred and revenge, what exactly are they making out of this
hatred and revenge? Did you hear these terms? Would you ever
suspect, if you attended only to their words, that you are among
men dominated by pure resentment?"

"I understand; I'll open my ears again (and close my nose!) Now
I hear, first, what they have so often said, 'We good ones—*we are
the just*'—they call that which they desire not retribution, but 'the
triumph of justice'; what they hate is not their enemy, but 'injustice,' 'godlessness'; what they believe in and hope for is not vengeance, sweet vengeance ('sweeter than honey,' as Homer calls it),
but the triumph of a just God over the godless; what they love on
earth is not their brothers in hate but their 'brothers in love,' all
the good and righteous on earth as they say."

"And what do they call that which offers them consolation
against all the sorrows of life—their fantasy of anticipated future
bliss?"

"What? Can I believe my ears? They call it 'the Last Judgment,'"
the coming of *their* kingdom, the 'kingdom of God'—meanwhile
they live 'in faith,'" 'in love,' 'in hope.' "

"Enough! Enough!"

14. Naturalism and moralism

"Lugubrious diagnosis of sordid impropriety." George Bernard
Shaw, *The Quintessence of Ibsenism* (1891)[1]

If any major literary figure in the era of naturalism shocked the
respectable, the "right-thinking" people, more than did Zola and
Nietzsche, he was the Norwegian dramatist Henrik Ibsen. All over
Europe in the 1870's and 1880's Isben's plays excited as much controversy as the music of Richard Wagner or the paintings of Edouard
Manet. Ibsen's play *Ghosts* reached Great Britain in 1891 against a
background of mounting Victorian alarm at immorality in literature.
Zola's *La Terre*, published in 1887, gave the greatest offense of any of
the French master's novels, and the National Vigilance Association suc-

[1] New York: Hill & Wang, 1958.

cessfully prosecuted a publisher of Zola and other "obscene" works. George Moore's *Esther Waters* marked the invasion of British letters by French naturalism. "These novels are fit only for swine," a Member of Parliament snorted, while *The Saturday Review* expressed fear that literary realism was turning into "dirt and horror pure and simple." The aged Tennyson was shocked:

> Rip your brother's vices open, strip your own foul passions bare;
> Down with Reticence, down with Reverence—forward—naked—let
>   them stare.

Amid the general condemnation of Ibsen's play, the young Irish playwright and pamphleteer George Bernard Shaw, near the beginning of his own brilliant career, pointed out that the Norwegian's message was a serious and searching one. The following extract is the portion of Shaw's *Quintessence of Ibsenism* dealing with *The Doll's House* and *Ghosts*.

Pillars of Society, as a propagandist play, is disabled by the circumstance that the hero, being a fraudulent hypocrite in the ordinary police court sense of the phrase, would hardly be accepted as a typical pillar of society by the class he represents. Accordingly, Ibsen took care next time to make his idealist irreproachable from the standpoint of the ordinary idealist morality. In the famous *Doll's House*, [1879], the pillar of society who owns the doll is a model husband, father, and citizen. In his little household, with the three darling children and the affectionate little wife, all on the most loving terms with one another, we have the sweet home, the womanly woman, the happy family life of the idealist's dream. Mrs. Nora Helmer is happy in the belief that she has attained a valid realization of all these illusions; that she is an ideal wife and mother; and that Helmer is an ideal husband who would, if the necessity arose, give his life to save her reputation. A few simple contrived incidents disabuse her effectually on all these points. One of her earliest acts of devotion to her husband has been the secret raising of a sum of money to enable him to make a tour which was necessary to restore his health. As he would have broken down sooner than go into debt, she has had to persuade him that the money was a gift from her father. It was really obtained from a moneylender, who refused to make her the loan unless she induced her father to endorse the promissory note. This being impossible, as her father was dying at the time, she took the shortest way out of the difficulty by writing the name herself, to the entire satisfaction of the money-lender, who, though not at all duped, knew that forged bills are often the surest to be paid. Since then she has slaved in secret at scrivener's work until she has nearly paid off the debt.

At this point Helmer is made manager of the bank in which he is employed; and the moneylender, wishing to obtain a post there, uses the forged bill to force Nora to exert her influence with Helmer on his behalf. But she, having a hearty contempt for the man, cannot be persuaded by him that there was any harm in putting her father's name on the bill, and ridicules the suggestion that the law would not recognize that she was right under the circumstances. It is her husband's own contemptuous denunciation of a forgery formerly committed by the moneylender himself that destroys her self-satisfaction and opens her eyes to her ignorance of the serious business of the world to which her husband belongs: the world outside the home he shares with her. When he goes on to tell her that commercial dishonesty is generally to be traced to the influence of bad mothers, she begins to perceive that the happy way in which she plays with the children, and the care she takes to dress them nicely, are not sufficient to constitute her a fit person to train them. To redeem the forged bill, she resolves to borrow the balance due upon it from an intimate friend of the family. She has learnt to coax her husband into giving her what she asks by appealing to his affection for her: that is, by playing all sorts of pretty tricks until he is wheedled into an amorous humor. This plan she has adopted without thinking about it, instinctively taking the line of least resistance with him. And now she naturally takes the same line with her husband's friend. An unexpected declaration of love from him is the result; and it at once explains to her the real nature of the domestic influence she has been so proud of.

All her illusions about herself are now shattered. She sees herself as an ignorant and silly woman, a dangerous mother, and a wife kept for her husband's pleasure merely; but she clings all the harder to her illusion about him: he is still the ideal husband who would make any sacrifice to rescue her from ruin. She resolves to kill herself rather than allow him to destroy his own career by taking the forgery on himself to save her reputation. The final disillusion comes when he, instead of at once proposing to pursue this ideal line of conduct when he hears of the forgery, naturally enough flies into a vulgar rage and heaps invective on her for disgracing him. Then she sees that their whole family life has been a fiction: their home a mere doll's house in which they have been playing at ideal husband and father, wife and mother. So she leaves him then and there and goes out into the real world to find out its reality for herself, and to gain some position not fundamentally false, refusing to see her children again until she is fit to be in charge of them, or to live with him until she and he become capable of a more honorable relation to one another. He at first cannot understand what has happened, and flourishes the shattered ideals over her as if they were as potent as ever. He presents the course most agreeable to him—that of her staying at home and avoiding a scandal—as her duty to her husband, to her children, and to her religion; but the magic of these disguises is gone; and at last even he understands what has really happened, and sits down alone to wonder whether that more honorable relation can ever come to pass between them.

In his next play, *Ghosts* [1881], Ibsen returned to the charge with such an uncompromising and outspoken attack on marriage as a useless sacrifice of human beings to an ideal, that his meaning was obscured by its very obviousness. *Ghosts*, as it is called, is the story of a woman who has faithfully acted as a model wife and mother, sacrificing herself at every point with selfless thoroughness. Her husband is a man with a huge capacity and appetite for sensuous enjoyment. Society, prescribing ideal duties and not enjoyment for him, drives him to enjoy himself in underhand and illicit ways. When he marries his model wife, her devotion to duty only makes life harder for him; and he at last takes refuge in the caresses of an undutiful but pleasure-loving housemaid, and leaves his wife to satisfy her conscience by managing his business affairs whilst he satisfies his cravings as best he can by reading novels, drinking, and flirting, as aforesaid, with the servants. At this point even those who are most indignant with Nora Helmer for walking out of the doll's house, must admit that Mrs. Alving would be justified in walking out of *her* house. But Ibsen is determined to show you what comes of the scrupulous line of conduct you were so angry with Nora for not pursuing. Mrs Alving feels that her place is by her husband for better for worse, and by her child. Now the ideal of wifely and womanly duty which demands this from her also demands that she shall regard herself as an outraged wife, and her husband as a scoundrel. And the family ideal calls upon her to suffer in silence lest she shatter her innocent son's faith in the purity of home life by letting him know the disreputable truth about his father. It is her duty to conceal that truth from the world and from him. In this she falters for one moment only. Her marriage has not been a love match: she has, in pursuance of her duty as a daughter, contracted it for the sake of her family, although her heart inclined to a highly respectable clergyman, a professor of her own idealism, named Manders. In the humiliation of her first discovery of her husband's infidelity, she leaves the house and takes refuge with Manders; but he at once leads her back to the path of duty, from which she does not again swerve. With the utmost devotion she now carries out an elaborate scheme of lying and imposture. She so manages her husband's affairs and so shields his good name that everybody believes him to be a public-spirited citizen of the strictest conformity to current ideals of respectability and family life. She sits up of nights listening to his lewd and silly conversation, and even drinking with him, to keep him from going into the streets and being detected by the neighbors in what she considers his vices. She provides for the servant he has seduced, and brings up his illegitimate daughter as a maid in her own household. And, as a crowning sacrifice, she sends her son away to Paris to be educated there, knowing that if he stays at home the shattering of his ideals must come sooner or later.

Her work is crowned with success. She gains the esteem of her old love the clergyman, who is never tired of holding up her household as a beautiful realization of the Christian ideal of marriage. Her own martyrdom is brought to an end at last by the death of her husband in the odor of a most sanctified reputation, leaving her free to recall her son from Paris and enjoy his society, and his love and gratitude, in the flower of his early manhood.

But when her son comes home, the facts refuse as obstinately as ever to correspond to her ideals. Oswald has inherited his father's love of enjoyment; and when, in dull rainy weather, he returns from Paris to the solemn strictly ordered house where virtue and duty have had their temple for so many years, his mother sees him show the unmistakable signs of boredom with which she is so miserably familar from of old; then sit after dinner killing time over the bottle; and finally—the climax of anguish—begin to flirt with the maid who, as his mother alone knows, is his own father's daughter. But there is this world-wide difference in her insight to the cases of the father and the son. She did not love the father: she loves the son with the intensity of a heart-starved woman who has nothing else left to love. Instead of recoiling from him with pious disgust and pharisaical consciousness of moral superiority, she sees at once that he has a right to be happy in his own way, and that she has no right to force him to be dutiful and wretched in hers. She sees, too, her injustice to the unfortunate father, and the cowardice of the monstrous fabric of lies and false appearances she has wasted her life in manufacturing. She resolves that the son's life shall not be sacrificed to ideals which are to him joyless and unnatural. But she finds that the work of the ideals is not to be undone quite so easily. In driving the father to steal his pleasures in secrecy and squalor, they had brought upon him the diseases bred by such conditions; and her son now tells her that those diseases have left their mark on him, and that he carries poison in his pocket against the time, foretold to him by a Parisian surgeon, when general paralysis of the insane may destroy his faculties. In desperation she undertakes to rescue him from this horrible apprehension by making his life happy. The house shall be made as bright as Paris for him: he shall have as much champagne as he wishes until he is no longer driven to that dangerous resource by the dulness of his life with her: if he loves the girl he shall marry her if she were fifty times his half-sister. But the half-sister, on learning the state of his health, leaves the house; for she, too, is her father's daughter, and is not going to sacrifice her life in devotion to an invalid. When the mother and son are left alone in their dreary home, with the rain falling outside, all she can do for him is to promise that if his doom overtakes him before he can poison himself, she will make a final sacrifice of her natural feelings by performing that dreadful duty, the first of all her duties that has any real basis. Then the weather clears up at last; and the sun, which the young man has so longed to see, appears. He asks her to give it to him to play with; and a glance at him shows her that the ideals have claimed their victim, and that the time has come for her to save him from a real horror by sending him from her out of the world, just as she saved him from an imaginary one years before by sending him out of Norway.

This last scene of *Ghosts* is so appallingly tragic that the emotions it excites prevent the meaning of the play from being seized and discussed like that of *A Doll's House*. In England nobody, as far as I know, seems to have perceived that *Ghosts* is to *A Doll's House* what the late Sir Walter Besant intended his own sequel[2] to that play to be. Besant attempted to show what might come of Nora's repudiation of that idealism of which he was one of the most popular professors. But the effect made on Besant by *A Doll's House* was very faint compared to that produced on the English critics by the first performance of *Ghosts* in this country. In the earlier part of this essay I have shown that since Mrs. Alving's early conceptions of duty are as valid to ordinary critics as to Pastor Manders, who must appear to them as an admirable man, endowed with Helmer's good sense without Helmer's selfishness, a pretty general disapproval of the moral of the play was inevitable. Fortunately, the newspaper press went to such bedlamite lengths on this occasion that Mr. William Archer, the well-known dramatic critic and translator of Ibsen, was able to put the whole body of hostile criticism out of court by simply quoting its excesses in an article entitled "Ghosts and Gibberings," which appeared in the *Pall Mall Gazette* of April 8, 1891. Mr. Archer's extracts, which he offers as a nucleus for a Dictionary of Abuse modeled upon the Wagner *Schimpf-Lexicon*, are worth reprinting here as samples of contemporary idealist criticism of the drama.

DESCRIPTIONS OF THE PLAY

"Ibsen's positively abominable play entitled *Ghosts*. . . . This disgusting representation. . . . Reprobation due to such as aim at infecting the modern theatre with poison after desperately inoculat-

---

[2] A forgotten production, published in the *English Illustrated Magazine* for January 1890. Besant makes the moneylender, as a reformed man, and a pattern of all the virtues, hold a forged bill *in terrorem* over Nora's grown-up daughter, engaged to his son. The bill has been forged by her brother, who has inherited a tendency to forge from his mother. Helmer having taken to drink after the departure of his wife, and forfeited his social position, the money-lender tells the girl that if she persists in disgracing him by marrying his son, he will send her brother to gaol. She evades the dilemma by drowning herself. The moral is that if Nora had never run away from her husband her daughter would never have drowned herself. Note that the moneylender does over again what he did in Ibsen's play, with the difference that, having become eminently respectable, he has also become a remorseless scoundrel. Ibsen shews him as a good-natured fellow at bottom. I wrote a sequel to this sequel. Another sequel was written by Eleanor, the youngest daughter of Karl Marx. I forget where they appeared.

ing themselves and others. . . . An open drain; a loathsome sore
unbandaged; a dirty act done publicly; a lazar-house with all its
doors and windows open. . . . Candid foulness. . . . Kotzebue turned
bestial and cynical. Offensive cynicism. . . . Ibsen's melancholy and
malodorous world. . . . Absolutely loathsome and fetid. . . . Gross,
almost putrid indecorum. . . . Literary carrion. . . . Crapulous stuff.
Novel and perilous nuisance." *Daily Telegraph* [leading article].
"This mass of vulgarity, egotism, coarseness, and absurdity." *Daily
Telegraph* [criticism]. "Unutterably offensive. . . . Prosecution
under Lord Campbell's Act. . . . Abominable piece. . . . Scanda-
lous." *Standard*. "Naked loathsomeness. . . . Most dismal and repulsive production." *Daily News*. "Revoltingly suggestive and
blasphemous. . . . Characters either contradictory in themselves,
uninteresting or abhorrent." *Daily Chronicle*. "A repulsive and
degrading work." *Queen*. "Morbid, unhealthy, unwholesome and
disgusting story. . . . A piece to bring the stage into disrepute and
dishonour with every right-thinking man and woman." *Lloyd's*.
"Merely dull dirt long drawn out." *Hawk*. "Morbid horrors of the
hideous tale. . . . Ponderous dulness of the didactic talk. . . . If any
repetition of this outrage be attempted, the authorities will doubtless
wake from their lethargy." *Sporting and Dramatic News*. "Just a
wicked nightmare." *The Gentlewoman*. "Lugubrious diagnosis of
sordid impropriety. . . . Characters are prigs, pedants, and prof-
ligates. . . . Morbid caricatures. . . . Maunderings of nookshotten
Norwegians. . . . It is no more of a play than an average Gaiety
burlesque." *Black and White*. "Most loathsome of all Ibsen's plays.
. . . Garbage and offal." *Truth*. "Ibsen's putrid play called *Ghosts*.
. . . So loathsome an enterprise." *Academy*. "As foul and filthy a
concoction as has ever been allowed to disgrace the boards of an
English theatre. . . . Dull and disgusting. . . . Nastiness and malo-
dorousness laid on thickly as with a trowel." *Era*. "Noisome corruption." *Stage*.

DESCRIPTIONS OF IBSEN

"An egotist and a bungler." *Daily Telegraph*. "A crazy fanatic.
. . . A crazy, cranky being. . . . Not only consistently dirty but
deplorably dull." *Truth*. "The Norwegian pessimist *in petto*"
[*sic*]. *Black and White*. "Ugly, nasty, discordant, and downright
dull. . . . A gloomy sort of ghoul, bent on groping for horrors by

night, and blinking like a stupid old owl when the warm sunlight
of the best of life dances into his wrinkled eyes." *Gentlewoman*. "A
teacher of the aestheticism of the Lock Hospital." *Saturday Review*.

DESCRIPTIONS OF IBSEN'S ADMIRERS

"Lovers of prurience and dabblers in impropriety who are eager
to gratify their illicit tastes under the pretence of art." *Evening
Standard*. "Ninety-seven per cent of the people who go to see
Ghosts are nasty-minded people who find the discussion of nasty
subjects to their taste in exact proportion to their nastiness." *Sporting and Dramatic News*. "The sexless. . . . The unwomanly woman,
the unsexed females, the whole army of unprepossessing cranks in
petticoats. Educated and muck-ferreting dogs. . . . Effeminate men
and male women. . . . They all of them—men and women alike—
know that they are doing not only a nasty but an illegal thing.
. . . The Lord Chamberlain left them alone to wallow in *Ghosts*. . . .
Outside a silly clique, there is not the slightest interest in the Scandinavian humbug or all his works. . . . A wave of human folly."
Truth.

15. Painting: The impressionists

"Life as it is, rendered in its actual conditions of light. . ." Emile
Zola, "Naturalism in the Salon" (1880)[1]

"The painter will become of more importance, the poet of less" in
modern times, John Ruskin predicted. Painting did become of extraordinary importance in the latter part of the nineteenth century. The
impressionists, who formally announced their "school" in 1874, can
be called the counterpart of the literary naturalists. That is to say, they
were bolder realists. Manet, Whistler, Pissarro, Cézanne, those who
were roughly known as impressionists between 1874 and 1886 began
as disciples of the realist, Courbet. But they added some rather daring
ideas and technical experiments. In rebellion against academic orthodoxy, they used strong colors freely and escaped from conventional
subjects. Often they painted in the open air, from "nature." They
painted peasant women, chorus girls, bridges in the sunlight, snow in

[1] The following translation is by the editor.

the suburbs rather than the fauns and satyrs or epochal battles of academic tradition. The impressionist's nudes were ordinary girls bathing rather than Greek goddesses. As usual, artistic conservatives refused to recognize the genius of the innovators. Museums which might have made a fortune by purchasing Renoirs and Cézannes for a pittance refused to do so and instead spent large sums for the canvasses of now forgotten artists. The impressionists were assailed for what was often mistakenly thought to be their sloppy technique as well as for their departure from academic traditions and for the "disgusting commonplaceness" of their subjects.

Zola, a close friend of Manet, Cézanne and other painters, took a keen interest in painting, as had Baudelaire and other French men of letters. Painting held a strong and glorious place in France by long tradition. The official salons, referred to in the selection that follows, reflected the long-standing role of the state in subsidizing the fine arts. Zola, as will be seen, tended to identify impressionism with naturalism, to hail it as the art of the future, and to predict its inevitable success. Many impressionist painters were indeed strongly under the influence of Positivist ideas, and spoke of painting scientifically. Quentin Bell has spoken of their "fact-finding and fact-loving materialism." Zola was in one sense wrong about the future. Academic traditionalism would never regain its hold, but the expressionists of the 1900's were to rebel against impressionism in the name of an inward reality, just as symbolism rebelled against naturalism in literature. The greater impressionists such as Paul Cézanne themselves developed toward a more subjective and visionary art. But Zola's cry of triumph, published in *Le Voltaire*, June 18–22, 1880, was uttered at the high point of naturalism in painting.

I COME now to the influence that the impressionists have at this time upon our French school of painting. This influence is considerable. And I use this word "impressionist" here because a label is necessary by which to designate the group of young artists who, following Courbet and the great landscape painters, dedicated themselves to the study of nature; otherwise, this term seems to me narrow in itself and not of any great significance. Courbet was a master craftman who has left imperishable works, in which nature is brought to life with an extraordinary power. But after him the movement has continued, as it continued in literature after Stendhal, Balzac, and Flaubert. Artists arrived who, without having quite the solidity and beauty of execution of Courbet, have enlarged the field, in making a more profound study of light, in banishing still more the badge of the academy. Basically, Courbet as a painter was a magnificent classicist, who stands in the larger tradition of Titian, Veronese and Rembrandt. The true revolutionaries of form appeared with M. Edouard Manet, and with the impressionists Claude Monet, Renoir, Pissarro, Guillaumin, and others. These men propose to leave the studio where painters have cooped themselves up for so many centuries, and go forth to paint in the open air, a simple act of which the consequences are considerable. In the open air, light is no longer of a single sort, consequently there are multiple effects which diversify and radically transform the appearance of things and beings. This study of light in its thousand decompositions and recompositions is what has been called more or less properly impressionism, because a picture becomes the impression of a moment experienced before nature. Newspaper humorists have used that point to caricature the impressionist painter as seizing impressions on the fly, in four crude strokes of the brush; and one is forced to concede that a few artists have unhappily justified these attacks, contenting themselves with too rudimentary drafts. In my opinion one ought to seize nature in the impression of a moment; only it is necessary to fix this moment forever on the canvas by a composition that is extensively studied. After all, without work no solidity is possible. . . . Note that the same evolution has taken place in painting as in literature, as I just suggested. Since the beginning of the century painters have step by step drawn closer to nature. Today our young artists have made a new step toward truth, in wishing that their subjects bathe in the real light of the sun, rather than the false light of the studio; it is like the chemist or physician who goes back to the sources, placing himself in the same conditions as the phenomena. If one wished to paint life, it is necessary to take life with its complete mechanism. Hence, in painting, the necessity of open air, of light studied in its causes and its effects. That is easy to say, but the difficulties begin with the execution. Painters have long declared that it is impossible to paint in the open, or even with the sun's rays in the studio, because of reflections and continual changes of light. Many even yet shrug their shoulders before the efforts of the impressionists. It is necessary to be in the profession in order to grasp effectively what has to be overcome if one wishes to accept nature with its diffuse light and its continual variations and colorations. In truth, it is easier to master light by the use of shades and curtains, so that one can stabilize it; but then one remains in the old convention, in a ready-prepared nature, in the commonplaceness of the schools. And what stupefaction for the public, when one places before them certain canvases painted in the open air, at particular hours; they stand gaping at blue grass, violet earth, red trees, water revealing all the colors of the prism. Yet the artist has been conscientious; he has perhaps exaggerated slightly the new tones which his eye has discovered, but the observation is at bottom quite accurate; nature has never had the simplified and purely conventional notation that the academic traditions have bestowed upon it. Hence, the crowd's laughter when faced with the pictures of the impressionists, despite the good faith and very sincere effort of the young painters. They are treated as jokers, charlatans making fun of the public and pretentiously puffing up their works, when on the contrary they are careful and earnest observers. What seems to be overlooked is that the majority of these strugglers are poor men who die of hardship, poverty, and weariness. Strange jesters, these martyrs to their beliefs!

Here then is what the impressionist painters exhibit: exact research into the causes and effects of light, flowing in upon the design as well as upon the color. They have been rightly accused of being inspired by the Japanese prints, so interesting, which today are in everyone's hands. It would be necessary here to study these prints and to show what this art of the Far East, so clear and fine, has taught us Occidentals, whose old civilization prides itself on knowing everything. It is certain that our black painting, our painting of the bituminous school, has been surprised and sent back to its studies by these limpid horizons, these lovely vibrant tints of the Japanese water-colorists. They have a simplicity of means and an intensity of effect which have struck our young artists and pushed them towards this way of painting drenched in air and light, which today engages all the newcomers of talent. And I do not mention the exquisite skill of the Japanese in detail, of their design so delicate and true, or of all this naturalistic fantasy which proceeds from direct observation into the most curious details. I would add only that if the Japanese influence has been an excellent thing to draw us away from the bituminous tradition and make us see the blond gayeties of nature, a deliberate imitation of an art which is not of our race or environment would end by being an insupportable mode. The Japanese style has merit, but it should not be introduced everywhere; if so, art would turn into a plaything. Our strength is not there. We cannot accept as the last word this too naive simplification, this curiosity of flat colors, this refinement of traits and of colored stain. All that is not life, and we ought to create life.

I restrain myself, I cannot here study each impressionist painter of talent. There are those of them who, like M. Degas, are enclosed in their specialties. Degas is above all a draftsman both meticulous and original, who has produced a series of most remarkable laundresses, dancers, women at their toilet, whose movements he has drawn with complete and delicate fidelity. Pissarro, Sisley, Guillaumin have followed in the footsteps of Claude Monet, whom I shall rediscover in a moment at the official Salon, and they have worked to reproduce corners of nature around Paris, under the true light of the sun, without flinching before the most unexpected effects of coloration. Paul Cézanne, with the temperament of a great painter, who still is struggling in search of composition, remains nearer Courbet and Delacroix. Mme. Berthe Morisot is a very personal student of Edouard Manet, while Mlle. Cassatt, an American I believe,[2] has lately made her debut with some remarkable works, of a singular originality. Finally M. Caillebotte is a very conscientious artist, whose composition is a little dry, but who has the courage to attempt large things and who searches with a most virile resolution.

I omit some names, certainly; but I am here concerned more with impressionism than with impressionists.

The great misfortune is that no artist of this group has completely and definitively realized the potential which they all carry scattered among their works. The prescription is there, divided in many parts; but nowhere, in no one of them, does one find it applied by a master. These are all the precursors; the man of genius has not yet arrived. We see very well what they aim at, we grant them their point, but we search in vain for the masterwork which realizes their formula and makes everyone bow his head before it. Here is the reason why the battle of the impressionists has not yet ended; they remain inferior to the task which they attempt, they

[2] Zola believed rightly; Mary Cassatt, much admired by the impressionists, was born in the United States though most of her life was spent in France. Today a number of American museums possess her canvases (Ed.).

stammer without being able to find the word. But their influence is none the less great, for they are in the only possible line of evolution, they are marching toward the future. One can regret their personal inabilities, but they remain the true creatures of the age; this explains how unknown painters, booed, driven from the Salons and forced to live in quarantine, remain so strong, even without a master at their helm yet, that from the little rooms where they hang their pictures they are little by little imposing on the official Salons the formula, still vague, which they apply. They have flaws, they are too often slack in their composition, they are too easily satisfied, they show themselves to be incomplete, illogical, exaggerated, impotent; no matter, it is enough that they are working in the vein of contemporary naturalism to place them at the head of a movement and to play a considerable role in our school of painting.

At present, we are witnessing the official Salon[3] being transformed under the direct influence of the impressionists, those pariah painters whom everybody makes fun of.

This is a fact. If one recalls the annual Salons of these last twenty years, since the *Salon des Refusés* of 1863[4] up to the present, for example, one is struck by the change of aspect, by the gradual evolution toward modern subjects and bright painting. Each year, we see diminishing the academic paintings, the groups of men and women served up to the public under a mythological etiquette, subjects classical, historical, romantic, paintings forced by tradition

[3] The system of official Academies, subsidized by the government and almost conferring a monopoly on their members, goes back to the time of Louis XIV and is a specifically French contribution to modern culture, though modeled on earlier Italian institutions. The Royal Academy of Painting and Sculpture, founded 1648–1663, offered training and lectures, but its more important function was to confer the badge of recognition and respectability on artists by admitting them to its privileged ranks. For a long time only by means of this acceptance was a successful career as an artist possible. Works were admitted to the official exhibition or Salon, in Zola's time, on the recommendation of a jury made up of recognized and accepted artists. There were bitter complaints that this perpetuated the rule of the past. The impressionists were among the first to organize independent exhibitions (Ed.).

[4] In 1863 a group of the rejected painters withdrew to set up their own exhibition, an event of revolutionary importance in the world of French art. Manet was the chief of the *Refusés* of 1863 (Ed.).

toward blackness; and, gradually, figures appear clothed in the style of the day and painted in open air, everyday and popular scenes, of the parks, the market places, our boulevards, our intimate life. It is a mounting tide of modernity, irresistible, which little by little is submerging the *École des Beaux-Arts*, the Institute, all the recipes and all the conventions. The momentum has started, the movement continues with a fatal force that no one can stop; and it is not a conspiracy, it is simply the influence of the age, which impels and reunites individuals. Note that I mention an evolution, without saying that all the painting which enters into the modern way has for that reason even any talent. Alas, talent is too often lacking. My first sensation, at this year's Salon, was a happy surprise at seeing that the pictures painted from nature outweighed those of the school. Next, I have to confess that not all these naturalistic efforts in painting are very good; that is inevitable. Masters remain rare, there are always many less gifted pupils. One can only say that the movement affirms itself with an invincible power; naturalism, impressionism, modernism, whatever one wishes to call it, is today master of the official Salons. We shall soon see that success is there, even for the multitude. If all the young painters are not masters, all, at least, apply the same formula, each with his different temperament. Let us wait, and perhaps a master of genius will come to utter powerfully the word that the present talents stammer.

M. Edouard Manet has been one of the tireless workers in naturalism, and he is still today the talent which is the purest, which reveals the finest and most original personality in the sincere study of nature. At this year's Salon he has a very remarkable portrait of M. Antonin Proust and an open-air scene, *At Father Lathuille's*, two figures at a cabaret table, which possesses a gaiety and a delicacy of charming tones. For fourteen years now I have been one of the foremost defenders of M. Manet against the imbecilic attacks of press and public. During that time, he has worked a great deal, always struggling, imposing himself on men of intelligence by his rare qualities as an artist, the sincerity of his efforts, the originality of his color, so clear and so distinguished, even the naivete which he had always had before nature. His is an existence entirely dedicated to art, courageously; and, one day, men will recognize what an important place he has held in the epoch of transition which our

French school is undergoing at this time. He will live as its most acute, most interesting, and most personable representative. But, as of today, one is able to measure his importance by the decisive role he has played during the last twenty years; it is enough to determine the influence which he has had on all the young painters who came after him. And I do not speak of certain painters among his elders, who have stolen from him with an incredible facility for assimilation, while affecting to laugh at him; these gentlemen have taken from him his blond color, his justness of tone, his naturalistic method, not honestly but to accommodate this painting to the taste of the public, in such a way that they have had the crowd on their side while they continue to scoff at Edouard Manet. It is always thus, the clever triumph upon the corpse of the sincere. As for the young painters who have profited so much from the work of Manet, they form today a vast school, of which he ought to be the real chief; they prefer not to recognize him as such, they discuss him, find him incomplete, say that he has not fulfilled his promise and that the artist in him has remained inferior to the new form which he introduced after Courbet and the landscapists. It is not the less true that they have all borrowed something from him and that he was the ray of truth which opened their eyes, when they were still groping along the banks of the *École des Beaux-Arts*. This is the real glory of M. Edouard Manet: his influence has reached the students of M. Gérome and M. Cabanel, not to mention the impressionists, who are his direct offspring.

At the head of the impressionists, I have just put M. Claude Monet, in observing that he decided this year to send two canvases to the Salon. One of these canvases only has been accepted, and that with difficulty, which caused it to be placed quite high on a wall, at an elevation which does not permit it to be seen. It is a landscape, Lavacourt, a bit of the Seine with an island in the middle, and some white houses of a village on the right bank. No one raises his head, the picture passes unnoticed. However, they did well to place it badly, for it wears up there an exquisite tone of light and open air; the more so as chance has surrounded it with some of those bituminous paintings, of a dismal mediocrity, which provide it with a framework of shadows among which it assumes the gaiety of a rising sun. M. Monet, too, is a master. He does not have the distinguished mark of Manet, he paints figures heavily; but he is an incomparable landscapist, with a clarity and truth of tone that is superb. Above all he paints seascapes marvelously; water sleeps, sings in his pictures, with a reality of reflections and transparency which I have seen nowhere else. Add that he is very competent, a master of his profession, who never gropes, and will please the public if it gives him the slightest chance. . . . M. Monet today pays the penalty of his haste, of his need to sell. If he wishes to conquer the high place he deserves, he will have resolutely to dedicate himself to important paintings, studied during the seasons, without any other preoccupation except to buckle entirely to his task. . . .

The other impressionist painter, M. Renoir, who is represented at the Salon, finds himself equally badly placed. His two canvases, *Fisherwomen at Berneval* and *Young Girl Sleeping*, have been hung in the circular gallery which extends around the garden; and the light of broad day, the reflections of the sun, do them a great injustice, since the palette of this painter embraces all the colors of the prism in a gamut of tones, often extremely delicate. But, again, what good is it to complain against the jury and the administration? It is a simple struggle, from which one always emerges the victor, by dint of courage and talent.

[Zola next describes several painters who are converts to "naturalism," if not exactly Impressionists.] . . . So then, there are the names, there are the facts. Each year the School diminishes. One sees all the young talents, all those who have need of life and success, coming over to the new formula, to modern subjects, to the exact observation of nature, to that painting in the open air which bathes individuals in the real light where they live. Certainly, I have said it, there are among these converts many false and feeble talents; but still it is necessary to thank them for opening their eyes and attempting reality. There are others, besides, who will come to accept this impressionist style, so often misunderstood: life as it is, rendered in its actual conditions of light. . . .

. . . I have verified the increasing progress of naturalism. Each year, at each Salon, we can see the evolution become more apparent. The painters in the academic tradition languish, producing more and more mediocre works, in the isolation which enlarges around them; while all life, all force come from the depicters of reality and modernity. The students of Messeurs Cabanel and Gérome abandon them one by one; the best, the most intelligent, the most talented, deserted the School first, drawing after them all their comrades of any merit, leaving to the professors only the mediocre ones, those troubled by no temperament; so that within ten years the desertion will be complete, the face of art transformed, naturalism triumphant, without adversaries. Likewise we have seen, by the examples of Messrs. Bonnat, Henner, and Vollon, that every artist of talent today relies upon observation and analysis; it is thanks to these gentlemen that naturalism, still stammering it is true, will doubtless soon enter into the Institute. And I have constantly insisted upon the large role that the impressionist painters play at this moment. If none of them has yet fully realized the formula of art which they uphold, this formula is not less in process of revolutionizing contemporary painting. . . . The future is there, one will see it later. After Delacroix, after Courbet, painters of genius who expressed nature with the old techniques, if one wished to advance farther it only remained to resume the study of realities and to strive to see them in the conditions of greatest truth. All researches ought to bear upon the question of light, upon this daylight which bathes objects and beings. All efforts ought to lead toward producing works that are stronger, more alive, which give the complete impression of figures and their surroundings, in the thousand conditions of existence in which they can present themselves.

16. A critique of naturalism

"Art moves towards its dissolution." Friedrich Nietzsche, *Human, All Too Human* (1878)[1]

A criticism of naturalism referred to in the Introduction is that since it aimed only to describe the world, and withheld moral judgments, it offered no basis for a criticism of society. Naturalists, for example Thomas Hardy, Joseph Conrad, and Theodore Dreiser, were pes-

[1] The translation which follows is by the author. See pp. 134, 270 for other translations of Nietzsche's work.

simists: in their books an inscrutable fate defeats man, making cruel mockery of his pathetic hopes and dreams. Moreover the collapse of Zola's genius in his later works seemed to point to a defect in his method. Naturalism seemed to lack any logical principle of selection, and thus to result in formless works.

Nietzsche argues that art has to escape from naturalism and bind itself by rules and standards. It had thrown off the shackles of classicism to enjoy the exhilarating freedom of romanticism—but how was it to progress after that? What was the future of a literature and art released from all standards, constantly forced to invent novelties, unable to tolerate discipline? Perhaps today we should be prepared to grant Nietzsche his point.

The strong force which the French dramatists exerted with regard to the unity of action, of place and time, style, verse, and sentence structure, choice of words and thoughts, was as important a school as that of counterpoint and fugue in the development of modern music, or the Gorgian figures in Greek rhetoric. Such limitations can seem absurd; and yet there is no other means for us to rise above naturalism, than first to limit ourselves in the strongest (perhaps the most arbitrary) way. Thus one learns gradually to walk gracefully on narrow paths over dizzying precipices, and gain the highest flexibility of movement, as the history of music in recent times shows. Here one sees how step by step the chains are unloosed, until they finally appear to fall off altogether; this *illusion* is the culminating point of a necessary development in art. In modern poetic art there has not been so happily gradual a release from the self-imposed shackles. Lessing made the French form, that is, the unique modern art form, a laughingstock in Germany and turned to Shakespeare, and so was lost the continuity of that unchaining; a leap was made into naturalism—i.e., back to the beginnings of art. From this Goethe sought to save us, knowing how to bind himself repeatedly in a variety of ways; but even the most gifted one of all brought us only to a continuous experimenting, once the thread of development had been broken. Schiller owed the vague security of his form to his unintentional honoring (even as he disowned them) of the examples of French tragedy, and held himself rather independent of Lessing, whose dramatic effects he notably disavowed. The French themselves failed to produce great talent after Voltaire, who had brought the development of tragedy

out of constraint to that illusion of freedom. They also followed the
Germans in making the leap to a sort of Rousseau-like state of
nature in art, and to experimentation. One need only reread Voltaire's *Mahomet* in order to get clearly in mind what European
culture lost, once and for all, by this break with tradition. Voltaire
was the last of the great humanists, many-sided, his great tragic
soul disciplined by Greek standards. He was able to do what no
German yet has done, because the nature of Frenchmen resembles
the Greek much more closely than does the German nature. He
was the last great writer who in his prose style revealed Greek
artistic conscientiousness, Greek simplicity and grace; as indeed he
was one of the last men who could unite in himself the highest
freedom of spirit with an utterly unrevolutionary temperament,
without being inconsistent or weak. Since then the modern spirit
with its restlessness, its hatred of standards and limits, has come to
supremacy in all areas, first unleashed by the fever of revolution
and then again applying the rein to itself when fear and terror
assailed it—but the rein of logic, no longer the standards of art.

We have enjoyed through that unleashing a long era of poetry of
all peoples, growing up in obscure places, original, wild-blooming,
strangely beautiful, sublimely irregular, from folk songs up to the
"great barbarian" Shakespeare; we taste the joys of local color and
period costumes, heretofore kept at a distance by all artistic peoples; we hugely enjoy these "barbarian advantages" of our time,
which Goethe urged against Schiller in order to put the formless-
ness of *Faust* in the most favorable light. But for how much longer?
The inflowing flood of poetry of all styles and all peoples *must*
gradually float away the earth in which a secret growth might
have been possible; all poets *must* become experimenting counterfeiters, foolhardy copyists, be their strength originally ever so great;
the public, finally, which had learned to see the true artistic act in
the *curbing* of representational strength, in the organizing power
of all artistic methods, *must* always more value strength for the
sake of strength, inspiration for the sake of inspiration; it accordingly will enjoy the elements and conditions of works of art only if
isolated, and finally comes to make the natural demand that the
artist *must* present them to it isolated. Yes, one has thrown off the
"irrational" fetters of French-Greek art, but thereby, unnoticed,

one finds that all fetters, all limitations have become irrational—and so art moves toward its dissolution, thereby revealing—a most instructive thing—all phases of its beginnings, its childhood, its incompleteness, its former daring and extravagances; it repeats, in its old age, its origin and growth.

17. Human nature in politics

"Knowledge of the complex and difficult world forces itself into their minds." Graham Wallas, "The Method of Political Reasoning," *Human Nature in Politics* (1908)[1]

Realism and naturalism did not come to an end, though rather different modes of thought and expression soon become fashionable. Perhaps their most enduring heritage lay in the "scientific" study of social phenomena. Around the turn of the century sociology became increasingly important, partially because of the work of such eminent practitioners as Emile Durkheim in France, Max Weber in Germany, Vilfredo Pareto in Italy, and Thorstein Veblen in the United States. As it diverged from traditional classical theory, economics became more realistic—less abstract and doctrinaire and more descriptive and historical. The study of politics followed suit. The Englishman Graham Wallas was one of the most important of those who called for a new approach to the study of politics. Wallas thought politics should be "quantitative" rather than "qualitative," stressing the realities of human nature rather than the ideal images of pure theory. His *Human Nature in Politics*, published in 1908, is in the grand tradition of British political thought. Eminently quotable, a delight to read, lucid yet original and stimulating, it is the offspring of David Hume, John Stuart Mill and Walter Bagehot.

Wallas thought political studies were in a most unsatisfactory state from a want of attention to the often irrational but intensely natural ways of men in actual situations. Men are not the rational atoms the utilitarians and political economists thought them to be. A. L. Rowse called Wallas' *Human Nature in Politics* "the most original and important contribution to be made to political thought by an Englishman in this century," and it has become a minor classic. Reprinted below is most of Chapter 5, "The Method of Political Reasoning." Bearing in mind our other criticisms of naturalism, the student might ask himself

[1] 4th ed., London: Constable, 1948.

whether Wallas' case for a purely "quantitative" science of politics is convincing.

THE TRADITIONAL method of political reasoning has inevitably shared the defects of its subject matter. In thinking about politics we seldom penetrate behind those simple entities which form themselves so easily in our minds, or approach in earnest the infinite complexity of the actual world. Political abstractions, such as justice, or liberty, or the state, stand in our minds as things having a real existence. The names of political species, "governments," or "rights," or "Irishmen," suggest to us the ideal of single "type specimens"; and we tend, like medieval naturalists, to assume that all the individual members of a species are in all respects identical with the type specimen and with each other.

In politics a true proposition in the form of "All A is B" almost invariably means that a number of individual persons or things possess the quality B in degrees of variation as numerous as are the individuals themselves. We tend, however, under the influence of our words and the mental habits associated with them to think of A either as a single individual possessing the quality B, or as a number of individuals equally possessing the quality. As we read in the newspaper that "the educated Bengalis are disaffected" we either see, in the half-conscious substratum of visual images which accompanies our reading, a single babu with a disaffected expression or the vague suggestion of a long row of identical babus all equally disaffected.

These personifications and uniformities, in their turn, tempt us to employ in our political thinking that method of a priori deduction from large and untried generalizations against which natural science from the days of Bacon has always protested. No scientist now argues that the planets move in circles, because planets are perfect, and the circle is a perfect figure, or that any newly discovered plant must be a cure for some disease because nature has given healing properties to all plants. But "logical" democrats still argue in America that, because all men are equal, political offices ought to go by rotation, and "logical" collectivists sometimes argue from the "principle" that the state should own all the means of production to the conclusion that all railway managers should be elected by universal suffrage. . . .

Since Jevons'[2] time the method which he initiated has been steadily extended; economic and statistical processes have become more nearly assimilated, and problems of fatigue or acquired skill, of family affection and personal thrift, of management by the entrepreneur or the paid official, have been stated and argued in quantitative form. As Professor Marshall said the other day, *qualitative* reasoning in economics is passing away and *quantitative* reasoning is beginning to take its place.[3]

How far is a similar change of method possible in the discussion not of industrial and financial processes but of the structure and working of political institutions?

It is of course easy to pick out political questions which can obviously be treated by quantitative methods. One may take, for instance, the problem of the best size for a debating hall, to be used, say, by the Federal Deliberative Assembly of the British Empire, assuming that the shape is already settled. The main elements of the problem are that the hall should be large enough to accommodate with dignity a number of members sufficient both for the representation of interests and the carrying out of committee work, and not too large for each member to listen without strain to a debate. The resultant size will represent a compromise among these elements, accommodating a number smaller than would be desirable if the need of representation and dignity alone were to be considered, and larger than it would be if the convenience of debate alone were considered.

A body of economists could agree to plot out or imagine a succession of "curves" representing the advantage to be obtained from each additional unit of size in dignity, adequacy of representation, supply of members for committee work, healthiness, etc., and the disadvantage of each additional unit of size as affecting con-

[2] Stanley Jevons, an economist at the University of London, pioneered in marginal utility theory using mathematical methods to chart the factors determining prices (Ed.).

[3] *Journal of Economics*, March 1907, pp. 7 and 8. "What by chemical analogy may be called qualitative analysis has done the greater part of its work. . . . Much less progress has indeed been made toward the quantitative determination of the relative strength of different economic forces. That higher and more difficult task must wait upon the slow growth of thorough realistic statistics." [Alfred Marshall, Cambridge economist, leading theoretician of his day; *Principles of Economics*, 1890 (Ed.).]

venice of debate, etc. The curves of dignity and adequacy might be the result of direct estimation. The curve of marginal convenience in audibility would be founded upon actual "polygons of variation" recording measurements of the distance at which a sufficient number of individuals of the classes and ages expected could hear and make themselves heard in a room of that shape. The economists might further, after discussion, agree on the relative importance of each element to the final decision, and might give effect to their agreement by the familiar statistical device of "weighting."

The answer would perhaps provide fourteen square feet on the floor in a room twenty-six feet high for each of three hundred and seventeen members. There would, when the answer was settled, be a "marginal" man in point of hearing (representing, perhaps, an average healthy man of seventy-four), who would be unable or just able to hear the "marginal" man in point of clearness of speech —who might represent (on a polygon specially drawn up by the Oxford professor of biology) the least audible but two of the tutors at Balliol. The marginal point on the curve of the decreasing utility of successive increments of members from the point of view of committee work might show, perhaps, that such work must either be reduced to a point far below that which is usual in national parliaments, or must be done very largely by persons not members of the assembly itself. The aesthetic curve of dignity might be cut at the point where the President of the Society of British Architects could just be induced not to write to *The Times*. . . .

It would be more difficult to induce a committee of politicians to agree on the plotting of curves, representing the social advantage to be obtained by the successive increments of satisfaction in an urban industrial population of those needs which are indicated by the terms socialism and individualism. They could, however, be brought to admit that the discovery of curves for that purpose is a matter of observation and inquiry, and that the best possible distribution of social duties between the individual and the state would cut both at some point or other. For many socialists and individualists the mere attempt to think in such a way of their problem would be an extremely valuable exercise. If a socialist and an individualist were required even to ask themselves the question, "How much socialism?" or "How much individualism?" a basis of real discussion would be arrived at—even in the impossible case that one should answer, "All individualism and no socialism," and the other, "All socialism and no individualism."

The fact, of course, that each step toward either socialism or individualism changes the character of the other elements in the problem, or the fact that an invention like printing, or representative government, or civil service examinations, or the utilitarian philosophy, may make it possible to provide greatly increased satisfaction both to socialist and individualist desires, complicates the question, but does not alter its quantitative character. The essential point is that in every case in which a political thinker is able to adopt what Professor Marshall calls the quantitative method of reasoning, his vocabulary and method, instead of constantly suggesting a false simplicity, warn him that every individual instance with which he deals is different from any other, that any effect is a function of many variable causes, and, therefore, that no estimate of the result of any act can be accurate unless all its conditions and their relative importance are taken into account.

But how far are such quantitative methods possible when a statesman is dealing, neither with an obviously quantitative problem, like the building of halls or schools, nor with an attempt to give quantitative meaning to abstract terms like socialism or individualism, but with the enormous complexity of responsible legislation?

In approaching this question we shall be helped if we keep before us a description of the way in which some one statesman has, in fact, thought of a great constitutional problem.

Take, for instance, the indications which Mr. Morley gives of the thinking done by Gladstone on Home Rule during the autumn and winter of 1885-1886. Gladstone, we are told, had already, for many years past, pondered anxiously at intervals about Ireland, and now he describes himself as "thinking incessantly about the matter" (vol. iii. p. 268), and "preparing myself by study and reflection" (p. 273).

He has first to consider the state of feeling in England and Ireland, and to calculate to what extent and under what influences it may be expected to change. As to English feeling, "what I expect," he says, "is a healthy slow fermentation in many minds working towards the final product" (p. 261). The Irish desire for self-government, on the other hand, will not change, and must be taken, within the time limit of his problem, as "fixed" (p. 240). In both England and Ireland, however, he believes that "mutual attachment" may grow (p. 292).

Before making up his mind in favor of some kind of Home Rule, he examines every thinkable alternative, especially the development of Irish county government, or a federal arrangement in which all three of the united kingdoms would be concerned. Here and there he finds suggestions in the history of Austria-Hungary, of Norway and Sweden, or of the "colonial type" of government. Nearly every day he reads Burke, and exclaims "what a magazine of wisdom on Ireland and America" (p. 280). He gets much help from "a chapter on semi-sovereign assemblies in Dicey's *Law of the Constitution*" (p. 280). He tries to see the question from fresh points of view in intimate personal discussions, and by imagining what "the civilized world" (p. 225) will think. As he gets nearer to his subject, he has definite statistical reports made for him by "Welby and Hamilton on the figures" (p. 306), has "stiff conclaves about finance and land" (p. 298), and nearly comes to a final split with Parnell on the question whether the Irish contribution to imperial taxation shall be a fifteenth or a twentieth.

Time and persons are important factors in his calculation. If Lord Salisbury will consent to introduce some measure of Irish self-government, the problem will be fundamentally altered, and the same will happen if the general election produces a Liberal majority independent of both Irish and Conservatives; and Mr. Morley describes as underlying all his calculations "the irresistible attraction for him of all the grand and eternal commonplaces of liberty and self-government" (p. 260).

It is not likely that Mr. Morley's narrative touches on more than a fraction of the questions which must have been in Gladstone's mind during those months of incessant thought. No mention is made, for instance, of religion, or of the military position, or of the permanent possibility of enforcing the proposed restrictions on self-government. But enough is given to show the complexity of political thought at that stage when a statesman, still uncommitted, is considering what will be the effect of a new political departure.

What then was the logical process by which Gladstone's final decision was arrived at?

Did he for instance deal with a succession of simple problems or with one complex problem? It is, I think, clear that from time to time isolated and comparatively simple traits of reasoning were followed up; but it is also clear that Gladstone's main effort of thought was involved in the process of coordinating all the laboriously collected contents of his mind onto the whole problem. This is emphasized by a quotation in which Mr. Morley, who was closely associated with Gladstone's intellectual toil during this period, indicates his own recollection.

"Historians," he quotes from Professor Gardiner, "coolly dissect a man's thoughts as they please; and label them like specimens in a naturalist's cabinet. Such a thing, they argue, was done for mere personal aggrandizement; such a thing for national objects; such a thing from high religious motives. In real life we may be sure it was not so" (p. 277).

And it is clear that in spite of the ease and delight with which Gladstone's mind moved among "the eternal commonplaces of liberty and self-government," he is seeking throughout for a quantitative solution. "Home Rule" is no simple entity for him. He realizes that the number of possible schemes for Irish government is infinite, and he attempts to make at every point in his own scheme a delicate adjustment between many varying forces.

A large part of this work of complex coordination was apparently in Mr. Gladstone's case unconscious. Throughout the chapters one has the feeling—which anyone who has had to make less important political decisions can parallel from his own experience—that Gladstone was waiting for indications of a solution to appear in his mind. He was conscious of his effort, conscious also that his effort was being directed simultaneously toward many different considerations, but largely unconscious of the actual process of inference, which went on perhaps more rapidly when he was asleep, or thinking of something else, than when he was awake and attentive. A phrase of Mr. Morley's indicates a feeling with which every politician is familiar. "The reader," he says, "knows in what direction the main current of Mr. Gladstone's thought must have been setting" (p. 236).

That is to say, we are watching an operation rather of art than of science, of long experience and trained faculty rather than of conscious method.

But the history of human progress consists in the gradual and partial substitution of science for art, of the power over nature acquired in youth by study, for that which comes in late middle age as the half-conscious result of experience. Our problem therefore involves the further question, whether those forms of political thought which correspond to the complexity of nature are teachable or not? At present they are not often taught. In every generation thousands of young men and women are attracted to politics because their intellects are keener, and their sympathies wider than those of their fellows. They become followers of liberalism or imperialism, of scientific socialism or the rights of men or women. To them, at first, liberalism and the empire, rights and principles, are real and simple things. Or, like Shelley, they see in the whole human race an infinite repetition of uniform individuals, the "millions on millions" who "wait, firm, rapid, and elate."

About all these things they argue by the old a priori methods which we have inherited with our political language. But after a time a sense of unreality grows upon them. Knowledge of the complex and difficult world forces itself into their minds. Like the old Chartists with whom I once spent an evening, they tell you that their politics have been "all talk"—all words—and there are few among them, except those to whom politics has become a profession or a career, who hold on until through weariness and disappointment they learn new confidence from new knowledge. Most men, after the first disappointment, fall back on habit or party spirit for their political opinions and actions. Having ceased to think of their unknown fellow citizens as uniform repetitions of a simple type, they cease to think of them at all; and content themselves with using party phrases about the mass of mankind, and realizing the individual existence of their casual neighbours. . . .

If this constantly repeated disappointment is to cease, quantitative method must spread in politics and must transform the vocabulary and the associations of that mental world into which the young politician enters. Fortunately such a change seems at least to be beginning. Every year larger and more exact collections of detailed political facts are being accumulated; and collections of detailed facts, if they are to be used at all in political reasoning, must be used quantitatively. The intellectual work of preparing legislation, whether carried on by permanent officials or Royal Commissions or Cabinet Ministers takes every year a more quantitative and a less qualitative form.

Compare for instance the methods of the present commission on the Poor Law with those of the celebrated and extraordinarily able commission which drew up the new Poor Law in 1833-1834. The argument of the earlier commissioners' report runs on lines which it would be easy to put in a priori syllogistic form. All men seek pleasure and avoid pain. Society ought to secure that pain attaches to antisocial, and pleasure to social conduct. This may be done by making every man's livelihood and that of his children normally dependent upon his own exertions, by separating those destitute persons who cannot do work useful to the community from those who can, and by presenting these last with the alternative of voluntary effort or painful restriction. This leads to "a principle which we find universally admitted, even by those whose practice is at variance with it, that the situation [of the pauper] on the whole shall not be made really or apparently so eligible as the situation of the independent laborer of the lowest class."[4] The a priori argument is admirably illustrated by instances, reported by the sub-commissioners or given in evidence before the commission, indicating that laboring men will not exert themselves unless they are offered the alternative of starvation or rigorous confinement, though no attempt is made to estimate the proportion of the working population of England whose character and conduct is represented by each instance.

This a priori deduction, illustrated, but not proved by particular instances, is throughout so clear and so easily apprehended by the ordinary man that the revolutionary Bill of 1834, which affected all sorts of vested interests, passed the House of Commons by a majority of four to one and the House of Lords by a majority of six to one.

The Poor Law commission of 1905, on the other hand, though it contains many members trained in the traditions of 1834, is being driven, by the mere necessity of dealing with the mass of varied evidence before it, on to new lines. Instead of assuming half consciously that human energy is dependent solely on the working of the human will in the presence of the ideas of pleasure and

---

[4] *First Report of the Poor Law Commission,* 1834 (reprinted 1894), p. 187.

pain, the commissioners are forced to tabulate and consider innumerable quantitative observations relating to the very many
factors affecting the will of paupers and possible paupers. They
cannot, for instance, avoid the task of estimating the relative industrial effectiveness of health, which depends upon decent surroundings; of hope, which may be made possible by state provision for
old age; and of the imaginative range which is the result of education; and of comparing all these with the "purely economic" motive
created by ideas of future pleasure and pain.

The evidence before the commission is, that is to say, collected
not to illustrate general propositions otherwise established, but to
provide quantitative answers to quantitative questions; and instances
are in each case accumulated according to a well-known statistical
rule until the repetition of results shows that further accumulation
would be useless.

In 1834 it was enough, in dealing with the political machinery
of the Poor Law, to argue that, since all men desire their own
interest, the ratepayers would elect guardians who would, up to the
limit of their knowledge, advance the interests of the whole community; provided that electoral areas were created in which all
sectional interests were represented, and that voting power were
given to each ratepayer in proportion to his interest. It did not then
seem to matter much whether the areas chosen were new or old, or
whether the body elected had other duties or not.

In 1908, on the other hand, it is felt to be necessary to seek for
all the causes which are likely to influence the mind of the ratepayer or candidate during an election, and to estimate by such
evidence as is available their relative importance. It has to be considered, for instance, whether men vote best in areas where they
keep up habits of political action in connection with parliamentary
as well as municipal contests; and whether an election involving
other points besides Poor Law administration is more likely to
create interest among the electorate. If more than one election,
again, is held in a district in any year it may be found by the record of the percentage of votes that electoral enthusiasm diminishes
for each additional contest along a very rapidly descending curve.

The final decisions that will be taken either by the commission
or by Parliament on questions of administrative policy and electoral
machinery must therefore involve the balancing of all these and

many other considerations by an essentially quantitative process. The line, that is to say, which ultimately cuts the curves indicated by the evidence will allow less weight either to anxiety for the future as a motive for exertion, or to personal health as increasing personal efficiency, than would be given to either if it were the sole factor to be considered. There will be more "bureaucracy" than would be desirable if it were not for the need of economizing the energies of the elected representatives, and less bureaucracy than there would be if it were not desirable to retain popular sympathy and consent. Throughout the argument the population of England will be looked upon not (as John Stuart Mill would have said) "on the average or en masse," but as consisting individuals who can be arranged in "polygons of variation" according to their nervous and physical strength, their "character" and the degree to which ideas of the future are likely to affect their present conduct.

Meanwhile the public which will discuss the report has changed since 1834. Newspaper writers, in discussing the problem of destitution, tend now to use, not general terms applied to whole social classes like the "poor," "the working class," or "the lower orders," but terms expressing quantitative estimates of individual variations, like "the submerged tenth," or the "unemployable"; while every newspaper reader is fairly familiar with the figures in the Board of Trade monthly returns which record seasonal and periodical variations of actual unemployment among trade unionists.

One could give many other instances of this beginning of a tendency in political thinking, to change from qualitative to quantitative forms of argument. But perhaps it will be sufficient to give one relating to international politics. Sixty years ago sovereignty was a simple question of quality. Austin had demonstrated that there must be a sovereign everywhere, and that sovereignty, whether in the hands of an autocracy or a republic, must be absolute. But the congress which in 1885 sat at Berlin to prevent the partition of Africa from causing a series of European wars as long as those caused by the partition of America, was compelled by the complexity of the problems before it to approach the question of sovereignty on quantitative lines. Since 1885 therefore everyone has become familiar with the terms then invented to express gradations of sovereignty: "effective occupation," "hinterland," "sphere of influence"—to which the Algeçiras Conference has perhaps added a lowest grade, "sphere of legitimate aspiration." It is already as unimportant to decide whether a given region is British territory or not, as it is to decide whether a bar containing a certain percentage of carbon should be called iron or steel.

Even in thinking of the smallest subdivisions of observed political fact some men escape the temptation to ignore individual differences. I remember that the man who has perhaps done more than anyone else in England to make a statistical basis for industrial legislation possible, once told me that he had been spending the whole day in classifying under a few heads thousands of "railway accidents," every one of which differed in its circumstances from any other; and that he felt like the bewildered porter in *Punch*, who had to arrange the subtleties of nature according to the unsubtle tariff schedule of his company. "Cats," he quoted the porter as saying, "is dogs, and guinea pigs is dogs, but this 'ere tortoise is a hinsect."

But it must constantly be remembered that quantitative thinking does not necessarily or even generally mean thinking in terms of numerical statistics. Number, which obliterates all distinction between the units numbered, is not the only, nor always even the most exact means of representing quantitative facts. A picture, for instance, may be sometimes nearer to quantitative truth, more easily remembered and more useful for purposes of argument and verification than a row of figures. The most exact quantitative political document that I ever saw was a set of photographs of all the women admitted into an inebriate home. The photographs demonstrated, more precisely than any record of approximate measurements could have done, the varying facts of physical and nervous structure. It would have been easily possible for a committee of medical men to have arranged the photographs in a series of increasing abnormality, and to have indicated the photograph of the "marginal" woman in whose case, after allowing for considerations of expense, and for the desirability of encouraging individual responsibility, the state should undertake temporary or permanent control. And the record was one which no one who had ever seen it could forget.

The political thinker has indeed sometimes to imitate the cabinetmaker, who discards his most finely divided numerical rule for some kinds of specially delicate work, and trusts to his sense of touch for a quantitative estimation. The most exact estimation possible of a political problem may have been contrived when a group of men, differing in origin, education and mental type, first establish an approximate agreement as to the probable results of a series of possible political alternatives involving, say, increasing or decreasing state interference, and then discover the point where their "liking" turns into "disliking." Man is the measure of man, and he may still be using a quantitative process even though he chooses in each case that method of measurement which is least affected by the imperfection of his powers. But it is just in the cases where numerical calculation is impossible or unsuitable that the politician is likely to get most help by using consciously quantitative conceptions.

An objection has been urged against the adoption of political reasoning either implicitly or explicitly quantitative, that it involves the balancing against each other of things essentially disparate. How is one, it is asked, to balance the marginal unit of national honor involved in the continuance of a war with that marginal unit of extra taxation which is supposed to be its exact equivalent? How is one to balance the final sovereign on the endowment of science with the final sovereign spent on a monument to a deceased scientist, or on the final detail in a scheme of old age pensions? The obvious answer is that statesmen have to act, and that whoever acts does somehow balance all the alternatives which are before him. The chancellor of the exchequer in his annual allocation of grants and remissions of taxation balances no stranger things than does the private citizen, who, having a pound or two to spend at Christmas, decides between subscribing to a Chinese mission and providing a revolving hatch between his kitchen and his dining room.

A more serious objection is that we ought not to allow ourselves to think quantitatively in politics, that to do so fritters away the plain consideration of principle. "Logical principles" may be only an inadequate representation of the subtlety of nature, but to abandon them is, it is contended, to become a mere opportunist.

In the minds of these objectors the only alternative to deductive thought from simple principles seems to be the attitude of Prince Bülow, in his speech in the Reichstag on universal suffrage. He is reported to have said:

Only the most doctrinaire socialists still regarded universal and direct suffrage as a fetish and as an infallible dogma. For his own part he was no worshipper of idols, and he did not believe in political dogmas. The welfare and the liberty of a country did not depend either in whole or in part upon the form of its constitution or of its franchise. Herr Bebel had once said that on the whole he preferred English conditions even to conditions in France. But in England the franchise was not universal, equal, and direct. Could it be said that Mecklenburg, which had no popular suffrage at all, was governed worse than Haiti, of which the world had lately such strange news, although Haiti could boast of possessing universal suffrage?[5]

But what Prince Bülow's speech showed, was that he was either deliberately parodying a style of scholastic reasoning with which he did not agree, or he was incapable of grasping the first conception of quantitative political thought. If the "dogma" of universal suffrage means the assertion that all men who have votes are thereby made identical with each other in all respects, and that universal suffrage is the one condition of good government, then, and then only, is his attack on it valid. If, however, the desire for universal suffrage is based on the belief that a wide extension of political power is one of the most important elements in the conditions of good government—racial aptitude, ministerial responsibility, and the like, being other elements—then the speech is absolutely meaningless.

But Prince Bülow was making a parliamentary speech, and in parliamentary oratory that change from qualitative to quantitative method which has so deeply affected the procedure of conferences and commissions has not yet made much progress. In a "full-dress" debate even those speeches which move us most often recall Mr. Gladstone, in whose mind, as soon as he stood up to speak, his Eton and Oxford training in words always contended with his experience of things, and who never made it quite clear whether the "grand and eternal commonplaces of liberty and self-government" meant that certain elements must be of great and permanent importance in every problem of church and state, or that an a priori solution of all political problems could be deduced by all good men from absolute and authoritative laws.

[5] *Times* (London), March 27, 1908.

18. The natural history of the soul

Sigmund Freud, "The Origin and Development of Psychoanalysis" (1910)[1]

Sigmund Freud is sometimes linked to an irrationalism akin to that of the symbolist poets; but in fact the Austrian physician was a thoroughly naturalistic scientist who explained the deeper workings of the human psyche in the language of physical forces and laws. His work began in 1880 at the peak of scientific naturalism's success and popularity, and he shared with the naturalists a basically pessimistic and determinist outlook; as a physician he hoped only to be able to moderate slightly the ludicrous tragedy of life. It seems best to place him in this book under the heading of naturalism, but at the end of that section.

Freud saw himself as standing in the line of Copernicus, Newton, and Darwin, extending their methods to the hitherto mysterious inner world. Novelists soon learned to apply his ideas to literature, as teachers did to education, and many others in their various fields. Freud had supplied them with a seemingly lucid guide to the mind's unconscious, or subconscious, features, including dreams and fantasies. In the following lecture he explains how, as a practicing physician, he came to his basic conclusions about the mechanisms of psychic disturbance.

At about the same time at which Breuer[2] was carrying on the "talking cure" with his patient, the great Charcot in Paris had begun the researches into hysterical patients at the Salpêtrière which were to lead to a new understanding of the disease. There was no possibility of his findings being known in Vienna at that time. But when, some ten years later, Breuer and I published our "Preliminary Communication" on the psychical mechanism of

---

[1] Freud's lectures on "The Origin and Development of Psychoanalysis," delivered at Clark University in 1910, and translated by Harry W. Chase, were printed in J.S. Van Teslar (ed.), *An Outline of Psychoanalysis* (New York: Random House, Modern Library, 1925); the lectures by themselves are available in *The Origin and Development of Psychoanalysis* (Chicago: Regnery 1960); Freud's works, the Standard Edition, translated and edited by James Strachey, are available from W.W. Norton, New York, in the Norton Library. The following translation is by Harry W. Chase.

[2] Dr. Joseph Breuer, a fellow Viennese physician of Freud's, who in 1880–1882 stumbled upon the method of curing mental disturbances by unearthing a buried memory and having the patient "talk it out." In the first lecture, preceding this one, Freud had described this case (Ed.).

hysterical phenomena [1893*a*], we were completely under the spell of Charcot's researches. We regarded the pathogenic experiences of our patients as psychical traumas, and equated them with the somatic traumas whose influence on hysterical paralyses had been established by Charcot; and Breuer's hypothesis of hypnoid states was itself nothing but a reflection of the fact that Charcot had reproduced those traumatic paralyses artificially under hypnosis.

The great French observer, whose pupil I became in 1885–1886, was not himself inclined to adopt a psychological outlook. It was his pupil, Pierre Janet, who first attempted a deeper approach to the peculiar psychical processes present in hysteria, and we followed his example when we took the splitting of the mind and dissociation of the personality as the center of our position. You will find in Janet a theory of hysteria which takes into account the prevailing views in France on the part played by heredity and degeneracy. According to him, hysteria is a form of degenerate modification of the nervous system, which shows itself in an innate weakness in the power of psychical synthesis. Hysterical patients, he believes, are inherently incapable of holding together the multiplicity of mental processes into a unity, and hence arises the tendency to mental dissociation. If I may be allowed to draw a homely but clear analogy, Janet's hysterical patient reminds one of a feeble woman who has gone out shopping and is now returning home laden with a multitude of parcels and boxes. She cannot contain the whole heap of them with her two arms and ten fingers. So first of all one object slips from her grasp; and when she stoops to pick it up, another one escapes her in its place, and so on. This supposed mental weakness of hysterical patients is not confirmed when we find that, alongside these phenomena of diminished capacity, examples are also to be observed of a partial increase in efficiency, as though by way of compensation. At the time when Breuer's patient had forgotten her mother tongue and every other language but English, her grasp of English reached such heights that, if she was handed a German book, she was able straightway to read out a correct and fluent translation of it.

When, later on, I set about continuing on my own account the investigations that had been begun by Breuer, I soon arrived at another view of the origin of hysterical dissociation (the splitting of consciousness). A divergence of this kind, which was to be decisive for everything that followed, was inevitable, since I did not start out, like Janet, from laboratory experiments, but with therapeutic aims in mind.

I was driven forward above all by practical necessity. The cathartic procedure, as carried out by Breuer, presupposed putting the patient into a state of deep hypnosis; for it was only in a state of hypnosis that he attained a knowledge of the pathogenic connections which escaped him in his normal state. But I soon came to dislike hypnosis, for it was a tempermental and, one might almost say, a mystical ally. When I found that, in spite of all my efforts, I could not succeed in bringing more than a fraction of my patients into a hypnotic state, I determined to give up hypnosis and to make the cathartic procedure independent of it. Since I was not able at will to alter the mental state of the majority of my patients, I set about working with them in their *normal* state. At first, I must confess, this seemed a senseless and hopeless undertaking. I was set the task of learning from the patient something that I did not know and that he did not know himself. How could one hope to elicit it? But there came to my help a recollection of a most remarkable and instructive experiment which I had witnessed when I was with Bernheim at Nancy [in 1889]. Bernheim showed us that people whom he had put into a state of hypnotic somnambulism, and who had had all kinds of experiences while they were in that state, only *appeared* to have lost the memory of what they had experienced during somnambulism; it was possible to revive these memories in their normal state. It was true that, when he questioned them about their somnambulistic experiences, they began by maintaining that they knew nothing about them; but if he refused to give way, and insisted, and assured them that they *did* know about them, the forgotten experiences always reappeared.

So I did the same thing with my patients. When I reached a point with them at which they maintained that they knew nothing more, I assured them that they *did* know it all the same, and that they had only to say it; and I ventured to declare that the right memory would occur to them at the moment at which I laid my hand on their forehead. In that way I succeeded, without using hypnosis, in obtaining from the patients whatever was required for establishing the connection between the pathogenic scenes they had forgotten and the symptoms left over from those scenes. But it was a laborious procedure, and in the long run an exhausting one; and it was unsuited to serve as a permanent technique.

I did not abandon it, however, before the observations I made during my use of it afforded me decisive evidence. I found confirmation of the fact that the forgotten memories were not lost. They were in the patient's possession and were ready to emerge in association to what was still known by him; but there was some force that prevented them from becoming conscious and compelled them to remain unconscious. The existence of this force could be assumed with certainty, since one became aware of an effort corresponding to it if, in opposition to it, one tried to introduce the unconscious memories into the patient's consciousness. The force which was maintaining the pathological condition became apparent in the form of *resistance* on the part of the patient.

It was on this idea of resistance, then, that I based my view of the course of psychical events in hysteria. In order to effect a recovery, it had proved necessary to remove these resistances. Starting out from the mechanism of cure, it now became possible to construct quite definite ideas of the origin of the illness. The same forces which, in the form of resistance, were now offering opposition to the forgotten material's being made conscious, must formerly have brought about the forgetting and must have pushed the pathogenic experiences in question out of consciousness. I gave the name of *"repression"* to this hypothetical process, and I considered that it was proved by the undeniable existence of resistance.

The further question could then be raised concerning what these forces were and what the determinants were of the repression in which we now recognized the pathogenic mechanism of hysteria. A comparative study of the pathogenic situations which we had come to know through the cathartic procedure made it possible to answer this question. All these experiences had involved the emergence of a wishful impulse which was in sharp contrast to the subject's other wishes and which proved incompatible with the ethical and aesthetic standards of his personality. There had been a short conflict, and the end of this internal struggle was that the idea which had appeared before consciousness as the vehicle of this irreconcilable wish fell a victim to repression, was pushed out of consciousness with all its attached memories, and was forgotten.

Thus the incompatibility of the wish in question with the patient's ego was the motive for the repression; the subject's ethical and other standards were the repressing forces. An acceptance of the incompatiable wishful impulse or a prolongation of the conflict would have produced a high degree of discomfort; this discomfort was avoided by means of repression, which was thus revealed as one of the devices serving to protect the mental personality.

To take the place of a number of instances, I will relate a single one of my cases, in which the determinants and advantages of repression are sufficiently evident. For my present purpose I shall have once again to abridge the case history and omit some important underlying material. The patient was a girl,[3] who had lost her beloved father after she had taken a share in nursing him—a situation analogous to that of Breuer's patient. Soon afterwards her elder sister married, and her new brother-in-law aroused in her a peculiar feeling of sympathy which was easily masked under a disguise of family affection. Not long afterwards her sister fell ill and died, in the absence of the patient and her mother. They were summoned in all haste without being given any definite information of the tragic event. When the girl reached the bedside of her dead sister, there came to her for a brief moment an idea that might be expressed in these words: "Now he is free and can marry me." We may assume with certainty that this idea, which betrayed to her consciousness the intense love for her brother-in-law of which she had not herself been conscious, was surrendered to repression a moment later, owing to the revolt of her feelings. The girl fell ill with severe hysterical symptoms; and while she was under my treatment it turned out that she had completely forgotten the scene by her sister's bedside and the odious egoistic impulse that had emerged in her. She remembered it during the treatment and reproduced the pathogenic moment with signs of the most violent emotion, and, as a result of the treatment, she became healthy once more.

Perhaps I may give you a more vivid picture of repression and of its necessary relation to resistance, by a rough analogy derived from our actual situation at the present moment. Let us suppose that in this lecture room and among this audience, whose exemplary quiet and attentiveness I cannot sufficiently commend, there is

[3] [This is the case of Fräulein Elisabeth von R., the fifth of the case histories fully reported in *Studies on Hysteria*, Standard Ed., 2, 135 ff.]

nevertheless someone who is causing a disturbance and whose ill-mannered laughter, chattering and shuffling with his feet are distracting my attention from my task. I have to announce that I cannot proceed with my lecture; and thereupon three or four of you who are strong men stand up and, after a short struggle, put the interrupter outside the door. So now he is "repressed," and I can continue my lecture. But in order that the interruption shall not be repeated, in case the individual who has been expelled should try to enter the room once more, the gentlemen who have put my will into effect place their chairs up against the door and thus establish a "resistance" after the repression has been accomplished. If you will now translate the two localities concerned into psychical terms as the "conscious" and the "unconscious," you will have before you a fairly good picture of the process of repression.

You will now see in what it is that the difference lies between our view and Janet's. We do not derive the psychical splitting from an innate incapacity for synthesis on the part of the mental apparatus; we explain it dynamically, from the conflict of opposing mental forces and recognize it as the outcome of an active struggling on the part of the two psychical groupings against each other. But our view gives rise to a large number of fresh problems. Situations of mental conflict are, of course, exceedingly common; efforts by the ego to ward off painful memories are quite regularly to be observed without their producing the result of a mental split. The reflection cannot be escaped that further determinants must be present if the conflict is to lead to dissociation. I will also readily grant you that the hypothesis of repression leaves us not at the end but at the beginning of a psychological theory. We can only go forward step by step however, and complete knowledge must await the results of further and deeper researches.

Nor is it advisable to attempt to explain the case of Breuer's patient from the point of view of repression. That case history is not suited to this purpose, because its findings were reached with the help of hypnotic influence. It is only if you exclude hypnosis that you can observe resistances and repressions and form an adequate idea of the truly pathogenic course of events. Hypnosis conceals the resistance and renders a certain area of the mind accessible; but, as against this, it builds up the resistance at the frontiers of this area into a wall that makes everything beyond it inaccessible.

Our most valuable lesson from Breuer's observation was what it proved concerning the relation between symptoms and pathogenic experiences or psychical traumas, and we must not omit now to consider these discoveries from the standpoint of the theory of repression. At first sight it really seems impossible to trace a path from repression to the formation of symptoms. Instead of giving a complicated theoretical account, I will return here to the analogy which I employed earlier for my explanation of repression. If you come to think of it, the removal of the interrupter and the posting of the guardians at the door may not mean the end of the story. It may very well be that the individual who has been expelled, and who has now become embittered and reckless, will cause us further trouble. It is true that he is no longer among us; we are free from his presence, from his insulting laughter and his *sotto voce* comments. But in some respects, nevertheless, the repression has been unsuccessful; for now he is making an intolerable exhibition of himself outside the room, and his shouting and banging on the door with his fists interfere with my lecture even more than his bad behavior did before. In these circumstances we could not fail to be delighted if our respected president, Dr. Stanley Hall, should be willing to assume the role of mediator and peacemaker. He would have a talk with the unruly person outside and would then come to us with a request that he should be readmitted after all: he himself would guarantee that the man would now behave better. On Dr. Hall's authority we decide to lift the repression, and peace and quiet are restored. This presents what is really no bad picture of the physician's task in the psychoanalytic treatment of the neuroses.

To put the matter more directly. The investigation of hysterical patients and of other neurotics leads us to the conclusion that their repression of the idea to which the intolerable wish is attached has been a *failure*. It is true that they have driven it out of consciousness and out of memory and have apparently saved themselves a large amount of unpleasure. *But the repressed wishful impulse continues to exist in the unconscious.* It is on the lookout for an opportunity of being activated, and when that happens it succeeds in sending into consciousness a disguised and unrecognizable *substitute* for what had been repressed, and to this there soon become attached the same feelings of unpleasure which it was hoped had been saved by the repression. This substitute for the repressed idea—the *symptom*—is proof against further attacks from the defensive ego; and in place of the short conflict an ailment now appears which is not brought to an end by the passage of time. Alongside the indication of distortion in the symptom, we can trace in it the remains of some kind of indirect resemblance to the idea that was originally repressed. The paths along which the substitution was effected can be traced in the course of the patient's psychoanalytic treatment; and in order to bring about recovery, the symptom must be led back along the same paths and once more turned into the repressed idea. If what was repressed is brought back again into conscious mental activity—a process which presupposes the overcoming of considerable resistances—the resulting psychical conflict, which the patient had tried to avoid, can, under the physician's guidance, reach a better outcome than was offered by repression. There are a number of such opportune solutions, which may bring the conflict and the neurosis to a happy end, and which may in certain instances be combined. The patient's personality may be convinced that it has been wrong in rejecting the pathogenic wish and may be led into accepting it wholly or in part; or the wish itself may be directed to a higher and consequently unobjectionable aim (this is what we call its "sublimation"); or the rejection of the wish may be recognized as a justifiable one, but the automatic and therefore inefficient mechanism of repression may be replaced by a condemning judgment with the help of the highest human mental functions and thus conscious control of the wish is attained.

You must forgive me if I have not succeeded in giving you a more clearly intelligible account of these basic positions adopted by the method of treatment that is now described as "psychoanalysis." The difficulties have not lain only in the novelty of the subject. The nature of the incompatible wishes which, in spite of repression, succeed in making their existence in the unconscious perceptible, and the subjective and constitutional determinants which must be present in anyone before a failure of repression can occur and a substitute or symptom be formed—on all this I shall have more light to throw in some of my later observations.

III. *Symbolism*

❦❦❦❦❦❦❦❦❦❦❦❦❦❦

The mood of the symbolist movement is startlingly different from that of naturalism. The writer is no longer considered a scientist but a seer, a mystic. He does not seek to describe the external world with clinical exatitude, but to grope among the shadows of the mind; Rimbaud says that the poet must deliberately derange his senses. He writes verses that, strictly speaking, have little if any meaning, but which drug and enchant the mind. Vast sociological treatises give place to small gems of verse. Poetry, the symbolists believed, is not meant to convey abstract thought. It should be "pure," in the sense that it should exist in its own right, not for some extrinsic purpose such as communicating knowledge or teaching a moral. It should not be vulgarized by contact with the masses, for only a few rare spirits can be poets. Yet from its mysterious visions may come images that will change the world. In a society grown corrupt and degenerate the poet must draw apart and proclaim his defiance of conventions, cultivating his own unique poetic sensibility.

19. The poet as seer

(a) ". . . a long, intensive, and reasoned disordering of all the senses." Arthur Rimbaud, in a letter to Paul Demeny, May 15, 1876[1]

[1] Rimbaud's "Illuminations," together with the letters, "Season in Hell," and "The Drunken Boat," have been trans. by Louise Varèse (New York; New Directions, 1940, 1952). The translation which follows is by the editor, who also made the translation of "The Drunken Boat."

Rimbaud was the archetypical *poète maudit* of the nineteenth century; his abnormal life and utter alienation from society made him the patron saint of all modern bohemians and aesthetic rebels. He was a great poet, revolutionary less in his belief that the poet is a seer who can invoke magical phrases (a Romantic notion) than in his willingness to pursue the search for poetic symbols through a deliberate derangement of the senses.

THE FIRST study for the man who wants to be a poet is to know himself, completely. He must search for his soul, scrutinize it, learn to know it. As soon as he knows it, he must cultivate it. . . . He must, I say, be a *seer;* he must make himself a seer.

The poet makes himself a seer by a long, intensive, and reasoned disordering of all the senses. Every kind of love, of suffering, of madness; he looks within himself, he devours all the poisons in him, keeping only their essences. Unspeakable torture in which he needs all his faith and superhuman strength, the great criminal, the great diseased, the utterly damned, and the supreme wise man! For he reaches the unknown! Since he has cultivated his soul, richer to begin with than any of the others! He reaches the unknown; and even if at last, half demented, he ceases to understand his visions, he has seen them! Let him die in his leap into these unutterable, numberless things; other accursed poets will come and will begin at the boundaries where he has left off. . . .

So, then, the poet is truly a stealer of fire.

Humanity is his responsibility, the animals too; he must take care that his inventions can be smelled, felt, heard. If what he brings back has form, he gives it form; if it is without form, he has made it so. A language must be discovered; indeed, every word being an idea, the day of a universal language will come! One has to be an academician—deader than a fossil—to finish a dictionary of any language. . . .

These poets are going to exist! When the eternal servitude of woman shall have ended, when she will be able to exist independently, when man—hitherto abominable—shall have given her freedom, she too will be a poet. Woman will discover the unknown. Will her world be different from ours? She will discover strange, unfathomable things, repulsive, delicious. We shall receive them, we shall understand them. . . .

LE BATEAU IVRE

Comme je descendais des Fleuves impassibles,
Je ne me sentis plus guidé par les haleurs:
Des Peaux-Rouges criards les avaient pris pour cibles,
Les ayant cloués nus aux poteaux de couleurs.

J'étais insoucieux de tous les équipages,
Porteur de blés flamands ou de cotons anglais.
Quand avec mes haleurs ont fini ces tapages,
Les Fleuves m'ont laissé descendre où je voulais.

Dan les clapotements furieux des marées,
Moi, l'autre hiver, plus sourd que les cerveaux d'enfants,
Je courus! Et les Péninsules démarrées
N'ont pas subi tohu-bohus plus triomphants.

La tempête a béni mes éveils maritimes.
Plus léger qu'un bouchon j'ai danse sur les flots
Qu'on appelle rouleurs éternels de victimes,
Dix nuits, sans regretter l'œil niais des falots!

Plus douce qu'aux enfants la chair des pommes sures,
L'eau verte pénétra ma coque de sapin
Et des taches de vins bleus et des vomissures
Me lava, dispersant gouvernail et grappin.

Et des lors, je me suis baigné dans le Poème
De la Mer, infusé d'astres et lactescent,
Dévorant les azurs verts; où, flottaison blême
Et ravie, un noyé pensif parfois descend;

Où, teignant tout à coup les bleuités, délires
Et rythmes lents sous les rutilements du jour,
Plus fortes que l'alcool, plus vastes que nos lyres,
Fermentent les rousseurs amères de l'amour!

Je sais les cieux crevant en éclairs, et les trombes
Et les ressacs et les courants: je sais le soir,
L'Aube exaltée ainsi qu'un peuple de colombes,
Et j'ai vu quelquefois ce que l'homme a cru voir.

THE DRUNKEN BOAT

As I floated down impassible rivers,
I felt the boatmen no longer guiding me:
After them came redskins who with war cries
Nailed them naked to the painted poles.

I was oblivious to the crew,
I who bore Flemish wheat and English cotton.
When the racket was finished with my boatmen,
The waters let me drift my own free way.

In the tide's furious pounding,
I, the other winter, emptier than children's minds,
I sailed! And the unmoored peninsulas
Have not suffered more triumphant turmoils.

The tempest blessed my maritime watches.
Lighter than a cork I danced on the waves,
Those eternal rollers of victims,
Ten nights, without regretting the lantern-foolish eye!

Sweeter than the bite of sour apples to a child,
The green water seeped through my wooden hull,
Rinsed me of blue wine stains and vomit,
Broke apart grappling iron and rudder.

And then I bathed myself in the poetry
Of the star-sprayed milk-white sea,
Devouring the azure greens; where, pale
And ravished, a pensive drowned one sometimes floats;

Where, suddenly staining the blueness, frenzies
And slow rhythms in the blazing of day,
Stronger than alcohol, vaster than our lyres,
The russett bitterness of love ferments.

I know the skies bursting into light, the jets of water
The breakers and the current; I know the night,
The dawn exalted like a flock of doves,
And sometimes I have seen what men have thought they saw!

J'ai vu le soleil bas, taché d'horreurs mystiques,
Illuminant de longs figements violets,
Pareils à des acteurs de drames très antiques
Les flots roulant au loin leurs frissons de volets!

J'ai rêvé la nuit verte aux neiges éblouies,
Baiser montant aux yeux des mers avec lenteurs,
La circulation des sèves inouïes,
Et l'éveil jaune et bleu des phosphores chanteurs!

J'ai suivi, des mois pleins, pareille aux vacheries
Hystériques, la houle à l'assaut des récifs.
Sans songer que les pieds lumineux des Maries
Pussent forcer le mufle aux Océans poussifs!

J'ai heurté, savez-vous, d'incroyables Florides
Mêlant aux fleurs des yeux de panthères à peaux
D'hommes! Des arcs-en-ciel tendus comme des brides
Sous l'horizon des mers, à de glauques troupeaux!

J'ai vu fermenter les marais énormes, nasses
Où pourrit dans les joncs tout un Léviathan!
Des écroulements d'eaux au milieu des bonaces,
Et les lointains vers les gouffres cataractant!

Glaciers, soleils d'argent, flots nacreux, cieux de braises,
Echouages hideux au fond des golfes bruns
Où les serpents géants dévorés des punaises
Choient, des arbres tordus, avec de noirs parfums!

J'aurais voulu montrer aux enfants ces dorades
Du flot bleu, ces poissons d'or, ces poissons chantants.
—Des écumes de fleurs ont bercé mes dérades
Et d'ineffables vents m'ont ailé par instants.

Parfois, martyr lassè de pôles et des zones,
La mer dont le sanglot faisait mon roulis doux
Montait vers moi ses fleurs d'ombre aux ventouses jaunes
Et je restais, ainsi qu'une femme à genoux . . .

Presque île, ballottant sur mes bords les querelles
Et les fientes d'oiseaux clabaudeurs aux yeux blonds.
Et je voguais, lorsqu'à travers mes liens frêles
Des noyés descendaient dormir, à reculons! . . .

I have seen the sinking sun, stained with mystic horrors,
Illuminating, with long purple thickenings
Like actors in ancient tragedies,
The shuddering waves shivering in the distance.

I have dreamed of the green night bedazzled with snow,
A kiss climbing slowly to the eyes of the sea,
The flow of unforgettable sap,
And the yellow-blue waking of singing phosphorous!

Long months I have followed, like maddened cattle,
The surge assaulting the rocks
Without dreaming that the Virgin's luminous feet
Could force a muzzle on the panting ocean!

I have struck against the shores of incredible Floridas
Mixing panther-eyed flowers like human skins!
Rainbows stretched like bridle reins
Under the ocean's horizon, toward sea-green troops!

I have seen the fermenting of monstrous marshes,
Nets where a whole Leviathan rots in the reeds!
The waters collapsing in the middle of the calm,
And horizons plunging toward the abyss!

Glaciers, silver suns, waves of pearl, charcoal skies,
Hideous beaches at the bottom of brown gulfs
Where giant serpents devoured by vermin
Tumble from twisted trees with black perfumes!

I would have liked to show the children those dolphins
On the blue waves, those golden singing fish.
—The froth of flowers lulled my voyagings,
Ineffable winds gave me wings by the moment.

Sometimes, a martyr weary of poles and zones,
The sea whose sob sweetened my listing
Raised toward me its shadow-flowers with yellow cups
And I paused, like a girl on her knees . . .

Island, tossing upon me the quarrels
And excrement of twittering birds with blond eyes.
And I sailed on, when across my frail bands
Drowned men descended to sleep, heads downward!

Or moi, bateau perdu sous les cheveux des anses,
Jeté par l'ouragan das l'éther sans oiseau,
Moi dont les Monitors et les voiliers des Hanses
N'auraient pas repêché la carcasse ivre d'eau;

Libre, fumant, monté de brumes violettes,
Moi qui trouais le ciel rougeoyant comme un mur
Qui porte, confiture exquise aux bons poètes,
Des lichens de soleil et des morves d'azur;

Quin courais, taché de lunules électriques,
Planche folle, escorté des hippocampes noirs,
Quand les juillets faisaient crouler à coups de triques
Les cieux ultramarins aux ardents entonnoirs;

Moi qui tremblais, sentant geindre à cinquante lieues
Le rut des Béhémots et les Maelstroms épais,
Fileur éternel des immobilités bleues,
Je regrette l'Europe aux anciens parapets!

J'ai vu des archipels sidéraux! et des îles
Dont les cieux délirants sont ouverts au vogueur:
—Est-ce en ces nuits sans fond que tu dors et t'exiles,
Million d'oiseaux d'or, ô future Vigueur?—

Mais, vrai, j'ai trop pleuré! Les Aubes sont navrantes.
Toute lune est atroce et tout soleil amer:
L'âcre amour m'a gonflé de torpeurs enivrantes.
O que ma quille éclate! O que j'aille à la mer!

Si je désire une eau d'Europe, c'est la flache
Noire et froide où vers le crépuscule embaumé
Un enfant accroupi plein de tristesses, lâche
Un bateau frêle comme un papillon de mai.

Je ne puis plus, baigné de vos langueurs, ô lames,
Enlever leur sillage aux porteurs de cotons,
Ni traverser l'orgueil des drapeaux et des flammes,
Ni nager sous les yeux horribles des pontons.

Now I, a boat lost under the tresses of the bay,
Tossed by the hurricane into the birdless sky,
I whose carcass neither the monitors nor Hansa ships
Would have salvaged, drunken, from the waters;

Steaming, free, mounted on violet mists,
I who pierced the sky reddening like a wall
Which bears, delicious sweets for good poets,
Lichens in sunlight and azure phlegm,

Who sailed, tarnished by electric crescents,
A crazy plank, escorted by black hippos,
When the Julys with cudgel blows made fall
The ultramarine skies with their fiery funnels;

I who trembled when I felt the moan
Of a distant behemoth in rut, and dense maelstroms,
Eternal spinner of blue immobilities,
I long for the Europe of ancient parapets!

I have seen sidereal archipelagos! Islands
Whose delirious skies open to the wanderer:
—Is it in these bottomless nights that you sleep, exiled,
O million golden birds, O Power of the future?

True, I have wept too much! Dawn breaks your heart.
Each moon is cruel, bitter every sun:
Sharp love has made me drunk with torpors.
O let my keel burst! Let me go to sea!

If I desire any European water, it's the pond
Black and cold where toward the perfumed twilight
A sad and cowering child sets sail
A boat as frail as butterflies in May.

I can no longer, bathed in your languors, o waves,
Obliterate the wake of cotton-carriers
Nor cross the pride of flags and banners,
Nor swim past the hateful eyes of hulks.

(b) Charles Baudelaire. Two poems from *Les fleurs du mal* (1857)[1]

Though he lived a generation before the symbolists, Baudelaire was the one poet of the 1850's and 1860's they all admired and thought of as their teacher. Certainly in many ways this great poet anticipated the symbolist mood and he taught them many of their ideas about poetry.

Baudelaire most directly influenced the "Parnassians" who, led by Paul Verlaine and later Paul Valéry, demanded a "pure" poetry and rebelled against the long narrative or didactic verse of the Victorians. Poetry should not be an alternative means of discourse; it has nothing to do with prose; it must be purged of everything that smacks of prose, including argument, description, narrative. This strain has been a powerful one in modern poetry. It is not quite the same thing as symbolism, but it has blended with the latter to shape the modernist revolution in poetry. Baudelaire also contributed something directly to the symbolists by his tendency to avoid direct statement and use a symbol or an image to suggest broader meanings. The short poem, "pure" in the sense of being utterly unprosaic, tightly packed, perfectly chiseled, and using some striking piece of imagery to convey powerfully an idea or emotional state—such is Baudelairean verse. T. S. Eliot later wrote of Baudelaire that he "gave new possibilities to poetry in a new stock of imagery of contemporary life" and that "his verse and language is the nearest thing to a complete renovation that we have experienced." [2]

XXIV

Je t'adore à l'égal de la voûte nocturne,
O vase de tristesse, o grande taciturne,
Et t'aime d'autant plus, belle, qu tu me fuis,
Et que tu me parais, ornement de mes nuits,
Plus ironiquement accumuler les lieues
Qui séparent mes bras des immensités bleues.

Je m'avance à l'attaque, et je grimpe aux assauts,
Comme après un cadavre un choeur de vermisseaux,
Et je chéris, o'bête implacable et cruelle!
Jusqu'à cette froideur par où tu m'es plus belle!

[1] Baudelaire's *Les fleurs du mal* have often been translated since they appeared in 1857 The greatest translation at present is by Robert Lowell; this type of translation is possible only for a poet, and is great poetry in its own right. The two following translations, which are much more literal, are by the editor.

[2] From Eliot's Introduction to Baudelaire's *Intimate Journals* (1930), reprinted in T. S. Eliot, *Selected Prose*, ed. John Hayward (Harmondsworth: Penguin Books, 1953).

XXIV

I adore you as the vault of night,
O vessel of sadness, o great silent one,
I love you the more, fair one, because you flee from me,
And because you seem, adornment of my nights,
More ironically to heap up the leagues
Between my arms and the blue immensities.

I advance to the attack, and climb to the assault,
As worms in a chorus after a corpse,
And I cherish, o beast implacable and cruel,
Even that coldness which makes you more fair!

SPLEEN

Quand le ciel bas et lourd pèse comme un civercle
Sur l'esprit gémissant en proie aux longs ennuis,
Et que de l'horizon embrassant tout le cercle
Il nous verse un jour noir plus triste que les nuits;

Quand la terre est changée en un cachot humide,
Où l'Espérance, comme un chauve-souris,
S'en va battant les murs de son aile timide
Et se cognant la tête à des plafonds pourris;

Quand la pluie étalant ses immenses traînées
D'un vaste prison imite les barreaux,
Et qu'un peuple muet d'infames araignées
Vient tendre ses filets au fond de nos cerveaux,

Des cloches tout à coup sautent avec furie
Et lancent vers le ciel un affreux hurlement,
Ainsi que des esprits errants et sans patrie
Qui se mettent à geindre opiniâtrement.

—Et de longs corbillards, sans tambour ni musique,
Défilent lentement dans mon âme; l'Espoir,
Vaincu, pleure, et l'Angoisse atroce, despotique,
Sur mon crâne incliné plante son drapeau noir.

SPLEEN

When a low and heavy sky weighs like a cover
On the groaning soul prey of long boredom,
And encompassing the whole circle of the horizon
Presses upon us a black day more dismal than the nights;

When the earth is changed into a humid dungeon,
Where Hope, like a bat,
Flies beating the walls with her frail wing
And dashing her head against the rotten ceiling;

When the endless lines of falling rain
Resemble the bars of a vast prison,
And like a silent race of loathsome spiders
Come to stretch their threads over the depths of our brains,

Bells suddenly leap with fury
And hurl a frightful howling at the sky,
Like homeless and wandering spirits
Who begin to whine childishly.

—And long funeral processions, without drums or music,
File slowly through my soul; Hope,
Vanquished, weeps, and atrocious Anguish, despotically,
Plants her black flag upon my lowered head.

(c) Paul Verlaine

Verlaine above all others taught the poets that verse should be pure
music, purged of rhetoric and exposition.[1]

LA LUNE BLANCHE

La lune blanche
Luit dans les bois,
De chaque branche
Part une voix
Sous la ramée . . .

O bien-aimée.

[1] The translation is by Jane Lilienfeld.

L'étang reflète,
Profond miroir,
La silhouette
De saule noir
Où le vent pleure . . .

    Rêvons, c'est l'heure.

Un vaste et tendre
Apaisement
Semble descendre
Du firmament
Que l'astre irise . . .

    C'est l'heure exquise.

THE WHITE MOON

The white moon
Glistens in the wood
From each branch
Comes a voice
Under the bough . . .

    O my beloved.

The pond reflects,
Infinite mirror,
The silhouette
Of the black willow
In which the wind cries . . .

    Let us dream, it is the time.

A vast and tender
Peacefulness
Seems to fall
From the heavens
Which the stars make iridescent . . .

    It is the exquisite hour.

20. The mystery of poetry

(a) "Poets, become disdainful." Stéphane Mallarmé, "Art for All" (1862)[1]

Everything sacred, and which wishes to remain sacred, is enveloped in mystery. Religions shelter behind arcana unveiled only before the initiates. Art too has its mysteries.

Music offers an example. Open Mozart, Beethoven, or Wagner, glance at the first page and you are struck by the sight of those macabre processions of severe, chaste, arcane signs. . . .

I have often asked why this necessary quality has been refused to the greatest art of all. This art is without mystery in the face of hypocritical curiosity, without terror against the impieties or before the smiles and grimaces of ignorant foes.

I am speaking of poetry. *The Flowers of Evil*, for example, is printed with the same type that blooms every morning in the garden of some utilitarian tirade, and is sold in black and white books exactly like those which serve to hold the prose of the Vicomte du Terrail or M. Legouvé.

Thus the first comers go right into a masterpiece, and never since there have been poets has anyone invented an immaculate language in order to keep these intruders away—some hieratic formulae whose arid study would blind the vulgar and spur on the faithful; these intruders continue to gain admission just by learning to read a page of the alphabet!

O golden clasps of ancient missals! O inviolate hieroglyphs of papyrus rolls!

What is the result of this absence of mystery?

Like anything that is absolutely beautiful, poetry commands admiration; but this admiration is distant, vague—it comes stupidly from the crowd. Thanks to this reaction, a weird and preposterous idea germinates in their minds, that poetry must be *taught* in the colleges, and inevitably, as is always the case with subjects taught to many people, poetry is reduced to the rank of a science. It is explained to all, equally and democratically, because it is difficult

---

[1] This translation is by the editor.

to distinguish under which scholar's tousled head the sybilline star gleams. . . .

A man need not have read a verse of Hugo's in order to be complete, just as he can be complete without having deciphered a note of Verdi's; and the course of basic studies should not include art, which is a mystery accessible only to rare individuals. The multitude would profit from not having to doze over Virgil for hours, and could devote the time to practical ends, while poetry would no longer suffer from hearing at its heels the baying of a crowd of beings who think, just because they are educated and intelligent, that they have the right to judge and even dictate to it. . . .

If a philosopher seeks popularity, I honor him for it. He should not close his fingers tightly over the fistful of radiant truths that he holds; he scatters them, and it is right that they leave a luminous mark on his fingers. But that a poet, a worshipper of the beauty inaccessible to the vulgar, should not be content with the approval of the Sanhedrin of art, this irritates me and I do not understand it.

Man can be democratic, but the artist goes his own way and ought to remain an aristocrat.

And yet we see around us the opposite. Cheap editions of the poets multiply, and this with the consent and to the satisfaction of the poets themselves. Do you think you are thereby gaining glory, O dreamers, O singers? When the artist alone possessed your book, cost what it might, even if he had to spend his last franc for your latest gems, you had true admirers. Now this mob which buys you because you are cheap, do they understand you? Already profaned by education, you are protected against their desires by one last barrier, the seven francs it takes to buy your book. And you, imprudent ones, would remove this barrier! You are your own worst enemies. Why (even more through your doctrines than through the price of your books, which does not depend on you alone) do you approve and preach this blasphemy, the vulgarization of art? You will then walk in the company of those who, effacing the mysterious notes from music (this is not a joke, the idea is spreading widely), open its mysteries to the common herd; or with those others who broadcast it to the country cost what it may, content that it be played out of tune just so long as it is played. What will happen one day, on the day of retribution? You too will be *taught*, like those great martyrs, Homer, Lucretius, Juvenal!

You think of Corneille, of Molière, of Racine, who are so popular and glorious? No, they are not popular. Their names are, perhaps, but not their poetry. The mob has read them once, I grant you, but without understanding them. Who rereads them? Only the artists.

And already you receive your punishment: among your exquisite and enchanting works you find yourself emitting some which do not have such high distinction. And these are the ones the crowd admires. You will mourn to see your true masterpieces accessible to a few exceptional souls and neglected by the vulgar who ought never to have been made acquainted with them. If it were not already true, if the masses had not already withered his poems, it is certain that Hugo's supreme creations would not be *Moses* or *Pray, My Child,* as is commonly said, but the *Faun* or *Tears in the Night.*

The hour is a serious one: the people are being educated, great doctrines are going to spread. Make sure that if there is vulgarization it is of morality, not art, and that your efforts do not tend toward making you, as I trust they have not, that grotesque and pitiful thing, a *working-class poet.*

Let the masses read works on morality, but for heaven's sake do not give them our poetry to spoil.

O poets, you have always been proud; now, even more, become disdainful.

(b) "A verse must not be composed of words, but of intentions." Stéphane Mallarmé, "Hérodiade" (1887)[1]

Stéphane Mallarmé, whose diatribe against the vulgar masses we have just heard, was a good example of the poet at odds with society. A very unsuccessful school teacher (the sons of the "vile bourgeoisie," whom he despised, booed him and threw spitballs!), he was a hypochondriac whose personality radiated unworldliness and preciosity; almost a mystic, he came close to madness at times. Mallarmé had none of Rimbaud's spectacular sinfulness, but dedicated himself austerely to the art of poetry. Like so many of the late nineteenth century aesthetes, he was sure that in a putrid society without beauty or stability there remained only art, which must be profoundly personal. He dreamed of writing the perfect poem, the perfect book. He wrote enough remark-

---

[1] The translation which follows is by the editor. Roger Fry has translated Mallarmé's *Poems* (New York: New Directions, 1951).

able poetry, combining daring experiments of form with a profound but rather schizophrenic spirituality, to make himself the leader of the symbolist school in the 1880's. Generous with praise of others' work, Mallarmé admired Zola, but said "naturalism is to symbolism as a corset to a beautiful bosom." The task of the poet, he believed, was to create, not to describe, to touch the mystery at the heart of existence by an art akin to music in its allusiveness. A poem should not mean but be. It is an incantation, a rite, a mystery, not an exposition. A disciple of Poe and Baudelaire, Mallarmé borrowed also from Verlaine and the Parnassians.

Below is the translation of a portion of his unfinished poetic drama, *Hérodiade*. The haughty, frigid female, beautiful but unapproachable, occurred frequently in symbolist and decadent literature and may be taken on the symbolic level to signify rejection of involvement, and an aristocratic disdain. Mallarmé's poetry floats in a luxuriant mist of semi-meanings, a blurred landscape of rich images from which meaning emerges only indirectly. To suggest, rather than to state definitely, was the essence of poetry to the symbolists, and Mallarmé said of his "completely new poetics" that it was to "describe not the object itself, but the effect it produces . . . a verse must not be composed of words, but of intentions. . . ." Though bathed in voluptuous and sometimes obscure imagery, the picture of the proud princess Herodias, who later asked for the head of John the Baptist, is clear and psychologically shrewd. The original text of the portion below is of course in rhyme and meter, which is not possible in a literal translation; but the mood comes through.

HÉRODIADE, II.

[The nurse finds Herodias in bed; she is concerned because the princess seems to have renounced life, or perhaps returned from a dangerous visit to the lions referred to in the poem, which may symbolize sensuality. In what follows it will be seen that Herodias abundantly indicates her pride, frigidity, sterility; she does not want to be touched, she "loves the horror of being virgin." Yet clearly she is tempted and feels the call of the flesh.]

NURSE: You live! Or do I see the shadow of a princess?
I'll kiss your fingers and their rings, and stop
Living in an age ignored.

HÉRODIAS: Hands off!
The blond torrent of my immaculate hair
Bathing my solitary body ices it
With horror, and my hair which the light enlaces

Is immortal. O woman, a kiss would kill me
If beauty were not death already. By what enchantment
Enticed, and what dawn forgotten of the prophets
Empties its sad rites upon the dying distances,
Do I know? You have seen me, O nurse of winter,
Go down into the heavy prison of iron and stone
Where my aged lions drag the tawny centuries,
And I walked, fatally, hands unscathed,
In the perfumed desert of these ancient kings;
But did you see what my fears were?
I pause dreaming of exiles, and I strip,
As if near a basin whose fountain welcomes me,
The pale lilies which are in me; while, love-smitten
From watching the languid debris fall
From me, across my reverie, in silence,
The lions dispel the indolence of my dress
And look at my feet which would calm the sea.

Calm, you, the shivering of your senile flesh
Come here and, my hair imitating the manner
Too fierce which makes you fear a lion's mane,
Help me, since you dare no longer look,
To comb me carelessly before a glass.

NURSE: If not the cheerful myrrh in its sealed bottles,
Will you not try, my child, the mournful virtue
Of essence ravished from the faded rose?

HÉRODIAS: Away with these perfumes! Do you not know
That I hate them, nurse, and would you have me feel
Their intoxication bathe my languishing head?
I want my tresses, which are not flowers
Scattering oblivion on human sorrows,
But gold, to be ever free of aromatics,
In their cruel sheen and dull pallor
Resembling the bleak frigidity of metal,
Reflecting you, the jewels of my natal wall,
Armour, vases, since my solitary infancy.

NURSE: Forgive me. Age, my queen, was dimming your command
From my mind grown pale as an old book or black. . . .

HÉRODIAS: Enough. Hold this mirror up before me.

O mirror,

Cold water frozen in your frame by ennui
How many times and through what lonely hours, desolated
By dreams, searching my memories which lie
Like leaves deeply buried under your ice,
I appeared in you like a distant shadow,
But, horror! evenings, in your austere pool,
I have known the nakedness of my scattered dreams!
Nurse, am I beautiful?

NURSE: In truth a star
But this lock's slipping down. . . .

HÉRODIAS: Stop your crime
Which freezes my blood in its source, repress
This gesture, notorious impiety! Ah, tell me,
What demon puts this sinister mood in you?
That kiss, those perfumes offered, and, shall I say it,
O my heart, this touch still more sacrilegious,
Because you wanted, I think, to touch me; all this foretells
A day which will not end without misfortune on the tower. . . .
O day Herodias looks upon with dread!

NURSE: Strange times, indeed, from which heaven shield you!
You wander, lonely shadow, with a new passion,
And looking in yourself, precocious with fear:
But always more than mortally adored,
O my child, fearfully lovely, such that. . . .

HÉRODIAS: But were you not about to touch me?

NURSE: I would love
To be the one for whom fate reserves your secrets.

HÉRODIAS: Oh! Be quiet!

NURSE: Will he ever come?

HÉRODIAS: Pure stars,
Do not listen!

NURSE: How, if not amid obscure
Alarms, to dream still more implacably,

And as a supplicant, of the god who awaits
The treasure of your favor!

                    For whom, devoured
By anguish, do you guard the unknown splendor
And futile mystery of your being?

HÉRODIAS: For myself!

NURSE: Sad flower which grows alone and knows no joy
Except its own reflection in the water, seen with apathy.

HÉRODIAS: Go, keep your pity and your irony.

NURSE: Yet tell me: Oh, no, naive child,
It must decrease, each day, this proud scorn. . . .

HÉRODIAS: But who would touch me, by the lions untouched?
Besides, I want nothing human, and, if you see me
Sculptured, with eyes lost in paradise,
That is when I call to mind your milk once drunk.

NURSE: Lamentable victim sacrificed to her fate!

HÉRODIAS: Yes, it's for me, for myself I bloom abandoned!
You know it, gardens of amethyst, hidden
Endlessly in the clever mazes, dazzled,
Unknown gold, guarding your antique glint
Under the sombre sleep of a primeval soil,
You stones from which my eyes, like pure jewels,
Borrow their melodious clarity, and you
Metals which impart to my young tresses
A fatal splendor and their massive charm!
As for you, woman born in an evil age
For the wickedness of sybilline grottoes,
You who speak of a mortal! You who would have
The chalices of my garments, redolent of fierce delights,
Reveal the white thrill of my nudity,
Prophesy that if the blue heat of summer
Toward which a girl instinctively unveils,
Should see me in my modesty trembling like a star,
I die!

       I love the horror of being virgin and I wish
To live among the dread my hair arouses

When, stretched at evening on my couch, a snake
Inviolate, I feel in my useless flesh
The cold scintillation of your pale light,
You who are dying, you who burn with chastity,
White night of icicles and cruel snow!

And your lonely sister, O my eternal sister
My dream will mount toward you: already
(Rare limpidity of a heart that dreamed it)
I think myself alone in my monotonous country
Where all around me lives in the idolatry
Of a mirror reflecting in its sleeping calm
Herodias of the clear diamond look. . . .
Oh, supreme joy, yes! I feel it, I am alone.

NURSE: Madame, will you then die so?

HÉRODIAS: No, poor grandam,
Calm yourself and, withdrawing, pardon this hard heart,
But first, if you will, close the shutters, the seraphic
Azure smiles in the deep window panes,
And I, I detest the beautiful azure!
                              Waves
Lap gently, and, there below, do you know a land
Where the sinister sky wears the hateful look
Of Venus, who, at evening, burns in the foliage?
I would go there.
                    More light, though you say
It's childish, those torches whose wax with subtle fire
Weeps some strange tear amid the fruitless gold
And. . . .

NURSE: Now?

HÉRODIAS: Farewell.
                    You lie, O naked flower
Of my lips.
          I await a thing unknown.
Or perhaps, unconscious of the mystery and your cries,
You utter the ultimate, bruised sobs
Of a childhood sensing among its reveries
Separate from each other, its cold gems.

21. A critique of symbolism

"Circles of ever decreasing diameter." Leo Tolstoy, "Symbolists and
Decadents," *What is Art* (1897)[1]

Tolstoy, a great novelist and one of the truly prophetic figures of
his era, was largely insensitive to poetry. Moreover *What is Art?*, published in 1897, is a product of his old age, perhaps revealing petulance
and failing powers, so it may be unfair to use it as an example of his
thought. No well-informed person could subscribe today to many of
its judgments. He seems as bewildered by Brahms and Liszt as by
Wagner and Richard Strauss, by Kipling as much as Baudelaire and
(more understandably) Mallarmé. Still, the old man's negative verdict
on the new literature and art registered some of his basic convictions
and expressed what was in many minds: literature should communicate
to all people; modern writers had become corrupt and decadent; over-
sophisticated art is bad art. The same theme was vigorously developed
in the polemic of Max Nordau, *Degeneration,* written in 1895, in which
he accused virtually all modern writers of having lost their sanity and
betrayed their heritage. (See pp. 259 f.). It is amusing that Nordau
placed Tolstoy among the decadent and corrupting influences!

As a result of the loss of faith of the upper classes the art of these
people has become poor in material. But besides this, becoming more
and more exclusive, it has become at the same time more complicated, capricious and obscure.

When a national artist, such as were the Greek artist and the
Hebrew prophets, composed his production, he naturally tried to
say what he had to say in such a way that his production might be
understood by everybody. But when an artist composed for a
small circle of people, who were living in exceptional conditions,
or even for a single personage and his court, for a pope, a cardinal,
a king, a duke, a queen, a king's mistress, he naturally tried to affect
these people who were known to him, and who lived in definite
circumstances with which he was familiar. And this easier means

[1] *What is Art?* was first published in 1897. The following translation by
Charles Johnston, which has been amended by the editor, was published in
Philadelphia, by Henry Altemus, in 1898. It is available in other translations,
including a Library of Liberal Arts paperback.

of evoking feelings involuntarily enticed the artist to express himself in veiled phrases, obscure for the many, and intelligible only for the insiders. To begin with, in this way he could say more, and then this form of expression contained a certain special charm of mystery for the cognoscenti. This means of expression which manifested itself in euphemism, in mythological and historical allusions, came more and more into use, and has recently reached what would appear to be its utmost limits in the art of the so-called decadence. In recent times, not only have mystery, obscurity, and inaccessibility to the masses been made a merit and condition of the poetical quality of works of art, but even inaccuracy, indefiniteness and absence of eloquence.

Théophile Gautier, in his preface to the famous *Les Fleurs du mal*, says that Baudelaire has as far as possible banished from poetry eloquence, passion, and truth too faithfully conveyed—"l'éloquence, la passion, et la vérité calqueè trop exactement."

And Baudelaire not only made this declaration, but showed it both in his verses and still more in his *Petits poèmes en prose*, the purpose of which must be guessed like riddles, and the majority of which have to be given up.

A poet following Baudelaire, and also held to be great, Verlaine, has even written a whole "Art Poétique" in which he advises us to write thus:

> Seek music before all else,
> Preferring the uneven line
> Vaguer and more soluble in air,
> Nothing in it that sinks or settles.
>
> This rule also: never choose
> Words without some faint disdain:
> Naught more precious than the grayish song
> Where blurred and clear are mingled.

And further on:

> Music, again and always music!
> Let your verse be on the wing
> Let it seem to speed from a soul in flight
> Toward other skies and other loves.

Let your verse be a lucky chance
Spread to the crisp morning wind
That smells as it blows of mint and thyme . . .
And all the rest is literature.[2]

And following these two, considered the most remarkable of
the younger writers, the poet Mallarmé says plainly that the charm
of verse consists in guessing its meaning, that there should always
be a riddle in poetry. . . .

So that among the new poets, obscurity is exalted to a dogma, as
the French critic René Doumic, who does not recognize the truth
of this dogma, quite justly remarks. "It is time," he says, "to have
done with this famous theory of obscurity which the new school
has practically exalted to the position of a dogma."

But not a single French writer thinks so.

The poets of all other nationalities think and act in the same way:
the Germans, and Scandinavians, and Italians, and Russians, and
English; all the artists of recent times in every department of art
think so too: in painting, and in sculpture, and in music. Relying on
Nietzsche and Wagner, the artists of recent times hold that they
need not be understood by the vulgar masses, that it is enough for
them to call forth the poetic mood of the best educated people: the
"best nurtured men," as an English aesthete says.

---

[2] Verses 1, 2, 8 and 9 of Paul Verlaine's "Art poétique," one of the most
famous manifestos of the new poetry:

De la musique avant tout chose
Et pour cela préfère l'Impair
Plus vague et plus soluble dans l'air
Sans rien en lui qui pèse ou qui pose.

Il faut aussi qui tu n'ailles point
Choisir tes mots sans quelque méprise:
Rien de plus cher que la chanson grise
Ou l'Indécis au Précis se joint.

De la musique encore et toujours!
Que ton vers soit la chose envolée
Qu'on sent qui fuit d'une âme en allée
Vers d'autres cieux à d'autres amours.

Que ton vers soit la bonne aventure
Éparse au vent crispe du matin
Qui va fleurant la menthe et le thym. . .
Et tout le reste est littérature.

In order that what I say may not seem mere empty words, I shall introduce here at least a few examples of the French poets, who are the leaders of this movement. . . .

[Tolstoy then cites two poems by Baudelaire from *Les Fleurs du mal* (xxiv and xxxv) which he finds both obscure and base; also two of his *Petits poèmes en prose*, and two of Verlaine's songs.]

All this is not only unintelligible, but under the pretext of conveying a mood it is a mere collection of false comparisons and words.

Besides these artificial and obscure poems there are other poems intelligible, but also quite bad in form and subject. Such are all the poems [of Verlaine] under the heading "La Sagesse." In these poems the chief place is taken by a very poor expression of the very lowest Catholic and patriotic feelings. In them there are verses like this for instance:

> I will think only of Mother Mary,
> Seat of wisdom and source of pardons,
> Mother of France, *to whom we look*
> *Steadfastly for the honor of our land.*

Before quoting examples of the other poets I cannot but linger over the wonderful fame of these two verse-writers: Baudelaire and Verlaine, counted now among the great poets. How can the French, who have had Chénier, Musset, Lamartine, and most of all Hugo, who have recently had the so-called Parnassiens: Leconte de Lisle, Sully Prud'homme, and others, ascribe such importance, and attribute greatness, to two poets very inartistic in form and altogether low and base in content? The world-concept of one, Baudelaire, consists in exalting coarse egotism into a theory, and replacing morality with an idea of beauty indefinite as a cloud, and of beauty necessarily artificial. Baudelaire preferred a woman's painted face to a natural one, and metallic trees and the stage semblance of water to the reality.

The world-concept of the other poet, Verlaine, consists in a wizened immorality, a recognition of his own moral impotence, and as a salvation from that impotence, the very grossest Catholic idolatry. Both are further not only quite devoid of innocence, sincerity and simplicity, but are filled to overflowing with artificiality, striving after originality and self-conceit. So that even in the least bad of their productions you see more of Messieurs Baudelaire or Verlaine than of what they are depicting. And these two poor verse-writers form a school and have hundreds of followers.

For this phenomenon there can only be one explanation: that the art of the society in which these versifiers work, is not a serious and important business of life, but only an amusement. And every amusement wearies you at every repetition. In order to make an amusement which has wearied you once more possible, you must somehow import novelty into it: if Boston wearies you, you must invent whist; if whist wearies you, you invent preference; if preference wearies you, you invent something else new, and so forth. The heart of the matter remains the same, only the forms are changed. And so in this art: its subject matter, becoming more and more limited, at last reached a point where it seemed to the artists of these exclusive classes that everything has been said already, and that nothing new can be said any more. And, in order to import novelty into this art, new forms are invented.

Baudelaire and Verlaine invent a new form, at the same time furbishing it up with hitherto unemployed pornographic details. And the critics and the public of the higher classes recognize them as great writers.

It is only in this way that we can explain the success not only of Baudelaire and Verlaine, but of the whole decadent school.

There are, for instance, poems of Mallarmé and Maeterlinck, which have no meaning at all, and in spite of this, or perhaps because of this, are printed not only in tens of thousands of separate editions, but in the selections of the best productions of the younger poets. . . .

Similar poems are published by the Germans, the Scandinavians, the Italians and by us Russians. And these productions are printed and circulated, if not by millions, then by hundreds of thousands of copies (several of them sold in tens of thousands). To set up in type, print, fold and bind these books, millions and millions of working days are spent, I think not less than were spent in building the great pyramid. But this is not all. The same thing happens in all the other arts, and millions of working days are spent on the production of equally unintelligible subjects, in painting, music and the drama.

Painting is not only not behind poetry in this, but even outstrips it. Here is an excerpt from the diary of a lover of pictures, who visited the Paris exhibition in 1894:

Today I was at three exhibitions: the symbolists, the impressionists, and the neo-impressionists. I looked at the pictures conscientiously and painstakingly, but again the same perplexity, and finally revolt. The first exhibition of Camille Pissarro was still the most intelligible, though there was no drawing, no subject, and the most improbable coloring. The drawing was so indefinite that sometimes you could not understand which way a hand or head was turned. The subjects were for the most part "effects": Effect of mist, evening effect, setting sun. There were some pictures with figures, but without subjects. . . .

From that gallery I went to look at the symbolists. I looked long, not questioning anybody, and trying to guess myself what the meaning of it all was, but this was too much for human imagination. One of the first things which caught my eye was a wooden haut-relief, formlessly executed, representing a woman (naked), who is pressing a stream of blood from her breast with both hands. The blood flows down and changes to a lilac color. Her hair is at first let down, and then raised upwards, where it turns into trees. The statue is painted a flat yellow color, the hair brown.

Then there is a picture: a yellow sea, with something floating on it, not quite a ship, and not quite a heart; on the horizon is a profile with an aureole and with yellow hair, which merges into the sea and is lost in it. The third is still less intelligible: a male profile; in front of it are flames and black stripes—leeches I was afterwards told. I finally asked a gentleman who was there what it meant, and he explained to me that the statue was a symbol, that it represented "The Earth," that the heart floating in the yellow sea was "Illusion," and the gentleman with the leeches was "Evil." There were some impressionist pictures here too: primitive profiles, with some kind of a flower in their hands. Of one tone, the drawing not finished, or altogether indefinite, or surrounded with a broad black coutour.

This was in 1894; at present this tendency has become even more strongly defined. . . .

The same thing is happening in the drama. Now it is an architect that is represented, who for some reason or other has not fulfilled his former high purposes, and in consequence climbs on the roof of a house he has built, and flies down again head over heels; or some unintelligible old woman, who rears rats, for some unintelligible reason leads a poetical child into the sea, and drowns him there; or some blind folk, sitting on the seashore, who keep on repeating something or other; or some kind of bell which sinks into a lake and sounds there.[3]

The same thing happens in music, the art which, it would seem, should be generally intelligible above all the others. . . .

The very same thing happens in a region where one would think it is difficult to be unintelligible, the region of romances and novels.

You read *Là-bas*, by Huysmans; or Kipling's stories, or "L'Annonciateur," by Villiers de l'Isle-Adam, from his *Contes Cruels* and so on; and all this is not only "abscons" (a new word of the new writers), but perfectly unintelligible, both in form and in subject matter. Such, for instance, is the novel *Terre Promise*, which has just appeared in the *Revue Blanche*, and such are the majority of recent novels: the style has plenty of swing, the feelings are apparently elevated, but you can never find out what happens, where, and to whom.

And such is all the young art of our times.

People of the first half of our century, admirers of Goethe, Schiller, Hugo, Dickens, Beethoven, Chopin, Raphael, da Vinci, Michelangelo, de Laroche, understanding absolutely nothing of this recent art often simply consider the productions of this art as mere tasteless foolishness and wish to ignore it altogether. But such an attitude towards recent art is entirely without foundation, because in the first place this art is spreading more and more, and has already won itself a firm position in society, such as the romanticism of the thirties won; and, in the second place, and chiefly, because if we are to decide in this way about the most recent productions of the so-called decadent art, simply because we do not understand it,

[3] Easily identifiable among these plays mentioned by Tolstoy are Ibsen's late play, *Little Eyolf* (1894), and one by the master of the symbolist drama, the Belgian Maurice Maeterlinck. The 1890's saw much daring new work in the theater, including the sexual-psychological plays of the great Swedish playright August Strindberg, as well as the symbolist drama. For some idea of the latter see Haskell M. Block, *Mallarmé and the Symbolist Drama* (Detroit: Wayne University Press, 1963); on Strindberg, see Borge G. Madsen, *Strindberg's Naturalistic Theater* (Seatttle: University of Washington, 1962). Ed.

there is an immense multitude of people—the whole of the toilers and many who are not toilers—who as little understand the art we consider beautiful: the poems of our favorite artists: Goethe, Schiller, Hugo, Dickens' novels, Beethoven's and Chopin's music, the pictures of Raphael, Michelangelo, da Vinci, and so on.

If I have a right to believe that the great masses of people do not understand or like what I recognize as undoubtedly good, because they are not sufficiently developed, then I have no right to deny that I may not understand and like the newest productions of art, simply because I am not sufficiently developed to understand them. And if I have a right to say that, with the majority of people who are of one mind with me, I do not understand the productions of the new art simply because there is nothing in it to understand, and because it is bad art, then with just the same right may the still larger majority, the whole of the toiling masses who do not understand what I consider fine art, say that what I consider good art is bad art and that there is nothing in it to understand.

I saw with especial clearness the injustice of condemning the new art, when once in my presence a poet, who composes unintelligible verse, with gay self-confidence laughed at some unintelligible music, and shortly after this the musician who composes unintelligible symphonies, with equal self-confidence laughed at unintelligible poetry. To condemn the new art because I, a person educated in the first half of the century, do not understand it, is something I have no right to do, and cannot do; I can only say that it is unintelligible for me. The sole superiority of the art which I recognize over the decadents, consists in this, that the art I recognize is understood by a greater number of people than the present art.

From the fact that I have been accustomed to a certain exclusive art, and understand it, and do not understand a more exclusive art, I have no right at all to conclude that my art is the genuine art, and that the art which I do not understand is unreal and bad; from this I can only conclude that art, becoming ever more and more exclusive, unintelligible for an ever greater and greater number of people, in its movements towards greater and greater unintelligibility, at one of the steps on which I stand with the art I am accustomed to, has gone so far that it is only understood by a very small number of select persons, and that the number of these select persons is ever growing less and less.

The moment the art of the higher classes separated itself from national art the conviction was reached that art may be art, and at the same time unintelligible to the masses. And the moment this position was admitted, the admission was inevitable that art may be intelligible only for a very small number of select persons, and finally only for two or one—one's best friend—one's self. And the present artists say openly: "I create and understand myself, and if anybody does not understand me, so much the worse for him."

The assertion that art may be good art, and at the same time be unintelligible for a great number of people, is so unjust, its consequences are so destructive to art, and at the same time it is so widely accepted, and has so eaten into our imaginations, that it is impossible to make all its inconsistency sufficiently plain.

There is nothing commoner than to hear it said of pretended productions of art that they are very good, but that it is very difficult to understand them. We have grown used to this sort of assertion, but at the same time to say that a production of art is good, but unintelligible, is the same thing as to say of some food, that it is very good, but no one can eat it. People may not like rotten cheese, high woodcock, and such viands, esteemed by gastronomists of corrupt taste, but bread and fruit are only good when people like them. It is the same with art: corrupt art may be unintelligible, but good art is always intelligible to everyone.

It is said that the very best works of art are such as cannot be understood by the majority, and are accessible only to the elect, prepared to understand these great productions. But if the majority does not understand it, we must explain it and give the majority the knowledge necessary for this understanding. But it seems that such knowledge does not exist, and that these productions cannot be explained, because those who say that the majority does not understand good works of art give no explanations, but say that in order to understand you must read, see and hear these very same works again and again. But this means not to explain, but to accustom. And you can accustom people to anything, however bad. As you can accustom people to rotten food, vodka, tobacco, and opium, so you can accustom people to bad art, and this is just what is done.

Besides it is wrong to say that the majority of people has not the taste to value the highest art. The majority always understood and understands what even we consider the very highest art: the artistically simple narratives of the Bible, the parables of the gospels, popular legends, stories, popular songs are understood by all. Then why should the majority suddenly have lost the ability to understand what is lofty in our art?

Of an oration, you can say that it is fine, but unintelligible, if you do not know the language in which it is pronounced. An oration pronounced in Chinese may be fine and remain for me unintelligible, if I do not know Chinese, but a production of art is distinguished from every other spiritual activity by the very fact that its language is understood by all, that it affects all alike. The tears and laughter of a Chinaman affect me in just the same way as the laughter and tears of a Russian; and in just the same way painting, and music, and poetry, if it is translated in a language I understand. The songs of the Kirghiz and Japanese touch me, though not so strongly as they touch the Kirghiz and Japanese themselves. I am equally touched by a Japanese painting, Indian architecture and Arabian tales. If a Japanese song and a Chinese novel touch me less strongly this is not because I do not understand these productions, but because I know and am accustomed to higher subjects of art, and not at all because this art is above me. The great objects of art are great only because they are accessible and intelligible to all. The story of Joseph, translated into Chinese, touches Chinamen. The story of Sakya Muni touches us. And there are buildings, pictures, statutes, music of the same kind. And if art does not touch us, it is wrong to say that this comes from the lack of understanding in the spectators and auditors, but we must and should conclude from this only that it is bad art, or not art at all.

Art is distinguished by this very thing from intellectual activity which demands preparation and a certain sequence of knowledge (so that you cannot teach trigonometry to a person who does not know geometry), that art acts on people independently of the degree of their development and education, that the charm of a picture, sounds, images, affects everybody in whatever degree of development he may be.

The business of art consists precisely in this, to make intelligible and accessible to all what might be unintelligible and inaccessible in an intellectual form. Usually on receiving a truly artistic impression it seems to the receiver that he has known it before, but could not express it.

And such was always good and high art: the Iliad, the Odyssey, the story of Jacob, Isaac, and Joseph, and the Hebrew prophets, and the Psalms, the gospel parables, the story of Sakya Muni, and the hymns of the Veda convey very lofty feelings, and in spite of this are perfectly intelligible to us now, educated and uneducated, and were understood by the people of those days, even less educated than our working classes. People talk of unintelligibility. But if art is the conveying of feelings, flowing from peoples' religious consciousness, then how can a feeling founded on religion, that is, on the relation of man to God, be unintelligible? Such art must be and in actuality always was intelligible to all, because the relation of every man to God is one and the same. And therefore churches and the images and singing in them were always intelligible to everybody. The obstacle to understanding the highest and best feelings, as is said in the gospel, lies not at all in lack of development and learning, but on the contrary, in false development, and false learning. A good and lofty artistic production may really be unintelligible, but not to simple, uncorrupted toilers of the people (to them the very highest is intelligible), but a real artistic production may be, and often is unintelligible to over-learned, corrupt people, who have lost the religious feeling, as often happens in our society, where the highest religious feelings are quite unintelligible to people. I know people, for instance, who consider themselves most refined, who say that they cannot understand the poetry of love of one's neighbor and self-abnegation; they do not understand the poetry of modesty.

So that good, great, universal, religious art can be unintelligible only to a small circle of corrupted people, but not the contrary.

Art cannot be unintelligible to the great masses because it is very good, as the artists of our time like to pretend. It may rather be affirmed that art is unintelligible to the great masses only because that art is very bad, or is not art at all. So that the favorite arguments, naively accepted by the cultivated crowd, that in order to feel art, you must understand it (which really means only to get used to it), are the most certain proof that what is supposed to be under-stood in this way is either very bad exclusive art or not art at all.

People say: Works of art do not please the people because the people are unable to understand them. But if a work of art has as its aim to affect people with the feeling which the artist experienced, how can we speak of not understanding?

A man of the people has read a book, has seen a picture, has heard a drama or symphony, and has received no feelings at all He is told that this is because he is unable to understand. You promise a man to show him a certain sight, he comes and sees nothing. He is told that this is because his eyes are not prepared for this sight. But the man knows that he sees perfectly well. If he does not see what you promised to show him he will only conclude (as is perfectly just), that the people who undertook to show him the sight did not fulfill what they undertook. In just the same way, and with perfect justice, a man of the people comes to a conclusion about our works of art, which do not call up in him any feeling at all. And therefore to say that a person is not touched by my art, because he is still stupid, besides being very conceited and also rude, means that you change the roles, and lay the blame of the sick head on the sound one.

Voltaire said that: "Tous les genres sont bons, hors le genre ennuyeux:"[4] with still greater right might one say of art that: "tous les genres sont bons, hors celui qu'on ne comprend pas"; or: "qui ne produit pas son effet,"[5] for what worth can there be in an object which does not accomplish what it is destined to do?

And most of all note this, that the moment you admit that an art may be good which is unintelligible to any mentally sound peo-ple, there is not the slightest reason to hinder any little circle of cor-rupted people producing works which tickle their corrupted feel-ings, and are unintelligible to everyone except themselves, the very thing that is done now by the so-called decadents.

The path on which art has traveled is like laying, on a circle of large diameter, circles of ever less and less diameter: so that a cone is formed, whose apex ceases to be a circle. This is what has hap-pened to the art of our time.

[4] Every form of art is good, except the boring one.
[5] Every form of art is good, except that which cannot be understood, or which does not produce its effect.

22. Against the grain

". . . the world is composed mostly of rascals and imbeciles." J. K.
Huysmans, *À Rebours* (1884)[1]

Tolstoy's plea for an art that all could understand, and an end to
literary snobbism, hardly represented the trend among writers and
poets near the end of the century. Much more familiar was the poetic
aesthete who withdrew from a world he believed to be hopelessly
corrupt to live in some sort of ivory tower. One of the most widely
read and influential manifestos of this retreat from society came from
the pen of Joris K. Huysmans, whose *À Rebours*, or *Against the Grain*,
might well claim to have been the model for poets of the 1890's. Huysmans had begun as a writer of documentary novels in the vein of the
Goncourts and Zola, but *À Rebours*, published in 1884, marked his
break with naturalism. Disgusted with "vulgar reality," he set forth
the alternate ideal of searching out the finest and most delicate of
private aesthetic experiences. Huysmans almost invented the "decadent"
type with des Esseintes, the "hero" of *Against the Grain*. How this
young man came to the conclusion that he must withdraw completely
from the world to a kind of monastic seclusion where he would cultivate his senses is told in the first chapter of this book. Huysmans, it is
interesting to note, revealed in his last works, written between 1898
and 1905, a return to fervent religion. But to the young men of the
1890's both *À Rebours*, and its sequel *Là-Bas* published in 1891, meant
something wickedly iconoclastic: the ultimate gesture of contempt and
defiance of conventional society.

Judging from several portraits preserved at their Chateau des
Lourps, the Floressa des Esseintes had been composed of stalwart
soldiers and stern cavalry men. Closely arrayed side by side, their
strong shoulders filling their picture frames, they frighten one with
their fixed, staring eyes, their chests bulging in the enormous shells
of their breast plates.

These were the ancestors. There were no portraits of their

---

[1] Robert Baldick has recently supplied an excellent translation of Huysmans' *À Rebours*, which he renders *Against Nature* though the customary
English title was *Against the Grain*. (Harmondsworth: Penguin Books,
1967). The translation which follows is by Jane Lilienfeld.

descendants. A gap existed in the series of faces of this race; one lone print served as intermediary, bridging the gap between past and present: a mysterious and cunning face, with elongated fervorless features, cheekbones punctuated by a comma of paint, hair plastered down and twined with pearls, and a long painted neck rising stiffly from a fluted ruff.

Already, in this picture of one of the most intimate familiars of the Duc d'Eperon and the Marquis d' O, the des Esseintes' vices of temperament and their impoverished constitution are apparent.

The decadence of this ancient house had doubtless followed a regular course; the men became ever more effeminate. As if to conclude the work of years, the des Esseintes had intermarried for two centuries, employing their remaining vigor in inbreeding.

Of this family, formerly so numerous that they occupied almost all the territory of the Isle de France and of la Brie, only one descendant remained. The Duke Jean was a frail thirty-year-old man, anemic and nervous, with sunken cheeks, cold, steel-blue eyes, a straight thin nose, and papery, thin hands.

By a strange freak of hereditary coincidence, this last descendant resembled his antique ancestor, the court favorite. He had the same pointed pale blond beard and ambiguous expression, at once world-weary and yet artful.

His childhood had been full of sickness. He was menaced by scrofula, struck by persistent bouts of fever. Thanks to fresh air and good nursing, he succeeded in clearing the hurdles of adolescence. He had overcome the langors and lethargy of sclorosis, and his body had reached its full physical development.

His mother, a tall woman, pale and silent, had died of nervous exhaustion. His father had succumbed to some obscure disease when des Esseintes was seventeen.

He remembered his parents only with fear, without gratitude and without affection. He hardly knew his father who had lived in Paris. His mother he remembered as she lay motionless in a darkened room of the chateau. Only rarely were husband and wife united; of those days he remembered colorless interviews. The father and mother sat facing each other, in front of a table on which was a dimmed lamp, for the duchess could not stand noise or light without having nervous crises. Seated in the gloom, they hardly exchanged two words. Then the duke went away, indifferent, and caught the first available train back to Paris.

At the Jesuit school where he was sent, Jean was treated with goodwill and gentleness. The Fathers coddled the boy, whose intelligence astonished them. In spite of their efforts they could not get him to concentrate on a disciplined course of study. He took readily to certain work, became precociously adept at Latin. As if to make up for this, he was absolutely incapable of translating two words in Greek, having no aptitude for living languages. He revealed himself impenetrable whenever one tried to force him to learn the first elements of science.

His family took little interest in him. Occasionally his father came to see him at school: "Hello, goodbye, be wise and work hard" was his sole message to Jean. During vacations and in the summer, Jean returned to the Chateau de Lourps. His presence failed to arouse his mother from her reveries. She hardly sensed his presence, or if she did, contemplated him for several seconds, with a sad smile and then became absorbed again in the artificial night which enveloped her room.

The servants were old and dull. The child, left to himself, riffled through the books in the library when it rained; in good weather he roamed the countryside.

His greatest joy was to descend into the valley to reach Jutigny, a village planted at the foot of the hills. It was a little cluster of houses capped with thatch, strewn with tufts of stonecrop and patches of moss. In the shadow of tall hayricks he would lie down in the meadow, listening to the muffled sounds of watermills and sniffing the fresh breeze from the Voulzie. Sometimes he went as far as the peat-bogs, up to the green and black hamlet of Longueville, or he climbed the windswept hills from which he could survey an immense expanse of land. There, below him to one side lay the Seine Valley, extending far into the distance where it merged with the blue sky. On the other side of him, above the horizon, were the churches and towers of Provins which seemed to shimmer in the sunlight, in the golden dust of the air.

He read or dreamed, steeped in solitude. By protracted meditation on the same thoughts, his mind grew sharp, his previously wavering ideas matured. After each vacation he returned to his masters more reflective and more stubborn. These changes did not escape his teachers. Shrewd, used by their work to sounding the depths of men's souls, they were not duped by his unresponsiveness. They understood that this student would never contribute to the glory of their order. As his family was rich and appeared uninterested in his future, they too gave up directing him to take up any of the profitable careers open to their successful scholars. He willingly discussed with them all the theological doctrines, which attracted him by their subtleties and hair-splitting. Yet the Fathers never dreamed of inducing him to take orders, because in spite of their efforts his faith had remained weak. As a last resort, from fear of the unknown, they let him study what subjects he liked and neglect the others, not wanting to alienate this independent spirit by the quibblings of lay schoolmasters.

Thus he lived, perfectly happy, hardly feeling the parental yoke of the priests. He continued studying Latin and French as he pleased. Since theology no longer figured in his schedule, he completed his apprenticeship to this science which he had begun in the Chateau de Lourps, in the library willed by his great-granduncle Don Prosper, former Prior of the Canons Regular of St. Ruf.

The time came for him to leave the Jesuit school; he had attained his majority and had become master of his fortune. His cousin and guardian the Comte de Montchevrel gave him the titles to his wealth. Relations between these two could not last long, as there could be no point of contact between one so old and one so young. But out of curiosity, idleness, courtesy, des Esseintes frequented this family. In his hotel on the rue de la Chaise, he suffered some oppressive evenings listening to female relatives gossip of quartering of noble arms, heraldic moons, and antiquated ceremonies.

Even more than the dowagers, the men gathered around a game of whist revealed themselves unalterably empty-headed. These, the descendants of ancient warriors, the last branches of feudal races, appeared to des Esseintes in the guise of catarrhal, crazy old men, repeating inanities and time-worn phrases. The fleur-de-lis was apparently the only thing that remained impressed on the softening pulp inside their ancient skulls.

An inexpressible pity filled the young man for these mummies buried behind rococo paneling in their Pompadour catafalques, for these tedious dullards who lived with their eyes constantly fixed on a vague Promised Land, on an imaginary Palestine.

After several such seances with his relatives, he resolved that in spite of invitations and reproaches, he would never again set foot in their society.

He took to consorting with young men of his own age and station.

These, raised like him in religious institutions, retained a special stamp from this education. They went to church regularly, took Easter Communion, haunted Catholic circles, and hid from one another their sexual activities which they considered sinful and criminal. For the most part they were unintelligent and submissive young men, victorious dunces who had exhausted their professors' patience, but had nevertheless satisfied their desire to send into the world dutiful and pious beings.

Others, raised in state-run colleges or *lycées,* were freer and less hypocritical, but they were neither more interesting nor less narrow-minded. These were gay young men, dazzled by operettas and races. They played lansquenet and baccarat, squandered fortunes on horses, on cards, on all the pleasures dear to hollow minds. After a year of such company he felt an immense weariness with their debauches which he found to be base and facile, engaged in indiscriminately, without fervor, without real stimulation of blood or nerves.

Little by little he left them, and approached the men of letters, expecting to find kindred spirits with whom he would feel more at ease. He suffered a new disillusionment. He was revolted by their mean and spiteful judgments, by conversations as banal as a church door, by their nauseating discussions, in which they judged a work's value according to the number of editions it had had, and the profits of its sale. At the same time he discovered free-thinkers, those doctrinaire bourgeoisie who claimed all the liberties in order to throttle others' opinions. They were arid and shameless puritans whose education he judged to be inferior to that of the corner shoemaker.

His contempt for humanity grew. He finally understood that the world is composed mostly of rascals and imbeciles. Decidedly, he could not hope to discover in others aspirations and aversions like his own, nor expect companionship from an intelligence exulting, as theirs did, in studious decrepitude, nor anticipate meeting a mind as keen as his own among the writers and scholars.

High-strung, ill at ease, indignant at the insignificance of the ideas which were exchanged, he became like one of those men whom Nicole discusses who are unhappy everywhere. He became incredibly thin-skinned and suffered terribly over the patriotic and social rubbish sold, each morning, in the newspapers. He began to exaggerate the significance of the success which an all-powerful public always reserved for works written without ideas and without style.

Already he dreamed of a refined solitude, of a comfortable desert, a motionless ark in which he could take refuge from the incessant deluge of human stupidity.

A single passion—women—might have been able to pull him from this universal disdain which constantly irritated him, but that too was exhausted. He had tasted carnal delights with the appetite of a crotchety man affected by depraved longings, obsessed by ravenous hungers, whose palate was quickly dulled and satiated. When he frequented country gentlemen, he had participated in unconventional dinners at which drunken women undressed themselves at dessert and banged their heads on the table. He had gone through theater-backstages, bedding with actresses and singers, and had suffered, in addition to the stupid inanity he had come to expect of women, the frenzied vanity common to women of the theater. Then he had kept mistresses celebrated for their depravity and had contributed to the fortunes of those agencies which furnish debatable pleasures, for a certain sum. Finally, satiated, tired of identical caresses, he had plunged into the lower depths, hoping that the contrast would revitalize his exhausted desires and stimulate his apathy by the exciting foulness of miserable poverty.

Whatever he tried, an immense boredom oppressed him. He persisted, he resorted to the perilous caresses of virtuosos, but his health weakened, and his nervous system was exacerbated. The nape of his neck became tender, and his hands, still firm when he seized a heavy object, became unsteady when he held anything as light as a small glass.

The doctors he consulted frightened him; it was time to stop this life, to renounce these pleasures which so sapped his vitality. For some time he lived peacefully by following their advice. But soon his brain took fire, calling him again to arms. Just as young girls under the blows of adolescence are famished for debased and coarse dishes, he began to dream of, and then to practice perverse pleasures and deviant joys. This time it was really the end. As if satisfied to have exhausted all experience, his senses fell into lethargy; impotence was near.

He recovered and found himself again on the road, disillusioned, alone, and abominably tired, imploring an end to this life which only the cowardice of his flesh kept him from terminating.

His ideas of snuggling far away from the world, of shutting himself up in a retreat, grew stronger. He dreamed of muffling the continuous uproar of inexorable life, just as one deadens the noise of traffic for sick people by covering the street with straw.

Besides, it was time to be resolved: the conditions of his fortune horrified him. In follies, in drinking bouts, in riotous living, he had devoured the major part of his patrimony. The remaining part was invested in land and brought in only an absurdly low income.

He determined to sell the Chateau de Lourps which he never visited and where he left behind no pleasant memories and no regrets. He liquidated his other assets and bought government bonds from which he was assured an annual income of fifty-thousand *livres*. In addition, he reserved a sum of money to pay for and to furnish the small house where he proposed to bathe himself in permanent peace.

He investigated the suburbs thoroughly and discovered for sale above Fontenay aux Roses a villa in a secluded spot near the fort, far away from all neighbors. His dream was realized: in this neighborhood, little ravaged by Parisians, he was certain to find shelter. The difficulty of communications, little eased by a comical railway situated at the foot of the village or by the streetcar routes which meandered as they liked, reassured him of his inaccessibility. In thinking of the new existence which he was arranging, he experienced a cheerfulness because he was already so withdrawn: the hurry of Paris no longer attracted him, and his closeness to the capital confirmed him in his solitude. And since as soon as it is impossible for one to attain something, one is seized by a desire for it, he felt that in not completely closing the road he stood less chance of being assailed by a desire to return to society.

He put local masons to work on the house he had bought. Then, brusquely, without making an announcement of his plans to anyone, one day he got rid of his furniture, dismissed his servants, and disappeared. He left no forwarding address.

23. The aesthetic ideal

"To burn always with this hard, gemlike flame, to maintain this ecstasy, is success in life." Walter Pater, from the Conclusion to *The Renaissance* (1873, 1888)[1]

In addition to Huysmans' *Against the Grain*, Walter Pater's books, *The Renaissance* (1873, 1877, and 1888), and *Marius the Epicurean* (1885), became bibles of the aesthetes of the 1890's. Pater was a scholar, and taught at Oxford for many years; these books exude an aristocratic, fastidious spirit derived from his literary studies of classicism and the Italian Renaissance. Youthful literary rebels read Pater as meaning that the chief value in life is aesthetic sensation, the last exquisite pleasure one can get from a dying civilization. Oscar Wilde and his circle perhaps misinterpreted Pater as meaning that "life is simply a *mauvais quart d'heure* made up of exquisite moments." Fearing that it might mislead the young, Peter removed the celebrated Conclusion from the second (1877) edition but restored it, with slight alterations, to the third edition in 1888. In it he is proposing the high ideal of a life lived every moment to the utmost of perceptiveness and intensity, and suggesting strongly that it is art which best provides this maximum of consciousness.

T o REGARD all things and principles of things as inconstant modes or fashions has more and more become the tendency of modern thought. Let us begin with that which is without—our physical life. Fix upon it in one of its more exquisite intervals, the moment, for instance, of delicious recoil from the flood of water in summer heat. What is the whole physical life in that moment but a combination of natural elements to which science gives their names? But these elements, phosphorus and lime and delicate fibers, are present not in the human body alone: we detect them in places most remote from it. Our physical life is a perpetual motion of them—the passage of the blood, the wasting and repairing of the lenses of the eye, the modification of the tissues of the brain by

---

[1] *The Renaissance* is available in several paperback editions.

every ray of light and sound—processes which science reduces to simpler and more elementary forces. Like the elements of which we are composed, the action of these forces extends beyond us; it rusts iron and ripens corn. Far out on every side of us those elements are broadcast, driven by many forces; and birth and gesture and death and the springing of violets from the grave are but a few out of ten thousand resultant combinations. That clear, perpetual outline of face and limb is but an image of ours, under which we group them—a design in a web, the actual threads of which pass out beyond it. This at least of flamelike our life has, that it is but the concurrence, renewed from moment to moment, of forces parting sooner or later on their ways.

Or if we begin with the inward world of thought and feeling, the whirlpool is still more rapid, the flame more eager and devouring. There is no longer the gradual darkening of the eye and fading of color from the wall—the movement of the shore side, where the water flows down indeed, though in apparent rest—but the race of the midstream, a drift of momentary acts of sight and passion and thought. At first sight experience seems to bury us under a flood of external objects, pressing upon us with a sharp and importunate reality, calling us out of ourselves in a thousand forms of action. But when reflection begins to act upon those they are dissipated under its influence; the cohesive force seems suspended like a trick of magic; each object is loosed into a group of impressions—color, odor, texture—in the mind of the observer. And if we continue to dwell in thought on this world, not of objects in the solidity with which language invests them, but of impressions unstable, flickering, inconsistent, which burn and are extinguished with our consciousness of them, it contracts still further; the whole scope of observation is dwarfed to the narrow chamber of the individual mind. Experience, already reduced to a swarm of impressions, is ringed round for each one of us by that thick wall of personality through which no real voice has ever pierced on its way to us, or from us to that which we can only conjecture to be without. Every one of those impressions is the impression of the individual in his isolation, each mind keeping as a solitary prisoner its own dream of a world. Analysis goes a step farther still, and assures us that those impressions of the individual mind to which, for each one of us, experience dwindles down, are in perpetual flight: that each of them is limited by time, and that as time is infinitely divisible, each of them is infinitely divisible also; all that is actual in it being a single moment, gone while we try to apprehend it, of which it may ever be more truly said that it has ceased to be than that it is. To such a tremulous wisp constantly reforming itself on the stream, to a single sharp impression, with a sense in it, a relic more or less fleeting, of such moments gone by, what is real in our own life fines itself down. It is with this movement, with the passage and dissolution of impressions, images, sensations, that analysis leaves off—that continual vanishing away, that strange, perpetual weaving and unweaving of ourselves.

"Philosophieren," says Novalis, "ist dephlegmatisieren, vivificieren."[2] The service of philosophy, of speculative culture, towards the human spirit is to rouse, to startle it into sharp and eager observation. Every moment some form grows perfect in hand or face; some tone on the hills or the sea is choicer than the rest; some mood of passion or insight or intellectual excitement is irresistibly real and attractive for us—for that moment only. Not the fruit of experience, but experience itself is the end. A counted number of pulses only is given to us of a variegated, dramatic life. How may we see in them all that is to be seen in them by the finest senses? How shall we pass most swiftly from point to point, and be present always at the focus where the greatest number of vital forces unite in their purest energy?

To burn always with this hard, gemlike flame, to maintain this ecstasy, is success in life. In a sense it might even be said that our failure is to form habits: for, after all, habit is relative to a stereotyped world, and meantime it is only the roughness of the eye that makes any two persons, things, situations, seem alike. While all melts under our feet, we may catch at any exquisite passion, or any contribution to knowledge that seems by a lifted horizon to set the spirit free for a moment, or any stirring of the senses, strange dyes, strange colors, and curious odors, or work of the artist's hands, or the face of one's friend. Not to discriminate every moment some passionate attitude in those about us, and in the brilliancy of their gifts some tragic dividing of forces on their ways, is, on this short day of frost and sun, to sleep before evening. With this sense of

[2] To philosophize is to de-phlegmatize, to bring life into.

the splendor of our experience and of its awful brevity, gathering all we are into one desperate effort to see and touch, we shall hardly have time to make theories about the things we see and touch. What we have to do is to be forever curiously testing new opinions and courting new impressions, never acquiescing in a facile orthodoxy of Comte, or of Hegel, or of our own. Philosophical theories or ideas, as points of view, instruments of criticism, may help us to gather up what might otherwise pass unregarded by us. "Philosophy is the microscope of thought." The theory or idea or system which requires of us the sacrifice of any part of this experience, in consideration of some interest into which we cannot enter, or some abstract theory we have not identified with ourselves, or what is only conventional, has no real claim upon us.

One of the most beautiful passages in the writings of Rousseau is that in the sixth book of the *Confessions*, where he describes the awakening in him of the literary sense. An undefinable taint of death had always clung about him, and now in early manhood he believed himself smitten by mortal disease. He asked himself how he might make as much as possible of the interval that remained and he was not biased by anything in his previous life when he decided that it may be by intellectual excitement, which he found just then in the clear, fresh writings of Voltaire. Well! we are all *condamnés*, as Victor Hugo says: we are all under sentence of death but with a sort of infinite reprieve—*les hommes sont tous condamnés à mort avec des sursis indéfinis:* we have an interval, and then our place knows us no more. Some spend this interval in listlessness, some in high passions, the wisest, at least among "the children of this world," in art and song. For our one chance lies in expanding that interval, in getting as many pulsations as possible into the given time. Great passions may give us this quickened sense of life, ecstasy and sorrow of love, the various forms of enthusiastic activity, disinterested or otherwise, which come naturally to many of us. Only be sure it is passion—that it does yield you this fruit of a quickened, multiplied consciousness. Of this wisdom, the poetic passion, the desire of beauty, the love of art for art's sake, has most; for art comes to you professing frankly to give nothing but the highest quality to your moments as they pass, and simply for those moments' sake.

24. The decadence

"All the cynicisms and petulances and flippancies of the decadence,
the febrile self-assertion, the voluptuousness, the perversity were,
consciously or unconsciously, efforts toward the rehabilitation of
spiritual power." Holbrook Jackson, *The Eighteen Nineties*
(1913)[1]

The 1890's have become a legend in English literary and social
history. It was the decade of *The Yellow Book*, Oscar Wilde, Aubrey
Beardsley, and of many other important writers, among them the
young poets Ernest Dowson, Lionel Johnson, John Davidson, and
Francis Thompson. In the exotic pages of *The Yellow Book* and *Savoy*
appeared such writers as George Moore, Henry James, William Butler
Yeats, George Bernard Shaw and Joseph Conrad, making this one of
the great generations of English letters. Exciting figures from across
the Channel—Verlaine, Nietzsche, Verhaeren—were introduced to the
British public. It was also the age of the dandies, those "super-
aesthetical young men" who wandered about seeking beauty and
quoting Huysmans or Pater. The decade came to a grand climax with
the arrest and trial of Oscar Wilde, its chief symbol. After this England
recoiled from everything associated with Wilde and the aesthetic
movement. The influence of the French had been strong, and the Irish
—Wilde, Shaw, Yeats and Moore—had participated prominently in the
literary movement of the nineties, so there seemed something rather
un-English about it. Yet for a time even the Victorian public had been
affected by this modern movement in literature and the arts, with its
aggressive assault on bourgeois philistinism.

Holbrook Jackson's book *The Eighteen Nineties*, subtitled "A Review of Art and Ideas at the Close of the Nineteenth Century," was
first printed in 1913 and went through many editions. Jackson took part
in the events of the nineties before becoming their historian. Therefore
he could and did recapture all the subtleties of mood. He even remembered and described something apparently as trivial as the part
played in the 1890's by that immortal song *Ta-ra-ra-boom-de-ay!*
"which, lit at the red skirts of Lottie Collins, spread like a dancing
flame through the land, obsessing the minds of young and old, gay
and sedate, until it became a veritable song-pest. . . . the absurd *Ça ira*

---

[1] *The Eighteen Nineties* has been in print ever since its publication in
1913; it is currently available in an edition by Penguin books.

of a generation bent upon kicking over the traces." His social and intellectual history of this decade that enchanted him includes other
things than the dandies and esthetes of the "decadence," but inevitably
focuses on them. Chapter III, reprinted below, was entitled "The
Decadence."

No ENGLISH writer has a better claim to recognition as an inter-
preter of the decadence in recent English literature than Arthur
Symons. He of all the critics in the eighteen-nineties was sufficiently
intimate with the modern movement to hold, and sufficiently removed from it in his later attitude to express, an opinion which
should be at once sympathetic and reasonably balanced without
pretending to colorless impartiality. But during the earlier phase
his vision of the decadent idea was certainly clearer than it was
some years later, when he strove to differentiate decadence and
symbolism.

"The most representative literature of the day," he wrote in
1893, "the writing which appeals to, which has done so much to
form, the younger generation, is certainly not classic, nor has it
any relation to that old antithesis of the classic, the romantic. After
a fashion it is no doubt a decadence; it has all the qualities that
mark the end of great periods, the qualities that we find in the
Greek, the Latin, decadence; an intense self-consciousness, a restless curiosity in research, an over-subtilizing refinement upon refinement, a spiritual and moral perversity. If what we call the classic
is indeed the supreme art—those qualities of perfect simplicity, perfect sanity, perfect proportion, the supreme qualities—then this
representative literature of today, interesting, beautiful, novel as
it is, is really a new and beautiful and interesting disease." [2]

Six years later Arthur Symons, like so many of the writers of
the period, was beginning to turn his eyes from the "new and
beautiful and interesting disease," and to look inwardly for spiritual
consolation. In the "Dedication" to *The Symbolist Movement in
Literature* he told W.B. Yeats that he was "uncertainly but inevitably" finding his way towards that mystical acceptance of
reality which had always been the attitude of the Irish poet. And
further on in the same book, as though forgetting the very definite

_____

[2] "The Decadent Movement in Literature," by Arthur Symons. *Harper's
New Monthly Magazine*, November 1893.

interpretation of decadence given by him in the article of 1893, he writes of it as "something which is vaguely called decadence," a term, he said, used as a reproach or a defiance:

> It pleased some young men in various countries to call themselves Decadents, with all the thrill of unsatisfied virtue masquerading as uncomprehended vice. As a matter of fact, the term is in its place only when applied to style, to that ingenious deformation of the language in Mallarmé, for instance, which can be compared with what we are accustomed to call the Greek and Latin of the decadence. No doubt perversity of form and perversity of matter are often found together, and, among the lesser men especially, experiment was carried far, not only in the direction of style. But a movement which in this sense might be called decadent could but have been straying aside from the main road of literature . . . . The interlude, half a mock-interlude, of decadence, diverted the attention of the critics while something more serious was in preparation. That something more serious has crystallized, for the time, under the form of symbolism, in which art returns to the one pathway, leading through beautiful things to the eternal beauty.

In the earlier essay he certainly saw more in decadence than mere novelty of style, and rightly so, for style can no more be separated from idea than from personality. The truth of the matter, however, lies probably between the two views. What was really decadent in the eighteen-nineties did seem to weed itself out into mere tricks of style and idiosyncrasies of sensation; and whilst doing so it was pleased to adopt the term decadence, originally used as a term of reproach, as a badge. But with the passing of time the term has come to stand for a definite phase of artistic consciousness, and that phase is precisely what Arthur Symons described it to be in his earlier article, an endeavor "to fix the last fine shade, the quintessence of things; to fix it fleetingly; to be a disembodied voice, and yet the voice of a human soul; that is the ideal of decadence."

The decadent movement in English art was the final outcome of the romantic movement which began the dawn of the nineteenth century. It was the mortal ripening of that flower which blossomed upon the ruins of the French Revolution, heralding not only the rights of man, which was an abstraction savoring more of the classic ideal, but the rights of personality, of unique, varied and varying men. The French romanticists, led by Victor Hugo, recognized

this in their glorification of Napoleon; but fear and hatred of the
great emperor generated in the hearts of the ruling classes in this
country and propagated among the people prevented the idea from
gaining acceptance here. At the same time decadence was neither
romantic nor classic: its existence in so far as it was dependent
upon either of those art traditions was dependent upon both. The
decadents were romantic in their antagonism to current forms,
but they were classic in their insistence upon new. And it must
not be forgotten that far from being nihilistic in aim they always
clung, at times with desperation, to one already established art form
or another. The French artists of the first revolutionary period
depended as much upon the traditions of republican Greece and
Rome as those of the revolution of July, and the poets of Britain,
led by Walter Scott and Byron, depended upon the traditions of
medieval feudalism. Romanticism was a reshuffling of ideals and
ideas and a recreation of forms; it was renascent and novel. It
could be both degenerate and regenerate, and contain at the same
time many more contradictions, because at bottom it was a revolt
of the spirit against formal subservience to mere reason. It is true
that there is ultimately an explanation for all things, a reason for
everything, but it was left for romance to discover a reason for
unreason. It was the romantic spirit in the art of Sir Walter Scott
which saw no inconsistency between the folk-soul and the ideals
of chivalry and nobility; that taught Wordsworth to reveal simplicity as, in Oscar Wilde's words, "the last refuge of complexity";
that inspired John Keats with a new classicism in *Endymion*
brighter than anything since *A Midsummer Night's Dream* and
Comus, and a new medievalism in *The Eve of St. Agnes* fairer than
"all Olympus' faded heirarchy." It taught Shelley that the most
strenuous and the most exalted individual emphasis was not necessarily antagonistic to a balanced communal feeling, and that the
heart of Dionysos could throb and burn in the form of Apollo;
and above all it taught Samuel Taylor Coleridge that mystery
lurked in common things and that mysticism was not merely a
cloistral property.

Though all of these tendencies of thought and expression went
to the making of the decadence in England, the influence, with
the exception of that of Keats, was indirect and foreign. In that it
was native the impulsion came directly from the Pre-Raphaelites,

and more particularly from the poetry of Dante Gabriel Rossetti and Swinburne. But the chief influences came from France, and partially for that reason the English decadents always remained spiritual foreigners in our midst; they were a product not of England but of cosmopolitan London. It is certain Oscar Wilde (hounded out of England to die in Paris), Aubrey Beardsley (admittedly more at home in the *brasserie* of the Café Royal than elsewhere in London) and Ernest Dowson (who spent so much of his time in Soho) would each have felt more at home in Paris or Dieppe than, say, in Leeds or Margate. The modern decadence in England was an echo of the French movement which began with Théophile Gautier (who was really the bridge between the romanticists of the Victor Hugo school and the decadents who received their inspiration from Edmond and Jules de Goncourt), Paul Verlaine and Joris Karl Huysmans. In short, Gautier, favorite disciple of Victor Hugo, represented the consummation of the old romanticism, and he did this by inaugurating that new romanticism, which had for apostles the Parnassians, symbolists and decadents. French romanticism begins with *Hernani*, and ends with *Mademoiselle de Maupin*. Decadence properly begins with *Mademoiselle de Maupin* and closes with *À Rebours*. In England it began by accident with Walter Pater's Studies in Art and Poetry, *The Renaissance*, which was not entirely decadent, and it ended with Oscar Wilde's *Picture of Dorian Gray* and Aubrey Beardsley's romance, *Under the Hill*, which were nothing if not decadent.

The accident by which Pater became a decadent influence in English literature was due to a misapprehension of the precise meaning of the famous Conclusion to the first edition of the volume originally issued in 1873, which led the author to omit the chapter from the second edition (1877). "I conceived it might possibly mislead some of those young men into whose hands it might fall," he wrote, when he reintroduced it with some slight modifications, bringing it closer to his original meaning, into the third edition of the book, in 1888. Nevertheless there was sufficient material in the revised version to stimulate certain minds in a direction only very remotely connected with that austere philosophy of sensations briefly referred to in *The Renaissance* and afterwards developed by Walter Pater under the idea of a "New Cyrenaicism" in *Marius the Epicurean* (1885). To those seeking a native sanction for their decadence, passages even in *Marius* read like invitations. "With the Cyrenaics of all ages, he would at least fill up the measure of that present with vivid sensations, and such intellectual apprehensions as, in strength and directness and their immediately realized values at the bar of an actual experience, are most like sensations." Such passages seemed in the eyes of the decadents to give a perverse twist to the aesthetic puritanism of the intellectual evolution of Marius, and to fill with a new naughtiness that high discipline of exquisite taste to which the young pagan subjected himself. It is not surprising then to find even the revised version of the famous Conclusion acting as a spark to the tinder of the new acceptance of life.

But misappropriation of the teaching of Walter Pater was only an incident in the progress of decadence in England. By the dawn of the last decade of the century susceptible thought had reverted to the original French path of decadent evolution which manifested itself from Théophile Gautier and Charles Baudelaire through the brothers Goncourt, Paul Verlaine, Arthur Rimbaud, Stéphane Mallarmé, to Huysmans, with a growing tendency toward little secret raids over the German frontier where the aristocratic philosophy of Friedrich Nietzsche was looted and made to flash approval of intentions and ideas which that philosopher, like Pater, had lived and worked to supersede. The publication of *The Picture of Dorian Gray* in 1891 revealed the main influence quite definitely, for, apart from the fact that Wilde's novel bears many obvious echoes of the most remarkable of French decandent novels, the *Á Rebours* of J.K. Huysmans, which Arthur Symons has called "the breviary of the decadence," it contains the following passage which, although *Á Rebours* is not named, is generally understood to refer to that book, even if the fact were not otherwise obvious:

His eyes fell on the yellow book that Lord Henry had sent him. What was it, he wondered. He went towards the little pearl-coloured octagonal stand, that had always looked to him like the work of some strange Egyptian bees that wrought in silver, and taking up the volume, flung himself into an arm-chair, and began to turn over the leaves. After a few minutes he became absorbed.

It was the strangest book he had ever read. It seemed to him that in exquisite raiment, and to the delicate sound of flutes, the sins of the world were passing in dumb show before him. Things that he had dimly dreamed of were suddenly made real to him. Things of which he had never dreamed were gradually revealed.

It was a novel without a plot, and with only one character, being, indeed, simply a psychological study of a certain young Parisian who spent his life trying to realise in the nineteenth century all the passions and modes of thought that belonged to every century except his own, and to sum up, as it were, in himself the various moods through which the world-spirit had ever passed, loving for their mere artificiality those renunciations that men have unwisely called virtue as much as those natural rebellions that wise men still call sin. The style in which it was written was that curious jewelled style, vivid and obscure at once, full of *argot* and of archaisms, of technical expressions and of elaborate paraphrases, that characterises the work of some of the finest artists of the French school of symbolists. There were in it metaphors as monstrous as orchids and as evil in colour. The life of the senses was described in the terms of mystical philosophy. One hardly knew at times whether one was reading the spiritual ecstasies of some mediaeval saint or the morbid confessions of a modern sinner. It was a poisonous book. The heavy odour of incense seemed to cling about its pages and to trouble the brain. The mere cadence of the sentences, the subtle monotony of their music, so full as it was of complex refrains and movements elaborately repeated, produced in the mind of the lad, as he passed from chapter to chapter, a form of reverie, a malady of dreaming, that made him unconscious of the falling day and the creeping shadows.

This book so revealed Dorian Gray to himself that he became frankly the Duc Jean des Esseintes of English literature. There are differences, to be sure, and the sensations and ideas of Dorian Gray are not elaborated so scientifically at those of des Esseintes, but there is something more than coincidence in the resemblance of their attitudes toward life.

Jean des Esseintes and Dorian Gray are the authentic decadent types. Extreme they are, as a matter of course, but their prototypes did exist in real life, and minus those incidents wherein extreme decadence expresses itself in serious crime, such as murder or incitement to murder, those prototypes had recognizable corporeal being.

In the eighteen-nineties two such types were Oscar Wilde and Aubrey Beardsley, each of whom approximated, if not in action, then in mind and idea, to des Esseintes and Dorian Gray. There was in both a typical perversity of thought, which in Wilde's case led to a contravention of morality evoking the revenge of society and a tragic ending to a radiant career. Both preferred the artificial to the natural. "The first duty in life is to be as artificial as possible," said Oscar Wilde, adding, "what the second duty is no one has as yet discovered." The business of art as he understood it was to put Nature in her proper place. To be natural was to be obvious, and to be obvious was to be inartistic. Aubrey Beardsley invented a new artificiality in black-and-white art, and in his romance, *Under the Hill*, only a carefully expurgated edition of which has been generally accessible to the public, he created an *À Rebours* of sexuality. And both possessed an exaggerated curiosity as to emotional and other experiences combined with that precocity which is characteristic of all decadents. The curiosity and precocity of the decadence were revealed in an English writer before the eighteen-nineties by the publication, in 1886, of the *Confessions of a Young Man*, by George Moore; but, apart from the fact that the author who shocked the moral susceptibilities of the people who control lending libraries, with *Esther Waters*, loved the limelight and passed throught enthusiasms for all modern art movements, he was as far removed from the typical decadent as the latter is removed from the average smoking room citizen who satisfies an age-long taste for forbidden fruit with a *risqué* story. George Moore played at decadence for a little while, but the real influences of his life were Flaubert and the naturalists on the one side, and their corollaries in the graphic arts, Manet and the impressionists, on the other. For the rest he insisted upon England accepting the impressionists; abandoned realism; introduced into this country the work of Verlaine and Rimbaud, and the autobiography of indiscretion; flirted with the Irish literary movement, and its vague mysticism— and remained George Moore.

The chief characteristics of the decadence were (1) perversity, (2) artificiality, (3) egoism and (4) curiosity, and these characteristics are not at all inconsistent with a sincere desire "to find the last fine shade, the quintessence of things; to fix it fleetingly; to be a disembodied voice, and yet the voice of a human soul." Indeed, when wrought into the metal of a soul impelled to adventure at whatever hazard, for sheer love of expanding the bound-

aries of human experience and knowledge and power, these characteristics become, as it were, the senses by which the soul may
test the flavor and determine the quality of its progress. In that
light they are not decadent at all, they are at one with all great
endeavor since the dawn of human consciousness. What, after all,
is human consciousness when compared with Nature but a perversity—the self turning from Nature to contemplate itself? And is
not civilization artifice's conspiracy against what is uncivilized and
natural? As for egoism, we ought to have learned by this time that
it is not sufficient for a being to say "I am." He is not a factor in
life until he can add to that primal affirmation a consummating "I
will." "To be" and "to will" exercised together necessitate action,
which in turn involves experience, and experience, not innocence,
is the mother of curiosity. Not even a child has curiosity until it
has experienced something; all inquisitiveness is in the nature of
life asking for more, and all so-called decadence is civilization rejecting, through certain specialized persons, the accummulated experiences and sensations of the race. It is a demand for wider ranges,
newer emotional and spiritual territories, fresh woods and pastures
new for the soul. If you will, it is a form of imperialism of the
spirit, ambitious, arrogant, aggressive, waving the flag of human
power over an ever wider and wider territory. And it is interesting
to recollect that decadent art periods have often coincided with
such waves of imperial patriotism as passed over the British Empire
and various European countries during the eighteen-nineties.

It is, of course, permissible to say that such outbreaks of curiosity
and expansion are the result of decay, a sign of a world grown *blasé*,
tired, played out; but it should not be forgotten that the effort demanded by even the most ill-directed phases of decadent action suggests a liveliness of energy which is quite contrary to the traditions
of senile decay. During the eighteen-nineties such liveliness was
obvious to all, and even in its decadent phases the period possessed
tonic qualities. But the common sense of the matter is that where
the so-called decadence made for a fuller and brighter life, demanding ever more and more power and keener sensibilities from its units,
it was not decadent. The decadence was decadent only when it
removed energy from the common life and set its eyes in the ends
of the earth, whether those ends were pictures, blue and white china,
or colonies. True decadence was, therefore, degeneration arising

not out of senility, for there is nothing old under the sun, but out of surfeit, out of the ease with which life was maintained and desires satisfied. To kill a desire, as you can, by satisfying it, is to create a new desire. The decadents always did that, with the result that they demanded of life not repetition of old but opportunities for new experiences. The whole attitude of the decadence is contained in Ernest Dowson's best-known poem: "Non sum qualis eram bonae sub regno Cynarae," with that insatiate demand of a soul surfeited with the food that nourishes not, and finding what relief it can in a rapture of desolation:

> I cried for madder music and for stronger wine,
> But when the feast is finished, and the lamps expire,
> Then falls thy shadow, Cynara! the night is thine;
> And I am desolate and sick of an old passion,
> Yea, hungry for the lips of my desire:
> I have been faithful to thee, Cynara! in my fashion.

In that poem we have a sort of parable of the decadent soul. Cynara is a symbol of the unattained and perhaps unattainable joy and peace which is the eternal dream of man. The decadents of the nineties, to do them justice, were not so degenerate as either to have lost hope in future joy or to have had full faith in their attainment of it. Coming late in a century of material pressure and scientific attainment, they embodied a tired mood, rejected hope beyond the moment, and took a subtle joy in playing with fire and calling it sin; in scourging themselves for an unholy delight, in tasting the bittersweet of actions potent with remorse. They loved the cleanliness in unclean things, the sweetness in unsavory alliances; they did not actually kiss Cynara, they kissed her by the proxy of some "bought red mouth." It was as though they had grown tired of being good, in the old accepted way, they wanted to experience the piquancy of being good after a debauch. They realized that a merited kiss was not half so sweet as a kiss of forgiveness, and this subtle voluptuousness eventually taught them that the road called decadence also led to Rome. The old romanticism began by being Catholic; Théophile Gautier strove to make it pagan, and succeeded for a time, but with Huysmans romanticism in the form of decadence reverted to Rome. In England the artists who represented the renaissance of the nineties were either Catholics like Francis Thompson and Henry Harland, or prospective converts to Rome, like Oscar Wilde, Aubrey Beardsley, Lionel Johnson and Ernest Dowson. If Catholicism did not claim them some other form of mysticism did, and W. B. Yeats and George Russell ("A. E.") became Theosophists. The one who persistently hardened himself against the mystical influences of his period, John Davidson, committed suicide.

The general public first realized the existence of the decadence with the arrest and trial of Oscar Wilde, and, collecting its wits and its memories of *The Yellow Book,* the drawings of Aubrey Beardsley, and the willful and perverse epigrams of *A Woman of No Importance,* it shook its head knowingly and intimated that this sort of thing must be stopped. And the suddenness with which the decadent movement in English literature and art ceased, from that time, proves, if it proves nothing else, the tremendous power of outraged public opinion in this country. But it also proves that English thought and English morality, however superficial on the one hand and however hypocritical on the other, would neither understand nor tolerate the curious exotic growth which had flowered in its midst. . . .

The decadence proper, in this country, was only one of the expressions of the liveliness of the times. It was the mood of a minority, and of a minority, perhaps, that was concerned more about its own moods than about the meaning of life and the use of life. At its worst it was degenerate in the literal sense—that is to say, weak, invalid, hectic, trotting with rather sad joy into the *cul de sac* of conventional wickedness and peacocking itself with fine phrases and professions of whimsical daring. As such it was open to satire, as such it would have suppressed itself sooner or later without the intervention of public opinion. At its best, even when that best was most artificial and most exotic, it realized much, if it accomplished little. True, it was a movement of elderly youths who wrote themselves out in a slender volume or so of hot verse or ornate prose, and slipped away to die in taverns or gutters—but some of those verses and that prose are woven into the fabric of English literature. And if it was a movement always being converted, or on the point of being converted, to the most permanent form of Christianity, even though its reasons were aesthetic, or due entirely to a yearning soul-weariness, it succeeded in checking a brazen rationalism which was beginning to haunt art and life with the cold shadow of logic. Ernest Dowson's cry for "Madder music and for stronger wine," Arthur Symons' assertion that "there is no necessary difference in artistic value between a good poem about a flower in the hedge and a good poem about the scent in a sachet," and Oscar Wilde's reassertion of Gautier's *l'art pour l'art* (with possibilities undreamt of by Gautier) are all something more than mere protests against a stupid philistinism; fundamentally they are expressions not so much of art as of vision, and as such nothing less than a demand for that uniting ecstasy which is the essence of human and every other phase of life. All the cynicisms and petulances and flippancies of the decadence, the febrile self-assertion, the voluptuousness, the perversity were, consciously or unconsciously, efforts towards the rehabilitation of spiritual power.

> I see, indeed [wrote W. B. Yeats] in the arts of every country those faint lights and faint colours and faint outlines and faint energies which many call "the decadence," and which I, because I believe that the arts lie dreaming of things to come, prefer to call the autumn of the body. An Irish poet, whose rhythms are like the cry of a sea-bird in autumn twilight, has told its meaning in the line, "The very sunlight's weary, and it's time to quit the plough." Its importance is great because it comes to us at the moment when we are beginning to be interested in many things which positive science, the interpreter of exterior law, has always denied: communion of mind with mind in thought and without words, foreknowledge in dreams and in visions, and the coming among us of the dead, and of much else. We are, it may be, at a crowning crisis of the world, at the moment when man is about to ascend, with the wealth he has been so long gathering upon his shoulders, the stairway he has been descending from the first days.

So it may be that this movement, which accepted as a badge the reproach of decadence, is the first hot flush of the only ascendant movement of our times; and that the strange and bizarre artists who lived tragic lives and made tragic end of their lives, are the mad priests of that new romanticism whose aim was the transmutation of vision into personal power.

25. Some Wilde epigrams (1890–1895)[1]

"My first meeting with Oscar Wilde was an astonishment," W. B. Yeats wrote. "I never before heard a man talking with perfect sentences, as if he had written them all overnight with labor, and yet all spontaneous." Wilde's whole life was an effort to astonish the Victorian age—shock it into an appreciation of art, beauty, culture. In the end he aroused its most brutal instincts against him and it crushed him. His epigrams, which Holbrook Jackson called "willful and perverse," were his trademark; even his plays, such as *Lady Winde-mere's Fan* and *The Importance of Being Ernest*, and even more *A Woman of No Importance*, are largely a succession of such witticisms. They remain eminently quotable. Some—perhaps most of them--Wilde meant seriously. He agreed with his fellow-Irishman Bernard Shaw that one should utter one's serious thoughts with the utmost levity, thereby disarming criticism. Perverse or serious, they all had the effect of scandalizing the bourgeoisie, and this was doubtless their basic intention.

There is no such thing as a moral or an immoral book. Books are well written, or badly written.

There is no sin except stupidity.

A little sincerity is a dangerous thing, and a great deal of it is absolutely fatal.

Don't say that you agree with me. When people agree with me I always feel that I must be wrong.

Any fool can make history. It takes a genius to write it.

The first duty of life is to be as artificial as possible. What the second is no one has yet discovered.

I don't like novels that end happily. They depress me so much.

The youth of America is their oldest tradition. It has been going on now for over three hundred years.

---

[1] The Penguin Books edition of Oscar Wilde's *Plays* includes *The Importance of Being Ernest, Lady Windemere's Fan, A Woman of No Importance, An Ideal Husband,* and *Salome.*

You should study the Peerage, Gerald. . . . It is the best thing in fiction the English have ever done.

As for the virtuous poor, one can pity them, of course, but one cannot possibly admire them.

Work is the curse of the drinking classes.

The only way to get rid of a temptation is to yield to it.

Nothing succeeds like excess.

Life is far too important a thing ever to talk seriously about it.

One should never take sides in anything. Taking sides is the beginning of sincerity, and earnestness follows shortly afterwards, and the human being becomes a bore.

I adore simple pleasures. They are the last refuge of the complex.

Children begin by loving their parents. After a time they judge them. Rarely if ever do they forgive them.

Really, now that the House of Commons is trying to become useful, it does a great deal of harm.

Science can never grapple with the irrational. That is why it has no future before it, in this world.

Women have a wonderful instinct about things. They can discover anything except the obvious.

Nothing is so dangerous as being too modern. One is apt to grow old-fashioned quite suddenly.

Morality is simply the attitude we adopt towards people whom we personally dislike.

She talks more and says less than anybody I ever met. She is made to be a public speaker.

To love oneself is the beginning of a life-long romance.

I remember having read somewhere, in some strange book, that when the gods wish to punish us they answer our prayers.

Duty is what one expects from others, it is not what one does oneself.

One can survive everything nowadays, except death, and live down anything except a good reputation.

Nowadays to be intelligible is to be found out.

To expect the unexpected shows a thoroughly modern intellect.

Youth isn't an affectation. Youth is an art.

26. The influence of Richard Wagner

(a) "Man passes here across this forest of symbols . . ." Charles Baudelaire, "Richard Wagner and *Tannhäuser*" (1869)[1]

Wagner truly came into his own in the 1880's. There was a *Revue Wagnerienne* in France, and the young George Bernard Shaw was defending Wagner in England. To the aesthetes and symbolist poets Wagner's was a "total art" in which all the genres were combined to achieve the fullest effect; Wagner stood, also, for the vital necessity of art in any civilized community, and a protest against the philistinism of bourgeois taste. That poetry must be akin to music—suggestive, allusive, carefully orchestrated in words to produce an emotional effect rather than to state some idea directly—was an article of faith among all the symbolist poets. They all admired Wagner as the master who had been among the first to make that link between the arts which was their ideal. For the same reason, they paid tribute to Edgar Allen Poe.

Baudelaire had leaped to the defense of the German composer when, in 1860 and 1861, a major battle broke out over Wagner's revolutionary music and an uproar greeted the performance of the opera *Tannhäuser* in Paris. Baudelaire's essay was first published in the *Revue européene* on March 18, 1861, and was slightly revised in the form in which it appears below for reprinting in his book *L'art romantique*, published in 1869.

THIRTEEN months ago, there was a great uproar in Paris. A German composer, who had once lived a long time among us without our knowledge, poor, unknown, working at miserable jobs, but whom for the last fifteen years the German public has been acclaiming as a man of genius, returned to our city, former witness of his youthful hardships, to submit his works to our judgment.

[1] For information on Baudelaire's essays see note 2, p. 385.

Until then Paris had heard little of Wagner; one knew vaguely that beyond the Rhine the question of a reform in musical drama was stirring, and that Liszt had enthusiastically adopted the views of the reformer. M. Fétis had launched a sort of indictment against him, and those curious enough to leaf through issues of the *Revue et gazette musicale de Paris* can verify once again the fact that writers who pride themselves on holding the wisest and most balanced opinions hardly are noted for either wisdom or moderation, or for that matter ordinary politeness, in the criticism of opinions different from their own. The articles by M. Fétis are little more than a painful diatribe; but the old dilettante's exasperation served only to prove the importance of the works which he consigned to anathema and ridicule. Richard Wagner has suffered other injuries during the thirteen months, during which public curiosity has not died down. Several years ago upon returning from a trip to Germany, Théophile Gautier, however, much moved by a performance of *Tannhäuser*, set forth his impressions in the *Moniteur* with that plastic certitude that gives all his writings such an irresistible charm. But these various documents, appearing at widely separated intervals, had made little impression on the crowd.

As soon as the posters announced that Richard Wagner was to have some portions of his compositions played in the hall on the Boulevard des Italiens, an amusing situation came about, which we have witnessed before, and which reveals the instinctive, precipitate necessity of Frenchmen to take sides on every issue before having deliberated or examined. Some spoke of marvels, and others prided themselves on disparaging to the utmost works which they had not yet even heard. This absurd situation still continues today, and one can say that never has an unknown subject been so much discussed. In brief, the Wagner concerts presented themselves as a veritable battle of doctrines, as one of those solemn crises in art, one of those mêlées into which critics, artists, and public are accustomed confusedly to throw all their passions; happy crises which testify to the sanity and richness of the intellectual life of a nation, and which we had almost forgotten since the great days of Victor Hugo. [Baudelaire had in mind the famous battle that accompanied the performance of *Hernani* in 1830.] I quote the following lines from a piece by M. Berlioz (February 9, 1860): "The lobby of the Theatre-Italien was curious to observe on the evening of the first concert. There were arguments, cries, discussions which seemed always on the point of degenerating into blows." Except for the presence of the emperor [Napoleon III], the same scandal might have been produced a few days ago at the Opera, the more so since it was a more expert audience. I recall having seen, at the end of one of the dress-rehearsals, one of the accredited Parisian critics planted pretentiously in front of the ticket office, meeting the crowd at the point of a narrow exit and laughing like a maniac, like one of those unfortunate persons who in mental hospitals are called "disturbed." This poor man, believing his face to be known to the multitude, seemed to be saying: "See how I'm laughing, I, the famous S. . . . ! So take care to conform your judgment to mine." In the review to which I just alluded, M. Berlioz, who however showed considerably less heat than one might have expected from him, added: "The nonsense, absurdities, and even lies which are spread about are truly prodigious, and prove convincingly that, with us at least, when it is a question of appreciating a different and unusual kind of music, passion and partisanship alone rule and prevent good sense and good taste from speaking. . . ."

I have often heard it said that music cannot boast of conveying anything with the precision of literature or painting. That is true to some extent, but it is not completely true. It communicates in its own manner, and by the means which are appropriate to it. In music, as in painting and even in the written word, which is the most explicit of the arts, there is always a lacuna to be filled in by the imagination of the listener.

Doubtless it was these considerations which impelled Wagner to consider dramatic art, that is to say the union, the *coincidence* of several arts, as the art par excellence, the most synthetic and the most perfect. Now, if we put aside for the moment the aid of the plastic arts, of scenery, the incorporation of imaginary types in living actors, and even the libretto, it remains incontestable that the more eloquent the music is, the more the suggestion is rapid and true, and the more chances there are for sensitive persons to conceive ideas in harmony with those that inspired the artist. An example that springs to mind is the famous overture to *Lohengrin*, on which Berlioz has written a magnificent eulogy in technical language. I will content myself here with showing its value by the suggestions it calls up.

I read in the program distributed at this time at the Theatre-Italien:

From the first measures, the soul of the pious recluse who searches for the Holy Grail *plunges into infinite space*. He sees taking shape little by little a strange apparition, which assumes a body, a figure. This apparition becomes clearer, and *the miraculous troop of angels*, bearing in their midst the sacred cup, passes before him. The holy procession approaches; the heart of the God-chosen man is uplifted little by little; it enlarges and expands, inexpressible aspirations are aroused in him; *he surrenders to an increasing beatitude*, finding himself closer and closer to *the luminous apparition*, and when finally the Grail itself appears in the middle of the holy procession, *he collapses in an ecstatic adoration, as if the whole world had suddenly disappeared.*

Meanwhile the Holy Grail bestows its blessing on the praying saint and consecrates him its knight. Then *the burning flames gradually moderate their brilliance;* in its holy joy, the troop of angels, smiling at the earth which they are leaving, regains the celestial heights. They have left the Holy Grail in the care of pure men, *in whose hearts the divine spirit is diffused*, and the august band vanishes *in the depths of space*, in the same way in which it had appeared.

The reader will soon understand why I underline these passages. I take now Liszt's book, and I open it at the page where the illustrious pianist (who is a philosopher as well as an artist) interprets the same passage in his own way:

This introduction includes and reveals the *mystic element*, always present and always hidden in the composition. . . . In order to teach us the inexpressible power of this secret, Wagner first shows us *the ineffable beauty of the sanctuary*, inhabited by a God who avenges the oppressed and asks only love and faith from his faithful. He introduces us to the Holy Grail; he makes shine before our eyes the temple of incorruptible wood, with its fragrant walls, its *golden* doors, its *asbestos* beams, its *cymophane* partitions, whose splendid porticoes are approached only by those with exalted hearts and pure hands. He does not make us perceive it in its real and imposing structure, but, as if out of compassion for our feeble senses, he first reveals it to us reflected in some *azure wave* or reproduced by some *iridescent cloud*.

At the beginning there is a *large dormant expanse* of melody, a *vaporous extended ether* as background in order that the sacred tableau may be delineated before our profane eyes; an effect exclusively assigned to the violins, divided into eight different sections which, after several measures of harmonies, continue in the highest notes of their registers. The motif is then repeated by the softest wind instruments; the horns and the bassoons, joining in, prepare the way for the trumpets and trombones, which repeat the melody for the fourth time, with a *dazzling flash of color*, as if in that single instant the sacred edifice *had blazed* before *our blinded eyes in all its luminous and radiant magnificence*. But the *vivid brilliance*, gradually brought to *the intensity of solar radiance*, fades quickly like a *flash in the sky*. The *transparent mist* of clouds form again, the vision gradually disappears in the same *variegated* incense in the midst of which it appeared, and the passage ends with a repeating of the first six measures, become *even more ethereal*. The quality of an *ideal mysteriousness* is conveyed above all by the steady pianissimo in the orchestra, interrupted only briefly when the *brasses light up* the marvelous notes of the single motif of this introduction. Such is the image which, as we listen to this sublime adagio, presents itself to our affected senses.

May I be allowed to relate, to render into words the inevitable translation my own imagination made of the same passage when I heard it for the first time, my eyes closed, and feeling as if I were lifted above the earth? I would not dare to speak complacently about my reveries, if it were not useful to compare them here with those just mentioned. The reader knows what goals we are after: to demonstrate that true music suggests similar ideas to different minds. Besides, it would not be foolish here to reason a priori, without analysis and without comparisons; for it would be really surprising if sound was *not* able to suggest color, if colors were *not* able to suggest a melody, and if sound and color were unsuited to conveying ideas; things being always expressed by a reciprocal analogy since the day when God created the world as a complex and indivisible totality:

Nature is a temple whose living pillars
Sometimes let confused words escape;
Man passes here across this forest of symbols
Which observe him with familiar looks.

Like long echoes which mingle from afar
In a profound and shadowy whole,
Vast as the night and as limpidity,
Perfumes, colors, and sounds speak to each other.[2]

To resume: I remember that, from the first measures, I experienced one of those pleasant sensations that almost every imaginative person has known, in dreams. I felt myself freed *from the bonds of weight,* and I recaptured the extraordinary *pleasure* which exists in *high places* (we may note in passing that I did not then know the programs just cited). Next I imagined involuntarily the delicious state of mind of a man in the grip of an intense dream in an absolute stillness, but a stillness with an *immense horizon* and a *great diffused light;* an *immensity* without anything present except itself. Soon I experienced the sensation of a sharper *brightness,* an *intensity of light* increasing with such rapidity that the vocabulary furnished by a dictionary would not suffice to express *this ever increasing excess of brilliance and whiteness.* Then I conceived fully the idea of a soul moving in a luminous atmosphere; of an ecstasy *compounded of pleasure and knowledge,* and soaring far above the natural world.

Among these three interpretations, you will readily note differences. Wagner indicates a troop of angels carrying a sacred vessel; Liszt sees a miraculously beautiful temple which is reflected in a hazy mist. My dream is a great deal less filled with material objects, it is more vague and abstract. But the important thing here is to observe the resemblances. They would constitute a sufficient proof even if they were few; but fortunately they are numerous and striking to the point of superfluity. In the three versions we find the sensation of a *physical and spiritual beatitude;* of *isolation;* of

[2] La Nature est un temple où de vivant pilliers
    Laissent parfois sortir de confuses paroles;
    L'homme y passe à travers des forets de symboles
    Qui l'observent avec des regards familiers.

    Comme de longs échos qui de loin se confondent
    Dans une ténébreuse et profonde unité,
    Vaste comme le nuit et comme la clarté,
    Les parfums, les couleurs et les sons se répondent.
The first and second stanzas of Baudelaire's "Correspondences," from *Les Fleurs du mal.*

the contemplation of *something infinitely great and infinitely beautiful;* of an *intense light* which delights *the eyes and the soul to the
point of rapture;* and finally the sensation of *space extended to the
utmost conceivable limits.*

No other musician rivals Wagner in *painting* depth and space,
material and spiritual. This is a remark that many minds, and the
best ones, have not been able to avoid making on numerous occasions. He possesses the art of conveying in the most subtle nuances
all that which is excessive, immense, aspiring, in natural and spiritual
man. It sometimes seems, while listening to this ardent and commanding music, that one recognizes painted upon a background of
shadows, torn·from a dream, the dizzy visions of opium. . . .

I see, from the notes that he has provided about his youth, that
when still a child Wagner lived in the bosom of the theatre, fre-
quenting the wings and composing plays. Weber's music and, later,
Beethoven's acted upon his spirit with an irresistible force and soon,
as the years and studies accumulated, he found it impossible not
to think in a double manner, poetically and musically— to view
every idea under two simultaneous forms, one of the two arts
beginning where the other leaves off. The dramatic instinct, which
occupies so large a place in his faculties, was bound to push him
into revolt against all the frivolities, the platitudes and the absurdities of the pieces written for music. Thus did Providence, which
presides over revolutions in the arts, nourish in the head of a certain
young German the problem which had so agitated the eighteenth
century. Anyone who has read attentively the *Letter on Music,*
which serves as the preface to *Four Operatic Poems Translated
into French Prose,* can retain no doubts about this. The names of
Gluck and Méhul are often cited there with a passionate sympathy.
Despite M. Fétis, who wishes fervently to establish for all eternity
the predominance of music in the lyric drama, the opinion of such
as Gluck, Diderot, Voltaire and Goethe is not to be disdained. If
the last two eventually retracted their favorite theories, this was
no more than an act of discouragement and despair on their part.
In leafing through the *Letter on Music,* I felt coming back to me,
like an echo of memory, various passages of Diderot which affirm
that true dramatic music cannot be anything but the cry or sigh of
passion, set to notes and rhythm. The same scientific, poetic, and
artistic problems recur again and again through the ages, and

Wagner does not pretend to be an innovator, but rather simply
the confirmer of an old idea which doubtless will be alternately
vanquished and victorious many more times in the future. All these
questions are indeed extremely simple, and it is not surprising to see
a revolt against the theories of "the music of the future" (to use an
expression as inexact as it is widely accepted) among those very
persons who have so often been heard complaining about the
tortures inflicted on every sensitive spirit by the triteness of the
usual opera libretto. In this same *Letter on Music*, where the author
gives a very brief and very clear analysis of his three previous
works, i.e., *Art and Revolution, The Work of Art of the Future,*
and *Opera and Drama*, we find a lively preoccupation with the
Greek theater, quite natural, indeed inevitable in a playwright-
musician who must have searched in the past for a vindication of his
disgust at the present, and for helpful advice for establishing the
new conditions of lyric drama. In his letter to Berlioz he had already said, more than a year earlier,

> I asked myself what should be the conditions of art which would
> enable it to inspire in the public an inviolable respect, and, in
> order not to risk too much speculation in the examination of this
> question, I took my point of departure from ancient Greece. I
> first encountered there the artistic work par execllence, the *drama*,
> in which the idea however profound it may be is able to manifest
> itself with the greatest clarity and in the most universally intel-
> ligible manner. We are rightly astonished today that thirty thou-
> sand Greeks were able to follow with sustained interest the per-
> formance of the tragedies of Aeschylus; but if we look for the means
> by which such results were obtained, we find that it is by the al-
> liance of all the arts working together toward the same end, that
> is to say, toward the production of the most perfect and only true
> work of art. This conducted me to study the relationships of the
> various branches of art .to each other, and, after having grasped
> the relation which exists between the *plastic* and the *mimetic*, I
> examined that which exists between music and poetry; from this
> examination came clarifications which completely dissipated the
> darkness which until then had disturbed me.
>
> I recognized, in fact, that precisely where one of the arts reaches
> its unsurpassable limits, the sphere of action of another begins,
> with the most rigorous exactitude; that, consequently, in the
> intimate union of these arts one would express with the most

satisfying clarity that which one could not express in each of them in isolation; that, on the contrary, every attempt to render by means of one of them what could only be rendered by two together was bound fatally to lead to confusion and obscurity, and thence to the degeneration and corruption of each art separately.

And in the preface to his last book, he returns to the same subject in these words:

I had found in a few rare artistic creations a firm foundation for my dramatic and musical ideal; now in its turn History offered me the model and type of ideal relations between the theater and public life as I conceived them. I found this model in the theater of ancient Athens. There, the theater opened its doors only on solemn occasions when a religious festival was celebrated accompanied by the pleasures of art. The most distinguished political leaders took a direct part in these solemn rites as poets or directors; they appeared as priests before the eyes of the people assembled from city and country, and this populace was filled with so great an expectation of the sublimity of the works which were going to be presented before them, that the most profound poetry, that of an Aeschylus or a Sophocles, could be offered to the people and assured of being perfectly understood.

This absolute, despotic taste for a dramatic ideal, where every detail, from a declamation notated and underscored by the music with so much care that the singer cannot omit a single syllable—a veritable arabesque of sounds formed by passion—to the most painstaking care about scenery and staging, is made to contribute constantly to the total effect, has shaped Wagner's destiny. It was as a perpetual demand on him. Since the day when he freed himself from the old routines of the libretto and courageously repudiated his *Rienzi*, an opera of his youth which had been awarded a great success, he has marched without deviating by a line, toward this imperious ideal. Without surprise, then, I found in those of his works which have been translated, particularly *Tannhäuser, Lohengrin*, and *The Flying Dutchman*, an excellent method of construction, a spirit of order and of division which is reminiscent of the structure of classical tragedies. But the phenomena and ideas that recur periodically throughout the ages assume at each resurrection an additional quality of circumstance and variation. The radiant Venus of old, Aphrodite born of the white foam, did not traverse

the dark shadows of the Middle Ages with impunity. She no longer
dwells on Olympus or on the banks of the perfumed archipelago.
She has retired to the depths of a cavern which is magnificent to
be sure, but illuminated by fires not those of the benevolent Phoe-
bus. In descending under the earth, Venus came close to hell, and
doubtless, in certain abominable rites, renders homage regularly to
the archdemon, prince of the flesh and lord of sin. Similarly, the
poems of Wagner, while revealing a sincere taste for and perfect
understanding of classical beauty, also participate very strongly in
the romantic spirit. If they make us dream of the majesty of
Sophocles and Aeschylus, at the same time they constrain our
minds to recall the mysteries of the most plastically Catholic era.
They resemble those great visions which the Middle Ages painted
on the walls of churches or wove into magnificent tapestries. They
wear a general look that is decidedly legendary: *Tannhäuser* a
legend, *Lohengrin* a legend, *The Flying Dutchman* also a legend.
And it is not only a propensity natural to every poetic soul that
has led Wagner toward this evident specialty; it is a deliberate
stance derived from the study of the conditions most favorable to
the lyric drama.

He himself has taken pains to elucidate this question in his books.
All subjects, of course, are not equally suited to provide a vast
drama endowed with a universal character. There would obviously
be an immense danger in translating the most delicate and perfect
genre painting into a fresco. It is above all in the universal human
heart and in the history of this heart that the dramatic poet will find
universally intelligible themes. In order to construct the ideal drama
in full freedom, it will be wise to eliminate all the difficulties that
might arise from technical, political, or even too positively historical
details. Let the master speak for himself:

> The only tableau of human life that may be called poetic is that in
> which motifs which have meaning only for the abstract intelligence
> give place to the purely human impulses which govern the heart.
> This tendency (relating to the invention of a poetical subject) is
> the sovereign law which presides over the poetic form and pre-
> sentation. . . . The rhythmic arrangement and the almost musical
> embellishment of rhyme are for the poet the means of endowing
> his verse, in the manner of music, with a power to captivate as
> by a charm and govern the feelings to its taste. Essential to the

poet, this proclivity leads him to the limits of his art, limits which
border immediately on music, and, consequently, the most complete work of the poet should be that which in its final achievement will be a perfect music.

Hence I saw myself necessarily led to designate the *myth* as the
ideal subject matter for the poet. The myth is the primitive and
anonymous poem of the people, and we rediscover it in every age,
revived, recast ever anew by the great poets of sophisticated eras.
In myth, human relations actually shed almost completely their
conventional form, intelligible only to the abstract reason; they
exhibit what is truly human in life, the eternally comprehensible
element, and they show it in that concrete form, free of all imitation, which gives to all myths their distinctive character recognizable at first glance.

And again, returning to the same theme, he says:

I quitted once and for all the terrain of history and established myself upon that of legend. . . . Every detail necessary to describe and
represent historical fact and its accidents, every detail which demands, in order to be understood, a special and remote epoch of
history, and which contemporary authors of dramas and novels
therefore set down in such a circumstantial manner—all this I was
able to leave aside. . . . The legend, to whatever epoch and whatever nation it belongs, has the advantage of embracing exclusively
that which that epoch and that nation possesses of the purely
human, and of presenting it in an original, exciting form, intelligible
therefore at the first glance. A ballad, a popular song, suffice to
show us in an instant this character in its most striking and enduring features. . . . The character of the scene and the tone of the
legend together contribute to projecting the mind into that *dream*-
like state which soon carries it to full *clairvoyance*, and the soul
discovers a new relationship between the phenomena of the world,
which the eyes could not perceive in the ordinary waking
state. . . .

Tannhäuser represents the struggle of the two principles which
have chosen the human heart for their battleground, that is to say
the struggle of the flesh with the spirit, hell with heaven, Satan with
God. And this duality is represented immediately, in the overture,
with an incomparable skill. What is there left to say about this
gem? In all likelihood it will furnish material for still more theses
and eloquent commentaries; for it is the property of truly great

works of art to be an inexhaustible source of suggestions. This overture, as I say, sums up the thought of the drama by two melodies, one religious and one voluptuous, which, to make use of an expression of Liszt's, "are here stated like two terms, and which, in the finale, find their equation." The "Pilgrim's Chorus" appears first, with the authority of the supreme law, as marking immediately the veritable meaning of life, the goal of the universal pilgrimage, that is to say, God. But just as the intimate sense of God is soon effaced in every breast by the concupiscence of the flesh, the melody representative of sanctity is little by little submerged by the sighs of sensual pleasure. The true, the terrible, the universal Venus raises herself already in every imagination. He who has not yet heard the marvelous overture to *Tannhäuser* must not imagine here a song of ordinary lovers, killing time under arbors, or the accents of a drunken gang flinging its defiance at God in the language of Horace. It is something quite different, at the sametime more valid and more sinister. Languorous notes, delights mixed with fever and mingled with anguish, returning incessantly toward a pleasure which promises to slake the thirst but never does; furious palpitations of the heart and senses, imperious commands of the flesh, the whole dictionary of the onomatopoeia of love is heard here. Finally the religious theme regains its empire little by little, slowly, by degrees, and absorbs the other in a peaceable victory, as glorious as that of the irresistible Being over the sick and disordered one, of Saint Michael over Lucifer.

At the beginning of this study, I noted the power with which Wagner in the overture to *Lohengrin* expressed the ardors of mysticism, the strivings of the spirit toward the ineffable God. In the *Tannhäuser* overture, in the struggle of the two contrary principles, he shows himself not less subtle or less powerful. Where did the master find this furious song of the flesh, this absolute knowledge of the diabolical part of man? From the first measures, nerves vibrate in unison with this melody; every body which remembers begins to tremble. Every normal brain carries in it two infinites, heaven and hell, and in every image of one of these infinites it quickly recognizes half of itself. To the satanic titillations of a vague love soon succeed raptures, transports, cries of victory, groans of gratitude, and then howls of ferocity, reproaches of victims and impious hosannas of sacrificers, as if barbarism must always take its place in the drama of love, and carnal enjoyment lead, by an ineluctable satanic logic, to the forbidden joys of crime. When the religious theme, making its attacks on this unchained evil, comes little by little to re-establish order and regain the ascendancy, when it raises itself again, with all its solid beauty, above this chaos of agonizing sensuality, the whole soul experiences a refreshment, a beatitude of redemption; an inexpressible sentiment which is repeated at the beginning of the second scene, when Tannhäuser, escaped from the grotto of Venus, finds himself again in real life, among the religious sound of the native bells, the naive song of the shepherd, the hymn of the pilgrims and the cross erected along the way, representative of all the crosses dragged over all the roads. In this last case, there is a power of contrast which acts irresistibly upon the spirit and which reminds one of the large and free manner of Shakespeare. A moment ago we were in the depths of the earth (Venus, as we have said, lives near to hell), breathing an atmosphere perfumed, yet suffocating, illuminated by a rose light that does not come from the sun; we were like the knight Tannhäuser himself, who, saturated with enervating pleasures, *aspires to sadness!*—a sublime cry which critics judge admirable in Corneille but which some would not perhaps wish to see in Wagner. Then we come back to earth; we breathe its fresh air, accept its joys with gratitude, its griefs with humility. Poor humanity has returned to its home.

Just now, in trying to describe the voluptuous part of the overture, I begged the reader to abandon his idea of common love songs, such as might be conceived by a gay lover; indeed, there is nothing trivial here; it is rather the overflowing of an energetic nature, which turns toward evil all the forces owed to the cultivation of good; it is love unrestrained, immense, chaotic, elevated to the stature of a counter-religion, a satanic religion. Thus, the composer, in the musical rendition, escaped that vulgarity which too often accompanies the depicting of the most *popular*—I was about to say the most vulgarized—of sentiments, and it is sufficient for him to paint the excesses of desire and energy, the ungovernable and immoderate ambition of a soul that has lost its way. Likewise in the plastic representation of the idea, he has freed himself, fortunately, from the tedious crowd of victims, the innumerable Elviras. The pure idea, incarnated in the single Venus, speaks much more strongly and with more eloquence. We do not see here an ordinary libertine, flitting from beauty to beauty, but the general, universal man, living morganatically with the absolute ideal of sensuality, with the queen of all the she-devils, all the female fauns and satyrs relegated to the earth since the death of the great Pan, that is to say, with the indestructible and irresistible Venus. . . .

It is to the great credit of Wagner that, despite the very proper importance he gives to the dramatic poem, the *Tannhäuser* overture, like that of *Lohengrin*, is perfectly intelligible even to one who does not know the libretto; and, also, that this overture contains not only the primary idea of the psychic duality that constitutes the drama, but also the principal themes, clearly accentuated, intended to depict the general sentiments expressed in the rest of the work. . . . The grand march of the second act has long since won the votes of even the most rebellious spirits, and one can apply to it the same eulogy as to the two overtures of which I have spoken, that it knows how to express, in a manner the most visible, the most colored, the most representative, what it wishes to express. Who in listening to these accents so rich and so proud, this stately rhythm elegantly cadenced, those regal fanfares, can imagine anything else but a feudal pageant, a parade of heroic men in brilliant garments, all of lofty height, all of great will and naive faith, as magnificent in their pleasures as terrible in their wars?

What shall we say of the story of Tannhäuser, of his voyage to Rome, where the literary beauty is so admirably complemented and sustained by the recitative that the two elements make a simple inseparable whole? One fears the length of this piece, and yet the story contains, as we have seen, an invincible dramatic power. The sadness, the oppressive sense of sin during his rude voyage, his happiness upon seeing the supreme pontiff who absolves sins, his despair when the latter shows him the irreparable character of his crime, and finally the almost unspeakably terrible sentiment of joy in his damnation; all is said, expressed, interpreted by words and music in a manner so positive that it is almost impossible to conceive another manner of saying it. One understands that such a woe can be repaired only by a miracle, and one excuses the unfortunate knight for searching for the mysterious path that leads to the grotto, in order to rediscover at least the graces of hell near his diabolical spouse.

(b) Max Nordau, *Degeneration* (1895)[1]

Wagner was the arch-fiend to the foes of the new spirit among the artists which they related to the "degeneration" of European civilization. The socialist and "rationalist" Max Nordau dedicated his book *Degeneration*, published in 1895, to Caesar Lombroso, the celebrated Italian professor of psychiatry, who believed, rather like Zola, that heredity determines character, that there are born criminal types, and that degenerates can pass as great artists. These criminal-artists, mad but able to seduce people, must be exposed. Nordau furiously denounced practically all nineteenth century art and literature, and regarded its more recent manifestations as evidence of the degeneration of an entire civilization.

Nordau's vigorous polemic, "The Richard Wagner Cult," occupies a prominent place in his book. What to Baudelaire was a stride forward, namely Wagner's use of music to communicate ideas and images like poetry or painting, was to Nordau a retrogression, evidence of hopeless, even maniacal confusion. The intermingling of the arts, which fascinated the symbolists, seemed to be a lapse from reason to their critics, who wished the arts to be clearly distinguished from one another.

We have seen in a previous chapter that the whole mystic movement of the period has its roots in romanticism, and hence originally emanates from Germany. In England German romanticism was metamorphosed into Pre-Raphaelitism, in France the latter engendered, with the last remains of its procreative strength, the abortions of symbolism and neo-Catholicism, and these Siamese twins contracted with Tolstoism a mountebank marriage such as might take place between the cripple of a fair and the wonder of a show booth. While the descendants of the emigrant (who on his departure from his German home already carried in him all the germs of subsequent tumefactions and disfigurements), so changed as to be almost unrecognizable, grew up in different countries, and set about returning to their native land to attempt the renewal of family ties with their home-staying connections, Germany gave birth to a new prodigy, who was in truth only reared with great trouble to manhood, and for long years received but little notice or appreciation, but who finally obtained an incomparably mightier

[1] New York: D. Appleton, 1895.

attractive force over the great fools' fair of the present time than all his fellow competitors. This prodigy is "Wagnerism." It is the German contribution to modern mysticism, and far outweighs all that the other nations combined have supplied to that movement. For Germany is powerful in everything, in evil as in good, and the magnitude of its elementary force manifests itself in a crushing manner in its degenerate, as well as in its ennobling, efforts.

Richard Wagner is in himself alone charged with a greater abundance of degeneration than all the degenerates put together with whom we have hitherto become acquainted. The stigmata of this morbid condition are united in him in the most complete and most luxuriant development. He displays in the general constitution of his mind the persecution mania, megalomania and mysticism; in his instincts vague philanthropy, anarchism, a craving for revolt and contradiction; in his writings all the signs of graphomania namely, incoherence, fugitive ideation, and a tendency to idiotic punning, and, as the groundwork of his being, the characteristic emotionalism of a color at once erotic and religiously enthusiastic.

For Wagner's persecution mania, we have the testimony of his most recent biographer and friend, Ferdinand Praeger, who relates that for years Wagner was convinced that the Jews had conspired to prevent the representation of his operas—a delirium inspired by his furious anti-Semitism. His megalomania is so well known through his writings, his verbal utterances, and the whole course of his life, that a bare reference to it is sufficient. It is to be admitted that this mania was essentially increased by the crazy procedure of those who surrounded Wagner. A much firmer equilibrium than that which obtained in Wagner's mind would have been infallibly disturbed by the nauseous idolatry of which Bayreuth was the shrine. The *Bayreuther Blätter* is a unique phenomenon. To me, at least, no other instance is known of a newspaper which was founded exclùsively for the deification of a living man, and in every number of which, through long years, the appointed priests of the temple have burned incense to their household god, with the savage fanaticism of howling and dancing dervishes, bent the knee, prostrated themselves before him, and immolated all opponents as sacrificial victims.

We will take a closer view of the graphomaniac Wagner. His *Collected Writings and Poems* form ten large thick volumes, and among the 4,500 pages which they approximately contain there is hardly a single one which will not puzzle the unbiased reader, either through some nonsensical thought or some impossible mode of expression. Of his prose works (his poems will be treated of further on), the most important is decidely *The Art-work of the Future*.[2] The thoughts therein expressed—so far the wavering shadows of ideas in a mystically emotional degenerate subject may be so called—occupied Wagner during his whole life, and were again and again propounded by him in ever new terms and phraseology. *The Opera and the Drama, Judaism in Music, On the State and Religion, The Vocation of the Opera, Religion and Art*, are nothing more than amplifications of single passages of *The Art-work of the Future*. This restless repetition of one and the same strain of thought is itself characteristic in the highest degree. The clear, mentally sane author, who feels himself impelled to say something, will once and for all express himself as distinctly and impressively as it is possible for him to do, and have done with it. He may, perhaps, return to the subject, in order to clear up misconceptions, repel attacks, and fill up lacunae; but he will never wish to rewrite his book, wholly or in part, two or three times in slightly different words, not even if in later years he attains to the insight that he has not succeeded in finding for it an adequate form. The crazed graphomaniac, on the contrary, cannot recognize in his book, as it lies finished before him, the satisfying expression of his thoughts, and he will always be tempted to begin his work afresh, a task which is endless, because is must consist in giving a fixed linguistic form to ideas which are formless.

The fundamental thought of the *Art-work of the Future* is this: the first and most original of the arts was that of dancing; its peculiar essence is rhythm, and this has developed into music; music, consisting of rhythm and tone, has raised (Wagner says "condensed") its phonetic element to speech, and produced the art of poetry; the highest form of poetry is the drama, which for the purpose of stage construction, and to imitate the natural scene of human action, has associated itself with architecture and painting respectively; finally, sculpture is nothing but the giving perma-

[2] Richard Wagner, *Das Kunstwerk der Zukunft* (Leipzig, 1850). The numbering of the pages given in quotations from this work refers to the edition here indicated.

nence to the appearance of the actor in a dead rigid form, while acting is real sculpture in living, flowing movement. Thus all the arts
group themselves around the drama, and the latter should unite
them naturally. Nevertheless they appear at present in isolation,
to the great injury of each and of art in general. This reciprocal
estrangement and isolation of the different arts is an unnatural and
decadent condition, and the effort of true artists must be to win
them back to their natural and necessary conjunction with each
other. The mutual penetration and fusion of all arts into a single
art will produce the genuine work of art. Hence the work of art
of the future is a drama with music and dance, which unrolls itself
in a landscape painting, has for a frame a masterly creation of
architectural art designed for the poetico-musical end, and is represented by actors who are really sculptors, but who realize their
plastic inspirations by means of their own bodily appearance.

In this way Wagner has set forth for himself the evolution of
art. His system calls for criticism in every part. The historical
filiation of the arts which he attempts to establish is false. If the
original reciprocal connections of song, dance and poetry be
granted, the development of architecture, painting and sculpture
is certainly independent of poetry in its dramatic form. That the
theater employs all the arts is true, but it is one of those truths
which are so self-evident that it is generally unnecessary to mention them, and least of all with profound prophetic mien and the
grand priestly gestures of one proclaiming surprising revelations.
Everyone knows from experience that the stage is in a theatrical
building, that it displays painted decorations which represent land-
scapes or buildings, and that on it there is speaking, singing and
acting. Wagner secretly feels that he makes' himself ridiculous
when he strains himself to expound this trite matter of first experience in the Pythian mode, with an enormous outlay of gush
and exaltation . . . ; hence he exaggerates it to such a degree as to
turn it into an absurdity. He not only asseverates that in the drama
(more correctly speaking, the opera, or the musical drama, as Wagner prefers to call it) different arts cooperate, but he asserts that it is
only through this cooperation that each individual art is advanced
to its highest capacity of expression, and that the individual arts
must and will surrender their independence as an unnatural error,

in order to continue to exist only as collaborators of the musical drama.

The first asseveration is at least doubtful. In the cathedral of Cologne, architecture produces an impression without the representation of a drama; the accompaniment of music would add nothing whatever to the beauty and depth of Faust and Hamlet; Goethe's lyric poetry and the *Divina Commedia* need no landscape painting as a frame and background; Michelangelo's *Moses* would hardly produce a deeper impression surrounded by dancers and singers; and the *Pastoral Symphony* does not require the accompaniment of words in order to exercise its full charm. . . .

Wagner's second assertion, that the natural evolution of each art necessarily leads it to the surrender of its independence and to its fusion with the other arts, contradicts so strongly all experience and all the laws of evolution, that it can at once be characterized as delirious. Natural development always proceeds from the simple to the complex—not inversely; progress consists in differentiation, in the evolution of originally similar parts into special organs of different structure and independent functions, and not in the retrogression of differentiated beings of rich specialization to a protoplasm without physiognomy.

The arts have not arisen accidentally; their differentiation is the consequence of organic necessity; once they have attained independence, they will never surrender it. They can degenerate, they can even die out, but they can never again shrink back into the germ from which they have sprung. The effort to return to beginnings is, however, a peculiarity of degeneration, and founded in its deepest essence. The degenerate subject is himself on the downward road from the height of organic development which our species has reached; his imperfect brain is incapable of the highest and most refined operations of thought; he has therefore a strong desire to lighten them, to simplify the multifariousness of phenomena and make them easier to survey; to drag everything animate and inanimate down to lower and older stages of existence, in order to make them more easy of access to his comprehension. We have seen that the French Symbolists, with their color-hearing, wished to degrade man to the indifferentiated sense perceptions of the pholas or oyster. Wagner's fusion of the arts is a pendant to this notion. His *Art-work of the Future* is the art work of times long past. What he takes for evolution is retrogression, and a return to a primeval human, nay, to a prehuman stage.

Still more extraordinary than the fundamental idea of the book is its linguistic form. For example, let us estimate the following remarks on musical art (p.68): "The sea separates and unites countries; thus musical art separates and unites the two extreme poles of human art, dancing and poetry. It is the heart of man; the blood which takes its circulation from it gives to the outward flesh its warm living color; but it nourishes with an undulating elastic force the nerves of the brain which are directed inward" [!!]. "Without the activity of the heart, the activity of the brain would become a piece of mechanical skill [!], the activity of the external limbs an equally mechanical, emotionless procedure." "By means of the heart the intellect feels itself related to the entire body [!]; the mere sensuous man rises to intellectual activity" [!]. "Now, the organ of the heart [!] is *sound*, and its artistic language is music." What here floated before the mind of Wagner was a comparison, in itself senseless, between the function of music as the medium of expression for the feelings, and the function of the blood as the vehicle of nutritive materials for the organism. But as his mystically disposed brain was not capable of clearly grasping the various parts of this intricate idea, and of arranging them in parallel lines, he entangled himself in the absurdity of an "activity of the brain without activity of the heart"; of a "relation between the intellect and the whole body through the heart," etc., and finally attains to the pure twaddle of calling "sound" the "organ of the heart." . . .

In the passages quoted, in which, in the most used-up style of Rousseau, he glorifies the masses, speaks of "unnatural culture," and calls "modern civilization" "the cruel oppressor of human nature," Wagner betrays that mental condition which the degenerate share with enlightened reformers, born criminals with the martyrs of human progress, namely, deep, devouring discontent with existing facts. This certainly shows itself otherwise in the degenerate than in reformers. The latter grow angry over real evils only, and make rational proposals for their remedy which are in advance of the time: these remedies may presuppose a better and wiser humanity actually exists, but, at least, they are capable of being defended on reasonable grounds. The degenerate subject, on the other hand, selects among the arrangements of civilization such as are either immaterial or distinctly suitable, in order to rebel against them. His fury has either ridiculously insignificant aims or simply beats the air. He either gives no earnest thought to improvement, or hatches astoundingly mad projects for making the world happy. His fundamental frame of mind is persistent rage against everything and everyone, which he displays in venomous phrases, savage threats, and the destructive mania of wild beasts. Wagner is a good specimen of this species. He would like to crush "political and criminal civilization," as he expresses it. In what, however, does the corruption of society and the untenableness of the condition of everything reveal themselves to him? In the fact that operas are played with tripping airs, and ballets are performed! And how shall humanity attain its salvation! By performing the musical drama of the future! It is to be hoped that no criticism of this universal plan of salvation will be demanded of me.

Wagner is a declared anarchist. He distinctly develops the teaching of this faction in the *Art-work of the Future* (p. 217): *All* men have but *one* common *need* . . . the need of *living* and *being happy*. Herein lies the natural bond between all men. . . . It is only the special needs which, according to time, place, and individuality, make themselves known and increase, which in the rational condition of future humanity can serve as a basis for special associations. . . . These associations will change, will take another form, dissolve and reconstitute themselves according as those needs change and reappear." He does not conceal the fact that this "rational condition of future humanity" "can be brought about only by force" (p. 228). "Necessity must force us, too, through the Red Sea if we, purged of our shame, are to reach the Promised Land. We shall not be drowned in it; it is destructive only to the *Pharaohs* of this world, who have once already been swallowed up—man and horse . . . the arrogant, proud Pharaohs who then forgot that once a poor shepherd's son with his shrewd advice had saved their land from starvation."

Together with this anarchistic acerbity, there is another feeling that controls the entire conscious and unconscious mental life of Wagner viz., sexual emotion. He has been throughout his life an erotic (in a psychiatric sense), and all his ideas revolve about woman. The most ordinary incitements, even those farthest removed from the province of the sexual instinct, never fail to awaken in his consciousness voluptuous images of an erotic character, and the bent of the automatic association of ideas is in him always directed towards this pole of his thought. In this connection let this passage be read from the *Art-work of the Future* (p. 44), where he seeks to demonstrate the relation between the art of dancing, music, and poetry: "In the contemplation of this ravishing dance of the most genuine and noblest muses, of the artistic man [?], we now see the three arm-in-arm lovingly entwined up to their necks; then this, then that one, detaching herself from the entwinement, as if to display to the others her beautiful form in complete separation, touching the hands of the others only with the extreme tips of her fingers; now the one entranced by a backward glance at the twin forms of her closely entwined sisters, bending towards them; then two, carried away by the allurements of the one [!] greeting her in homage; finally all, in close embrace, breast to breast, limb to limb, in an ardent kiss of love, coalescing in one blissfully living shape. This is the love and life, the joy and wooing of art," etc. (Observe the word-play: *Lieben und Leben, Freuen und Freien!*) Wagner here visibly loses the thread of his argument; he neglects what he really wishes to say, and revels in the picture of the three dancing maidens, who have arisen before his mind's eye, following with lascivious longing the outline of their forms and their seductive movements.

The shameless sensuality which prevails in his dramatic poems has impressed all his critics. Hanslick speaks of the "bestial sensuality" in *Rheingold*, and says of *Siegfried:* "The feverish accents, so much beloved by Wagner, of an insatiable sensuality, blazing to the uttermost limits—this ardent moaning, sighing, crying, and sinking to the ground, move us with repugnance. The text of these love-scenes becomes sometimes, in its exuberance, sheer nonsense." Compare in the first act of the *Walküre*, in the scene between Siegmund and Sieglinde, the following stage directions: "Hotly interrupting"; "embraces her with fiery passion"; "in gentle ecstasy"; "she hangs enraptured upon his neck"; "close to his eyes"; "beside himself"; "in the highest intoxication," etc. At the conclusion, it is said, "The curtain falls quickly," and frivolous critics have not failed to perpetrate the cheap witticism, "Very necessary, too." The amorous whinings, whimperings and raving of *Tristan und*

Isolde, the entire second act of *Parsifal,* in the scene between the hero and the flower girls, and then between him and Kundry in Klingsor's magic garden, are worthy to rank with the above passages. It certainly rebounds to the high honor of German public morality, that Wagner's operas could have been publicly performed without arousing the greatest scandal. How unperverted must wives and maidens be when they are in a state of mind to witness these pieces without blushing crimson, and sinking into the earth for shame! How innocent must even husbands and fathers be who allow their womankind to go to these representations of "lupanar" incidents! Evidently the German audiences entertain no misgivings concerning the actions and attitudes of Wagnerian personages; they seem to have no suspicion of the emotions by which they are excited, and what intentions their words, gestures and acts denote; and this explains the peaceful artlessness with which these audiences follow theatrical scenes during which, among a less childlike public, no one would dare lift his eyes to his neighbor or endure his glance.

With Wagner amorous excitement assumes the form of mad delirium. The lovers in his pieces behave like tomcats gone mad, rolling in contortions and convulsions over a root of valerian. They reflect a state of mind in the poet which is well known to the professional expert. It is a form of sadism. . . .

In spite of the unfavorable judgments of many of his professional brethren, Wagner is incontestably an eminently gifted musician. This coolly expressed recognition will certainly seem grotesque to Wagnerian fanatics, who place him above Beethoven. But a serious inquirer into truth need not trouble himself about the impressions provoked by Wagner among these persons. In the first period of his productivity Wagner much oftener achieved compositions of beauty than subsequently, and among these many may be termed pearls of musical literature, and will for a long time enjoy the esteem of serious and rational people. But Wagner the musician had to confront a life-long enemy, who forcibly prevented the full unfolding of his gifts, and this enemy was Wagner the musical theorist.

In his graphomaniacal muddle he concocted certain theories, which represent so many fits of aesthetic delirium. The most important of these are the dogmas of the *leitmotif* and of the unending melody. Everyone now undoubtedly knows what Wagner understood by the former. The expression has passed into all civilized languages. The *leitmotif*, in which the threshed-out discarded "program music" was bound logically to culminate, is a sequence of tones supposed to express a definite conception, and appears in the orchestration whenever the composer intends to recall to the auditor the corresponding conception. By the *leitmotif* Wagner transforms music into dry speech. The orchestration, leaping from *leitmotif* to *leitmotif*, no longer embodies general emotions, but claims to appeal to memory and to reason, and communicate sharply defined presentations. Wagner combines a few notes into a musical figure, as a rule not even distinct or original, and makes this arrangement with the auditor: "This figure signifies a combat, that a dragon, a third a sword," etc. If the auditor does not agree to the stipulation, the *leitmotifs* lose all significance, for they possess in themselves nothing which compels us to grasp the meaning arbitrarily lent them; and they cannot have anything of this kind in them, because the imitative powers of music are by its nature limited to purely acoustical phenomena, or at most to those optical phenomena ordinarily accompanied by acoustical phenomena. By imitating thunder, music can express the notion of a thunderstorm; by the imitation of the tones of a bugle, it can call up that of an army in such a way that the listener can hardly have a doubt as to the significance of the corresponding sequences of tones. On the other hand, it is absolutely denied to music, with the means at its disposal, to produce an unequivocal embodiment of the visible and tangible world, let alone that of abstract thought. Hence the *leitmotifs* are at best cold symbols, resembling written characters, which in themselves say nothing, and convey to the initiated and the learned alone the given import of a presentation.

Here again is found the phenomenon already repeatedly indicated by us as a mark of the mode of thought among the degenerate—the unconscious moon-struck somnambulous way in which they transgress the most firmly established limits of the particular artistic domain, annul the differentiation of the arts arrived at by long historical evolution, and lead them back to the period of the lacustrines, nay, of the most primitive troglodytes. We have seen that the Pre-Raphaelites reduce the picture to a writing which is no longer to produce its effect by its pictorial qualities, but must express an abstract idea; and that the symbolists make of the word, that conventional vehicle of a conception, a musical harmony, by whose aid they endeavor to awaken not an idea, but a phonetic effect. In precisely the same way Wagner wishes to divest music of its proper essence, and to transform it from a vehicle of emotion into a vehicle of rational thought. The disguise produced by this interchange of costumes is in this way complete. Painters proclaim themselves writers; poets behave like the composers of symphonies; the musician plays the poet. Pre-Raphaelites wishing to record a religious apothegm do not make use of writing, which leaves nothing to be desired in the way of convenience, and by which they would be distinctly understood, but plunge into the labor of a highly detailed painting, costing them much time, and which, in spite of its wealth of figures, is far from speaking so clearly to the intelligence as a single line of rational writing. Symbolists desirous of awakening a musical emotion do not compose a melody, but join meaningless, though ostensibly musical words, capable, perhaps, of provoking amusement or vexation, but not the intended emotion. When Wagner wishes to express the idea of "giant," "dwarf," "tarn-cap which makes the wearer invisible," he does not say in words universally understood "giant," "dwarf," "tarn-cap" (which makes the wearer invisible), but replaces these excellent words by a series of notes, the sense of which no one will divine without a key. Is anything more needed to expose the complete insanity of this confusion of all the means of expression, this ignorance of what is possible to each art? . . .

A searching examination has thus shown us that this pretended musician of the future is an out-and-out musician of long ago. All the characteristics of his talent point not forward, but far behind us. His *leitmotif*, abasing music to a conventional phonetic symbol, is atavism; his unending melody is atavism, leading back the fixed form to the vague recitative of savages; atavism, his subordination of highly differentiated instrumental music to music-drama, which mixes music and poetry, and allows neither of the two art forms to attain to independence; even his peculiarity of almost never permitting more than one person on the stage to sing and of avoiding vocal polyphony is atavism. As a personality he will occupy an important place in music; as an initiator, or developer of his art, hardly any, or a very narrow one. For the only thing that musicians of healthy capacity can learn from him is to keep song and accompaniment in opera closely connected with the words, to declaim with sincerity and propriety, and to suggest pictorial ideas to the imagination by means of orchestral effects. But I dare not decide whether the latter is an enlargement or an upheaval of the natural boundaries of musical art, and in any event disciples of Wagner must use his rich musical palette with caution if they are not to be led astray.

Wagner's mighty influence on his contemporaries is to be explained, neither by his capacities as author and musician, nor by any of his personal qualities, with the exception, perhaps, of that "stubborn perseverance in one and the same fundamental idea" which Lombroso cites as a characteristic of graphomaniacs, but by the peculiarities of the present nervous temperament. His earthly destiny resembles that of those strange Oriental plants known as "Jericho roses" (*Anastatica asteriscus*), which, dingy brown in color, leathery and dry, roll about, driven by every wind, until they reach a congenial soil, when they take root and blossom into full-blown flowers. To the end of his life Wagner's existence was conflict and bitterness, and his boastings had no other echo than the laughter not only of rational beings, but, alas! of fools also. It was not until he had long passed his fiftieth year that he began to know the intoxication of universal fame; and in the last decade of his life he was installed among the demigods. It had come to this, that the world had, in the interval, become ripe for him—and for the madhouse. He had the good fortune to endure until the general degeneration and hysteria were sufficiently advanced to supply a rich and nutritious soil for his theories and his art.

27. Just before the war

(a) "We rejoice in all that loves danger, adventure . . ." Nietzsche,
"We Homeless Ones," *The Joyful Wisdom* (1887)[1]

Some people have associated Nietzsche with the alleged ruthlessness of German militarism. How little he appreciated German nationalism

[1] First published in 1882; this section was added to the 1887 edition. The following translation is by the editor; see pp. 134, 163 for other translations of Nietzsche's work.

can be seen in the following passage from "We Fearless Ones," a section of *Die Fröhliche Wissenschaft* (*The Joyful Wisdom* or *The Gay Science*). Still, there is much in this passage by the era's foremost prophetic voice that reflects the restless idealism of European youth on the eve of 1914. Despising the dull society in which they lived, embracing visions of total destruction, they were ready to march off to war and adventure.

THERE are those among today's Europeans who have a right and who feel it a distinctive honor to call themselves Homeless—the same ones exactly who lay my secret wisdom, my "gay science" to their hearts! For their lot is hard, their hope uncertain, for them to find consolation is a difficult art—and what does it help? We children of the future, how can we be *permitted* to stay at home at this hour? We are hostile to all ideals with which anyone can feel at all at home in this brittle, broken time of transition; we don't believe that their "reality" will endure. The ice that supports us today is wearing very thin; the thawing wind blows, and we ourselves, we homeless ones, are instruments that break the ice and other all-too-thin "realities. . . . We "conserve" nothing, we will return to no past, but we are in no sense "liberal" either, we do not work for "progress," we do not need to stop our ears against the commercial sirens whose songs about "equal rights," "the free society," "no more lords and no more knights" do not in the least tempt us. Nor do we have any use for the Kingdom of Justice and Peace on Earth, since in any case this would be a kingdom of the most appalling mediocrity; we rejoice in all that like us loves danger, war, adventure, all that is never satisfied, never fenced in, reconciled, emasculated; we count ourselves among the conquerors, we dwell on the need for a new order and also a new slavery—since every strengthening and elevating of the human species requires a new kind of enslavement, does it not? With all that, must we basely stay at home, in an age that prides itself on being the most humane, the mildest, the most lawful that has ever been known? Bad enough that we harbor such contempt for these pretty phrases! That we see in them only an expression, a mask, for profound weakness, decadence, old age and sinking strength. What can it matter to us what kind of tinsel a sick man decorates himself with! Let him wear his virtue for the sake of appearances—there is not the slightest doubt that weakness is mild, oh so mild, so law-abiding, so inoffensive, so "human." The religion of "compassion," to which they would have us converted—we know well enough the hysterical little men and women who today need this religion as a disguise and a pretense. We are no humanitarians; we would never think of allowing ourselves to prate of our "love for humanity"—we are not hypocritical enough for that. Or not Saint-Simonist enough, not French enough. One must be afflicted with a Gallic excess of erotic susceptibility and amorous impatience, in order even to approach in an honest way this humanity with its lust. . . . Humanity! Is there an uglier old hag among all old hags? . . . No, we do not love mankind; on the other hand we also are not "German" enough either, as the word is used currently, to talk of nationalism and race-hatred, to be able to take pleasure in the national diseases and blood poisoning, because of which peoples are now quarantined against peoples in Europe, isolated and walled off from one another. For that we are too impartial, too angry, too spoiled, too well educated, too well traveled; we much prefer to live on mountains, to dwell, "out of season," in past or future ages, if thereby we can be spared the quiet madness to which we know we will be condemned as witnesses of a politics which wearies and empties the German spirit, a politics of pettiness. In order that its own creation might not immediately be destroyed again, has it not been forced to plant it between two deadly hatreds?[2] *Must* it not will the perpetuation of Europe's system of separate states? . . . . We homeless ones, we are a race and breed too complex and mixed, "modern men," consequently little tempted to take part in that mendacious racial self-admiration and prostitution which today parades in Germany as the mark of German sentiment, a doubly false and indecent illusion. We are, in a word—and it shall be our word of honor!— *good Europeans*, heirs of Europe, richly, even too richly indebted to the millennia of European thought. We have outgrown Christianity as such, but exactly because we have grown *out* of it, because our ancestors were Christians of ruthless integrity, who willingly sacrificed their lives and property, class and fatherland, for their religion, we—do likewise. For what? For our unbelief? For any sort of unbelief? No, you know better, my friend! The hidden

---

[2] An evident reference to the French and Russians, who soon after Nietzsche wrote this formed an alliance aimed at Germany (Ed.).

Yes in you is stronger than all No's and Perhaps's, of which you and your age are sick; and if you must go to sea, you wanderer, conquer there, you also—a *faith!*

(b) Gabriele d'Annunzio. *The Triumph of Death* (1896)[1]

Gabriele d'Annunzio, "the archangel Gabriel," was the most flamboyant figure to flash across the pre-1914 literary scene, and represents almost all the "decadent" themes at their most decadent. Nietzschean and Wagnerian, preaching love, life and art, he also enacted these themes in a tempestuous life that cast him in the roles of great lover, great adventurer, and finally—and most sinister—political activist. His call for an Italian imperialism in 1910 helped set in motion the forces that led to the First World War; after the war, he invented the gestures and mood of Fascism, which Benito Mussolini largely borrowed from d'Annunzio's 1919 march on Fiume. In his book on *The Romantic Agony*, Mario Praz discusses d'Annunzio at length; no one else fits so well into this category of *fin de siècle* madness. His widely read novels featured lushly described love affairs between exceptional individuals, the amoral, artistic hero being always an obvious copy of d'Annunzio himself. They are profoundly "decadent" in that, for example, barren and diseased women are the most sexually attractive; they are haunted by themes of sadism and death, as will be seen in the following conclusion to a novel entitled *The Triumph of Death*, published in 1896. Wearying of sexual pleasure, the hero becomes obsessed by a desire to mutilate and destroy his beautiful, completely sensual mistress.

W HEN she spoke of the things that pleased her or of the caresses that she preferred, she had in her voice a singular delicacy; to modulate the syllables, her lips moved in a manner that expressed profound sensuality. Now, in every one of these words, in each of these movements, George found a motif of the keenest suffering. That sensuality which he had himself aroused in her he believed had now come to the point where desire, untiring and tyrannical, could no longer support any bridle and claimed immediate satisfaction. Hippolyte appeared to him like a woman irresistibly addicted to pleasure in all its forms, no matter what degradation it might cost her. When he had gone away, or when she had tired of his

[1] The following excerpt from *The Triumph of Death*, published by G. H. Richmond, appeared in 1896. More recently, this novel was published by Modern Library (1926) but it is no longer in print.

"love," she would accept the most generous and most practical offer. Perhaps she would even succeed in raising the price very high. Where, in fact, could a rarer instrument of voluptuousness be found? She possessed at present every seduction and every science; she had that beauty which strikes men at sight, which disturbs them, which awakens in their blood implacable covetousness; she had feline elegance of person, refined taste in dress, exquisite art in colors and styles that harmonized with her grace; she had learned to modulate, in a voice suave and warm as the velvet of her eyes, the slow syllables that evoked dreams and lulled pain; she bore in the depths of her being a secret malady that seemed at times to mysteriously illumine her sensibility; she had, by turns, the languors of the malady and the vehemence of health; and, finally, she was barren. United in her, then, were the sovereign virtues that destine a woman to dominate the world by the scourge of her impure beauty. Passion had refined and complicated these virtues. She was now at the zenith of her power. If, all at once, she found herself free and untrammeled, what road would she choose in life? George had no longer the slightest doubt; he knew what that choice would be. He was confirmed in the certitude that his influence over her was bounded by the senses and by certain factitious attitudes of her mind. The plebeian foundation had persisted, impenetrable in its thickness. He was convinced that this plebeian foundation would permit her to adapt herself without compunction to the contact of a lover who would not be distinguished by any superior qualities, physical or moral: in short, a commonplace lover. And, while he filled her empty glass again with the wine she preferred, the wine that one uses to enliven secret suppers, to animate little modern orgies behind closed doors, he attributed, in imagination, attitudes of outrageous immodesty to "the pale and voracious Roman, incomparable in the art of tiring the loins of men."

"How your hand trembles," observed Hippolyte, looking at it.

"It's true," he said, with a convulsion that simulated gaiety. "I think I've already had too much. Why don't you drink? That's not fair."

She laughed, and drank for the third time, filled with a childish joy at the thought of getting tipsy, at feeling her intelligence become gradually obscured. The fumes of the wine were already operating in her. The hysterical demon began to move her.

"See how sunburnt my arms are!" she cried, drawing her large sleeves up to the elbows. "Just look at my wrists!"

Although she was a carnation brunette, of a warm, dull-gold color, the skin at her wrists was extremely transparent and of a strange pallor. The sun had burnt the parts exposed; but on the under side the wrists had remained pale. And on that fine skin, through that pallor, the veins shone through, subtle, and yet very visible, of an intense azure slightly approaching a violet. George had often repeated the words of Cleopatra to the messenger from Italy: "Behold, here are my bluest veins to kiss."

Hippolyte held out her wrists to him and said:

"Kiss them!"

He seized one, and made a motion with his knife as if about to cut it off.

She dared him to.

"Cut, if you want to. I won't move."

During the gesture he looked fixedly at the delicate blue network on her skin, so clearly defined that it seemed to belong to another body, to the body of a blond woman. And that singularity attracted him, tempted him aesthetically by the suggestion of a tragic image of beauty.

"It is your vulnerable spot," he said with a smile. "It is a sure indication. You will die from cut veins. Give me the other hand."

He placed the two wrists together, and again made a gesture as to cut them off with a single blow. The complete image arose in his imagination. On the marble threshold of a door, full of shadow and expectation, the woman who was about to die appeared, extending her naked arms; and at the extremities of the arms, from the slashed veins, spouted and palpitated two red fountains. And, between these red fountains, the face slowly assumed a supernatural pallor, the cavities of the eyes were filled with an infinite mystery, the phantom of an inexpressible word was outlined on the closed mouth. All at once the double jet ceased to flow. The exsanguined body fell backwards like a mass, in the shadow.

"Tell me your dream!" begged Hippolyte, seeing him absorbed.

He described the image to her.

"Very beautiful," said she, with admiration, as if before an engraving,

And she lit a cigarette. She puffed a wave of smoke from between her lips against the lamp around which the night-moths were whirling. She watched for a moment the agitation of the little variegated wings between the moving veils of the cloud. Then she turned toward Ortona, which scintillated with fire. She arose and raised her eyes to the stars.

"How warm the night is!" she said, breathing heavily. "Aren't you warm too?"

She threw away her cigarette. Again she uncovered her arms. She came close to him; she suddenly threw his head back; she enveloped him in a long caress; her mouth glided over all his face, languishing and ardent, in a multiple kiss. Feline-like, she clung to him, entwined him, and with an almost inexplicable movement, agile and furtive, she seated herself on his knees, intoxicating him with the perfume of her skin, that perfume, at once irritating and delicious, that always had the same exhilarating effect on him as the scent of the tuberose.

Every fiber of his being trembled, like a few moments before when she had clasped him ardently in the room filled with the last shadows of twilight. She noticed his emotion and it aroused desire in her. Her hands became bold.

"No, no; let me be!" he stammered, repulsing her. "We shall be seen."

She tore herself away. She tottered slightly, and appeared really influenced by the wine. It seemed as though a mist, passing over her eyes and into her brain, obscured her sight and thought. She put her hands to her forehead and burning cheeks.

"How warm it is!" she sighed. "I wish I had nothing on."

Possessed from now on by that one fixed idea, George repeated to himself: "Must I die alone?" As the fatal hour drew nearer, the deed of violence seemed more necessary. Behind him, in the shadow in the bedroom, he heard the ticktack of the clock; he heard the rhythmic blows of a flax brake on a distant field. These two sounds, cadenced and dissimilar, intensified in him the sensation of the flight of time, gave him a sort of anxious terror.

"Look at Ortona aflame!" cried Hippolyte. "What a number of rockets!"

The festive city illuminated the sky. Innumerable skyrockets, parting from a central point, spread out in the sky like a broad golden fan, that slowly, from top to bottom, dissolved into a shower of scattered sparks, and, suddenly, in the midst of the golden rain, a new fan was formed, entire and splendid, to dissolve again and reform again, while the waters reflected the changing picture. One heard a low crepitation, like a distant fusillade, interspersed with deeper reports that followed the explosions of multicolored bombs in the heights of the sky. And at every report the city, the port, the great stretched-out mole, appeared in a different light, fantastically transfigured.

Upright against the parapet, Hippolyte admired the spectacle, and saluted the brighter splendors with exclamations of delight. From time to time it spread over her person like the reflection of a fire.

"She is overexcited, a little inebriated, ready for any madness," thought George as he watched her. "I could suggest a walk, which she has often wanted to take: to go through one of the tunnels by the light of a torch. I would go down to the Trabocco to get a torch. She could wait for me at the end of the bridge. I would lead her then to the tunnel by a path that I know. I would manage that the train should come upon us while we were in the tunnel—foolhardiness, accident."

The idea seemed to him easy of realization; it had presented itself to his imagination with extraordinary clearness, as if it had formed an integral part of his consciousness since that first day when, before the shining rails, he received the first confused glimmer from them. "She must die, too." His resolution became strengthened, immutable. He heard behind him the ticking of the clock. He felt a feeling of intense anxiety he could not master. It was getting late. Perhaps there was scarcely time for them to go down. He must act without delay, assure himself immediately as to the precise time indicated by the clock. But it seemed impossible for him to rise from his chair; it seemed to him that if he spoke to her carelessly, his speech would fail him.

He started to his feet as he heard in the distance the well-known rumbling. Too late! And his heart beat so fast that he believed he would die of anguish as he heard the rumbling and whistling draw nearer.

Hippolyte turned.

"The train!" she said. "Come and see!"

He went; and she encircled his neck with her bare arm, leaning on his shoulder.

"It is entering the tunnel," she said again, prompted by the difference in sound.

In George's ears the rumbling increased in a frightful manner. He saw, as in a hallucination, his mistress and himself beneath the dark roof, the rapid approach of the headlight in the dark, the short struggle on the rails, the simultaneous fall, the bodies crushed by the horrible violence; and, at the same time, he felt the contact of the supple woman, caressing, always triumphant. And, added to the physical horror of this barbarous destruction, he felt an exasperated rancor against her who seemed to escape his hate.

Both leaning against the parapet, they watched the deafening train, rapid and sinister, that shook the house to its very foundations, and even imparted the shock to them.

"All night," said Hippolyte, pressing still closer to him, "I'm afraid when the train shakes the house as it passes. Aren't you, too? I have often felt you tremble."

He did not hear her. An immense tumult stirred his whole being; it was the rudest and most obscure agitation that his soul had ever experienced. Incoherent thoughts and images whirled in his brain, and his heart writhed beneath a thousand cruel punctures. But one fixed image dominated all the others, invaded the center of his soul. What was he doing at this hour five years before? He was holding vigil over a cadaver; he was contemplating a face hidden beneath a black veil, a long, pale hand—

Hippolyte's restless hands touched him, crept into his hair, tickled his neck. On his neck, on his ear, he felt a warm mouth. With an instinctive motion that he could not repress, he drew aside, walked away. She laughed that singular laugh, ironical and immodest, which burst out and resounded from between her teeth whenever her lover refused himself to her. And under this obsession he heard once more the slow and limpid syllables: "For fear of my kisses!"

A low crepitation, mingled with the distinct reports, still came from the festive town. The fireworks were beginning again.

Hippolyte turned toward the spectacle.

"Look! One would think that Ortona were on fire."

A vast crimson glare lit up the heavens and was reflected in the waters, and in the midst of the light the profile of the flaming town was outlined. The rockets burst overhead like splendid large roses.

"Shall I live through this night? Shall I recommence to live to-morrow? And how long? A disgust, bitter as a nausea, an almost savage hate, arose from his heart at the thought that the following night he would again have that woman near him on the same pillow, that he would again smell the odor and feel the contact of that heated skin, and then that the day would break again and pass by in the usual idleness, amidst the torture of perpetual alternatives.

A burst of light struck him, attracted his gaze to the spectacle outside. A vast pink lunary light blossomed over the festive town, and yonder, on the shore, illuminated the succession of little indented bays and jutting points as far as the sight could reach. Cape Moro, the Nicchiola, the Trabocco, the rocks, near or distant, as far as the Vasto point, appeared a few seconds in the immense irradiation.

"The promontory!" suggested a secret voice to George suddenly, while his gaze was carried to the heights crowned by the twisted olive trees.

The white light faded away. The distant town became silent, still outlined against the shadows by its illuminations. In the silence, George perceived again the oscillations of the pendulum and the rhythmic beats of the flax brake. But now he was master of his anguish; he felt himself stronger and his mind clearer.

"Shall we go out a little?" he asked Hippolyte, in a slightly changed voice. "We'll go to some spot in the open; we'll stretch ourselves out on the grass, and breathe in the fresh air. Look! The night is almost as light as if it were full moon."

"No, no; let us stay here!" she answered nonchalantly.

"It's not late. Are you sleepy already? I cannot go to bed too early, you know: I do not sleep, I suffer. I would gladly take a little walk. Come, do not be so lazy! You could come just as you are."

"No, no; let us stay here."

And, once more, she passed her bare arms around his neck, languishing, seized by desire.

"Let us stay here. Come indoors; let us lie down a little. Come!"

She tried to coax him, to entice him, seized by desire that became all the fiercer as she noticed George's resistance. She was all ardor, and her beauty was at its best, illuminated as by a torch. Her long, serpentine body trembled through her thin wrapper. Her large dark eyes shed the fascinating charm of the supreme hours of passion. She was the sovereign Sensualism repeating: "I am forever the unconquered. I am stronger than your thought. The odor of my skin has the power to dissolve a world in you."

"No, no; I do not want to," declared George, seizing her wrists with an almost brutal violence that he could not moderate.

"Ah! you don't want to?" she echoed mockingly, amused by the struggle, sure of conquering, incapable of giving way in her caprice.

He regretted his roughness. To draw her into the snare, he must be mild and coaxing, must simulate ardor and tenderness. After that, he would certainly induce her to take the nocturnal walk—the last walk. But, on the other hand, he also felt the absolute necessity of not losing that nervous momentary energy that was indispensable for the approaching *action*.

"Ah! So you don't want to?" she repeated, throwing her bare arms about him, gazing up at him, looking into the depths of his eyes with a species of repressed frenzy.

George permitted himself to be led into the room.

Then all the Enemy's feline lasciviousness broke loose over him whom she believed already vanquished. She let down her hair, loosened her dress, permitted her natural perfume to be exhaled like a shrub of odoriferous flowers. She seemed to realize that she must disarm this man, that she must enervate him, and that she must crush him to prevent him from becoming dangerous.

George felt he was lost. Once more the Enemy had asserted her superiority.

Suddenly she was seized with laughter, nervous, frantic, ungovernable, lugubrious as the laughter of the insane.

Frightened, he let her go. He looked at her with manifest horror, thinking, "Is this madness?"

She laughed, laughed, laughed, writhing, hiding her face in her hands, biting her fingers, holding her sides; she laughed, laughed in spite of herself, shaken by long, sonorous hiccoughs.

At intervals, she stopped for a second; then recommenced with renewed violence. And nothing was more lugubrious than these mad laughs in the silence of the magnificent night.

"Don't be afraid! Don't be afraid!" she said, during the pauses, at the sight of her perplexed and frightened lover. "I am calmer now. Go out, please. Please go out!"

He went back on the loggia, as if in a dream. Nevertheless, his brain retained a strange lucidity and strange wakefulness. All his acts, all his perceptions had for him the unreality of a dream, and assumed at the same time a signification as profound as that of an allegory. He still heard behind him the ill-repressed laughter; he retained still in his fingers the sensation of the impure thing. He saw above and around him the beauty of the summer evening. He knew what was on the point of being accomplished.

The laughs ceased. Again, in the silence, he perceived the vibrations of the pendulum and the beats of the flax-brake on the distant area. A groan coming from the house of the old people made him shudder: it was the pain of her who was now in childbirth.

"All must be accomplished!" he thought.

And, turning, he crossed the threshold with a firm step.

Hippolyte lay upon the sofa, recomposed, pale, her eyes half closed. At the approach of her lover, she smiled.

"Come, sit down!" she murmured, with a vague gesture.

He bent over her, and saw tears between her eyelashes.

"Are you suffering?" he asked.

"I feel a slight suffocation. I have a weight here, as if a ball were rising and falling."

She pointed to the center of her chest. He said: "It is suffocating in this room. Make an effort, and get up. Let us go out. The air will do you good. Come!"

He rose, and held out his hands. She gave him hers, and let him raise her. When on her feet, she shook her head to throw back her hair, which was still untied. Then she bent down to search for her lost hairpins.

"Where can they be?"

"What are you looking for?"

"My hairpins."

"Let them be! You'll find them tomorrow."

"But I need them to fasten my hair."

"Leave your hair as it is. It pleases me that way."

She smiled. They went out into the loggia. She raised her face towards the stars and breathed the perfume of the summer night.

"You see how beautiful the night is!" said George, in a hoarse yet gentle voice.

"They are beating the flax," said Hippolyte, listening attentively to the continuous rhythm.

"Let us go down," said George. "Let us walk a little. Let us go as far as the olive trees, yonder."

He seemed to hang on Hippolyte's lips .

"No, no. Let us remain here. You see in what a state I am!"

"What does that matter? Who will see you? We shall not meet a living soul at this hour. Come as you are. I'd go without my hat. The country is almost like a garden for us. Let us go down."

She hesitated a few seconds. But she, too, felt the need of fresh air, of getting away from this house that still seemed to resound with the echo of her horrible laughs.

"Let us go down," she finally consented.

At these words, George felt as if his heart had ceased to beat.

With an instinctive movement he approached the threshold of the illuminated room. He cast toward the interior a look of anguish, a look of farewell. A hurricane of recollections arose in his distracted soul.

"Shall we leave the lamp lit?" he asked, without thinking of what he was saying.

And his own voice gave him an indefinable sensation as of some distant and strange thing.

"Yes," answered Hippolyte.

They went down.

On the staircase they took each other by the hand, slowly descending step by step. George made so violent an effort to repress his anguish that the effort caused in him a strange exaltation. He considered the immensity of the nocturnal sky, and believed it to be filled by the intensity of his own life.

They perceived on the parapet of the courtyard the shadow of a man, motionless and silent. They recognized old Colas.

"You here at this hour, Colas?" said Hippolyte. "Are you not sleepy?"

"I am keeping vigil for Candie, who is in childbirth," responded the old man.

"And is everything going well?"

"Yes, very well."

The door of the habitation was lit up.

"Wait a minute," said Hippolyte. "I want to see Candie."

"No, do not go there now," begged George. "You will see her on your return."

"That is so; I will see her on my return. Good-by, Colas."

She stumbled as she entered the path.

"Take care," cautioned the shadow of the old man.

George offered her his arm.

"Do you want to lean on me?"

She took George's arm.

They walked several steps in silence.

The night was bright, glorious in all directions. The Great Bear stone on their heads in all its sextuple mystery. Silent and pure as the heaven above, the Adriatic gave as the only indication of its existence its respiration and its perfume.

"Why do you hurry so?" asked Hippolyte.

George slowed down his step. Dominated by a single thought, pursued by the necessity of the act, he had only a confused consciousness for everything else. His inner life seemed to disintegrate, to decompose, to dissolve in a heavy fermentation that invaded even the deepest depths of his being, and brought to the surface shapeless fragments, of diverse nature, as little recognizable as if they had not belonged to the life of the same man.

All these strange, inextricable, abrupt, violent things he vaguely perceived, as if in a half-slumber, while at the same time one single point in his brain retained an extraordinary lucidity, and, in a rigid line, guided him toward the fatal act.

"How melancholy the sound of the flax brake in that field is," said Hippolyte, stopping. "All night long they beat the flax. Does that not make you feel melancholy?"

She abandoned herself on George's arm, brushed his cheek with her tresses.

"Do you recall, at Albano, the pavers who were beating the pavement from morning to night beneath our window?"

Her voice was veiled with sadness, somewhat tired.

"We became accustomed to that noise."

She stopped, restless.

"Why do you keep turning around?"

"It seems to me that I hear a man walking barefoot," responded George in a low voice. "Let us stop."

They stopped, listened.

George was under the empire of the same horror that had frozen him in front of the door of the funereal chamber. All his being trembled, fascinated by the mystery; he seemed to have already crossed the confines of an unknown world.

"It is Giardino," said Hippolyte, on perceiving the dog, which approached. "He has followed us."

And, several times, she called the faithful animal, which came running up friskily. She bent down to caress him, spoke to him in the special tone she habitually used when she petted animals she was fond of.

"You never leave your friend, do you? You never leave her?"

The grateful animal rolled in the dust.

George made a few steps. He felt a great relief on feeling himself free from Hippolyte's arm; up to now, this contact had given him an indefinable physical uneasiness. He imagined the sudden and violent act he was about to accomplish; he imagined the mortal embrace of his arms around the body of this woman, and he would have liked to touch her only at the supreme instant.

"Come, come; we'll soon be there," he said, preceding her in the direction of the olive trees, whitened by the moonlight and stars.

He halted on the edge of the plateau, and turned around to assure himself that she was following him. Once more he gazed around him distractedly, as if to embrace the image of the night. It seemed to him that, on this plateau, the silence had become more profound. Only the rhythmic beats of the flax brake could be heard from the distant fields.

"Come!" he repeated in a clear voice, strengthened by a sudden energy.

And, passing between the twisted trunks, feeling beneath his feet the softness of the grass, he directed his steps towards the edge of the precipice.

This edge formed a circular projection, entirely free in every direction, without any kind of railing. George pressed his hands on his knees, bent his body forward on this support, and advanced his head cautiously. He examined the rocks below him; he saw a corner of the sandy beach. The little corpse stretched out on the sand reappeared to him. There appeared to him also the blackish spot he had seen with Hippolyte from the heights of the Pincio, at the foot of the wall; and he heard again the answers of the teamster to the greenish-looking man; and, confusedly, all the phantoms of that distant afternoon repassed before his soul.

"Take care!" cried Hippolyte, as she came up to him. "Take care!"

The dog barked among the olive trees.

"Do you hear me, George? Come away!"

The promontory fell perpendicularly down to the black and deserted rocks, around which the water scarcely moved, splashing feebly, rocking in its slow undulations the reflections of the stars.

"George! George!"

"Have no fear!" he said in a hoarse voice. "Come nearer! Come! Come and see the fishermen, fishing by torchlight among the rocks."

"No, no! I am afraid of vertigo."

"Come! I will hold you."

"No, no."

She seemed frozen by the unusual tone in George's voice, and a vague fright commenced to invade her.

"Come!"

And he approached her, his hands extended. Suddenly he seized her wrists, dragged her several steps; them he seized her in his arms, made a bound, and attempted to force her towards the abyss.

"No! no! no!"

She resisted with furious energy.

She succeeded in disengaging herself, jumped back, panting and trembling.

"Are you mad?" she cried, choked by anger. "Are you mad?"

But when she saw him come after her without speaking a word, when she felt herself seized with more brutal violence and dragged again toward the precipice, she understood all, and a great, sinister flash of light struck terror to her soul.

"No, George, no! Let me be! Let me be! Only one minute! Listen! Listen! One minute! I want to tell you—"

Insane with terror, she supplicated him, writhing. She hoped to stop him, to move him to pity.

"One minute! Listen! I love you! Forgive me! Forgive me!"

She stammered incoherent words desperately, feeling herself becoming weaker, losing her ground, seeing death before her.

"Assassin!" she then shrieked, furious.

And she defended herself with her nails, with her teeth, like a beast.

"Assassin!" she shrieked, as she was seized by the hair, thrown to the ground on the edge of the precipice, lost.

The dog barked at the tragic group.

It was a brief and fierce struggle, like the sudden outburst of supreme hate which, up to then, had been smoldering unsuspected, in the hearts of implacable enemies.

And they both crashed down to death, clasped in each other's arms.

(c) "Soldiers marching, all to die." A. E. Housman, *A Shropshire Lad* (1896)

A stiff, reserved, withdrawn professor of Latin at University College, London, published in 1896 a thin volume of verses under the title *A Shropshire Lad*. The verses are exquisitely classical in their simplicity and economy, but beneath the simplicity lie coiled springs of deep emotion, and an almost unbearable poignancy. In writing these remarkable stanzas A. E. Housman must have listened to the voices of prophecy, for the image of death is present almost as much (in its very different way) as it is in the wild romantic exuberance of d'Annunzio.

ON THE IDLE HILL OF SUMMER

On the idle hill of summer,
Sleepy with the flow of streams,
Far I hear the steady drummer
Drumming like a noise in dreams.

Far and near and low and louder
On the roads of earth go by,
Dear to friends and food for powder,
Soldiers marching, all to die.

East and west on fields forgotten
Bleach the bones of comrades slain,
Lovely lads and dead and rotten;
None that go return again.

Far the calling bugles hollo,
High the screaming fife replies,
Gay the files of scarlet follow;
Woman bore me, I will rise.

(d) "There is no longer any Christianity left." Charles Péguy,
Clio (1910)[1]

"The death of God," the extinction of Christianity, was felt by many
in this era, but by none, perhaps, save Nietzsche and Dostoyevsky, so
keenly as by the French man of letters Charles Péguy. Péguy, who
died at the battle of the Marne in 1914, began as a socialist, but was too
free a spirit to be bound by the dogmas of a faction and left the party
in 1899 to become finally an ardent Christian mystic. Between 1900 and
1910 he edited France's leading journal of ideas and literature, the
Cahiers de la Quinzaine, opening it to all shades of opinion. He was a
patriot who more than any other one person was responsible for popu-
larizing the cult of Joan of Arc, mystic, Christian and patriot. He can
also be described as a Christian socialist or Christian democrat, exerting
a large influence on these movements. The following passage, written
in 1910, is from a version of his *Clio*, a work in which he reveals an
almost terrifying awareness of the spiritual crisis the Western world
faces.

W HAT WE mean is that the modern world has given up, renounced
the whole system, the whole mystique. Which means that from
now on there is a new and different world; that the modern world
is not just a bad Christian world, which would be nothing, but an
unchristian world, literally, absolutely, totally de-Christianized.
That is what it means. That is what needs to be said and seen. If it
were only the old story, if it was merely that sin had once again
encroached, it would mean nothing, my dear child; we are used to
that, the world is used to it. One more bad Christian century after
many others. If people knew history as well as I do, they would
know perhaps that it has always been so, that all those twenty

[1] Charles Péguy's *Clio* was written between 1909 and 1912; he later took
one part of it out. See the Pléiade edition of his works, 1909-1914 (Paris:
Gaillimard, 1961.) The selection used was translated by Alexander Dru, in a
book titled *Temporal and Eternal* (London: Harvill Press, 1958.) Other
writings of Péguy, but not the *Clios*, were translated by Anne and Julian
Green in 1943 and 1944: *Basic Verities* and *Men and Saints* (New York:
Pantheon Books).

centuries have really been centuries of miserable Christianity, evil
centuries, terribly wanting in mysticism. Which means that the
contingent of saints has always been minute compared with the
sinners. And while, no doubt, a few saints triumphed eternally, no
doubt, whole masses, whole peoples of sinners held power and
dominated temporally; while a few saints saved themselves eternally
(and others too perhaps), and made their salvation eternal, the
sinners, the innumerable sinners risked temporally being lost. That,
alas, is unfortunately the regime itself. Those were Christian
miseries. And the grandeur of Christianity too. But the regime is
no more, and the disaster is that even our miseries are no longer
Christian. That is the truth of it. That is what is new. As long as
our misery was a Christian misery, as long as vices created sins, and
what was base was also Christian, as long as crime meant perdition,
there was, so to speak, something good about it. You see what I
mean, my friend. There was some hope, there was something; there
was matter for grace, naturally. Whereas nowadays everything is
new and everything is different. Everything is modern. That is
what one must see. What must be said. Everything is completely
unchristian. Alas, alas, if it were merely bad Christianity, one could
see a way out, one could begin to talk. But when we talk of de-
Christianization, when one says there is a modern world, and that
it is completely de-Christianized, that simply means that it has
given up the whole system altogether, that it moves and has its
being outside the system; it means that everybody has renounced
the whole of Christianity. It implies the constitution of a totally
different, new, free, entirely independent system. Were it only
bad Christianity, my child, it would not (yet) be very interesting;
it would no longer be interesting. You understand, my poor, dear
friend, what I am driving at.

What is interesting, what is new, is that there is no longer any
Christianity left. That expresses not only the extent but the nature
of the disaster. Once the Catholics have consented to see and
measure and admit the disaster and where it comes from, once
they have given up their cowardly diagnosis, then, and only then
will they perhaps be able to work usefully; then they will no
longer be lazy, and we shall, perhaps, be able to talk. But what
they will not recognize, what is new and interesting, alas, my son,
alas, you know what I mean, is that there is a modern world, a

modern society (I do not say a modern city, and as the song says: "You know what I mean"), is that that world, that society, has constituted itself entirely exteriorly outside Christianity. For it is no longer a question of internal difficulties, but of something complete and exterior; not even of an exterior difficulty, which would still imply some relationship, some link, but on the contrary, of a complete absence of relationship, of link, of binding, and even in point of fact of difficulties; a very curious lack therefore, very disturbing, in the highest degree unsettling: a mutual, reciprocal independence, very singular and strange.

My child, we have seen a world, a society, I do not say a city, a perfectly viable and entirely unchristian society instituted, if not *founded*, under our very eyes; seen it being established, functioning, living. That must be conceded. Those who deny it are hopeless. And just as the world, as I, history, had seen the world, whole worlds, whole humanities live and prosper before Jesus, so we have the sorrow of seeing whole worlds, humanities, living and prospering *after* Jesus. Both the ones and the others without Jesus. Just as one has seen whole worlds, whole *cities* founded, born, assembled, prosper and increase and decrease, like plants, be born and die unchristian, ante-Christian, so we, the first, have seen, the first since Jesus, and see every day, a whole world, if not a city, a wholly unchristian, post-Christian society, be born and grow and not decrease, prosper and not perish, And between the two there is a chasm.

(e) "I have need to busy my heart with quietude."
Rupert Brooke (1913)

Integrity is the last resort of the idealist without ideals. Nietzsche is, among other things, the philosopher of integrity. The theme may be found in almost all the poetry of the pre-1914 War era. The Georgian poets in Britain, such as Robert Bridges, Rupert Brooke, Walter de la Mare, W. H. Davies, and Harold Monro, limited themselves to subjects that they knew and trusted and could therefore, they felt, write about with integrity. These subjects were mostly rural England, nature, the sea, and love. They spurned the prophetic and didactic functions of poetry, for they mistrusted the gods and morals of the Victorian age.

Rupert Brooke, probably the most talented of the Georgian poets, died in the Dardanelles expedition in 1915. He was only twenty-seven. He went to the war, like so many young Europeans in 1914, full of a vague idealism, half glad to have found an heroic cause better than "A world grown old and cold and weary." Before the war he had written about the personal, immediate, and sensory, like all the Georgians and like almost all the poets of the symbolist age. This "filling of the mind with thoughts that will not rend," this search for the homely enduring truths in a confused society, is reflected in the following poem, typical of the pre-1914 English poets.

THE BUSY HEART

Now that we've done our best and worst, and parted,
I would fill my mind with thoughts that will not rend.
(O heart, I do not dare go empty-hearted)
I'll think of Love in books, Love without end;
Women with child, content; and old men sleeping;
And wet strong plowlands, scarred for certain grain;
And babes that weep, and so forget their weeping;
And the young heavens, forgetful after rain;
And evening hush, broken by homing wings;
And Song's nobility, and Wisdom holy,
That live, we dead. I would think of a thousand things,
Lovely and durable, and taste them slowly,
One after one, like tasting a sweet food.
I have need to busy my heart with quietude.

Bibliography

General

ALLEN, WALTER. *The Modern Novel in Britain and the United States*. New York: Dutton, 1964

CECIL, DAVID. *Victorian Novelists*. Chicago: University of Chicago Press, 1958

DAICHES, DAVID. *The Novel and the Modern World*. Chicago: University of Chicago Press, 1939, 1960

—— *Poetry and the Modern World*. Chicago: University of Chicago Press, 1940

FUERST, NORBERT. *The Victorian Age of German Literature*. University Park, Pa.: Pennsylvania State University Press, 1966

GIFFORD, HENRY. *The Novel in Russia*. London: Hutchinson, 1964

GRAÑA, CÉSAR. *Bohemian versus Bourgeois: French Society and the French Man of Letters in the Nineteenth Century*. New York: Basic Books, 1964; Harper Torchbooks, 1967

GRAY, R. D., *The German Tradition in Literature 1871–1945*. Cambridge: Cambridge University Press, 1961

HELLER, ERICH. *The Disinherited Mind*. Cambridge: Cambridge University Press, 1952

HOUGHTON, WALTER E., *The Victorian Frame of Mind*. New Haven: Yale University Press, 1957

MILLER, JOSEPH H., *The Disappearance of God*. Cambridge: Belknap Press of Harvard University, 1963

MOERS, ELLEN. *The Dandy: Brummell to Beerbohm*. New York: Viking Press, 1960

PASCAL, ROY. *The German Novel*. Manchester: Manchester University Press, 1956

PECKHAM, MORSE. *Beyond the Tragic Vision*. New York: Brazilier, 1962

ROUBICZEK, PAUL. *The Misinterpretation of Man: Studies in Eu-*
ropean Thought of the Nineteenth Century. New York:
Scribner's, 1947

SHATTUCK, ROGER. *The Banquet Years: The Arts in France 1858–*
1918. New York: Doubleday Anchor Books, 1961.

SIMON, WALTER M., *European Positivism in the Nineteenth Cen-*
tury. Ithaca: Cornell University Press, 1963

SLOANE, JOSEPH C., *French Painting between the Past and Present*.
Princeton: Princeton University Press, 1951

SLONIM, MARK L., *Modern Russian Literature*. New York: Oxford University Press, 1953

STARKIE, ENID. *From Gautier to Eliot*. London: Hutchinson, 1960

WILLEY, BASIL. *Nineteenth Century Studies*. New York: Columbia University Press, 1949; Harper Torchbooks, 1966; London: Chatto & Windus, 1949

—— *More Nineteenth Century Studies*. New York: Columbia
University Press, 1956; Harper Torchbooks, 1966; London:
Chatto & Windus, 1956

WIND, EDGAR. *Art and Anarchy*. London: Faber & Faber, 1963

Realism

AUERBACH, ERIC. *Mimesis: The Representation of Reality in*
Western Literature. Princeton: Princeton University Press,
1953

CASSAGNE, ALBERT. *La théorie de l'art pour l'art en France chez*
les derniers romantiques et les premiers réalistes Paris: Dorbon,
1959

CHARLTON, D. C., *Positivist Thought in France, 1852–1870*. Oxford: Clarendon Press, 1959

DUMESNIL, RENÉ. *Le realisme et le naturalisme* Paris: Del Duca
de Gigard, 1955)

FREDEMAN, WILLIAM E., *The Pre-Raphaelites*. Cambridge: Harvard University Press, 1965

LEVIN, HARRY. *The Gates of Horn: A Study of Five French Real-*
ists. New York: Oxford University Press, 1963

MARTINI, FRITZ. *Deutsche Literatur im bürgerlicher Realismus,*
1848–1898. Stuttgart: J. B. Metzler, 1962

PRAZ, MARIO. *The Hero in Eclipse in Victorian Literature*. London and New York: Oxford University Press, 1956

SIMMONS, ERNEST. *Introduction to Russian Realism*. Bloomington: Indiana University Press, 1964

Naturalism

BEUCHAT, CHARLES. *Histoire du naturalisme français*. Paris: Correa, 1949

BRANDES, GEORGE M. C., *Naturalism in Nineteenth Century English Literature*. New York: Russell & Russell, 1957

COGNY, PIERRE. *Le Naturalisme*. Paris: Presse Universitaires de France, 1963

HENKIN, L. J., *Darwinism in the English Novel 1860–1910*. New York: Russell & Russell, 1963

HIMMELFARB, GERTRUDE. *Darwin and the Darwinian Revolution*. New York: Macmillan, 1959

REWALD, JOHN. *A History of Impressionism*. New York: Museum of Modern Art, 1961

ZOLA, ÉMILE. *The Naturalist Novel*. ed., Maxwell Geismar. Montreal: Harvest House, 1965

Symbolism

BOWRA, C. M., *The Heritage of Symbolism*. London: Macmillan, 1943

CARTER, A. E., *The Idea of Decadence in French Literature 1830–1900*. Toronto: University of Toronto Press, 1958

CHIARI, JOSEPH. *Symbolism from Poe to Mallarmé*. London: Rockcliff, 1956

CLOUARD, HENRI. *Histoire de la littérature française du Symbolisme à nos jours*. Vol. 1, Paris: Albin Michel, 1947

HOUGH, GRAHAM. *Image and Experience: Studies in a Literary Revolution*. London: Duckworth, 1960

PRAZ, MARIO. *The Romantic Agony*. London and New York: Oxford University Press, 1957

REWALD, JOHN. *Post-Impressionism*. New York: Museum of Modern Art, 1956

SYMONS, ARTHUR. *The Symbolist Movement in Literature*. New York: Dutton, 1919

WILSON, EDMUND. *Axel's Castle*. New York: Scribner's 1931

Individual studies

MACKWORTH, CECILY. *Apollinaire and the Cubist Life*. London: J. Murray, 1951

TRILLING, LIONEL. *Matthew Arnold*. New York: Columbia University Press, 1949

BUCHAN, ALASTAIR. *The Spare Chancellor: The Life of Walter Bagehot*. East Lansing: Michigan State University Press, 1960

FAIRLIE, ALISON. *Baudelaire: Les Fleurs du Mal*. London: Edward Arnold, 1960

STARKIE, ENID. *Baudelaire*. London: Faber & Faber, 1957

HASSALL, CHRISTOPHER V., *Rupert Brooke, A Biography*. New York: Harcourt, Brace, 1964

COHEN, JOHN M., *Robert Browning*. London: Longmans, Green, 1952

REWALD, JOHN. *The Ordeal of Paul Cézanne*. London: Phoenix House, 1950

SIMMONS, ERNEST. *Chekhov: A Biography*. Boston: Little, Brown, 1962

HOUSE, HUMPHREY. *The Dickens World*. London: Oxford University Press, 1960

FRAZER, DONALD. *Dostoyevsky and Romantic Realism*. Cambridge: Harvard University Press, 1966

MAGARSHACK, DAVID. *Dostoyevsky*. London: Secker & Warburg, 1962

SIMMONS, ERNEST. *Dostoevski: The Making of a Novelist*. London–New York: Oxford University Press, 1940

ALLEN, WALTER. *George Eliot*. New York: Macmillan, 1964

BROMBERT, VICTOR. *The Novels of Flaubert: A Study of Themes and Techniques*. Princeton: Princeton University Press, 1967

SPENCER, PHILIP H., *Flaubert, a Biography*. London: Faber & Faber, 1952

STARKIE, ENID. *Flaubert: The Making of the Master*. London: Weidenfeld & Nicolson, 1967

THORLBY, ANTHONY. *Gustave Flaubert and the Art of Realism*. New Haven: Yale University Press, 1957

JONES, ERNEST. *Life and Works of Sigmund Freud*. New York: Basic Books, 1953–1955

WHYTE, LANCELOT L., *The Unconscious before Freud*. New York: Basic Books, 1960

RICHÁRDSON, JOANNA. *Théophile Gautier: His Life and Times*. London: Max Reinhardt, 1958

BILLY, ANDRÉ. *The Goncourt Brothers*. New York: Horizon Press, 1960

BROWN, DOUGLAS. *Thomas Hardy*. London and New York: Longmans, Green, 1954

MALIA, MARTIN. *Alexander Herzen and the Birth of Russian Socialism 1812–1855*. Cambridge: Harvard University Press, 1961

LAMPERT, EUGEN. *Studies in Rebellion*. New York: Praeger, 1957

WATSON, GEORGE L., *A. E. Housman, A Divided Life*. London: Rupert Hart-Davis, 1957

BIBBY, CYRIL. *T. H. Huxley: Scientist, Humanist, Educator*. New York: Horizon, 1960

BALDICK, ROBERT. *Life of J.-K. Huysmans*. Oxford: Clarendon Press, 1955

LAVER, JAMES. *The First Decadent*. New York: Citadel Press, 1955

BRANDES, GEORG. *Henrik Ibsen, A Critical Study*. New York: B. Blom, 1964

LUCAS, F. L., *The Drama of Ibsen and Strindberg*. New York: Macmillan, 1962

EDEL, LEON. *Henry James*. Minneapolis: University of Minnesota Press, 1960

BLOCK, HASKELL M., *Mallarmé and the Symbolist Drama*. Detroit: Wayne University Press, 1963

FOWLIE, WALLACE. *Mallarmé*. Chicago: University of Chicago Press, 1953

HAMILTON, GEORGE HEARD. *Manet and His Critics*. New Haven: Yale University Press, 1954

TUCKER, ROBERT G., *Philosophy and Myth in Karl Marx*. New York: Cambridge University Press, 1961

BALDICK, ROBERT. *The First Bohemian*. London: Hamish Hamilton, 1961

HOLLINGDALE, R. J., *Nietzsche, the Man and His Philosophy*. London: Routledge, 1965

LEA, F. A., *The Tragic Philosopher*. London: Methuen, 1957

KAUFMANN, WALTER. *Nietzsche*. Princeton: Princeton University Press, 1950

BENSON, A. C., *Walter Pater*. London: Macmillan, 1926

DRU, ALEXANDER. *Péguy*. London: Harvill Press, 1956

VILLIERS, MARJORIE. *Charles Péguy: A Study in Integrity*. New York: Harper & Row, 1965

WARDMAN, H. W., *Ernest Renan: A Critical Biography*. London: Oxford University Press, 1964

ÉTIEMBLE, RENÉ. *Le mythe de Rimbaud*. Paris: Gallimard, 1952–1961

FROHOCK, WILBUR M., *Rimbaud's Poetic Practice*. Cambridge: Harvard University Press, 1963

STARKIE, ENID. *Rimbaud*. New York: New Directions, 1962

GRYLLS, ROSALIE. *Portrait of Rosetti*. London: Macdonald, 1965

ROSENBERG, JOHN D., *The Darkening Glass* [Ruskin]. New York: Columbia University Press, 1961

COPLESTON, FREDERICK. *Schopenhauer: Philosopher of Pessimism*. London: Burns & Oates, 1947

GARDINER, PATRICK. *Schopenhauer*. Baltimore: Penguin Books, 1963

MADSEN, BORGE G., *Strindberg's Naturalistic Theater: Its Relation to French Naturalism*. Seattle: University of Washington Press, 1962

SIMMONS, ERNEST. *Leo Tolstoy*. Boston: Little, Brown, 1946

FREEBORN, RICHARD. *Turgenev: The Novelist's Novelist* London: Oxford University Press, 1960

NEWMAN, ERNEST. *Life of Richard Wagner*. New York: Knopf, 1933–1946

BARZUN, JACQUES. *Darwin, Marx, Wagner: Critique of a Heritage*. Boston: Little, Brown, 1941

MANN, THOMAS. *Freud, Goethe, Wagner*. New York: Knopf, 1937

ADAM, ANTOINE. *The Art of Paul Verlaine*. New York: New York University Press, 1961

HYDE, H. MONTGOMERY. *Oscar Wilde: The Aftermath*. New York: Farrar, Straus, 1963

GRANT, ELLIOTT M., *Zola's Germinal: A Critical and Historical Study*. Leicester: Leicester University Press, 1962

HEMMINGS, F. W. J., *Zola*. Oxford: Clarendon Press, 1966

LAPP, JOHN C., *Zola before the Rougon-Macquart*. Toronto: Toronto University Press, 1965

69 70 71 72 73   12 11 10 9 8 7 6 5 4 3 2 1